# WHOLE FOODS

# natural foods guide

### What happens to natural food products from farm to consumer

Compiled
from the pages of
WHOLE FOODS magazine
The Natural Foods Business Journal

**Published by AND/OR PRESS, Berkeley, California**

Printed in the United States on recycled paper.

Copyright© 1979 Whole Foods Publishing Company. All rights reserved.
ISBN: 0-915904-46-2

Library of Congress Catalog Card Number: 79-19013
Printed in the United States of America
First printing August 1979

**Whole foods guide**
   **1. Food, Natural. 2. Organic gardening.**
**3. Food industry and trade—United States. I. Whole**
**foods.**
**TX369.W45        640        79-19013**
**ISBN 0-915904-46-2**

Book and cover design by Henrietta Haines

Published and distributed by
  And/Or Press
  P.O. Box 2246
  Berkeley, CA 94702

This book is dedicated
to all the people of integrity
in the natural foods industry
who are doing their best to
provide unadulterated,
whole foods to the consumer.

# Table of Contents

# Introduction

The *Whole Foods Natural Foods Guide* gives an inside look at the food products and production methods of the natural foods industry. Hundreds of current books and magazine articles talk about nutrition and diet, but only a small handful consider the ingredients and processing involved in bringing foods from their birth as seeds, through the manufacturing facilities, to the grocery store shelf. This *Guide* is the first to take a close look at each step in that process as it applies to the special products sold as "natural."

The chapters in the *Natural Foods Guide* are articles compiled from *Whole Foods* magazine, a trade journal written primarily for retailers and wholesalers of natural foods. The articles have been selected for their interest and use to the consumer, on subjects ranging from detailed descriptions of the manufacture of specific kinds of products to discussions of problems in advertising these products. The purpose of the book is to give the natural foods consumer a complete picture of the realities of the industry.

Unlike many trade journals, *Whole Foods* has never served as a mere pollyanna mouthpiece for the trade it speaks to. From the first issue in January 1978, the staff of the magazine has taken the position that their job is to provide the readers with the most thorough and accurate information available, so that the buyers of the various products could make an informed choice based on the facts about such foods. The assumption from the start has been that the interests of the consumer and the interests of the businesses in this particular industry are identical: As an alternative to the mainstream of food technology, the natural foods industry is grounded in a minimum of processing and a maximum of disclosed information about what goes into the making of the final product.

It came as a surprise to the writers of many of these chapters that retailers, wholesalers, and even manufacturers were not fully aware of the constitutuents and processing of the items they sell. Retailers and wholesalers handle too many products to delve into all the details about each one; manufacturers have to rely on the information given to them by the suppliers of the materials they process further; growers might not be sure about what is in that sack sold to them as "organic" fertilizer. Even the simplest of foods are involved in a technological and ecological system which is so elaborate and complicated that an almost encyclopedic knowledge is required on the part of the buyer who would be fully informed.

Many studies and surveys show that information about our foods is becoming increasingly sought after by consumers as more public concern focuses on the many problems in the American diet. The growing market for natural foods reflects not only a desire for the positive aspects of health, but also an increasing alarm over the many substances added to what we eat, to the extent that the side panel on a box of breakfast cereal may read like a chemist's dictionary.

In reporting on its industry, *Whole Foods* magazine decided to advocate no particular dietary philosophy, but to provide as much information as possible in order to help the buyer know what is being bought. To be complete, that knowledge had to include more than statements about substances added—or not added—to the final product. It may make a difference if the food has at some point been fumigated, heated, hammered, filtered, ground, fermented or subjected to other treatments which might alter its character. The natural foods industry is not able to avoid the complex machineries of food technology, many of which were a mystery to many retailers.

One result of this obscurity and complexity in the natural foods trade is that many of the articles written for *Whole Foods* turned into exercises in investigative journalism. And it very soon became clear that the new information being presented to the retailers in the pages of the magazine was often exactly the kind of information which would be of value to the consumer. This book is an obvious consequence of that discovery.

The articles themselves, which are the chapters in this *Guide*, have been authored by a variety of people with differing views of the industry. Some are written by officers of companies in the industry, others are written by free-lance journalists who are not part of the industry, and still others are written by the staff of the magazine. One difficulty faced by the writers of several of these articles was the translation of technical terms and procedures into words that mean something to people with no scientific training—that is, most of us. The usual procedure was to use the technical vocabulary when necessary, explain what it means in plain English, and give an analogy. The goal was to make the foods that end up in our stomachs comprehensible to persons without a Ph.D. in chemistry.

Readers of the *Whole Foods Natural Foods Guide* will share an important realization with the writers of these chapters: The natural foods store cannot be expected to be a Garden of Eden.

In order to provide adequate supplies of food to a growing mass-market, the farmers, wholesalers, and shopkeepers in the natural foods industry face relentless realities, and must make choices among a limited range of options. All of them fall short of the perfection we may imagine. If this book makes clear to the reader what the realities are about the foods available in the shops, making an informed choice a possibility at last, it will have served its purpose.

A special acknowledgement for chapters in this book is due to the writers who are also executives of companies in the industry. They were assigned the especially difficult task of maintaining a balance in their reports on subjects in which grinding their particular axes must have been a constant temptation.

The Art Department of Whole Foods Publishing Company has earned our gratitude for its design and production of this *Natural Foods Guide*. They worked late into each night under the strict pressure of deadlines, and somehow produced the monthly magazine and other creative projects at the same time this book was on their drawing boards. It was their job to make the book handsome, and to assure that its information would be readily accessible to the reader. This sleepless burden was carried mostly by Henrietta Haines and Tom Glass, supported solidly by Katie Godfrey, Cheryl Nichols, Shiela Timony, and Kit VanBuskirk.

The people at And/Or Press deserve thanks for their patience and their guiding hand in the making of a first full-sized book by the *Whole Foods* staff, whose previous experience was in newspapers and magazines. And/Or will always be regarded as our original mentors in the book-publishing field.

Acknowledgements for the creation of this book would not be complete without special thanks to Steven Haines and Janice Fillip. Steven Haines, the publisher of *Whole Foods* magazine, saw an unmet need in the natural foods industry and set out two years ago to meet it. Both the magazine and this book first took shape in his brain, and became real largely as a result of his endless hard work. Janice Fillip, the associate editor of the magazine and author of many of the chapters in this book, has been the reliable editorial right hand, left hand, keen eyes and swift feet of both of these publishing ventures.

Particular thanks are also due to Miftah Henley, Susan Juve-Hu, and Eileen Mitro for their special contribution.

The final and deepest thanks for the creation of this book go to the scores of people in the natural foods industry—store owners, wholesalers, growers and manufacturers—who dedicate themselves to bringing the highest quality unadulterated foods to the consumer, and took the time to offer their help and to answer our questions with complete candor. They are the ultimate source of our best knowledge and of our best nourishment.

Jim Schreiber
Berkeley, California
July 1979

# WHOLE FOODS

# natural foods guide

# Section I: From the Ground Up

The growing concern about pollutants in our bodies and in our environment has helped to generate an increasing interest in organic farming—the growing of foods without the use of synthetic fertilizers, herbicides and pesticides, most of which did not exist 40 years ago. Excluding chemical additives at the manufacturing stage of food processing may not be enough if the farmlands themselves have been doused with poisons. Nobody knows what the accumulation of these synthetic trace chemicals do to a human being over a lifetime. But it is known that organic farming methods do not harm our foods or our countryside.

Although many food technologists insist that their tests show that organically-grown foods are no more nutritious than their chemical force-fed cousins, people in the natural foods industry suggest that there is more to the story than shows up in standardized laboratory measurements. Analytic procedures isolate one item at a time, and require conditions far removed from the ordinary daily uses of foods. Scientific methods, it is argued, do not show the full interaction between foods and their eaters. Some have even been so bold as to suggest that foods involve something called "life," which does not show up in gas-liquid chromatography.

For people aware of ecological problems, there is no doubt that organic farming methods help to build a living soil, whereas the methods of chemical-intensive farming result in an artificially imbalanced soil that drifts away in the wind, washes into the rivers, leaches chemicals into the water supply, and has to be continually replenished by the products of petrochemical companies. The chemical-intensive, energy-intensive type of farming continues to dominate agriculture in the USA despite studies which show that organic methods are just as economical and produce yields-per-acre equal to chemical methods.

The consumer who wants to choose organically-grown foods faces several difficult problems. First, in most areas of the nation, it is not easy to find a store which offers an adequate selection of organically-grown produce, if any. Second, it is often hard to be sure that the seller of fruits, nuts, grains and vegetables is accurately representing them as organic. Third, despite the best efforts of growers, distributors and retailers, the use of synthetic herbicides, fertilizers and pesticides is so widespread that they drift and ooze into neighboring fields, oblivious of property lines.

The first few chapters in this section of the *Natural Foods Guide* look at the problems of setting and maintaining organic standards, from the viewpoint of growers, wholesalers and retailers. Two further chapters focus on specific hazards resulting from the lack of control of the spread of pesticides. This section also includes an account of a successful community experiment with a solar-heated greenhouse, and a three-way discussion of the present and future place of meat in the American diet, including the views of meat-industry officers, advocates of vegetarianism, and officials of the US Department of Agriculture.

3

# 1

# Overture to Organics

## by Larry Eggen

Farming in America is taking some small steps in the right direction—for the wrong reasons. Not a concern for ecology, but the high and rising costs of chemical fertilizers produced by the major oil companies are driving farmers to a "transitional" form of farming, using methods that include increasing amounts of allegedly organic fertilizers. Some chemical manufacturers, seeing big money in the transition toward organic farming, are offering products aimed at that growing market. Since the switch to organic cannot be made overnight on farms where the crops have become, like drug addicts, dependent on abnormally high levels of nitrogen-phosphorus-potassium fertilizers, there will be time for the oil companies to adapt their products to where the money is.

**Addicted crops need fertilizer fix**

Integrated Pest Management programs, too, have been gaining popularity not due to the environmental effects of pesticides, but because IPM costs less. IPM methods include crop rotation, insect traps, interruption of insect life-cycles, and poisons as a final resort.

Regardless of the reasons for the move toward organic commercial farming, the problems faced by the farmer and the wholesale or retail buyer remain the same. People concerned with providing organic products not only have to determine exactly what "organic" is, but also have to verify that organic standards are met at every step of the way, beyond the farmer's fields to the companies which sell soil conditioners under the "organic" banner.

**Fertilizer labels give no clue to secret formulas**

The farmer, acting in good faith, has little choice but to accept the word of the seller of the soil conditioner. When companies are asked about their ingredients, they invoke the words "secret formulas" and adopt a none-of-your-business stance. Fertilizer labels need not list ingredients or give the sources of them. All that is required on labels is the ratio of nitrogen, phosphorus, and potassium.

The US Senate has passed informative labeling for pesticides—not fertilizers. Senate Bill 1678 provides that names of active ingredients in pesticides would not be trade secrets, and would be subject to disclosure to federal agencies and to the

4

public. At present, there seems to be no alternative to the natural food industry's seeking government intervention in the labeling of soil conditioners, too, urging the Federal Trade Commission to enforce truth-in-labeling regulations, and the Department of Agriculture to specify what ingredients cannot be used in organic production.

We are a long way from the ultimate in production that is free from chemical fertilizers and pesticides. DDT and other poisons have spread throughout the planet, and have half-lives stretching into decades. Since World War II, the soil has been mined, and all that has been replaced is massive doses of nitrogen, phosphorus and potassium. The topsoil, a complex structure of trace minerals, clay colloids, bacteria, enzymes and ions, will rebuild itself if left alone, but it grows less deep every year. Now, to grow anything at all in such mined-out soil, some farmers expend more than six units of primary energy for every single unit of food energy they produce—which is an ample demonstration of the kind of energy-intensive methods which the organic farmer seeds to reverse.

Energy-intensive farming takes a toll

# PROHIBITIVE COSTS

Verifying that a product is in fact organic is expensive. Most producers' associations are not fully capable of carrying out a complete certification program, because they lack full-time staff and are greatly under-funded. New Life Foods, which has an unsurpassed certification program, has spent $200,000 using a full-time staff over a couple of years, and cannot begin to examine every claim made. Each of the 100 farms is visited once in about three years.

About 1,000 soil conditioners are listed in *Acres* magazine—of which about half are probably uncertifiable as truly organic—and the products are constantly changing, which would require constant monitoring. My estimate is that about 200 companies sell such products, and none are required to reveal anything about their ingredients or their sources.

The buyer rarely has the expertise to judge the organic quality of purchased production, and even the organic farmer often does not know that such "natural" conditioners as fish emulsion and kelp may be chemically fortified, sometimes to meet state requirements. The unsuspecting farmer may be buying and using soil conditioners which contain synthetic urea, ammonium sulfate, triple super phosphate, or other chemicals manufactured synthetically.

Although organic farming still has to devote many years to reaching the final goal of perfectly balanced soil, free from all synthetic fertilizers, herbicides, insecticides, fungicides, and rodenticides, there are some rules-of-thumb to apply immediately. A minimum standard for organic certification would be crops grown in fields which are at least three years away from the use of chemicals, and a minimum of three years of strict, balanced crop rotation. By increasing these minimum times, each year the organic products will continually increase their distance from all synthetic chemicals.

Certified organic soil enrichment can be accomplished by the use of organic matter, bacteria and algae cultures, and natural rock products which have not been processed with synthetic chemicals. Insect control can be limited to predators, disease cultures, and attractants, allowing the use of non-synthetic pesticides like pyrethrum only in emergencies. Similarly, certifiable rodent control can be restricted to natural enemies, natural repellants, and traps. Weed control can be limited to crop rotation, cultivation, and cutting of weed patches.

All grain production will contain some insect eggs. Commercial production is typically fumigated with poisons like cyanide gas. This is clearly unacceptable for organic products, and should even be banned from commercial production. The use of diatomaceous earth is completely effective against insects in stored grains, and it is totally non-toxic. Diatomaceous earth is pure calcium, consisting of ground up fossil remains of single-cell plankton. It scratches the insects microscopically, causing them to dehydrate and die.

Field drying is the best way to attain an acceptable moisture content of a crop, but weather does not always permit this. Normal or warm air aereation in bins can take care of

Standards for organic certification

a small amount of moisture. Large amounts of moisture require artificial drying to prevent spoilage, but temperatures higher than 160°F. will result in a serious loss of nutrients. Since some vitamins will be destroyed even at lower temperatures, artificial drying should not be used unless unavoidable.

# PESTICIDE TESTS

**Laboratory tests have limited value**

The laboratory testing of the product is of limited value, because lab tests cannot determine the source of the elements which have been applied to the soil. Such tests can only show the amounts present. Large amounts of chlorinated hydrocarbons, the usual insecticides, will show up in such tests, but spraying weed patches with 2-4-D could easily escape detection. For reasons of this kind, the National Farm Organization gave up on lab testing for organic production several years ago.

Current laboratory tests, which are already expensive, commonly measure amounts as small as 0.02 parts per million. For pesticides current in use, this is not nearly refined enough. These pesticides accumulate in the human body throughout a lifetime, and affect the body in yet unknown ways on a cellular level. Already, chemicals like DDT are known to cause caner and chromosome damage, and herbicides were discovered to produce birth defects. To be an effective screen against long-term, cumulative effects, lab tests of all ''organic'' production would have to measure parts per billion—at a cost that nobody in the natural foods business could afford.

Most farmers who offer organic production are sincere, but there can be mistakes, accidents, and occasional deceptions. For this reason, thorough cross-checking is necessary. The certifying agency can talk with the farmer's neighbors and the fertilizer companies in the area, and can check with the soil conditioner company the farmer buys from. These people are usually quite cooperative in giving information about what the farmer has been doing.

An additional safeguard is a legal affidavit, signed by the farmer at the time of sale, which is stringent enough to discourage lying. At New Life Foods, a classification would mean that the farmer would lose certification, would pay the shipping costs, and would be subject to suits for loss of business. Fortunately, this has never happened.

To make the word organic truly mean something will require a major effort of cooperation and coordination among the entire natural foods industry. Working together, we can lean on the Federal Trade Commission to enforce strict, thorough truth-in-labeling by suppliers of soil conditioners. This full disclosure can be pursued immediately, without waiting for industry-wide agreements about organic certification standards.

**Agreeing on a definition of ''organic''**

That—agreement about organic certification standards—is perhaps the largest step the industry can take as a whole. I hope to see the nationwide adoption of the highest level of standards, like those outlined in this article. I envision something like an industry-wide vote on organic standards by all of the organizations concerned with certification.

Once a consensus is reached in the natural foods industry, we will be in a strong position to propose standards to such federal agencies as the Food and Drug Administration and the Environmental Protection Agency. The US government is the one organization which is nationwide and has the staff and money to oversee organic standards. If our industry can reach agreement about it first, those standards can be our own.

I want to share information with people concerning with these problems and issues. My office is at New Life Foods, 736 Craig Ave., (Hwy. 14), Tracy, MN 56175.

# 2

# On the Organic Trail

## by Rick Purvis

The old cultivating tractor creaked, groaned, made one last feeble attempt to extricate itself from the predicament I had driven it into, and then died. Stuck. Mud oozed up around the axles as I sat there knowing that I would have to explain myself to the tractor's owner.

Climbing down from the Allis-Chalmers "G," I looked around at the hilly landscape crowded with orderly squares of vegetable crops. A closer look revealed rows of leafy broccoli, patches of parsley-topped carrots, and beds of mature white-stalked leeks, growing on this 12-acre truck farm just north of San Diego. Amidst all the greenery, a man approached me.

The aging but spry farmer of Japanese-American ancestry crinkled his weathered brow and smiled. He slapped me on the back, chided me, and then reassured me. Joe Hamada's relaxed attitude about the bogged tractor made me break into an easy laughter. He has been farming vegetables organically all his life, and because of this is regarded as somewhat of a legend in organic farming circles.

Joe Hamada's easygoing nature becomes uncompromising, though, when he speaks of the prevailing use of chemical pesticides, herbicides and fertilizers on farms: "I've never used chemicals on my farm, and don't plan to. Growing food does not involve poisoning the land and environment. Working with what raw materials nature so generously provides, I try to achieve a productive balance."

He is one of the many organic farmers I met during a research tour I made early in 1979. During January and February, I was sponsored by 27 organic/natural food distributors and retailers to go on an agricultural fact-finding mission that took me to Southern and Central California. The main emphasis of my trip focused on possible misrepresentation of organic produce by growers.

In one of the world's richest agricultural regions, Southern and Central California are areas of major organic fruit and vegetable production. I researched four locations, each of which contains specific crops. Fallbrook-San Diego: avocados, citrus, exotic fruit, and

*An agricultural fact-finding mission*

vegetables; Desert (Coachella Valley): dates, citrus, and grapes; Santa Barbara: avocados, citrus, vegetables, and mushrooms; Porterville-Lower San Joaquin Valley: citrus, avocados, and raisins.

In my travels, I visited over 30 farms, ranging in size from a half acre to 150 acres. My sponsors, mainly from the San Francisco Bay Area, included small community co-op food stores, privately-owned natural food stores, and larger produce distributors such as Veritable Vegetables, 3:30 A.M. Produce, and Community Produce in Seattle.

# THE RIGHT QUESTIONS

Research at the farm level

As distributors and retailers of "organic produce," they were concerned about what they were really selling to their customers. David Lansky, an energetic worker at Veritable Vegetable Produce Collective in San Francisco, puts it this way: "How can we feel good about representing fruits and vegetables as organic when we don't know what's going on at the farming level—and besides, we don't even know the right kinds of farming questions to ask the grower."

Although there were obvious economic and business considerations in standing behind the products they sell, the sponsors of my study were prompted as much by their individual, personal motivations as by a desire to make a buck off organic produce. On the consumer level, as recent polls indicate, customers are increasingly concerned about the quality of foods, and are often quite knowledgeable in making purchasing decisions. In fact, it is the purchasing power of the consumers which will either encourage or discourage the industry.

Secondary areas of my research focused on providing general information on organic and chemical agricultural technology. These included machinery, soil management, crop culture, packing operations, and support services. Problems and solutions in distribution and marketing were a third area of study.

# WHAT'S ORGANIC?

"Organic"—a catchword?

Ask the next person you meet what "organic" means, and the answer is likely to differ from what you had in mind. Apparently there is no commonly understood definition, and different people—consumers, distributors, retailers, and farmers—use variations loosely based on the idea that no chemicals are used in the production of fruits and vegetables. "Organic" is definitely a catchword in the present marketing climate of the industry.

A popular desk-top dictionary defines organic as "of, relating to, or derived from living organisms," and as "of, relating to, or containing carbon compounds." By the latter definition, any pesticide that contains carbon, such as DDT, is organic. That definition is, of course, very different from what most people think of when they're talking about organic produce.

Toward a legal definition

Another definition is found in the proposed California Organic Food Bill of 1979, introduced by Assemblyman Mike Gage of Sonoma County and supported by many organic growers throughout the state. That bill defines organic produce as raw agricultural commodities which are produced, stored, processed, and packaged without the use of synthetically compounded fertilizers, herbicides, fungicides, or pesticides for one year prior to the appearance of flower buds in the case of perennial crops and one year prior to seed planting in the case of annual crops.

Let's start with the farmer's perspective, based both on what I saw during my tour and my own experience as a grower. First of all, growers operate basically from one of three broad frames of reference:

Personal commitment to an organic philosophy

● Some farmers grow organically by what I call active definition. They act according to a philosophy which usually stems from a personal commitment which affects their growing methods. This approach involves promoting sound ecological soil management programs, protecting and increasing the fertility of the land, and eliminating the introduction of toxic chemicals into the environment.

Steve Taft, president of Eco Farms, Inc., voiced a strong commitment to such a philosophy. "Our company operates a grove management service for 300 acres of avocados and citrus which we see as a testing ground to incorporate our beliefs on an actual farming level," he said. "What is interesting—much of the fruit we produce cannot be handled through organic outlets as the volume is too large, so as much as 80 to 90 percent goes to nonorganic commercial retailers and distributors."

Organic farming for profit

● The second category includes farmers who grow organically primarily for the market value. The motivations involved are higher prices for organic production and an increased number of outlets.

Albert Palalay, whose tanned face tells a story of having farmed all his life under the desert sun in Coachella Valley, commented on his practices. "I grow my tomatoes organically with cow and chicken manure because my customers find the taste superior to chemically fertilized ones. My other crops—Oriental vegetables for the San Francisco market—may get sprayed if I have a pest problems."

In the same locale I found some date growers who may not include last year's methods in this year's definition of "organic." If it's a dry summer, these non-organic growers may eliminate Malathion, an insecticide used on pest beetles, and then sell the dates as organic, fetching a higher price.

● The third category includes farmers who grow organically by neglect. Absentee landowners are usually involved in these instances. The land was likely to have been bought for speculation—one of the most serious threats to farming today—and the existing orchards are left untended. A local organic produce broker will get a crew in to pick what they can.

Organic by default

# CERTIFICATION

Organic farming, by its very nature, means diversity. For this reason, a complete study would require looking at each farm on a case-by-case basis. Still, there are important definitive guidelines which are widely recognized by the growers themselves.

One of the most successful current grower certification programs in Northern California is being carried on by the California Certified Organic Farmers (CCOF). Sy Wiesman, state secretary for CCOF, describes it as a democratic association of chartered grassroots chapters, whose membership includes organic growers and supporting members. Its stated purpose is to promote and support a healthful, ecological, accountable and permanent agriculture. This is done by establishing standards and grower-certification programs, and through open meetings, research, education, and marketing assistance.

In Southern California, similar programs have not yet worked well. This is unfortunate, since that area is a major supplier of organically grown fruits and vegetables.

California Certified Organic Farmers

# A CULTURAL GAP

One key problem in the Southern California area is usually overlooked. It is important to understand that the vast majority of retailers, distributors, and consumers of organic produce are white, formally educated, health-conscious, relatively young, middle-class people with a limited knowledge of farming. Their views on the issues involved are generally much more demanding than the perspectives of many of the growers in Southern California. A majority of the farmers there are older, and have an ethnic background which is quite different from that of the purchasers of their crops. And all are very busy in their fields.

A certification program would undoubtedly develop markets, but many of these farmers talk of such programs as an invasion of their privacy, and as a possible limitation on their freedom in longstanding cultural practices.

An organic avocado and mixed fruit grower in Fallbrook puts it bluntly: "You like my fruit, you buy it. If you don't like it, don't buy it."

Certification programs— an invasion of privacy?

Organic certification programs have worked better in Northern California, probably because there has been a large, recent influx of new farmers who share a white, middle-class background with their chief buyers. New to farming, they are likely to be more willing to try different approaches, and are often motivated to organize together on a basis of idealism.

Some lack of interest in Southern California is the result of absentee landowners. Farms of this sort are under management services programs, and are guided by hard economic decisions. Jim McDonald, of McDonald Master Farmer, an avocado-grove management service in Fallbrook, outlined it this way: "Why should we pay labor for hand-weeding trees at $200 an acre per year, when we can use Simazine (a residual herbicide) for half that cost?"

# ORGANIC—MAYBE

Growers themselves express different opinions about what is legitimately sold as organic. A controversy rages over urea, a synthetically compounded nitrogen fertilizer commonly used on crops like avocados, citrus, and vegetables. One grower uses the insecticide Malathion on his dates which have citrus planted right underneath the date-palms—a common inter-planting technique employed in Coachella Valley; this grower represents his citrus as organic. A grower who has organic tomatoes in one field uses Simazine or the insecticide Sevin in another field less than a hundred yards away. A citrus grower represents his navel oranges as organic and uses weed oil for his Bermuda grass problem. Another organic grower gets heavy chemical drift from his neighbors.

Despite these cases, growers are generally quite honest, and the actual frequency of deliberately misrepresented "organic" produce is very small at the farm level. By chance, I happened to walk into one of Sunburst's beautiful natural food stores in Santa Barbara after visiting one of their non-organic suppliers, and I noticed an "organic" sign over that particular farmer's navel oranges. Did this prove a lack of integrity somewhere? The Sunburst manager answered me that he was aware that the fruit was not organic, but had not been aware of the sign. He attributed the incident to a lack of communication between their produce person and the warehouse. Failures of communication between growers, distributors, and retailers is probably the single largest source of misrepresentation in produce.

**Misrepresentation due to lack of communication**

# ALTERNATIVES TO FACTORY FARMS

Some of the problems faced by the independent farmer are different from those found on corporate farms. Corporate farms operate on an industrial factory model of farming which lends itself very well to chemical monoculture. Smaller, independent farmers have a certain amount of freedom to experiment, and are not as tied to strict guidelines and formula management. Almost all organic fruit and vegetable farmers are independent, and seldom farm more than 150 acres. Organic farming cannot be readily reduced to the input-output system of factory farming. Organic farming runs contrary to excessive bigness in agriculture. As a result, the retailer and distributor cannot expect to be supplied with organic produce in volume except by supporting many small farmers.

George Hitachi, an independent, non-organic vegetable grower on 60 acres in Coachella Valley, took a break from his irrigation work to tell me about the realities he has to deal with. He said he realizes that pesticides are poisonous and expensive, and are sometimes ineffective, but that he did not feel economically secure enough to try organic technology, since he had no previous experience in organic methods.

**Biological pest control**

Growers like Mr. Hitachi are discovering consultants such as Rincon-Vitova Insectaries who have the experience and technology to help a farm convert to biological pest management programs. Dr. Everett Dietrick, director of Rincon-Vitova, overwhelmed me during our hour together with the extent of his direct knowledge of agriculture. When cotton was on the way to becoming one of California's largest crops in the 1940's, he was on the scene promoting biological pest control. He and his associates have also pioneered citrus pest control.

Within the University of California system—long known for its research in the development of mechanized farming techniques—whole new departments have been created for the study of biological control. Some sources say that biological control is now one of the number-one research topics in agricultural studies.

# THE COST OF CHEMICALS

Diverse people, from the grower to the US Secretary of Agriculture, are slowly realizing that it is becoming ever more uneconomical to continue conventional chemical farming practices. Although personal philosophy may not motivate growers to use organic techniques, the rising costs of herbicides, insecticides, fumigants, fertilizers, and other economic considerations are prompting growers to look for innovative approaches.

White Chinese geese are being rediscovered as an alternative to herbicides—now the fastest-growing group of chemicals used on farms. These waterfowl were long used in California for weeding in orchards, vineyards and cotton fields before the herbicide revolution. John Mason, a Barstow tomato grower, is totally enthusiastic about using these geese. He grows his tomatoes in greenhouses for the winter market. He has found that three geese per acre will do the weeding job of one full-time person.

**An organic future?**

Growers still have to confront a multitude of problems: the cost and availability of labor, the price of land and machinery, weather, marketing, and inflation. Bill Kirst of Koening Ranch in Valley Center noted that high-quality organic produce is expensive to grow, and that he needs to receive a higher price for his fruit if he is going to stay in business.

In spite of problems, there are many encouraging signs for California organic agriculture. Technical help is available, retailer and distributor interest is strong, consumers are increasing their demand for organic produce, land taxes are lower, and an organic food bill is in the legislative works. And most of all, the industry is seeing a small but serious group of new people moving into commercial organic production.

Eric and Jack Kuhrst, organic farmers for two years, typify this trend. Although they made low returns on their carrot-growing operation for Pure & Simple before its demise, these brothers are still determined to make their farming venture a success, now concentrating on offseason melons, zucchini and tomatoes at their Borrego Springs farm. With committed young farmers like these, organic farming seems destined to grow.

# 3

# Raising Rice:
# Lundberg Farm

## by Leonard Jacobs

Lundberg Farm is nationally known for its high quality organic brown rice. Despite increasing production, Lundberg and the other four or five major organic brown rice growers in the country have not been able to keep up with the growing demand. At the same time, questions are being raised almost daily about just what the term "organic" means when applied to rice or other grains.

To find out what is involved in increasing production without sacrificing organic quality, Leonard Jacobs, publisher of *East West*, interviewed Harlan Lundberg, one of four Lundberg brothers who jointly own and manage Lundberg Farm in Richvale, California. California.

**LEONARD: Do you all own the farm collectively?**

**HARLAN:** No, each brother owns his own property. We pool all the machinery and milling equipment. We have a corporation that we call WEHAH Farms, Inc. That's the first letters of all our names—Wendell, Eldon, Harlan, Albert—that's our dad who's now deceased—and Homer. Some people think "Wehah" is an Indian tribe, and we say it's the only Indian tribe with all chiefs and no Indians.

**LEONARD: Is the organic rice generally yours, or is it all four of you?**

**HARLAN:** All four of us. I work more in the fields, watching the crops grow, making sure that the cultivation is done when it's needed. I just finished up being in charge of the harvest crew and the harvesting with the oats. The other brothers work more with marketing, going to shows and things like that, working with accounts, making sure the

All chiefs and no Indians

12

office work gets done every day—although that's passed around too. But we do have specialized areas that either fit us best or where we like to work best.

Out in the production, we have a winter crew and a summer crew. The winter crew works with maintenance, maybe repairing some spouting or working on elevators. That crew runs about three. The summer crew and the harvest crew will probably go as high as 20 fellows, but they aren't full time. That's for everything, the organic and the commercial. The three on full time are pretty much milling rice to order 52 weeks out of the year.

Two crews for year-round production

**LEONARD: What's the total rice output of the farm?**

**HARLAN:** We're trying to run about 1,000 to 1,300 acres of rice, and out of that we'd like to have a ton and a half to two tons to the acre. That comes out to about 40,000 hundred-weight of rice to market.

**LEONARD: And that's economical for you?**

**HARLAN:** Yes, that would give us all a good living.

**LEONARD: Would you explain a bit about how your organic brown rice is grown and processed?**

**HARLAN:** Okay. First of all, I'd like to go into the cultivation and some of the preparations we'd have. Early, say in the late fall, we would be getting the land as level as possible, and getting at the dikes and things like that. One thing we want is very careful water management, because you can drown out certain weeds with water—just certain weeds.

Preparing the land for an organic rice crop

We like to put our compost manures on in winter, well ahead of the planting. We don't like to put them on just prior to the planting because we like the cover crops—the enriching crops—to use the compost, and let the enriching crops fix the nitrogen in the soil. We think we get a more rounded use of the manures through feeding the legumes instead of just feeding the rice plants. The legumes grow very slowly in the winter because of the cold and foggy conditions. Then, preferably in late March or early April, we'll be turning the green enriching crop into the ground, preparing the ground for seeding.

In the past we ran into a problem with aquatic sedges that caused us to make a drastic turn-around in our cultivation in the organic production. This sedge is a weed that competes with the rice, and it had really pushed us up against a brick wall. Its seed won't generate unless it's in a few inches of water. You put four inches of water in a rice field, and the sunlight comes through and triggers its germination. We had been building up this population of sedges through our organic farming until they caused us almost to have a crop failure.

Now, prior to going organic, we were in regular commercial production, but now that we're in organic there's no way to eliminate sedge like the other farmers do. Our neighbors use a chemical called MCPA, a weed killer. But we don't spray it, so the aquatic sedge population has been building up. In the organic field I was taking care of, I would take plant counts. I would measure a square foot and count all the sedge leaves, and I would count all the rice plants, and I'd get as many as 500 sedge to about ten rice plants. You see that you just can't go that way. So after that harvest we sat down as brothers and decided we're going to have to come up with some new technology.

Rooting out the weeds

**LEONARD: You weren't using anything at that time to hold back the sedge?**

**HARLAN:** A couple of things. One was trying varieties of rice that would be more competitive with this weed. We went to a variety that's a little longer growing—about 150 days to maturity—and it was more competitive, but it was finally being pushed out, too. We still like to use it if it's an early spring, because it's a very good user of plant food in the ground. But if it's a late spring we go to another variety, which we don't think is quite as efficient a plant. We try to go pretty much half and half.

Another thing we tried was summer irrigation to eliminate sedges. In summer, we'd run water into our fields and then go in and cultivate down the sedge, thinking that we could eliminate the plants and seeds that way, but it didn't work. As a matter of fact, it seemed to make it worse. We didn't really have a good explanation for it.

**LEONARD: You didn't use any kinds of weed killers?**

**HARLAN:** Oh, no. We just lived with what we had.

**LEONARD: You have some fields that aren't organic. Would you use weed killers in those fields? Do you have similar problems there?**

**Commercial and organic crops farmed separately**

**HARLAN:** Yes, it's a rice industry problem all over California. With our commercial fields, we have to go out and evaluate, and if we find areas that are heavy in sedges we'd have to spray them, because we have to have the production or the price of the rice would be out of range. The year before on some of our commercial fields we didn't use any weed spray, but last year there were some fields that had to be spotted.

We have a separate area that is all organic production. We don't go from organic growing to commercial growing on the same field. We keep records on all those fields, and the organics have a history of no spray and of crop rotation. We have two different farms, actually.

Right now we're rotating with a legume, vetch, and some of the fields have oats. We're working now with the Canadian or yellow pea. I think it's going to be an important crop to a number of farms. I'm hoping it has a market value, so it will help with some of the expenses of the organic programs.

**LEONARD: How has the demand changed since you've been in the rice-growing business?**

**HARLAN:** It's growing steadily. We see a continued interest in organic. The people who buy our rice are very slow to pick up on our commercial grade brown rice, 'though I believe our commercial is superior to any other type of commercial rice you could buy in the market. But people really do want the organic.

**LEONARD: What is the "new technology" you mentioned?**

**Developing new technology for organic farming**

**HARLAN:** That was the number-one priority of our get-togethers as brothers for awhile. Many, many weeks we spent on throwing ideas around, and meeting with other farmers.

Last April, we started in preparing the ground. We didn't let the vetch grow profusely to about three foot. Instead, we disced it under when it was about six inches, when it was setting very good nitrogen nodules. There wasn't as much organic matter to work in, but we had the composted chicken manure that we'd put on earlier. We disced it heavy, disced it light, and took a land planer across it to make it very smooth.

Then we used what we called a disc opener—two discs that run together at an angle, with a tube in the angle that places the seed in the groove. On one field we also tried a hole-opener, which is just a shovel that makes holes the seed drops in, just to make sure our thinking was right, but we liked the disc opener best. The optimum, we found, is to drill the rice in to about an inch and a half. Some of it we got in too deep, and it ruined our stand, but we didn't know that at the time.

After the rice was in the ground, we flash flooded the field. We put the water on as fast as we could, and took it off as fast as we could, trying to do the whole thing in twelve hours. If we had left the water on, the rice wouldn't have germinated. It'll germinate if you sow it on top of the ground, in an irrigated situation, but if you put it in the ground, you have to take the water off for it to germinate.

We didn't want the water to puddle for, say, 36 hours, because then the sedge would liable to have started. The sedge was the thing we were trying to eliminate and, since it is an aquatic, with no water it wouldn't germinate. And we proved this theory out. It worked for us.

Earlier, we had bought some special equipment. Instead of the large, heavy equipment we usually would use in rice-producing areas, we bought a very small John Deere tractor with a very wide track. You see them in the snow areas; they use them to groom the snow slopes. We bought that kind of tractor so we could get in on that ground after flooding and just very lightly hoe out the seeds and not distrub the rice. Just before it came out of the ground we cultivated with a rotary hoe, and then after it emerged from the ground we gave it the same kind of flash-flood irrigation, at about 30 or 35 days. Then we just let it grow, and when we thought it needed another irrigation we put the water back on to stay at about four to six inches, so it's finally growing in paddies just like it usually does.

**LEONARD: Do you anticipate any problems with this new technique?**

**HARLAN:** The real problem with rice is, in its infancy the weeds seem to push it out in competition. But this new way the rice is shading out the weeds, although we do have some water grass. We don't have 100 percent control.

**LEONARD: What happens after the rice has been flooded for the last time?**

**HARLAN:** It stays flooded and grows up until around a hundred days. That's when it starts to head. Around then we take the water off into a drainage system that ends up in the Sacramento River. A couple of other farmers will pick it up down below us and put it through some more rice fields. We're the first users of the water that comes out of the High Sierras. Matter of fact, we drink it right out of the canal. It's that clean.

It's another 30 or 40 days to harvest and maturity, and the ground then will be firm enough to support the harvesters that we use to cut the grain with. Then it's picked up in our trucks and taken to our own facilities where it's stored and handled.

Probably we'll cut the rice at about 17 percent moisture, optimum. It stores really well at 14 percent moisture, so we'll only have to take out about three percent in our storage facilities. A regular commercial farmer would cut that rice at about 30 percent moisture. Then he would use huge amounts of energy to dry that down from 30 to 14 percent, where it'll store. That's the reason you can look at our competitors' rice and see green kernels, shriveled. And what causes that? It's because he went out and cut it at 30 percent moisture. At 30 percent, those kernels haven't really finished doing what they need to do.

You'd think all the farmers would cut it at 17 percent, except for one point: At 30 percent they can dry it and their salvage of whole kernels is much higher than if you wait until it's dry. If it dries out in the field, the way we do it, it becomes a little brittle, and when you put it through the mill, it will break up. All of us are paid on whole kernels. What breaks up goes into seconds, and you don't get much more than feed price for something like that.

But we're looking for a consistent brown rice, and actually you could sprout ours, and it would make a beautiful seed rice because it has been left to mature in the fields. The stuff that's cut at 30 percent moisture has a very poor germination rate. It wouldn't make a good seed rice at all. This is what we're talking about: A complete rice.

We have different types of storage facilities to take out that three percent moisture, bringing it down from 17 to 14 percent. We have baffle-type driers where a column of air runs up through the drier and the rice comes down on baffles and the air is blown through it. If it is a wet, foggy day, some heat will be added carefully, to not ruin the germ or anything like that. And we have other facilities called air bins, where nothing but air is used to dry the rice.

**LEONARD: After it's dried, then it still has to be hulled?**

**HARLAN:** Right. We have our own driers, so we can hold things in isolation. We know exactly where that bin of rice is, and where it came from, and when somebody wants a lot of rice, we mill to order.

At the mill, the rice runs over a monitor or cleaner, and the water grasses and sedges are taken out. The first screen it passes over is larger than the rice. The rice will fall through those screens, but things like mud and rocks will roll on over, and they're separated out. The next set of screens are smaller than the rice, so the rice flows over on top of those screens and the smaller pieces fall through. Then dust and things like that are aspirated—blown out.

It's taken from there to the Kiowa rubber-roller huller. This is really the heart of the operation. It has to be delicate to pop that hull off. There are two large, soft rubber rollers. One runs at a very high rate of speed. The other, right beside it, runs at a slower speed. The rice is dropped through the rollers and they strip off that hull. If you scratch the bran layer, the rice is going to deteriorate much faster than if you are very, very careful that you don't disturb that bran layer. Those soft rubber rollers are so simple, and work so beautifully.

Huller, gravity tables and screening operations— untouched by human hands

So you've got the hulls and the brown rice coming out the bottom of the Kiowa huller, and the hulls have to be blown off, so there's another aspirator underneath. We get about 80 percent of the hulls off there.

Next, the rice is taken over to the gravity tables. They're at a slight angle, and they shake, and the heavier things tend to run uphill. At the top of the gravity table the heavy, beautiful brown rice comes off, and some of it that's quality brown goes right into the bag. The lower end of the table has the 20 percent of the hulls that were left, and we put them into the hull bin.

There's one more process. It's called a Rotex, another screening operation that takes the bran dust off, so if you bang your cellophane bag of rice around you don't get that dust and stuff settling out in the bag. In other rices you'll see that.

**LEONARD: So, after all this, the last rice is fairly clean? Do you think it's necessary to wash it?**

**HARLAN:** No. When it goes through that process, it's untouched by human hands, and you can't beat the packaging that the hull represents. Everything would have been taken out except the stuff that would be exactly the same specific gravity and exactly the same size as a rice berry.

**LEONARD: In view of the difficulty in developing the technology to grow organic rice, the difficulties in distributing and marketing it, and the overall economic problems involved with it, why are you growing organic brown rice?**

**HARLAN:** I think if I really got into the philosophy of it, I'd say that one of these days that ground out there will be so poisoned that nothing is going to grow on it. In our areas, especially. I talk to my neighbors, and they're using more chemicals all the time, and I can't believe they're not starting to get really frightened. A few of them are. It's really the basic thing to living, as far as I'm concerned. You can't mine the soil—you've got to take care of it and make sure the micro-organisms are fed.

One thing is residues. The straw, after the grain has been taken off, is all burned by those farmers. Rice stubble, they'll burn it. They just set a match to it. You go out there and it looks like an atomic bomb went off. It just makes you sick.

We've never burned a field. We bought some very heavy, huge discs, and we run choppers on the back of our harvesters. It cuts the rice straw into about six inch stubble, where originally it was about two feet long. We work it in and feed that ground. It needs that organic matter. Just some ideas like that may seem like small things, but I think in the long run that's what's going to make the difference. So that's the story.

Improving on a heritage

**LEONARD: So it's not only in terms of personal health of the people eating it, but also the health of the planet . . .**

**HARLAN:** Right. We're pretty much committed to it. It's a way of life for us. I want to pass this ground on, this heritage on, in better shape than it was. I think we'd be doing it even if we were just breaking even, although I think it should maintain a decent living for all of us. Dad taught us there's a better way than the chemical way.

# Sunburst Farms

## by Janice Fillip

Sunburst Farms is a multifaceted corporation owned and largely operated by members of the Sunburst Community, a theocratic society located near Santa Barbara, California. Since its beginning in 1969, Sunburst has grown from a communal living/farming enclave in the Santa Inez mountains into a major supplier and distributor of organic produce within California and across the country.

In addition to the farming operation, Sunburst owns and operates six retail stores, a juice factory, a bakery, the Pierce Fisheries, a wholesale warehouse which serves as a clearing house for local organic farmers and distributes a full line of natural food products, and Gaviota Village which includes the Farmer & Fisherman Restaurant and General Store, Craft Shop and Gas Station. Recent acquisition of a distribution warehouse in Los Angeles has directed Sunburst into another new area of expansion.

Steve Terre, director of sales and marketing, has been with the Sunburst Community for eight years. Terre explained that Sunburst's remarkable business activities are an outgrowth of the goal of the Community "for spiritual beings to be in a position to set up sanctuaries on the earth, free from development and destruction. We want to set aside land masses. If we do it, other people will, and there will be a massive trend toward undevelopment. Owning the land is not the trip. We own it as a stewardship, a protectorate. That's our goal."

None of the properties occupied by Sunburst—Tajiguas Ranch, Gaviota Village, stores and small ranch and farm properties—are owned free and clear. Sunburst's business enterprises evolved as a means of paying for the land which the Community has acquired. Operation of Sunburst's businesses and the Sunburst Community are intertwined, but it is the goals of the spiritual Community which motivate and direct the business operations.

Perhaps prophetically, the first piece of land acquired by Sunburst was saved from real estate developers planning to use it for a different sort of community development. Raising vegetables to feed the Community and selling the surplus to pay for Tajiguas Ranch formed the embryo that was to grow into Sunburst Natural Foods.

**Business activities grow out of a spiritual commitment**

# BACK TO THE GARDEN

The decision to farm organically at Tajiguas reflects the Community's attitude toward living in harmony with the earth. "Organic farming represents a concept consistent with the spiritual beliefs of our community," said Steve Terre. "It embraces the basic law of nature: Whatever you sow, that also do you reap. It doesn't mean only that if you plant beet seed you will harvest beets.

"With organic farming, a person not only builds his soil and strengthens his plants, but improves his relationship with nature by promoting the natural balances. In short, organic farmers treat the earth with respect and do their part in healing our pillaged planet."

Crops grown organically at Tajiguas include corn, tomatoes, summer and winter squash, cucumbers, bell peppers, eggplant, melons, broccoli, cauliflower, cabbage, kale, beets, watercress, six types of lettuce, lemons and avocados. Due to excellent local growing conditions and the high dollar value they command in the marketplace, avocados are becoming the ranch's main crop.

Sunburst's produce is certified organic by the California Organic Growers Association standards. At Tajiguas, soil is enriched with cover crops, green manure, chicken manure and well-composted goat, horse and cow manure. The avocado trees are fertilized with fish emulsion, zinc and kelp.

Biocontrol methods which are used to contain insects include lady bugs and lace larvae, and "sprays" made from flowers, tree roots and garlic. Probably the most effective methods of pest control is what the Tajiguas farmers describe as "plain old two-fingered bug squishing."

Modern equipment, including tractors and trucks, are used at Tajiguas when appropriate. In keeping with their belief in self-sufficiency, Community members do most of the equipment repairs, with parts being made in the Community's machine shop.

But the draft horses popularized in Sunburst's advertising campaign continue to be used at Tajiguas. "We use draft horses as much as possible for discing, furrowing and seeding," Terre said. "We are trying to produce the feed for the horses, so that they will become more economical than the tractors. They are more ecological already, of course, in that they don't compact the soil or pollute the air, and they fertilize as they go."

# FARMING WITH FRIENDS

Sunburst also distributes produce grown by 20 to 25 other organic farmers. There are three principles in Sunburst's Organically Grown Code: "The grower will practice farming methods which improve and preserve the health of the soil and increase or maintain a high humus content. The grower will not use particular fertilizers, insecticides, herbicides or any other substances that endanger the health of the soil, environment, farmworkers or consumers. The farmer will strive to produce, harvest, and handle foods in such a way to insure high quality, full flavor and nutrition."

While these guidelines are rather broad, personal contact with associated growers helps insure they are observed. "The local farmers grow mainly mixed vegetables for us, so we are making frequent visits to check on the quality and the processing of the produce. This helps us keep in contact and also helps us monitor farming practices," said Terre.

"With farmers at greater distances, we have less opportunity for personal visits, but they aren't usually as necessary. Our distant suppliers are raising a large monoculture, and we have long-term commitments to them. They know what we want, and how we want it grown. For example, we use apples from Washington and potatoes from Idaho. These crops are planted and harvested only once a year—by our same growers every year—so a visit every year or two will suffice."

Sunburst also requires its growers to sign an affadavit of origin, first developed by the state of Oregon to define specific organic farming practices. Copies of the affadavits are available from Jacob Collier at Sunburst.

One of the main problems Sunbursts faces is having an adequate, constant supply of produce to meet its customer's needs. "Organic farmers do have some real problems with distribution," Terre observed. "The main problem is getting someone who can handle the peaks of production and someone who can go for produce elsewhere when a farmer has no production. Farmers also need someone that can give them a good, honest return, season after season, paying fairly and promptly so they can keep farming."

# DEWORMING THE IMAGE

Organic produce creates a marketing challenge because, according to Terre, "it is often a totally different product from its conventionally grown counterpart. Organic produce has a long list of nutritive and vibrational benefits beyond those of commercial produce. It will also vary in appearance.

"Here lies one of the most difficult problems in marketing organic produce. Many consumers want the best of both worlds, insisting that their produce be as large, shiny and cosmetically attractive as supermarket produce, and that it be organically grown as well.

"The wholesale suppliers is put into the awkward position of having to deal with a public whose orientation has always been superficial and appearance oriented. Over the years, this pressure has resulted in many fraudulent misrepresentations at the wholesale level. It even gets back to the grower who is encouraged to come up with a product of cosmetic perfection, at the sacrifice of purely organic cultural practices, if needs be.

"At Sunburst Farms, we have attacked this problem on two levels. First, at the farm, we make every effort to come up with a product that is pleasing to the eye. By having a high humus content in the soil and harvesting only fully mature crops, we can generate produce of an acceptable size.

"We try to keep all pests down to as minimal levels as possible by using biocontrols so that our customers don't feel that they are the second or third one to be eating the vegetables.

"We are also very careful about our packaging. For leafy vegetables, we use waxed cartons which seal in the moisture and freshness in transit. We also put ice on the leafy vegetables to perk them up. Other fruits and vegetables are packaged in conventional fashion so that they are not damaged or squashed before the consumer sees them.

"At the retail level, we use many signs over the produce displays which explain the unfamiliar appearance of a certain item. For example, over the seedless grapes there might be a sign saying: 'These grapes may appear smaller than most grapes because they were not sprayed with gibrellic acid, a growth hormone used on commercial grapes to cause them to retain more water as they reach maturity.'

"In this way we are able to slowly change the buying habits and attitudes of our customers. It is, however, a painful process, and I'm sure we lost hundreds of customers, both wholesale and retail, because we gave them the genuine article.

"Natural foods mean that nature is put back in control of the growing environment; that certain acts of God will not be interfered with; that produce is not stamped out in a factory, but is subject to the forces of air, earth, fire and water. So if you want giant seedless grapes, shining perfect apples or peppers in February, please, go to your local supermarket."

# THE FARMERS' MARKETS

Currently, Sunburst has six retail outlets in the Santa Barbara area. Their newest store in Goleta is a modern, spacious natural foods supermarket, designed to serve as a prototype for future natural food markets. As with all Sunburst's construction, the Goleta market was built by Community members using recycled materials and equipment whenever possible.

"Our customers are coming from an increasingly wide range of sociological groups as the popularity and the rationality of natural foods becomes more widely accepted," said

Terre. "Five years ago it was mostly young people who were concerned with their health and living a natural life. It seems now that more of your average middle-aged and elderly citizens are taking advantage of the good wholesome food that our stores offer."

Geared to serve the local population, the Goleta market offers a variety of products not usually found in a natural food store, including a complete meat section featuring naturally-fed beef.

No dietary philosophy

While some people were surprised that a spiritual community would sell meat, Sunburst espouses no dietary philosophy and Community members pursue the diet of their choice. Sunburst's policy on meat is expressed in their Community brochure: "The reason we're all here primarily is to inspire other peole toward self-realization, not to make them meat eaters or vegetable eaters. And this has been an age old argument and a continual problem. That's why Jesus confronted it, no doubt, because there were vegetarians and meat eaters then. He solved it by saying that it's not what you eat that defiles you, it's what you do with it after you eat it—with your words, thoughts and deeds."

# THE RED EYE EXPRESS

When most people in the Los Angeles area are snuggling into their beds and drifting off to sleep, the commercial produce distribution center begins to buzz with activity. An eerie parade of semi-trailers lumbers out of the night, dwarfing the men waiting to unload them. As box after box of fruits and vegetables arrives from growing regions in the Western US and Mexico, the warehouses begin to resemble the vegetable crisper in a giant's refrigerator. Most of the produce shipped from California passes through these warehouses on its way to feed our nation. Nowhere is it more evident that agribusiness is big business.

The giant's refrigerator

A few blocks away from the center of commercial produce activity is a smallish warehouse identified by a colorful sign as Sunburst Organic Produce. From this loading dock, organic produce is shipped by truck and by air to natural and health food stores across the country. A recent addition to Sunburst's enterprises, the LA warehouse marks a new direction for the Community and is the focal point for what is probably one of the most efficient distribution networks in the natural foods industry.

"We became a distributor because, as a retailer, we were concerned that we were offering the best possible produce to the public and that growing methods should also be publicly known, to give people who are concerned a fair shake, and to give people on a chemical/pesticide-free diet a chance to survive," Terre remembers.

"We felt at the time (1971-72) that no such outlet was available to us. So we undertook a circuit of Southern and Northern California farmers to procure organic produce. We started bringing oranges and avocados from the south to the people up north, and apples and stone fruit to people down south. Since Santa Barbara is in between, we were dropping off everything to our stores on the way."

From these modest beginnings, Sunburst now operates six trucks—three leased, and three owned by the Community—which distribute produce, juice, bakery products and other dry goods from San Diego to San Francisco.

In the early morning hours, five times a week, Sunburst trucks rendezvous at the warehouse with LD-3 air cargo containers, capable of carrying up to 3000 pounds of produce. Since LD-3's can only be flown in wide-bodied DC-10 aircraft, large airfreight deliveries are limited to cities with major airports. However, cardboard containers holding from 300 to 400 pounds of produce are shipped into small airports, bringing Sunburst produce to individuals and stores in less urban areas.

Sunburst distributes commercial, as well as organic produce. Terre explained that both types of produce are clearly marked on computerized invoices to avoid confusion. The computer listing is designed to make it "impossible to unknowingly sell one for the other."

Some customers have arranged a commercial substitution program with Sunburst. If the preferred organic produce is not available, these customers authorize Sunburst to fill the order with clearly marked commercial product instead. Terre emphasized that the substitution is done "only if the people authorize us to do it."

Terre ruefully observed, "There are a million problems in distribution. The most difficult is probably keeping on top of all sources of supply so that we can represent all of our products honestly. It is solved by constant communication with all our sources of supply, by knowing the problems on the farm level, and by helping with practical solutions within the framework of organic methods."

It is tempting to credit Sunburst's success to the free labor provided by the Community, but Terre maintains that "the free labor notion is basically false." While some Community members provide voluntary labor and the rest donate their paychecks to the Community, Terre points out that the Community provides its members with food, clothing, housing, medical and dental care, and recreation—"We provide them with a life and the means to live it."

About 200 Community members participate in some phase of Sunburst's diverse businesses, but most Community members prefer to remain at Tjiguas Ranch pursuing their spiritual life. Already expanded beyond the point where business can be handled solely by Community members, Sunburst has about 150 paid employees who do not belong to the Community. Association with people like Bob Kreiger, the LA sales representative, has provided practical experience that serves as a valuable addition to Sunburt's operation and helps balance the community's spiritual orientation. As a waiter at Sunburst's restaurant explained, employees are not treated as outsiders simply because they do not belong to the Communiy.

The Farmer & Fisherman Rastaurant at Gaviota Village is managed by a Sunburst Community member—a delightful elderly woman called Ma—but most of its employees do not belong to the Community. Located 25 miles north of Santa Barbara, the restaurant is on one of the two main highways connecting Southern and Northern California.

"The restaurant is another way to turn the public on to natural foods and to introduce them to our way of life," said Terre. "The restaurant is a very effective tool because it is on a main highway to attract a random sample of hungry motorists. And once they stop, they have the opportunity to actually taste natural food meal prepared in an appetizing fashion. This helps people over the barriers of not knowing what to do with the raw materials such as whole grains, tofu, seaweed, etc. There is also a general store right there where they can purchase the ingredients of their meal." Also available at the store is *The Sunburst Farm Family Cookbook*, a collection of recipes created in the Community's kitchens.

Honest product representation

A labor of love

An introduction to whole foods

# DISAPPEARING ACT

The spiritual values which sustain the Sunburst Community form the basis for their business philosophy. Terre reflects that Sunburst's main contribution to the natural food industry may go beyond producing and distributing organic produce.

"We are a people of our word," said Terre, "applying a spiritual ethic—honesty—to the business world." Terre speculates that Sunburst's policy of honoring all their contracts and paying bills on time has helped the image of new age business people and the image of the natural foods movement.

"We conduct our business in a fair, humane, civilized fashion," Terre said. "We're new age business people for the reason we're in business to begin with. We're not plugged in to profit for the sake of profit. Profit is not the goal."

The goal of the Sunburst business enterprises is, ironically, to go out of business: to pay for the land they have acquired and to retreat to the sanctuary of Tajiguas Ranch. Yet the very success of their enterprise may prevent the people at Sunburst Natural Foods from attaining their ultimate goal of returning to the land. Sunburst has brought the fruits of Tajiguas to many people across the country and their success is not without responsibility. As Terre concludes, "As the business grows, our obligations also grow."

Applying a spiritual ethic to the business world

# 5

# *Beyond Farming*

## by Jim Schreiber

"To supply organically and naturally grown produce and farm products primarily from New England to the people of New England.

"To provide a market for the varied traditional and new age products harvested and manufactured on New England farms and in small cottage industries from the 3,000 miles of rocky Maine coast to the beautiful green mountains of Vermont, with the independent creative spirit New Englanders are famous for."

That is the twofold purpose of the New England Organic Produce Center (NEOPC), headquartered in Gardner, Massachusetts. These purpose illustrate a key viewpoint shared by many new age observers—a viewpoint which may be called ecological regionalism.

Less than three years ago, NEOPC started distributing produce from a single 75-acre farm. Now it is the clearinghouse for nearly 2000 acres throughout the USA. According to company president Gene Fialkoff, business multiplied six times during the first year, four times more during the second year, and is expected to double again by the end of the third year. This swift growth demonstrates the need for an efficient distribution network to get the organic produce beyond the farm.

**Ecological regionalism**

The focus on the New England region is consistent with the idea that it makes the most sense to eat foods grown nearby. It is an ecological and economic boondoggle to live in Alaska and try to subsist on tropical fruits. The pride of the mainstream American food business is bland uniformity, which boasts that you can buy the same Big Mac or artificial egg substitute from Nome to Key West. The unavoidable result of this uniformity is energy-guzzling trucks, ships, trains, and jet planes whisking for thousands of miles across the nation, burning fossil fuels and spewing pollutants. Preservatives and additives are also an essential part of the long-haul uniformity picture—or at least the energy and dollar cost of refrigeration.

By keeping within a limited region, the New England Organic Produce Center keeps the distribution lines of fresh foods to a minimum length that fit into a distinctive ecological area. At present, NEOPC is devoting attention to storage, in order to extend local distribution through time as well as space. When winter comes to New England, local fresh produce is not available. Rather than bringing in tons of vegetables from warmer climates, NEOPC is expanding its capabilities to store cabbages, carrots, onions, and other local crops for use through the snowy months. That is why sauerkraut and "The Pickle Eater's Pickle" are important items on their list. And that is one reason why "Back to our roots" is their motto—root crops keep well off season.

# HELP FOR FARMERS

NEOPC tries to take non-farming burdens off the farmers, Fialkoff says, to help them have more time for the farming itself. In addition to the usual distribution services, they provide farmers with carrot washers, mechanical packers, conveyors, and baggers, which are taken to the farmsite. "This is a direction we'd like to follow," Fialkoff says, "making a few expensive pieces available to a number of farmers on a cooperative basis. Although we're not against using machinery, we feel that the more human contact there is, the better the quality and the more joy we have in selling the product."

From the beginning, NEOPC has been labor-intensive, although there are now about a dozen workers doing farmwork and another dozen doing the distribution—twice as many people as there were in the summer of 1978. Appropriately, they are looking at a 20,000 square-foot warehouse to move into, which is double the size of their present warehouse space.

At present their three leased 20-foot refrigerated trucks, and their own 14-foot reefer and one van, are used to service about 250 outlets in New England. And now there's New York City.

"New York City is asking for us," Fialkoff says. Fresh produce is in notoriously short supply in New York City, and it has apparently developed a hunger which is eyeing the New England greenery. NEOPC has no sales people there, but New Yorkers are on the phone asking for distribution in their area.

That city is, of course, a special case for new age problem-solvers. Except for some neighborhood gardens, the concept of locally-grown food cannot be applied. That city, and others like it, fit into no new age ecological niche, and the only currently plausible transaction seems to be to pump greenery in and pump greenbacks out. The nearby distribution network of the New England Organic Produce Center is a logical, if not ecological, tie-in.

New York City is not the only connection NEOPC has outside its provinces. New England does not subsist on roots, and the firm does "import" exotic produce including avocados and artichokes from such foreign lands as Mexico, Florida and California. Their network links up with Sunburst Farms on the West Coast.

# KEEPING IN TOUCH

Although they do not stay strictly in their own backyard, the strong NEOPC emphasis on local produce has the added advantage of keeping them in touch with practices at the farm level. They know which nearby farms are organic because they conduct soil analyses and work along with the farmers. For outlying areas, they rely more heavily on affidavits and on that old standby of the natural foods industry— trust. Many of the farms are members of statewide and regional organic farmers' associations, which adds further assurance of the authenticity of the produce as organic.

Getting back to roots, Fialkoff says, "My basic standards for 'organic' are no use of synthetic fertilizers, presticides, or herbicides—with the intention of creating a naturally balanced soil." Their main farming problem is insects such as the cabbage butterfly, root maggot, and cucumber beetle. Organic sprays and "biodynamic seaweed sprays" are

Taking non-farming burdens off the farmer

New York City—a case for new age problem-solvers

Getting back to roots

used, but, again, the emphasis is on healthy soil. "When you have healthy soil, you don't have as many bugs and crop diseases." So far, only two crops, totaling not more than an acre, have been reported destroyed by insects.

Spoilage—a major problem

The major problem for NEOPC as a distributor is spoilage. They aim to design their warehouses to simulate natural root cellars. This strategy has been successful enough that they can sometimes offer items more cheaply than commercial wholesale markets. But it is still true that produce starts to go limp as soon as it is harvested.

Fialkoff points out that, even with refrigeration, a leafy green will not last for more than a week, and cucumbers will last not more than two. At the Chang farm, in South Deerfield, 45 minutes away from the warehouse, vegetables are picked at night or early in the morning, and placed in a refrigerated space on the farm. They are then trucked to the warehouse and kept in another cold space. The goal, which is usually met, is to deliver the produce to the stores on the same day as the morning harvest.

As a successful distributor of organic foods, the New England Organic Produce Center continues to serve as a informative study in new age agribusiness alternatives. It already offers an example of local emphasis with short lines of supply, along with some long-range imports. It will be equally instructive as NEOPC attempts to bite into the Big Apple.

# Solar Green

## by Gary M. Garber

On Sun Day, May 3, 1978, as America was officially beginning the "solar age," the sun broke through the clouds over Cheyenne, Wyoming just long enough for dedication ceremonies at the nation's largest community solar greenhouse.

Cheyenne received 17 inches of snow that afternoon, but while the sun was shining, hundreds of people visited the 5,000 square foot greenhouse and harvested bushels of vegetables that had been growing since January. Even more amazing than the fact that these crops were reaped a full month before the growing season usually begins, is the fact that they were grown in a greenhouse heated entirely by the sun!

The Cheyenne Community Solar Greenhouse was built by Community Action of Laramie County after a successful greenhouse project involving 15 low-income youths brought the group national acclaim in 1976. The young people, all in the program as an alternative to jail, built three 16 by 20 foot solar greenhouses that worked so well they are still being used to provide food for a home of 35 handicapped people. That fall the teenagers addressed the National Energy Policy Advisory Board for Community Service Administrations (CSA) and laid the groundwork for similar projects all over the country.

The people at Community Action anticipated success even before it was realized. Executive Director Al Duran negotiated with the regional CSA office in Denver for money to begin planning a commercial-scale solar greenhouse to provide a continual source of low cost food for Cheyenne's poor. The concept has involved the people of Cheyenne in all phases of the program including planning, design, construction and operation. In December 1976, Community Action received $42,700 from CSA's Community Food and Nutrition Program and immediately set up a one-week workshop to develop program goals and objectives.

The workshop group included high school students, as well as unemployed, retired and professional people. They developed a scale model of the proposed greenhouse and decided to build the greenhouse in three sections. This design not only allowed for

**Community Action builds solar greenhouse**

construction in three phases (to compensate for the anticipated lack of money), but provided for three complete growing climates. The plan to build the greenhouse a section at a time proved to be a wise decision—the project ran short of money twice. The Laramie County Commissioners allocated $2,000 to keep the work going while Community Action's staff worked on additional funding through CSA's Community Food and Nutrition Program to secure another $13,000 to complete the construction.

The final day of the workshop was spent briefing local and state officials. This was the beginning of a working relationship with key agencies whose cooperation would be necessary for the duration of the program. Community interest was maintained by constant news releases and radio and TV talk-show appearances until actual construction began in the spring of 1978.

Locating a suitable construction site proved frustrating. Miles of red tape stood in the way of acquiring any government land, and negotiations with various city and county officials were fruitless. Just as it was beginning to look hopeless, a family that had heard of the project offered two acres of land, and construction was underway.

**The community pitches in**

The surveying was done by a retired highway engineer who had participated in the workshop. By the middle of May 1977, all the sketches and ideas had been converted into architectural drawings, and actual construction, under the supervision of two carpenters, was started. The labor force consisted of high school students, retired people, and weekend volunteers.

The foundation, requiring 120 yards of concrete, was insulated all along the outside with discarded polyurethane and then back-filled to create an earth berm to retain heat within the greenhouse.

The plumbing was supervised by 57-year-old Molly Rivera, who was assisted by her retarded son. All plumbing, including a gray water recovery system, was in place by mid-summer. Molly's dedication to the project won her Cheyenne's Volunteer of the Year Award.

Electrical work was supervised by an electrician off his job because of a leg injury. His crutches were ideal for holding the wiring while volunteers worked to fasten wires permanently into place.

# READY FOR WINTER

The eight-inch studs and ten-inch rafters on four foot centers allowed the Community Action weatherization crew to amply insulate the north, east, and west walls, and ceilings. The building was then caulked and weather-stripped to stop possible infiltration. Inner surfaces were painted white to reflect incoming light throughout the greenhouse. The complete south side of the building was double-glazed with corrugated "Filon" on the outside and Monsanto 602 on the inside.

Volunteers, working with 45 squares of multicolored shingles and six cases of beer, created an unique patchwork design that makes the greenhouse very easy to locate.

**A garden in the snow**

As Wyoming's winter began closing in, workers moved inside to begin readying the greenhouse for planting. More than 200 55-gallon oil drums, painted black and filled with water, were placed inside to capture the sun's heat during the day and reradiate it back into the greenhouse at night and on cold, cloudy days. A local high school welding class constructed two wood-burning stoves from oil barrels to serve as a backup heating system.

The center greenhouse was planted in January 1978 with crops being harvested by March. The west section was planted in March, and bedding plants and food were ready in May. The east greenhouse was finished in early 1979. It is used commercially to raise and sell bedding and ornamental plants, and organic gardening supplies. The income is helping to make the greenhouse financially self-sufficient.

With 1979 recorded as the coldest winter in Cheyenne's history, it has become apparent that solar greenhouses are the wave of the future. Even with outside temperatures remaining below zero for weeks at a time, the inside temperatures never dipped below freezing. The backup wood stoves have only been needed on two occasions!

Soil fertility at the greenhouse is maintained by an ongoing compost operation. Companion planting is used extensively, and the beneficial effects that different plants have on each other are being documented. Since little is known about which plant varieties do best in the fluctuating temperatures of a solar greenhouse, plant performance is constantly tested.

Food crop scheduling makes a big difference in yields, quality, insect and disease resistence, and in heat and cold tolerance. Biological insect control is used extensively. Armies of lady bugs, spiders, lacewing flies, and hoover flies constantly patrol the greenhouse for aphids and other harmful insects.

# FOOD AND JOBS

The food grown at the greenhouse is used to pay volunteers, donated to local feeding programs, or sold to the public. Volunteers are generally older people looking for worthwhile activities that will directly benefit them, as well as the community. They develop their own jobs and work schedules, or help the greenhouse staff perform routine tasks. Juvenile offenders can work off sentences and fines while learning new job skills. Community gardens outside the greenhouse provide space for low-income people to grow their own food during summer months. Organic gardening classes are held regularly to help Cheyenne gardeners cope with the harsh 90-day growing season.

The Community Solar Greenhouse means much to the people of Cheyenne. It is an alternative energy park where people can learn not only how to save energy, but how to create it. It is a center where senior citizens can find meaningful work, and where young people can gain work experience and interact with older people. The greenhouse not only provides fresh food for Cheyenne's poor, it is an information center and botanical garden where children can gain insight into their daily food. It is a place where people can gather not only to work, but to share in the fruits of their labor at monthly "solar dinners."

*An alternative energy park*

The potential of Cheyenne's Solar Greenhouse Program has not yet been fully realized, but the people already demonstrated that communities can solve their own problems if only given the chance. As long as the costs for food and energy continue to rise projects like this will become increasingly popular all over the country.

Community Action has produced a slide show to be used as an organizing tool by groups undertaking similar projects. All profits generated by sales and rentals are put back into the greenhouse. Community Action also plans to conduct a series of workshops on community organization and greenhouse management. For further information, contact Community Action of Laramie County, Inc.; 1603 Central Avenue; Bell Building, Suite 400; Cheyenne, Wyoming 82001. Phone: (307) 635-9291 or 635-9292.

# *Dimilin*

## by Janice Fillip

In an effort to exterminate gypsy moths, the Michigan Department of Agriculture last spring decided to spray a recently-developed pesticide over three counties. In response, organic farmers and other concerned people went to court, an action which may lead to "the test case that every organic farmer has been waiting for."

Gypsy moths feed on hardwood trees. Although this dietary philosophy does not directly threaten the public health, it does affect the aesthetic, recreational and timber values of forests, woodlands and ornamental trees. So the Michigan Department of Agriculture (MDA) proposed to spray Dimilin-25 over Montcalm, Isabella, and Gratiot counties.

Compared to its chemical ancestors, DDT, Carbaryl, and Dylox—all highly toxic insecticides formerly used for gypsy moth control—Dimilin is a scientific wonder-child. Over the past seven years, extensive field and laboratory studies have been conducted with Dimilin in Europe and the United States by universities, government agencies and private companies. The results are impressive: Dimilin's high selectivity makes it relatively harmless to nontarget insects; it has a low mammalian toxicity; there appears to be no significant bioaccumulation; and soil and water residues are virtually absent.

But "virtually" is not good enough for many of the property owners whose land was slated for a Dimilin-shower. These organic farmers and concerned property owners formed CACC—Citizens Against Chemical Contamination—to see what they could do about it.

Aerial-spraying was objected to on economic, as well as ecological, grounds: Farmers were threatened with loss of their organic certification. Most of the farmers involved market their crops through New Life Foods in Tracy, MN and Eden Foods in Ann Arbor, MI. According to New Life's general manager Larry Eggen, farmers would lose their organic certification for at least 36 months from the last application of Dimilin spray. The use of Dimilin on these lands could "ruin the organic economy of Michigan," and

**Scientific wonder-child threatens crops**

28

practically eliminate East Coast supplies of organically-grown wheat, rye, corn, edible beans and soybeans.

Tim Redmond, chairman of Eden Foods, said spraying with Dimilin would "substantially and adversely effect the economic wellbeing of Eden Foods and the farmers who grow crops for Eden." Redmond estimated that close to one million pounds of organic crops, worth approximately $250,000, would lose their organic status, and that Dimilin spraying would prohibit entry of new farmers into the organic marketplace for at least three years.

# SPRAY FOR ALL

CACC objected to the aerial-spraying program, but MDA was unimpressed. Dean Lovitt, Chief of the Plant Industry Division of MDA, summarized the Department's position: "We work for all the people. There are hundreds of land owners in these areas. Their welfare has to be protected in protecting their valuables from gypsy moths. If we leave islands of untreated territory, this compromises the objective of getting rid of gypsy moths." Although MDA planned "no intentional spraying of fields," all woodlots, fences and sentinal trees would be sprayed. Drift could reasonably we expected to spread to surrounding fields.

Sometimes when you think, "there oughta be a law," there is. CACC enlisted the aid of James Olson and William Rastetter, prominent environmental attorneys who had worked with Ralph Nader. Armed with a number of state and federal laws, Olson and Rastetter went to court seeking an injunction to stop the aerial-spraying program. They presented some powerful arguments:

**Arguments against aerial-spraying**

● MDA gained authority to conduct the aerial-spraying program from the Michigan Insect Pests and Plant Disease Act, which approves the use of aerial sprays to remove "nuisance pests." However, the gypsy moth problem is not severe enough to quality the moths as a "nuisance" under the terms of that Act.

● The National Environmental Policy Act of 1969 requires that an environmental impact statement be made for aerial-spray programs. MDA did not provide such a statement.

● Because Dimilin is registered as a "restricted use" pesticide by the Environmental Protection Agency (EPA), its use in an aerial-spray program is contrary to the provisions of the Michigan Pest Control Act and the Federal Insecticide, Fungicide, Rodenticide Act. Pesticides which pose an "environmental hazard" are designated for "restricted use" by EPA. This designation prohibits Dimilin from being applied by aerial-spray and limits its application solely to forested lands. Fields are not forests.

Douglas Campp, Director of the Pesticide Registration Division of EPA, said that in May 1978 a decision was made that Dimilin "could not be used in residential and crop land application at this point." Campp said the decision was based on the fact that "information was not presented to allow the establishment of permanent tolerance (for Dimilin) in food crops." Apparently the EPA does not consider "virtually" to be good enough, either. EPA is "continuing to review the evidence" on Dimilin, said Campp.

# NATURAL ALTERNATIVES

Under the Michigan Environmental Protection Act, pesticides designated as "environmental hazards" may not be used if there are feasible and prudent alternatives. Natural preditors and diseases which can be used to control gypsy moths include bacillus thuringiensis (bacteria which paralyze the digestive tract of any leaf-chewing insect), gypchek (a virus which specifically attacks gypsy moths), pheronomes (a sex attractant used in trapping moths), and possibly Trichograma Wasps, diatomaceous earth and rotenone. When they first objected to the aerial-spray program, the organic farmers expressed a willingness to cooperate with MDA by using these alternative control methods, which would enable them to keep their organic certification.

Ultimately, the most serious objection to aerial-spraying is that citizens and landowners cannot protect themselves and their property from chemical intrusion by the state. According to some legal opinion, spraying an organic farm with a pesticide without permission, compensation, or due process of law violates the Fifth and Fourteenth Amendments to the United States Constitution.

On June 1, 1978, a court order halted the Dimilin spraying program in Michigan. In the future, organic farmers may not be so lucky. Large parts of Nebraska, Kansas, Colorado and Oklahoma have been besieged by the greatest grasshopper plague in twenty years. With damage expected to run into millions of dollars, state agricultural officials asked the EPA to authorize the use of more potent pesticides to fight the grasshoppers.

**Violating Constitutional rights?**

Sometimes when you think, "there oughta be a law," there isn't. CACC is presently soliciting funds to obtain a declaratory judgment in federal court on the constitutionality of public agencies—at any level—spraying any private property with anything, either by direct spraying or by wind-blown drift from adjacent areas. Larry Eggen feels this is "the best case that every organic farmer has been waiting for. It can, once and for all, put an end to the spraying of road ditches and the harassment by county and state officials that forces some organic farmers to spray toxic chemicals over their organic land because of weed contamination."

Legal battles aren't cheap. Obtaining an injunction to stop the Dimilin spraying program in Michigan cost over $4,700. Taking the issue to the US Supreme Court could cost from $10,000 to $12,000—maybe more. That is a lot of money for a small group of organic farmers to raise. Securing the rights of organic farmers to continue to grow their crops without the threat of government intrusion into their methods is important, not only to those farmers, but to the entire natural foods industry, which seeks to provide its customers with the purest, healthiest foods possible.

# A LOST CROP

Is there any chance of the Supreme Court deciding in favor of the organic farmer? An encouraging precedent was set in 1977 by the Supreme Court of the State of Washington. Patrick and Dorothy Langan own a farm in the Yakima Valley, certified organic by the Northwest Organic Food Producers Association (NOFPA). In June of 1973, a neighbor of the Langans was having his fields sprayed by helicopter with a chemical pesticide, Thiodan. During one pass, the helicopter began spraying while over the Langan property, contaminating their tomato, bean, garlic, cucumber and Jerusalem artichoke rows. NOFPA revoked the Langans' organic certification and they had to pull their crops to prevent soil contamination. Since the Langans had no commercial contract to sell their produce, the entire crop was lost.

**Court upholds farmers' right not to spray crop**

With the support of NOFPA, the Langans brought a law suit for damages against their neighbor, the chemical company, and the aerial-spraying company. Ruling in favor of the Langans, the Washington Supreme Court concluded, "Given the nature of organic farming, the use of pesticides adjacent to such an area must be considered an activity conducted in an inappropriate place... We realize that farmers are statutorily bound to prevent the spread of insects, pests, noxious weeds and diseases . . . But the fulfillment of that duty does not mean that the ability of an organic farmer to produce organic crops must be destroyed without compensation."

What has happened before might happen again, this time on a federal level. Donations to support the proposed court case may be made to the CACC, c/o Farwell State Savings Bank, Farwell, MI 48622. As Tim Redmond sees it, "People are beginning to open their ears to our industry: We should begin to talk."

# Pesticides for Baby

## by Jim Schreiber

Among the patrons and operators of natural foods businesses are many people who seek to live their whole lives in a more natural way. It is no surprise to meet many mothers who are weighing the merits of breast feeding their babies.

Unfortunately, the informed mother, deciding how to feed her infant, is faced with a three-horned dilemma. The usual choice is made between breast feeding, cows' milk, and fabricated formulas. Each one offers both risks and benefits. The natural way of nursing has been made potentially dangerous to children by the widespread use of industrial and agricultural chemicals—yet another reason to support organic farming methods.

Given these three alternatives, studies have shown the following hazards:

● Of the three, mothers' milk in the USA has the highest concentration of pesticides, exceeding the "acceptable daily intake" established *for adults* by the World Health Organization.

● Cows' milk induces allergic reactions in up to seven percent of babies in the USA, and has a different balance of nutrients than human milk.

● Formula preparations have sometimes been found to contain lead from unknown sources, typically contain large amounts of white sugar, and may be subject to whatever chemicals are in the local water supply.

Agricultural chemicals like DDT, Dieldrin, and other chlorinated hydrocarbons build up great concentrations in fatty tissue, persist for many years, and are toxic and cancer-producing in test animals. Inside the human body, DDT becomes DDE. Recent studies by the federal Environmental Protection Agency showed an average of 2½ times the acceptable adult daily intake of DDE in mother's milk among the women tested in the USA. The average amount of Dieldrin was more than nine times the acceptable intake— and in the most extreme case was more than 7000 times higher than the acceptable adult level.

A French report in 1974 showed that a diet containing 70 percent or more of oganically grown foods reduced pesticide residues in human milk to less than half that of

**Poisoning mother's milk**

the median among the samples in France. The most general advice given to nursing mothers who want to minimize pesticides in their milk is to avoid eating animal fats as much as possible, because that is where chlorinated hydrocarbons concentrate most.

Organic foods reduce pesticide residue in human milk

Cows' milk lacks the human colestrum which some studies indicate has anti-infection properties, and lacks other substances which are beneficial to digestion and help ward off disease. It is common to recommend soy milk formulas for babies who develop allergic reactions to cows' milk, but one study indicates that about 40 percent of the children allergic to cows' milk also become allergic to soy milk. Soy milk formulas, in addition, resemble the composition of human milk even less than cows' milk.

# LEAD IN FORMULA

Liquid formulas may contain industrial chemicals

Although investigators do not agree about how lead gets into liquid formulas, FDA studies indicate that canned formula contains an average of .05 parts per million of lead—about half the FDA standard. Water used to prepare formulas at home can also be a source of industrial chemicals in infant diets. Few communities in the USA use the activated carbon filtration which would eliminate such chemicals. Polychlorinated biphenyls and polybrominated biphenyls—PCBs and PBBs—are found in the air, in waterways, and in human milk. They are toxic and carcinogenic. The average amounts ingested by infants are less than the amount the FDA sees as the maximum acceptable amount, but little study has gone into the health effects of the ingestion of these chemicals.

Data are not available on what was once a commonly suggested alternative to mothers' milk: Goats' milk. Apparently, so little goats' milk is consumed in the USA that studies of its contamination levels have had zero priority. Even if it were given a clean bill of health, the current supply could not meet the needs of a chemical-laden nation.

Greater detail on this subject is given in a booklet published by the Environmental Defense Fund, 1525 - 18th St. NW, Washington, DC 20036. The 55-page booklet, *Birthright Denied: The Risks and Benefits of Breast-feeding*, contains informative charts and shows substantial documentation in its 100 footnotes.

# Meat vs Meatless

## by Howard Summerfield

The question of the ethical and economic problems of meat consumption was hotly debated at a symposium during the 1978 annual meeting of the prestigious American Association for the Advancement of Science (AAAS) in Washington.

With $35 billion in sales, the meat industry represents an important sector of the US economy and affects substantially the health and welfare of most Americans. In recent years, the meat industry has experienced its most severe challenges since the publication of *The Jungle* by Upton Sinclair, and the subsequent enactment of the Wholesome Meat Act.

In *Diet for a Small Planet*, Frances Moore Lappe documented the inefficiencies of protein conversion by livestock; and the ethical case against killing for food has been made by Peter Singer in *Animal Liberation*. More recently, the Report on Dietary Goals for the US by the Senate Select Committee on Nutrition and Human Needs challenged the commonly-assumed health aspects of meat consumption.

The AAAS symposium provided a forum to discuss the complex and controversial issues between proponents and opponents of meat consumption.

**Ethics and economics of meat consumption**

## NOT IDEAL FOOD

"Next to tobacco, the use of meat is the greatest single cause of mortality in the United States," M.A. Scharffenberg, M.D., M.P.H., Assistant Professor of Applied Nutrition, Loma Linda University, told the AAAS. He took issue with those claiming that meat is an ideal food. He explained that meat is the cause of many diseases, it wastes energy, is defficient in two major food components (carbohydrates and fiber), and its cost is excessively high.

Dr. Scharffenberg listed the following diseases as being potential from the use of meat: cancer, atherosclerosis, decreases in longevity or life expectancy, kidney problems, and salmonellosis, and trichinosis. He noted that the mechanisms by which meat could increase the cancer potential are chemical carcinogens, cancer virus, lessened host resistance, lack of fiber, rapid maturation, high fat diet and high prolactin levels. Meat is the main source of food with little fiber in it, he said.

The risk of breast cancer obviously increases among users of meat and apparently in proportion to the amount used, he told the AAAS symposium. "Since meat is probably a major causative factor in cancer, especially of breast and colon cancers," he said, "Americans are well advised to adopt the Prudent Diet, a diet low in meat, low in fat, low in cholesterol, but high in fruits, unrefined grains and vegetables."

"Meat is a high protein food and when used in large quantities may not be conducive to long live," he said. As long as man eats meat as a food, he added, we will not be able to conquer the salmonellosis problem. Meat inspection is of no value in the prevention of salmonellosis and trichinosis, he said.

Addressing the economics, he said that, next to sugar and sweets, meat and fish are the poorest buy nutritionally, not because there is not some good nutrition in meat, but because for the dollar it is expensive.

Meat, he said, is a food without carbohydrates, and their lack in the diet, or a diet high in fat or protein, is not conducive to well-being and endurance.

It is now known that serum cholesterol can be reduced by diet, Dr. Scharffenberg said. He added that it is known that morbidity and mortality rates from coronary heart disease can be lowered, and total mortality reduced, increasing life expectancy. Reversal of atherosclerosis has been done in monkeys, based on the saturated fat theory, he said.

Prof. Thomas H. Jukes of the University of California, Berkeley, however, concluded that residues in meat do not constitute a consumer problem and "are certainly decidedly less than toxic substances in vegetables products." The main problem with meat, he said, is that it is a good culture medium for bacteria that cause food poisoning. This is much more common in other countries than here, because the US food industry has developed advanced refrigeration and food handling technology.

# ELIMINATE MEAT FROM DIET

The elimination of meat from the diet pursuant to the "Vegetarian Outlook" eliminates many ethical and economic problems, and provides some alternatives to our present relations with nature, James B. Mason, executive Vice President of Friends of Animals, Inc., told the AAAS session. He took issue with those who call the meatless diet quackery or a fad, and pointed out that vegetarianism is not a new idea and "has always had a solid place in Eastern cultures."

Mason said that nutritionists do not believe, as they once did, that meat provides some nutrients necessary to the human diet. "Reasons of pure self-interest," he said, should be strong enough to motivate change in diet when you consider the increased risk of harm to our health from a diet of meat with its pathogenic organisms, cellular wastes, chemical residues, heavy fats and lack of fiber." And, he added, "there are strong economic reasons for the elimination of meat from diet that go beyond self-interest reasons that are moral or ethical in character."

The progressive specialization of domestic animal breeds is causing gene pools to become vulnerably narrow, he said. Deprived of their genetic diversity, he warned, "new pests and diseases could cause epidemics and losses in unprecedented numbers."

Looking at the economics, Mason said, "the economic case against meat interweaves with the ethical sections because waste is unethical." He pointed out that meat consumption results in wasted protein and grain, wasted energy, costly meat inspections, and diseases. While we would have to use energy, he explained, if we fed directly and exclusively from plants, we would recover more of our investment at the dinner table.

Meat inspection in 1975, he said, cost $26 million, and a thorough inspection "would be prohibitively costly."

# MEAT IS A GOOD FOOD

There is "an outstanding economic and ethical case for meat consumption," according to Richard Lyng, President of the American Meat Institute. He said that "meat is a good food—efficiently produced food—food desired by most human beings. Meat animals—storehouses of vegetable plants not available directly to humans as food—contribute immensely to human well-being."

Lyng pointed out that "we often become rather emotional about an ethical approach to the subject," and there has been a lot of that in Washington lately with such issues as the Equal Rights Amendment, abortion, nuclear energy, and even food additives argued from both sides on "ethical" grounds.

Those who advance the general idea that meat animals consume grains that could otherwise be exported to needy people abroad, the Former US Department of Agriculture official said, forget "that beef and dairy cattle and sheep make use of our natural resources that humans cannot. They have the unique ability to convert inedible cellulose and nonprotein nitrogen to edible protein. They are the only practical means of deriving human food from most of the millions of acres of grazing land in the United States."

From more than 300 million acres of cropland, we produce huge quantities of plant residue which only these animals can digest. Corn ensilages is an obvious example. Most fruits and vegetables produce by-products—such as leaves, hulls, and pulp—which are not acceptable for human consumption, yet are very desirable as livestock feed. "and," he added, "the fact is that while we did not stop eating meat, we did during the the years 1975, 1976 and 1977 reduce our livestock population."

There is no way that the poor throughout the world can pay US farmers to produce grain, and there have been no indications that US consumers wish to give up meat and, at the same time, pay for grain to be given away, Lyng said.

The meat industry association executive told the AAAS members: "Meat is a goodtasting, popular method for upgrading the diets of an advancing world. Pound for pound, in amount and quantity, meat protein cannot be matched by any single vegetable, fruit or grain. It is the most important source of iron and contains abundant amounts of B vitamins and other minerals. Given a choice, most people prefer meat."

Addressing the ethical question of the propriety of killing animals for food, Lyng said it is impossible to deal logically with this issue. AMI's position, he explained, "is that it is morally justified to raise and use animals for food because it helps to provide a better life for human beings."

Professor P. Vincent J. Hegarty, University of Minnesota, St. Paul, said that "meat contributes many important nutrients to the diet." However, he added, the "evidence for the detrimental effect of meat in the diet is inconclusive, but worthy of further extensive investigation."

# USDA'S VIEW

The US Department of Agriculture's position was explained by Dr. Robert Angellotti, Administrator of the Food Safety and Quality Service.

Dr. Angellotti told the AAAS session: "The fact that food is perceived by most people in the US firstly as a source of pleasure and secondly as fuel for life weighs against the acceptance of abrupt radical changes in dietary habits." He pointed out that "we are a nation of meat-eaters, and most people in our society would consume some meat at every meal if they could afford it," and that the high volume of meat sales results from national dietary habits and preferences built around meat as the main course in our meals.

In addition, he added, "meat is the single most important source of protein for our teenage, adult and elderly populations For the present, and for a significant time in the future, meat is and will remain a desired and sought-after item in the American diet and is tied to us through deeply rooted cultural attachments associated with our history and economic development."

Putting aside the question of whether it is or is not ethical to use sentient animals as our major source of dietary protein, he said, "it is not realistic to assume that major changes in American dietary habits relative to the source of dietary protein can occur in the time frames of less than generations," because in addition to the basic desire of people for meat, such factors as geography, climate, arability, and economics weigh against quick change.

**Is a meatless diet in the national interest?**

He warned that "any changes in national policy that would swing the dietary habits of people away from meat toward grain consumption would have to first identify and then provide alternatives to current land-use practices, to disruption of farm, ranch and rural communities, and to disruption of economic and industrial entities which are directly or indirectly tied to meat consumption." It is not a question of can we move away from meat as a major dietary protein source, he explained, but rather should we, and is it in the best national interest?

# IMPROVING MEAT

Dr. Angelotti forecast that meat and poultry consumption will remain with us for some time to come. There are no national programs on the drawing boards in the Department of Agriculture, nor are any proposed for the immediate future, he said. Thus, he added, "the question to be addressed is, if meat and poultry are to remain with us as the major source of dietary protein for the foreseeable future, what should be done to improve upon this already excellent source of protein?"

**Potential changes in meat grading**

Reviewing USDA activities, Dr. Angellotti pointed to proposed changes in meat grading. The current grading system, he explained, supports the production of fat cattle. To complete the process of providing leaner meat, it might be desirable to have an incentive program for producers to raise leaner cattle than grade "Choice" but at the same time are eligible for yield grades of 1, 2 or 3. Marketing incentives, he said, will have to be developed in order for producers, packers and wholesale buyers to benefit financially from such a change.

**Genetic improvement of cattle**

The USDA can conduct and support research on genetic improvement of cattle, it can provide educational programs to producers on the benefits accrued to them through raising the new hybrids, and it can provide marketing incentive through the purchases the Department makes in its national food assistance activities such as the school lunch program, according to Angellotti. Another incentive that USDA can create, he said, would be to modify the current quality standards so that leaner meat is included under the Choice quality grade.

He concluded by saying that the Agriculture Department intends "to continue its commitment to guiding the development and implementation of national food and nutrition policies. Within these policies, meat and poultry foods are important because of the nutrition they provide, because they are the preferred protein source of the American People, and because a nationally integrated production and economic system has developed to respond to this demand." USDA intends to pursue programs which will improve the nutrition provided by meat.

# Section II: Rules and Regulations

The role of governmental regulatory officials is seen with double-vision by members of the natural foods industry. The regulators may be viewed either as guardian angels or as perverse demons, depending...

It is the legitimate job of such agencies as the Food and Drug Administration (FDA), Federal Trade Commission (FTC), and state and local health departments to assure the safety of products, to ensure truthful labeling and advertising, and to protect the public from the spread of illnesses. But, to many critics, such agencies also arbitrarily limit the consumer's freedom of choice, enforce vague and contradictory rules willy-nilly, and selectively act upon the prejudices of individual government agents or local offices.

As Yul Brynner sang in *The King and I*:
> I need allies to protect me,
> But they might protect me out of all I own.

This double-vision is partly the result of an unhappy fact about the industry itself: Not all of its members are angels, either. As the following chapters by attorney Dennis Warren suggest, some people have used the guise of natural foods to hawk wares in the manner of Snake Oil. Such people live under the same industry roof as the most conscientious and honest dealers in whole foods. There is no copyright on the word "natural" or the other terms commonly used to describe or promote the industry's products. Only a few states have passed or even considered legislation to regulate the use of such words to label foodstuffs. The doors of entry to the industry have no lock.

38

Self-regulation is much talked about in the trade, but is a long time coming. The beginnings, happening right now, are small and lack muscle. The industry's largest trade organization, the National Nutritional Foods Association (NNFA), is now compiling information about vitamin and mineral supplements, and about cosmetics. The NNFA Standards Committee—which does not set standards—has sent questionnaires to manufacturers, asking them to volunteer a full disclosure about their products. There is no penalty for not offering this information, and the NNFA lacks the facilities to verify the accuracy of the responses they do receive.

Other efforts to set standards are being made by such new special trade groups as the Herb Trade Association and the Soycrafters Association of North America, but it is too early to judge the results. The most clear-cut and thorough standards now in use are probably those established by the various associations of organic growers and some of their distributors; the use of prohibited chemicals by members minimally denies them the use of the group's "organically grown" seal.

The lack of thoroughgoing self-regulation leaves the field clear for government agencies, whose officers often seem to have little comprehension of or sympathy for a diet of natural foods. The selling of grains straight from bulk containers in the store may strike them as suspicious and dangerous, while the selling of sterilized, bleached, hydrogenated, artificially preserved, colored and flavored edibles seems ordinary and safe. Their view of the entire industry may be artificially colored by their encounters with the present-day equivalent of Snake Oil pitchmen. And the legitimate side of the industry may still be seen as "health food nuts."

It would be a mistake for the buyer or seller of natural products to expect the regulations to be logical, clear, or consistent. Synthetic chemicals may meet with FDA approval and later be stricken from the acceptable list. Botanicals which have been in use for centuries, such as sassafrass and ginseng, may be curtailed or strictly limited in their use or labeling. It sometimes looks as if the enforcers of the regulations, looking at a can of carrots and peas, would insist that either the carrots or the peas must be listed as an additive.

The consumer who goes into a natural foods or health foods store looking for some kinds of information may be disappointed. If a customer says, "I have a bad cold. What would you recommend for it?" the retailer is prohibited by law from saying, "Eat a lot of oranges." That would be practicing medicine without a license. The rules prevent the retailer from saying that anything in the store will help or cure any ailment. The retailer can only give information about nutrition.

*Report on the Regulators*, the first chapter in this section, tells of one state's attempt to devise a system of regulation which will fairly separate the wolves from the lambs, rather than choking the whole industry in the same snare. The author, Dennis Warren, served as a prosecutor of food-product fraud cases for the State of California. He is now a consultant to businesses in the natural foods industry.

Other chapters in this section show the problems met by the major raw-milk dairy when faced with zealous regulation, the basic federal rules that apply to vitamin and mineral formulations, how the courts deal with misleading advertising by major corporations, an attempt to establish standards for cheese in the natural foods industry, a review of recent federal-level policies and actions concerning foods, and the details of a court case involving mislabeling. The special status of regulations as applied to herbs is discussed later in this book, in the section titled *Herbs*.

# 10

# *Report on the Regulators*

## by Dennis M. Warren

Much has been made of the increasing role of governmental intervention at every level of business, from the mom and pop grocery store to nationally-known manufacturers and distributors. During the production and distribution of a single product, a business may be faced with rules and regulations promulgated by the Occupational Safety and Health Agency, the Environmental Protection Agency, the Food and Drug Administration, and any number of state agencies and commissions. While all of these agencies provide a valuable service to consumers and the business community alike, there is now a growing resentment of the power of government and the manner in which that power is used.

While regulatory agencies create one type of problem for businesses, members of industry create another and possibly more serious problem. There are those in industry who intentionally deceive the public through their marketing programs, and attempt to gain a competitive advantage in the marketplace by continually violating existing rules, regulations, or generally accepted practices in the trade.

Those who fraudently sell their products to the public as "organic" and "natural" when, in fact, these products are laced with preservatives, additives and food colorings give the entire industry a black eye. They invite regulatory investigations of the legitimate as well as the illegitimate, and they court over-reaction on the part of the state legislators who then pass restrictive legislation. Those in the industry who engage in and encourage deceptive and illegal practices also encourage the growth of special consumer protection units and "strike forces" in the offices not only of the United States Attorney, but also in the offices of the Attorney General and District Attorneys in the various states.

I believe that it is also of considerable importance to acknowledge that there are powerful economic sections of our society which have a substantial vested interest in encouraging adverse criticism of healthful dietary and lifestyle changes in American patterns of life. There should be no question of this fact after witnessing the awesome and frequently irrational and emotional attacks by powerful special interest groups upon the

**Governmental
intervention on rise**

McGovern report on national dietary goals. The presence of this vocal and organized opposition to the thoughtful re-evaluation of our nutritional habits presents clear obstacles to the economic growth of some segments of the food industry.

One of the major characteristics of the relationship between regulatory agencies and members of the food industry is the presence of an atmosphere of suspicion and the absence of effective communication. Many industry members feel that government has failed to recognize many practical considerations that govern marketing decisions and strategy in developing rules and regulations affecting the industry. Government officials, on the other hand, constantly see questionable industry practices, and they criticize the failure of responsible industry members to speak out in opposition to these practices or to develop industry self-policing methods to prevent them. But an analysis of state and federal regulatory and prosecution trends, and newly-implemented investigatory systems, reveals a shift in this ostensible adversary relationship between government and industry.

One of the major tools of prosecutors is the filing and persuance of criminal actions based on a flood of legislation in the health and consumer-protection field since the late 1940's. Frequently, these criminal actions against corporations and corporate officials, or the threat of such actions, have been used to end what amount to technical and sometimes obscure violations of laws concerning the manufacturing, packaging, labeling and advertising of foods. These actions, by their very nature, are matters of considerable concern to the corporate official who must be arraigned in court for a "criminal offense" which is frequently entered on his "rap sheet." There is often a stigma attached to this type of action.

**Trends in regulatory prosecution**

A review of federal documents reflects a trend since 1973 toward a constant decrease in the number of criminal prosecutions filed in the food field. The number of seizure actions and injunctions has remained relatively constant.

What has developed, however, is a more liberal attitude about taking more informal actions to obtain corrective action on the part of a particular business. The main form this has taken is the use of regulatory letters of warning from members of the Food and Drug Administration to corporate officials. Another form of this more informal approach has allowed a number of companies to resolve controversies with federal authorities short of formal legal action by agreeing to certain corrective conduct which is reflected in a "commitment letter."

# SHIFT IN ATTITUDE

On the state level, there are several developments which deserve considerable attention, particularly in California. With its activist legislature and executive branch, California tends to be a weather vane for state developments in the food, drug and cosmetic field. I have personally witnessed a substantial shift in attitude among legislators and regulatory officials about policy questions in the food and drug field.

During the last two years, the California Department of Health has successfully experimented with a new training program for investigators and policy-level personnel. The program's objectives have been to broaden the legal perspective of its personnel and to create a more in-depth, equitable and uniform statewide approach to the investigation and resolution of cases dealing with foods, drugs and cosmetics.

The program consists of a series of two-day workshops held in Sacramento, San Francisco, Berkeley and Los Angeles. The program features some three hours of slide presentations, a seventy-odd page training manual, and various workshops encouraging group participation.

**Sequential investigation method—new training for regulators**

One of the underlying premises of these seminars is that many traditional investigations mistakenly aimed at the symptom rather than the origin of a particular illegal practice. The alternative approach developed in these trainings programs is a methodical and systematic investigatory approach to cases called the "Sequential Investigation Method," or SIM.

Under this concept, a single business—located at any level of the chain of distribution—which as become the focus of investigatory attention is considered a potential symptom of a larger industry-wide problem or the symptom of an organized or coordinate illegal practice involving the manufacturer, distributor and retailer. Attention is then given to developing the investigation on a step-by-step basis, to explore the entire range of potential violators and illegal practices.

While industry members may, upon first hearing of this development, experience feelings of discomfort, SIM works to the advantage of the legimate business operation. The reason is simple: this step-by-step investigatory method allows the regulatory official to gain a clearer view of the entire marketing and distribution program of a particular company. A particular company action, when considered only by itself, may appear to be improper or questionable. The same action, when considered from the larger perspective of SIM, can be clarified and reasonably explained. As a result, corporate and business actions are evaluated from a more equitable viewpoint.

# GREATER FAIRNESS

Another viewpoint emerging from these programs is the value of alternatives to the traditional criminal actions in the food field. These alternatives are based on approaches to regulation which stress similarities to consumer protection actions on the state and federal level. This includes the use of informal conferences which attempt to resolve potential legal problems with a particular business. If this fails, civil rather than criminal legal action is taken, which allows for a more open exploration of the factors affecting possible settlement of the dispute.

The enhanced fairness of SIM can be seen in a recent California regulatory action against a New York corporation. A group of New York businessmen began offering a service in California which included the distribution of various food products to promote overall consumer health and well-being. More than eighty retail outlets and other distributors were enlisted to sell the products. Complaints were received about the marketing techniques being employed by distributors, and a regulatory review resulted.

A review of the sales methods being used by the retail outlets showed considerable violations of California law, raising the potential of prosecutions. A SIM's approach was employed. It revealed that the actions of the retailers and distributors were taken upon the direction and recommendations of the New York corporation. As a result, civil action halting the conduct of the New York firm was instituted and obtained. The retail outlets and California distributors who had relied in good faith upon the presentation of the New York corporation, and had no reason to know their actions violated California law, were spared the legal difficulties that would have resulted under a more traditional regulatory approach.

# DECEPTIVE SCHEMES

The SIM approach will be particularly effective in cases such as this, where the responsibility for improper and questionable conduct lies with the manufacturer rather than the distributor or retailer who has taken reasonable measures to verify the reliability of the manufacturer. In many respects, this situation is like the relationship of the doctor and drug company in the medical community. The national drug companies in this country have learned well the art of manipulating the physician. These companies take advantage of the fact that the general physician has neither the time nor the inclination to examine critically the detailed and extensive product literature accompanying each product. As a result, the doctor relies upon the representations provided to him by the drug companies.

The same dangerous situation exists in parts of the food and "health" product industries. As a prosecutor, I repeatedly saw companies promoting the grossest and most deceptive marketing schemes, which were subsequently relied upon by the distributor, retailer and consumer alike. The SIM approach can be as effective in proving illegal conduct on the part of unscrupulous members of the business community as it can be equitable to the honest. Those who seek to gain a competitive advantage over other industry competitors through the use of deceptive and unfair business practices should thoughtfully consider the implications of SIM before acting.

The California Department of Health is also considering a series of new approaches to developing better lines of communication and cooperation with industry. One such idea is the distribution to retailers of an informational newsletter concerning areas of legal concern in the manufacturing, packaging, labeling and advertising of foods, drugs and cosmetics held for sale or sold within the State of California. The idea is currently under discussion within the Department, and the views of a number of industry members have been solicited concerning the project.

A review of the developments cited in this article reflect a gradual shift in attitude and emphasis among regulatory officials about the most effective, fair and workable methods for dealing with problems and controversies within the food industry. There appears to be a growing consensus that businesses should be given a greater opportunity to correct unintentional violations before regulatory officials resort to the harsher forms of correcting problems—criminal and civil litigation.

As an attorney and educator in this field, I believe that members of industry should encourage these trends in government and take affirmative steps to open lines of communication and cooperation with regulatory agencies. Industry also needs to take a close took at itself, at its attitudes and beliefs. Members of industry need to question and examine their own business structures and operations, with a view to preventing regulatory problems from developing and stopping them before they result in regulatory intervention. Despite the more liberal attitude developing in government regulatory circles, those who fail to practice prevention will find themselves saddled with time-consuming and costly regulatory problems.

**Business and government can work together**

# 11

# *Alta Dena's Curdling Tale*

## by Jim Schreiber

Such noted dairy names as Borden, Adohr, Arden, and Sealtest built their reputations on raw milk. Now they are out of the raw milk business. As pasteruization became the easier choice in the face of regulation, raw milk producers, one after another, closed their doors.

In the major agricultural state of California, there is now only one producer of raw certified cow's milk—Alta-Dena Dairy. For more than a decade, Alta-Dena has been strugging against a remarkably zealous state department of health, although several experts have called Alta-Dena the cleanest dairy they have ever seen. So far, the dairy is winning, at a cost of half a million dollars and temporary losses of sales.

In 1968, the California Department of Health raised the alarming cry of "Q-fever," a pneumonia-like disease from the rickettsia parasite *Coxiella burnetti*. Last year, the cry was an equally alarming "Salmonella." Both times the health department tried to link these ailments to the drinking of raw milk, and sought to end Alta-Dena's raw milk production and force them to pasteurize like the rest of the dairy industry.

Although the Q-fever bug was detected in May and June 1968, the health department order to ban raw milk did not come down until January 1969—a bit of a lag if there was a real danger to public health. But the wheels suddenly turned faster when Alta-Dena decided to defy the ban. The state swiftly got a temporary restraining order to halt their raw milk production. Then for two days the judge heard evidence, to decide whether to lift the ban or to make it permanent.

The judge heard that prison inmate volunteers ingested *C. burnetti* in tests, and that antibodies appeared in their blood, but they developed no clinical manifestations of Q-fever, no symptoms of illness. The judge heard that personnel at the Milwaukee health department voluntarily consumed the Q-fever parasites in milk, and also developed no ailments. The judge heard that guinea pigs were given doses of *C. burnetti* directly into their stomachs and developed no illness. (The way to give guinea pigs Q-fever is to pour the contaminated milk onto the bottom of the cage, let it dry out, and make sure the

**Health Department hassles—pasteurize or perish**

44

animals inhale the powder.) The judge heard that in 1966 six people living around dairies in the San Fernando Valley were diagnosed as having Q-fever—but that none of them had consumed raw milk. A health agency nevertheless recommended pasteurization.

After hearing the arguments of the state's five attorneys and the sole Alta-Dena attorney, the judge noted that there had been nothing shown that would link the drinking of raw milk with Q-fever. He denied the state's request for a permanent injuction banning raw milk.

No link shown between raw milk and disease transmission

There is apparently no case on record anywhere that a person has contracted Q-fever as a result of drinking raw milk. Studies indicate, on the contrary, that the human digestive system destroys the parasite, and that the disease is airborne.

After winning that round, the Alta-Dena Dairy got little rest. In the early 1970's, armed with more-refined tests, the state health department began trying to link the drinking of raw milk with ailments produced by *Salmonella dublin*. A telephone call from the health department informed the Alta-Dena management that a patient who had consumed their raw milk had gotten ill from *S. dublin*. Alta-Dena got a copy of the patient's case history, interviewed the patient, and could not find the alleged connection between raw milk and the patient's Salmonella ailment.

When this was mentioned at a Milk Commission meeting, the result was that the hearing officer informed Alta-Dena that they were not supposed to have access to case histories, that the reports were confidential. The dairy was never able to see any more case histories.

# HEALTH DEPARTMENT MISINTERPRETS EVIDENCE

As a result of this and other instances, Paul Virgin at Alta-Dena expresses some scepticism about health department interpretations of clinical and laboratory evidence. In 1974, Milk Commission tests reportedly showed *Brucellosis*—undulant fever—in three cows in Chino. Tests of the same cows by other labs showed no Brucellosis, but showed results of the animals' having been vaccinated *against* Brucellosis. Meanwhile, the health department had banned the sale of raw milk. In September 1977, the Milk Commission reportedly found Salmonella in two in two samples of raw non-fat milk. Other labs, including the State Department of Agriculture, found no trace of Salmonella. But Alta-Dena complied with the health department's request to pasteurize.

A compromise with the health department

A compromise with the health department was finally reached, requiring testing of the feces of the cows. Over 25,000 tests of about 7000 cows at a cost of some $200,000 have detected five or six animals excreting Salmonella one time. This testing, according to Mr. Virgin, "doesn't prove a thing." He emphasized that there is no correlation between Salmonella in cows' feces and Salmonella in cows' milk. But there is a danger that the costs brought about by this regulation could raise prices beyond what the consumer is willing to pay, eventually driving even Alta-Dena out of the certified raw milk business.

# PUBLIC HEALTH AND SAFETY

Is Salmonella in milk a danger to the public health? According to microbiologist R. Dean Thomas, writing in *Feedstuffs*, people eat small amounts of Salmonella nearly every day. The organism is found in meats, poultry, vegetables, and in the air we breathe. Serious human illness from Salmonella usually comes from the feces of household pets. A statement from Alta-Dena cites experiments reported in a veterinary journal showing that adult humans may ingest from two to four billion Salmonella organisms without showing symptoms. In addition, Salmonella dwindles away in cold milk, and will not grow unless the temperature reaches around 80° F., the statement asserts.

The risk of Salmonella and other disease organisms comes not from the cow's lower digestive system, but from contamination of the milk itself, especially during the milking

Federal regulations vary
for raw milk and
pasteurized milk

process. The amount of such organisms in the milk taken from healthy animals depends upon the cleanliness of the dairy. Under federal regulations, pasteurized milk must keep its final plate count—a test of the amount of living bacteria—below 100,000 bacterial colonies. Raw milk is required to have plate counts below 20,000 for the final product. According to Mr. Virgin, the standard plate count at Alta-Dena is in the 400 to 800 range.

By another measure, milk is tested for coliform bacteria at the farm. Pasteurized milk is allowed by law to contain up to 750 organisms per milliliter. (A milliliter is about 2/3 of a cubic inch.) The maximum number of coliform bacteria allowed per milliliter of certified raw milk at the farm is ten. At Alta-Dena, says Mr. Virgin, tests find from one to three organisms per milliliter.

# RAW MILK LEGISLATION

In an effort to undo the triplicate over-regulation by the state Department of Health, and by the California Department of Food and Agriculture, and by the Los Angeles County Milk Commission, Alta-Dena Dairy is supporting legislation now before the state senate. A bill introduced by William Campbell, a Republican from Whittier, would limit raw milk regulation to the county milk commission. Commenting on the need for his Senate Bill 2214, Campbell said that it was absurd that junk foods can be so easily obtained while there are delays and obstructions keeping certified raw milk from the consumer. The bill was approved by the Agriculture Committee, but was vetoed by Governor Jerry Brown.

A similar bill, passed by the California legislature, was vetoed by then-Governor Ronald Reagan ten years ago. Reagan remarked at the time that the bill had apparently been generated by a case of alleged harrassment, and that the problem should perhaps be handled administratively, with the possibility that the responsible officer be relieved of duty. He expressed concern that the bill might hinder the legitimate activities of state health officers.

# PASTEURIZATION

Pasteurization makes it less essential for dairies to reach near-absolute levels of cleanliness. By heating the milk above 161° F. for 15 seconds, the federal minimum, organisms in the milk are destroyed—along with some nutrients. In order to surpass, by far, the stricter standards set for raw milk, Alta-Dena takes special care to attain the highest degree of cleanliness, which draws words of praise from people in the natural foods industry who visit their dairy.

At a typical dairy—not Alta-Dena—which relies on pasteurization, cows may be treated to dry-lot feeding. In rainy weather, such cows would slog around in a confined sea of mud and excrement, all of which slops onto the cows' udders. Before milking, each udder is sprayed with cold water or sponged with an iodine solution, often dipping the sponge repeatedly into the same bucket of antiseptic solution. The udder may still be dripping wet when attached to the milking machine.

At Alta-Dena, the udders of cows brought in from pasture are first sprayed with water. Ten cows at a time are herded onto a platform where they can be reached from a pit beneath them. Their udders are hosed with an iodine solution, and are then wiped with towels dipped in iodine solution. One towel is used for five cows only, and is then discarded. A different area of the towel is used for each of the five udders. To prevent the dripping of liquid from the wrinkled surface of the udder onto the teats, and so into the cups of the milking machine, fluffy terrycloth towels are used to dry the udder. Only after this dry, antiseptic state is reached, is the cow attached to the milking machine. They use about 20,000 towels each day.

The point of this comparison is not to suggest any danger of disease from dairies which pasteurize, but to show the extreme care taken by Alta-Dena in its certified raw milk production. In light of this cleanliness, it seems odd that state health agents are so ready to sound alarms, ban raw milk, and urge pasteurization on the basis of questionable evidence for diseases which are not even transmitted by drinking certified raw milk.

An Alta-Dena officer wrote, "If we had contaminated milk, we would be the first to remove it from stores . . . The people who want pasteurized milk can get it. Why force pasteurized milk on people who know the superior food value of raw milk?"

# THE GRINDING AXE

When asked about possible reasons for the state health department's repeated attentions to Alta-Dena, Paul Virgin said, "I really don't know why they have an axe to grind." He speculated that Alta-Dena might "rub people in the dairy industry the wrong way" by offering a certified raw milk that does not have nutrients destroyed by pasteurization, and by their example of extreme cleanliness.

While the federal standards allow a plate count of 100,000 for pasteurized milk, the California law requires a stricter count of no more than 50,000. Members of the mainstream dairy industry are urging that the California requirements be changed to match the less stringent federal requirements.

Paul Virgin expressed confidence that Alta-Dena Dairy would more than survive the current squeeze. After the 1969 Q-fever episode, reports in the press were highly favorable to the dairy, and their business increased around 300 percent.

**Surviving the regulatory squeeze**

# 12

# Regulating Supplements

## by Janice Fillip

Labeling requirements and standards of identity for vitamin/mineral products are found in *Code of Federal Regulations (CFR)*, Title 21, Section 105, and are administered by the Food and Drug Administration. The Federal Trade Commission, concerned with protecting the public from unfair and deceptive acts and practices, regulates advertising claims for vitamin/mineral products. *CCH Trade Regulations Reporter*, Volume 2, contains the FTC cases relating to vitamins/minerals. The following summary is based on these two sources. Supplement labels are permitted to state that the product is a source of an essential nutrient and that the nutrient is important for good nutrition and health. But the labels may **not** state:

--that the presence (or absence) of certain vitamin/minerals is adequate or effective in prevention, cure, mitigation or treatment of any disease or sympton;

--that a balanced diet of ordinary foods cannot supply adequate amounts of nutrients;

--that the soil in which a food is grown is or may be responsible for an inadequacy or deficiency in the quality of the daily diet;

--that storage, transportation, processing or cooking of food is or may be responsible for inadequacy or deficiency in the quality of the daily diet;

--that a food has dietary properties when such properties are of no significant value or need in human nutrition.

It is considered misleading to claim that a natural vitamin in a food is superior to an added or synthetic vitamin, or that there is a difference between vitamins naturally present and those that have been added. According to R. E. Newberry, Assistant to the Director, Division of Regulatory Guidance, FDA's Bureau of Foods, "There are no specific regulations governing the manufacturing of either natural or synthetic vitamins. Such preparations must meet labeled potency. FDA regularly examines such products for potency and removes subpotent products from the market whenever such are encountered... Synthetic vitamins are very pure. They contain virtually no contaminants of the substance from which they were synthesized. This is not true for 'natural' vitamins."

**Vitamin/mineral labeling requirements**

48

# PERCENTAGE REQUIRED

Supplement labels are required to state the percentage of US Recommended Daily Allowance (RDA) of each vitamin/mineral in the product, on the basis of how much of that vitamin/mineral is consumed in the recommended daily dosage. Regulations allow for a "reasonable" variation between the percentage listed on the label and the actual percentage in the product, caused by heat, light, oxidation, storage, transportation or "unavoidable deviations in good manufacturing practice."

RDAs are established by the Food and Nutrition Board, National Academy of Sciences/National Research Council. If no RDA's are established for a vitamin/ mineral, the label must state the percentage of the nutrient consumed in the recommended daily dosage and state that no RDA has been established for this nutrient. According to the CFR, "vitamins and minerals recognized as essential or probably essential in human nutrition in their biologically active forms but for which no US RDA's have been established are: vitamin K, choline, and the minerals chlorine, chromium, fluorine, manganese, molybdenum, nickel, potassium, selenium, silicon, sodium, tin and vanadium."

**Recommended Daily Allowance (RDA)**

# STANDARDS OF IDENTITY

The standards of identity established for vitamin/ mineral supplements apply to tablets, capsules, wafers or other similar uniform units and products in powder, granular, flake or liquid form. Standards of identity do not apply to conventional foods to which one or more nutrient(s) are added to improve the nutritional quality, unless the total level of the nutrient(s)--including any naturally occurring amounts--exceeds 50 percent of the RDA for that nutrient. Nor do standards of identity apply to foods with nutrients restored to pre-processing levels or added so it is not nutritionally inferior to food for which it substitutes and which it resembles.

Vitamin and mineral preparations can be offered only in the following combinations: all vitamins and minerals, all vitamins, all minerals, or all vitamins and the mineral iron. A vitamin combination, termed "multivitamin," must contain the mandatory vitamins A, D2, E, C, folic acid 3, thiamine, riboflavin, niacin, B6, and B12. Optional vitamins include D, biotin, and pantothenic acid. Mandatory minerals in a mineral combination ("multimineral") include calcium, phosphorus, iodine, iron and magnesium. Optional minerals are phosphorus (in preparations for pregnant or lactating women), copper and zinc. If one optional vitamin or mineral ingredient is used in a combination, all the optional ingredients must be used. The term "multivitamin and multimineral" supplement refers to products containing all the mandatory vitamins and minerals.

**Multivitamins, multiminerals, liquid formulas and timed release vitamins**

Liquid vitamin formulations have the option of not including folic acid because it is unstable in liquid preparations. If the liquid preparation does not contain folic acid, that must be stated on the label. If a liquid preparation contains alcohol, the label must state the percentage-by-volume of alcohol in the product.

According to Newberry, "The FDA has concluded that timed release vitamins serve no useful purpose that is not already served by ordinary vitamin preparations . . . Vitamin preparations sold as USP (US Pharmacopeia) drugs must comply with the specified disintegration and dissolution times. However, most vitamins are sold as foods and no specific disintegration time need be met except that such preparations must be bioavailable."

There are no specific requirements concerning binders, fillers, and excipients used in dietary supplements, according to Newberry. The ingredients must be safe and suitable in compliance with food additives regulations, cannot exceed the amount reasonably required to serve their function, and cannot impair the biological availability of the vitamins/minerals in the preparation.

# 13

# Advertising and the Law

## by Dennis M. Warren

When I first started working on legal problems dealing with foods, drugs and cosmetics, I naively assumed that only the fly-by-night suede shoe operation would deceptively advertise and promote its products. As I began to research court actions, legal documents and case histories, I soon discovered—much to my chagrin—that the nationally known and advertised brands of bread, mouthwash, vitamins, headache remedy and shaving cream used by family had all been deceptively advertised and their makers successfully sued.

This chapter deals with the unfair business practices of deceptive advertising. It also concerns a stunning US Supreme Court case involving Listerine that has major implications for the food industry. But first some background.

**Deceptive advertising— an unfair business practice**

The two acts most pressing on the food industry involve laws enforced by the Food and Drug Administration and the Federal Trade Commission. Individual corporate officers may be named in criminal and civil complaints under the Food, Drug and Cosmetic Act. The maximum individual penalty allowed per violation is a $1,000 fine and/or one year in prison for a first offense and $10,000 and/or three years in prison for violations after the first conviction. Under the Federal Trade Commission Act, the remedies available are civil, and are limited to actions against the corporation itself rather than the corporate officers and executives. The penalties include restitution to consumers; injunctions to halt objectionable commercial conduct; divestiture; and a potential $10,000 per day fine for violations of the rules and orders of the Commission.

State prosecutions, in many instances, also have access to broad consumer protection statutes similar to those of the Federal Trade Commission. In California, for example, actions may be taken against the corporation as well as its officers. Civil penalties of up to $2,500 per violation may be levied against the offender.

In the last five years, a series of prosecutions of industry members for "deceptive or misleading" advertising has resulted in FTC ordering "corrective advertising." A corrective advertising order requires a business to correct previous misleading advertising by affirmative disclosure in future advertising. This amounts to limited regulation of what can and cannot be said in a particular advertisement or advertising campaign.

The concept of "corrective advertising" strikes at the core of consumer motivation. It is an accepted fact that the objective of effective advertising is to create a cumulative impression in the mind of the consumer that long outlasts the advertisement itself. The advertising message has a residuary effect that is stimulated and re-enforced with each new viewing of the advertisement. I call this the Mr. Whipple principle.

# SQUEEZED BY CHARMIN

Mr. Whipple is the friendly grocer who maintains an eternal vigil near the Charmin bathroom tissue display to prevent eager customers from squeezing and generally mugging the soft and loveable four-roll packs of toilet tissue. I hate Mr. Whipple. And because I hate Mr. Whipple, I hate Charmin bathroom tissue. But every time I walk through the grocery store and reach the toilet tissue section, the first thing I see is the Charmin.

Even today, I still read "Carter's Little Liver Pills" when I see "Carter's Little Pills" even though the pills have no value for your liver and the word "liver" was taken out of the title years ago by FTC mandate. My mind also keeps playing back a childhood tape about Wonder-bread "helping build strong bodies 12 ways" even though that advertisement too was put to sleep by the FTC.

The message of these experiences is clear: Advertising captures the consumer's attention, then cultivates and develops an image and a purchasing habit. If a company can make its product appear more attractive by exaggerations, tricky photography, demonstrations or misleading statements, commercial history shows that a substantial number of businessmen will employ these techniques to increase sales and gain an advantage over their competitors.

A few illustrations:

In the late sixties, Campbell Soup ran an advertisement showing a beautiful closeup of its soup. The government alleged that Campbell had placed huge marbles in the bowl with the soup to force the solid ingredients in the soup to the top of the liquid, creating the image of a richer looking soup. Campbell's executives stopped humming "Hmmm Hmmm Good" after entering into a consent order prohibiting the "marbles and soup" advertisement technique.

Can any of us forget Palmolive Rapid Shave and the television commercial which asked the burning question: "Who's the man behind the sandpaper mask?" Well, it was Frank Gifford. He had the same problem that many of us do—"a beard tough as sandpaper." The commercial went on to say: "To prove Rapid Shave's super-moisturizing power, we put it right from the can onto this tough, dry sandpaper." The next thing we saw was a hand, maybe even Frank Gifford's, with a razor cutting through the sandpaper with hardly and pressure at all—amazing! If Rapid Shave could do that to dry sandpaper, imagine what it could do for us.

*Advertising's cumulative impression develops purchasing habits*

# AN UNKIND CUT

The government's complaint against Colgate-Palmolive for this commercial revealed that the viewer was not seeing sandpaper being shaved at all. The razor in the commercial was cutting through loose sand on a plexiglass plate. The complaint also pointed out that an application of Rapid Shave to tough sandpaper and an attempt to shave the sandpaper with a razor would fail miserably.

Manufacturers hit with lawsuits for deceptive advertisements and deceptive advertising practices have been quick to use the "everybody is doing it" and the "I'm only doing it to compete" defenses. The courts have consistently held that this is no defense at all. The fact that a competitor is also engaging in illegal conduct does not excuse illegal conduct. Fairness and honesty in the trade can not be legitimately downgraded for sheer economic expediency.

These cases deal only with stopping offensive advertisements from continuing on the air or in print. The "corrective advertising" cases require manufacturers to take steps to correct the deceptive image of their product which was created through a planned course of improper advertising. This regulatory action assumes that simply stopping the particular advertising campaign does nothing to remedy the false impression already created in the mind of the consumer. The company may continue to reap the benefits of its previous deceptive and illegal practices by using advertising messages that seem to abandon the objectionable practice but, in fact, recall and reinforce the previous deceptive claim in the consumers' memory.

The case that most clearly established the authority of the FTC to require corrective advertising involved a struggle in 1971 with ITT Continental Baking Company and Ted Bates and Company, an ad agency, on the one hand and government attorneys on the other. The lawsuit was brought not only against ITT for its commercials for Profile Bread, but also against the agency which had prepared the advertisement.

The government alleged that the Profile Bread advertisements were false and misleading concerning that product's "dietetic value." The advertisements showed a sleekly built model posing with a package of the bread. The actress enthusiastically told the listener how the product was lower in calories than ordinary bread and that, by merely taking two slices of Profile Bread before meals, the listener could lose weight without dieting. The actress suggested that Profile Bread had "significant value" in weight control.

# HOW YOU SLICE IT

The government's case alleged that each slice of Profile Bread did, in fact, contain fewer calories than its competitors—but only because it was sliced thinner. The representation that the bread was an effective dietetic product was strongly condemned.

ITT Continental agreed to devote 25 percent of its advertising expenditures for the year following the settlement of the law suit to finance FTC-approved corrective ads. The agreement required that corrections must be run in the same markets, media, time periods and seasons as other Profile advertising currently used by the company. The ads were required to carry the following message: "Profile is not effective for weight reduction, contrary to possible interpretations of prior advertising . . ."

At the same time the FTC was negotiating corrective advertising agreements with various manufacturers, the US Supreme Court was making judicial history by expanding the coverage of the first amendment to include various types of advertising. Prior to 1976, the Supreme Court had consistantly held that commercial speech was "wholly outside the protection of the first amendment." Then came a series of cases reversing this long-held position, based on the public's right to accurate and truthful information in advertising messages. In *Virginia State Board of Pharmacy vs. Virginia Citizens Consumer Council, Inc.*, for example, the court held that restrictions on price advertising for pharmaceutical products and services were unconstitutional. Many industry members hailed these cases as establishing, in the words of *Advertising Age*, "advertising's new first amendment rights." Many began to believe that traditional restrictions placed on advertising would soon be overturned.

The Court has been careful to point out, however, that its rulings were not to be interpreted as restricting the ability of prosecuting agencies to move against advertising that was false, deceptive, or misleading. The court went so far as to state that much commercial speech is not proveably false or even wholly false, but is nontheless deceptive, misleading, and actionable. The Court added that, in certain circumstances, it may be necessary "to require that a commercial message appear in such a form, or to include such additional information, warnings, and disclaimers, as are necessary to prevent its being deceptive."

# GIANT GERM-KILLER

It was in this context that the FTC moved against Warner-Lambert for its advertising of Listerine. Warner-Lambert had advertised its prized product as a mouthwash that "kills germs by the millions," and as effective "for relief of cold symptoms and minor sore throats due to colds." Primarily as a result of this advertising since the early 1920's, Listerine remained a dominating influence on the mouthwash market.

In 1972 the FTC filed an action against Warner-Lambert for misrepresenting the efficacy of Listerine. FTC questioned the validity of the claim that the product prevented, cured, or alleviated the common cold and its unpleasant side effects. The action wound its way through administrative appeals, federal circuit court of appeal hearings, and finally to the US Supreme Court.

Warner-Lambert contested the FTC action. Administrative hearings were held and the administrative law judge ordered Warner-Lambert to do the following:

Showdown between government and industry

> 1. Cease and desist from representing that Listerine will cure or prevent colds or sore throats; will have any significant beneficial effect on the symptoms of colds or sore throats; or that Listerine's ability to "kill germs" is of medical significance in the treatment of colds or sore throats or their symptoms.
>
> 2. Cease and desist from any advertisement for Listerine unless the exact language cited below is clearly and conspicuously present in the advertisement:
>
> CONTRARY TO PRIOR ADVERTISING, LISTERINE WILL NOT HELP PREVENT COLDS OR SORE THROATS OR LESSEN THEIR SEVERITY.

The order required that this language be contained in the next ten million dollars of Listerine advertising! Warner-Lambert decided to appeal the case.

Industries' big guns swung behind the Warner-Lambert appeal to make the Listerine case a showdown at high noon between government and industry on the issue of the First Amendment. Both the Association of National Advertisers and the American Advertising Federation joined the appeal to overturn the FTC position. High-powered legal counsel in New York and Washington, DC, went to bat for Listerine.

First came an appeal to the full Federal Trade Commission. The administrative ruling was upheld. Then came an appeal to the Federal District Court of Appeals. The FTC's position was upheld. Then came a second appeal to the Federal District Court. Again, the FTC's position was upheld.

# NO MEDICAL VALUE

The Court's rulings at the federal level in August and September of 1977 were particularly devasting to Warner-Lambert. The Court first attacked the advertising claims made by the company. It upheld the Commission's findings upon specific medical data that Listerine has no therapeutic effect in curing or preventing colds or sore throats or of lessening the severity of their symptoms. In particular, the Court upheld the Commission's finding that the ability of Listerine to "kill germs by the millions on contact" is of no medical significance. Expert testimony showed that the bacteria in the mouth, the "germs" which Listerine proports to kill, do not cause colds and play no role in cold symptoms.

Court rules against Listerine's deceptive advertising

In defence of over fifty years of this advertising campaign, Warner-Lambert presented one four year study of school children who had gargled with Listerine. The Court upheld the FTC's position that the poor design and execution of the study made its results unreliable and inconclusive. The Court concluded:

> In this case it has been found that Warner-Lambert has, over a long period of time, worked a substantial deception upon the public; it has advertised Listerine as a cure for colds and consumers have purchased its product with that in mind . . . Listerine continues to enjoy a reputation it does not deserve . . .

The Court also upheld the requirement that nearly ten million dollars of corrective advertising was to be undertaken by Warner-Lambert. This sum was equal to the average annual Listerine advertising budget for the period from April 1962 to March 1972. The Court estimated that such an expenditure would take approximately one year to disperse and found that this "is not unreasonably long time in which to correct a hundred years of [deceptive] cold claims."

The Court did, however, rescind the FTC order requiring Warner-Lambert to include the wording "contrary to prior advertising" in the corrective advertising message since this would unduly "humiliate" the manufacturer.

The Court found no validity in the argument that these regulatory actions infringe upon the First Amendment constitutional rights of advertisers. The Court was quick to point out that allowing consumers to continue to buy Listerine on the strength of the impression built up by prior advertising—an impression which was now known to be false—would be unfair and deceptive.

# CORRECTION REQUIRED

The Court also pointed out that, without corrective advertising, advertisers would remain free to misrepresent their products to the public through false and deceptive claims, knowing full well that even if the FTC chose to prosecute they would be required only to cease the advertising campaign, which had already done its damage by deceiving the public and promoting a false image of the product. The Court ultimately decided that the corrective advertising approach was essential to provide a deterrent against future deceptive advertising and insure the flow of "truthful" information.

Still feeling the sting of this ruling, Warner-Lambert appealed the case to the U.S. Supreme Court. The Supreme Court, in such instances, has two alternatives. First, it may accept the appeal and hear argument before the full Court. This is done in those limited number of cases that the Justices perceive as presenting issues of such importance that a Supreme Court ruling is required. The second alternative is to simply deny the appeal. This is routinely done in cases that, in the Justices' opinions, have been clearing and properly resolved in the lower district Court of Appeals or the respective state court.

In April of last year, the Supreme Court denied the appeal of Warner-Lambert. The affect of this denial is to give full force and effect the Federal District Court decision against Warner-Lambert. The rulings in the Warner-Lambert case represent hard realities that must be faced not only by Warner-Lambert but by all people involved in product development and promotion.

**Legal realities of promotional claims**

# 14

## *Seal of Approval for Cheese*

### by Jim Schreiber

People in the natural foods trade often talk of the need for self-regulation within the industry. Efforts along these lines are at present most visible among producers of cosmetics and marketers of organically grown vegetables.

Leo J. Nuttall, who has spent most of his life in the dairy business, recently decided to assure self-regulation in the natural dairy products industry. He established the National Raw Milk Products Institute, designed primarily to ensure truth in labeling of raw milk cheeses.

When he started manufacturing raw milk cheese about four years ago, Nuttall realized that the market for that product was going to grow. He noticed that supermarkets were starting to take an interest when demand increased—but supermarkets are geared to sell to the fast flow of consumer traffic rather than to focus on quality. And a packager of cheese may think it is raw milk cheese coming from the supplier, when in fact it is not.

**National Raw Milk Institute—focus on quality**

## FALSE LABELING

Nuttall declined to give names citing instances of false labeling, but said, emphatically, "I know for sure that it's been done." The purpose of the National Raw Milk Products Institute is to make sure that it is not being done in Institute-licensed plants, by means of contractual agreements, inspections and lab tests, and adherence to agreed minimum standards.

One problem was to set up a program which would not cost vast amounts of money to administer. Although Nuttall estimates that there are less than 50 plants nationwide that produce strictly raw milk cheese, it would be impossible to monitor every manufacturer, cutter and distributor. The solution to the problem is, in part, the use of a special seal of approval by the Institute, a seal which is transmitted at every step from manufacture through cutting and distribution to the consumer. The seal is green on gold. Since sticking a label on each piece of cheese costs time and money, the Institute is urging its members to incorporate the seal in their own labels on raw milk products.

As a member of the Institute, a manufacturer agrees to prepare the raw milk cheese at temperatures less than 120° F. in all stages of preparation, to send samples of the raw milk cheeses to the Institute for testing, and to meet or exceed all local, county, state and federal standards. The cheese must also be able to meet a test for the presence of alkaline phosphatase. This test, made at the Logan, Utah lab of the Institute, shows reliably whether the cheese has been pasteurized.

The US Department of Agriculture will not permit raw milk cheese to be sold until it is aged for 60 days. That minimum aging is also required by the National Raw Milk Products Institute.

Seal of approval—
protection from false
labeling

The verification that certain cheese is indeed a raw milk product will have significance to the consumer at the point of sale. In addition to the assurance generated by the Institute's seal—once the buyer recognizes its meaning—the Institute offers flyers to display at the counter. The flyers, headed "Is It Really Raw Milk Cheese?" and depicting the Institute seal, explain what raw milk and the seal of approval are all about.

# PRODUCTION COSTS

The production and marketing of raw milk cheese is at present more costly than pasteurized cheese. A processed cheese is typically re-melted, pasteurized, and dosed with water and whey protein to the point that it needs no refrigeration.

The required 60-day aging of authentic raw milk cheese creates large storage costs, on the order of 12 cents per pound additional. For a small family plant producing raw milk cheese, this added inventory cost is magnified by what may be 100 days from the time of distribution to the time of payment for the cheese. Leo Nuttall remarks that some distributors, almost traditionally, "love to never pay on time." Transportation costs are, as usual, a larger proportion of their costs for smaller companies, and the breakdown of a vehicle carrying cheese that requires refrigeration can be a disaster, while a processed cheese might just sag a little.

The normal pricing of cheese is based on the price of a 40-pound on the Green Bay, Wisconsin, market. Other costs are then added onto that standard price. Among the initial costs for the maker of quality raw milk cheese is the employment of an experienced cheesemaker—not required for mass production of a processed product—and the purchase of good-quality raw milk.

It is already difficult for the small raw milk cheese manufacturer to compete in price with the giants of the dairy industry, who market through supermarket chains. Competing is made even more difficult if a cheaper product, improperly labeled "raw milk cheese," is on display under false colors, making it impossible for the consumer to tell the difference. The Institute hopes to end that by making the real thing easy to identify.

Most manufacturers do not package their own cheese for retail sale. Cheese-makers generally sell 40-pound blocks to cutting/packaging operations which slice the cheese blocks into the smaller packages for the consumer. Under the Institute membership program, the 40-pound blocks of raw milk cheese bear a large seal, and the package places smaller seals on the smaller packs cut from the block—or has the seal as part of the pre-printed label.

On behalf on the Institute, Leo Nuttall and his assistants drop in on plants to inspect their operations, and they take samples from retail stores in their travels across the nation. If any cheese is not up to standard, the Institute can revoke the license of the offender, who cannot then use the seal of approval. If a license is ever revoked, members of the National Raw Milk Products Institute will be notified by mail.

No system that does not monitor each block of cheese can give a 100 percent guarantee, but this program of self-regulation is likely to reach Nuttall's goal of offering a high degree of protection from false labeling to the manufacturer, packager, retailer and consumer of raw milk products.

# 15

# *Federal Almanac*

## by Howard Summerfield

The nutrition education efforts of the American food industry appear to be "nothing more than just product promotion," according to Rep. Fred Richmond (D-NY). He reached that conclusiong after reviewing a comprehensive survey of nutrition education done by the subcommittee on Domestic Marketing, Consumer Relations and Nutrition of the House Agriculture Committee, of which he is chairman.

Under the guise of nutrition education, food companies are promoting their products to captive audiences, he said. He cited as examples the classroom material furnished by such leading food firms as Campbell Soup and Del Monte. The House Nutrition Subcommittee recently released the results of a comprehensive survey of the nutrition education efforts of 38 of the "giants of the American food industry" and five trade associations. The Subcommittee questionnaire was sent to 53 leading food companies and ten trade associations in order to obtain an objective assessment of what these firms were doing in nutrition education, and what they believed the role of private industry, education, and the government should be.

The Subcommittee conducted a comprehensive examination on what the role should be of the federal government in nutrition education. As part of this investigation, the House group also held a public hearing to get the views of top food industry executives. Rep. Richmond did not like what he learned at hearings and from Subcommittee investigation, and is pushing for legislation to improve nutrition education.

**Products promoted under guise of nutrition education**

# LACK OF A
# NATIONAL POLICY

Rep. Richmond explains that the Subcommittee's survey of nutrition policies gives "a disturbing insight" into the food industry by "uncovering a lack of stated nutritional policies by most companies." Of the 28 companies replying to this question, he said, 23 had no written policy. As a result, Rep. Richmond "fears that now it is the chemist, the marketing analyst and the advertiser" who are responsible for the nutritional makeup of our food.

# NO NUTRITION POLICY

According to Rep. Richmond the results of the Congressional survey indicate that:

"1) Nutritional education is viewed as a means of encouraging consumers to purchase a certain product rather than to maintain healthy diet.

"2) The food companies on the whole lack any stated nutrition policy.

"3) Those food companies which engage in so called nutrition education believe the only message consumers need is to eat... without any consideration as to health problems such as obesity.

"4) Most of the nutrition education in the public schools by large food companies is designed to promote their product rather than a healthy diet."

Rep. Richmond, reporting on the survey, said that under the guise of nutrition education, food companies are promoting their products to captive audiences. In at least one instance, he said, the survey found that the total advertising budget for two product brands, Fleishmann's margarine and Egg Beaters, was offered as nutrition education expenditures.

The food industry's concept of nutrition education is frequently nothing more than an excuse for such self-serving concepts as "Breakfast Nutrition," "Dairy Nutrition," or even "Wiener Nutrition," Rep. Richmond said. In the face of a rising incidence of obesity and other diet-related health problems, he added, "food company messages say eat something of everything. Rarely is emphasis given to diet and health."

Rep. Richmond did say that the Subcommittee's survey showed that there were a number of individual industry activities that are praiseworthy for their scope, quality and accuracy.

However, Rep. Richmond said, he was "disturbed to find on an industry-wide basis the same lack of focus, confusion of message and duplication of effort which plagues government programs." He explained that the Subcommittee's survey of the federal government could not determine accurate expenditures for nutrition education, and the survey did not produce any "meaningful figures" for the private sector.

Rep. Richmond cited low expenditures for nutrition education by General Foods, Campbell Soup Co., and Pillsbury, in comparison to product advertising.

# GOVERNMENT'S ROLE

Replies from the food industry said the role of the federal government should be to:

• Conduct nutrition research.

• Insure the accuracy of the nutrition information provided on labels and in advertisements.

• Provide for nutrition education at the primary, secondary, college and professional school levels.

• Disseminate basic information about nutrients.

Most often cited by those replying to the House questionnaire as being the responsibility of industry were:

● To provide safe, nutrition, and appealing products.

● To inform "consumers" of the nutritional composition and merits of its products.

● To communicate to the public information about the principles of good health and the importance of a balanced diet.

● To assist the government in its educational functions by providing information about specific products.

Replies to the House Subcommittee indicated that most of the food companies did not consider the present program of nutritional labeling as needing improvement to become useful to consumers. It was pointed out that the program was only five years old, and more time was needed for consumers to get used to it. Responses from some said they were unaware of consumer dissatisfaction.

Corporations "unaware" of consumer dissatisfaction

Thirteen companies said that the present labeling program "definitely should be improved" and five others said that it might be desirable, but only after considerable research was undertaken to determine what kind of improvements would be most valuable to the consumer.

During its hearings, the Congressional group heard a number of criticisms of the nutritional labeling program. Spokesmen for food retailers and manufacturers pointed to difficulties due to regulatory restrictions and conflicts.

# REGULATORY PROBLEMS

George W. Koch, President of the Grocery Manufacturers of America, called for resolving conflicts in the approaches of the Agriculture Department and the Food and Drug Administration to nutrient education themes. He explained that USDA's nutrition education programs embrace a food-based approach, currently the four food groups, while FDA's programs revolve around "an incompatible system based on nutrients." An early decision needs to be made, he said, as to what strategy should be followed. Pointing out that nutrition education must by necessity be a long-range effort, Koch urged both nutrition education and food technology be enlisted in any effort to improve the nutritional status of the American people.

Robert Aders, President of the Food marketing Institute, stressed to the Richmond Subcommittee the importance of finding different ways to present nutrition information and labeling in the marketplace so that it will better meet consumer needs. Companies are now restricted in what they can do in this area, he said, because of restrictions already in place or proposed by the Food and Drug Administration, US Department of Agriculture, and the Federal Trade Commission. It might be helpful, he said, to have a moratorium for a period of time on nutritional labeling and information regulations to provide for such marketplace experimentation.

A food-based or a nutrition-based policy?

Both Kraft and the Grocery Manufacturers told the House Subcommittee that they do not believe that print or television advertisements can be effective in improving nutrition education. Both strongly objected to a rule proposed by the Federal Trade Commission which would require the listing of nutrients in advertising.

GMA's George W. Koch urged the Subcommittee not to make any such recommendation in order not to encumber brand advertsising, since the FTC proposal "is impractical from a communications standpoint," and "commercials cannot serve as vehicles for providing detailed information."

William O. Beers, Chairman and Chief Executive Officer of Kraft, warned that "an attempt to convey explicit information through product advertising is more likely to result in confusion than education."

# GENERAL FOODS QUESTION

An integrated effort by the public, voluntary, education, and private sectors that would focus on nutrition education activities was suggested by Andrew J. Schroder III, Vice President, Public Affairs, General Foods Corp. Replying to the questionnaire of the House Subcommittee, Schroder said, "the urgent question is not whether there should be greater coordination and focus in nutrition education activities, but how such a necessary result should be organized."

**Nutrition Education Council proposed**

Schroder suggested that a joint council might be named the "Nutrition Education Council" and could be governed by its own board of trustees composed of educators, government and industrial representatives, together with representatives from other professional organizations having a broad profile of skills related to nutrition, education, communications and equipment. The task groups, he added, would be organized by this board to compile a comprehensive nutrition information data bank, to develop ongoing systems to reach specific target audiences, and to monitor the effectiveness of resulting educational activities.

The Subcommittee's investigation, Rep. Richmond said, revealed that current nutrition education efforts have ignored the relationship of food, diet and health, and almost never deal with nutrition as it pertains to prevention. "Processed foods," he added, "are not in themselves bad, but they're made with chemical additives of unknown health value and have uncertain nutritional qualities. Some say that all foods have a place in our diets, but I believe that some foods are better for us that others."

Rep. Richmond said that nutrition education means different things to different people. For example, he said that to consumers it means staying healthy and avoiding being ripped-off in the marketplace, while to the food industry it is a "strategy for selling products."

Based on the comprehensive investigation of the House Subcommittee, Rep. Richmond has concluded that the "Government is not providing effective information to those who need it most."

# THE FTC

Once one of the quietest of government agencies, the Federal Trade Commission began last year to change its image. The food industry became a prime subject for the FTC under Chairman Michael Pertschuk and a new, aggressive staff.

**Marketing systems running amok**

Pertschuk has said that the problems of food marketing today are different from the past, and they do not represent the classic consumer-deception issue where an advertsier knowingly deceived or misled the public "as to either the good's qualities or the blatant hazards of his product." The concerns we have, he said, "are the product of a marketing system which seems to be running amok."

There is a growing concern by government regulators, spurred by members of Congress, about food, diet and health. The FTC's action will certainly encourage other agencies to act, especially is the Commission is successful.

Pertschuk last year explained to the Board of Directors of the Grocery Manufacturers that the Commission is "not about to engage in a rampage of random mayhem on the food industry." However, he added that "the food marketing revolution has produced a series of by-products that raise serious concerns," and the FTC is addressing these concerns.

**Radical transformation of the food supply**

"Consumers," he said, "are concerned about what they view as a radical transformation in the food supply that reaches their tables—are fearful about the health impact of restructured, reprocessed, chemically-altered food products, and they seek—in some cases, despairingly seek—information on which they can rely. They are concerned about a marketing system which employs its most powerful persuasive resources to sell its families the least nutrition foods. They are concerned about attitudes and knowledge about nutrition implanted in the very early years by commercial messages whose object is to sell, not educate, their very young children."

# ADVERTISING RULE

The report of the Presiding Officer on Phase I of the FTC's proposed trade regulation rule on food advertising was published in March, 1978, marking the completion of a major stage in development of these rules which will have a significant impact on all segments of the natural food industry.

Covered in the proposal is the advertising of energy, calorie, organic and health-related claims.

● Food advertising containing energy claims should be required to disclose the number of calories the product contains.

● The hearing record does support a finding that representations concerning the diet-heart relationship can be made which are factually true and do not otherwise have the tendency or capacity to deceive if such representations include and are limited to statements that a particular product which is low in cholesterol and/or saturated fat may, as part of a total dietary plan designed to reduce cholesterol intake, serve to lower serum cholesterol levels and reduce the risk of heart disease.

● That the record does not support the ban proposed by the FTC staff on the use of "natural," "organic" and similar description for foods.

● That no food should ever be described as a "health food" because this expressly represents that such products are "superior to other products and that claim could not be justified under any standard."

● That infant formulas be included in the definition of "food."

# ADVERTISING TO CHILDREN

A petition from Action for Children's Television and the Ralph Nader-backed Center for Science in the Public Interest requested the Commission to promulgate a trade rule regulating the advertising of candy and other sugared products. After an extensive study of the petition, the FTC's Bureau of Consumer Protection recommended that the Commission proceed with the rule "to eliminate harms arising out of television advertising to children."

Responding to the staff recommendations, the Commission has voted to proceed with speeded-up rule-making proceedings for regulating children's advertising, including the consideration of less drastic alternatives than outright ban.

The Commission called for comments on these proposals:

1. A prohibition on all TV commercials addressed to children too young to understand the selling purpose of advertising;

2. A prohibition on TV commercials addressed to older children under 12, for sugared products which pose most serious danger to dental health; and

3. A requirement that advertisers selling other sugared products to children, also be required to fund the broadcast of affirmative health and nutritional messages to tell children both sides of the sugar story.

The Commission also called for comment on several additional proposals, including disclosures in the body of commercials, limitation on the number of commercials addressed to children, and limitations on particularly deceptive or unfair techniques or messages used in children's advertising.

The less drastic alternatives considered are: affirmative disclosures within the bodies of the ads; separate affirmative disclosures on nutritional information funded by advertisers for all carcinogenic products; limitation on techniques used in advertising to merchandise to very young children and all children for highly-sugared foods; limitations on the number or amounts of ads directed to very young children and on the number or amount of sugared food ads directed to children.

The FTC would be far less concerned about the advertising of sugared products if the mix of products advertised reflected roughly what accepted nutritional wisdom tells us is a healthful diet, according to Pertschuk. But even then, he added, there are those concerned that advertising distorts the role of food in our society—the overconsumption, stimulated by advertising, is as serious a problem as the mix of foods in our diet.

Advertising distorts the role of food in our society

"It is not the individual ads, not the individual products, that raise concern," he said, "but the cumulative impact of hundreds and thousands of ads on the foods we eat and the role food plays in our lives."

There is very strong support from consumer groups and parents. While no one likes the idea of prohibiting the advertising of any product, it will be very difficult for the advertisers and the media to show the benefit of their promotions.

Don't look for any results for some time. A spokesperson for the Kellogg Co. is quoted as saying that the firm doesn't expect any changes before five years.

The FTC action will be the subject of legal action for at least two years. In the meantime, the warnings are clear—when diet and health are concerned, especially to a vulnerable audience, extra care must be taken.

# FOOD COMPETITION

A Bureau of Competition Task Force has been studying its food program and is preparing recommendations for future antitrust actions, but in the meantime the FTC has an active program dealing with competition throughout the food marketing chain.

**Food monopoly challenged**

According to Alfred P. Dougherty, Jr., the Bureau's Director, "we will continue our substantial effort to maintain and increase competition in food manufacturing and processing. Among such efforts is one of the most significant cases brought by any antitrust agency." He was making reference to the Kellogg, or the cereal case, in which the FTC alleged that major producers of ready-to-eat cereal, who controlled 90 percent of the market in 1979, used that joint market position to avoid price competition, to deter new entry, and to maintain artificially low prices in violation of Section 5.

"Our goal in this 'shared monopoly' case," he explained, "is deconcentration of the industry through divestiture of some assets and products and compulsory licensing of certain additional products."

Mr. Dougherty promised that the FTC will continue its "strong enforcement presence in food manufacturing" and will act decisively whenever the competitive process is threatened.

# DIETARY GOALS

A revised edition of a set of controversial dietary goals for the United States was released by the Senate Select Committee on Nutrition just before the group went out of business in January 1978. The dietary goals, which are backed up by research and documentation, are of major importance to the natural foods business since they will be hotly debated as part of efforts to get a national nutrition policy.

**Dietary goals revised to reflect criticism**

The first edition of the goals raised a considerable amount of criticism from representatives of the meat, sugar, salt, egg, canning, and dairy industries. A task force of professors from land grant colleges warned that the goals, if adopted by government, would have severe economic consequences to specialized food producers, with the processing and fabrication segment being hardest hit.

The revised edition of the Senate Nutrition Committee's dietary goals reflected some of the criticisms received after it issued its first report in January 1977. The report in general stresses that the less a food is refined, the more nutrition it is. It updates the orginal report and adds sections on obesity and alcohol consumption.

The revised Dietary Goals are:
• To avoid overweight, consume only as much energy (calories) as is expended; if overweight, decrease energy intake and increase energy expenditure.
• Increase the consumption of complex carbohydrates and "naturally occurring" sugars from about 28 percent of energy intake to about 48 percent of energy intake.

- Reduce consumption of refined and processed sugars by about 45 percent to account for about 10 percent of total energy intake.
- Reduce overall fat consumption from approximately 40 percent to about 30 percent of energy intake.
- Reduce saturated fat consumption to account for about 10 percent of total energy intake; and balance that with poly-unsaturated and mono-unsaturated fats, which should account for about 10 percent of energy intake each.
- Reduce cholesterol consumption to about 300 mg. a day.
- Limit the intake of sodium by reducing the intake of salt to about 5 grams a day.

# FOOD SELECTION

The goals suggest the following changes in food selection and preparation:
- Increase consumption of fruits and vegetables and whole grains.
- Decrease consumption of foods high in total fat, and partially replace saturated fats whether obtained from animal or vegetable sources, with polyunsaturated fats.
- Decrease consumption of refined and other processed sugars and foods high in such sugars.
- Decrease consumption of animal fat, and choose meats, poultry and fish which will reduce saturated fat intake.
- Except for young children, substitute low-fat and non-fat milk for whole milk, and low-fat dairy products for high-fat dairy products.
- Decrease consumption of butterfat, eggs and other high cholesterol sources. Some consideration should be given to easing the cholesterol goal for pre-menopausal women, young children and the elderly in order to obtain the nutritional benefits of eggs in the diet.
- Decrease consumption of salt and foods high in salt content.

Suggested changes in food selection and preparation

The goals say that "persons with physical and/or mental ailments who have reason to believe that they should not follow guidelines for the general population should consult with a health professional having expertise in nutrition regarding their individual case."

In releasing the new goals, Sen. George McGovern (D-S.D), Chairman of the Senate Nutrition Committee, noted that six of the ten leading causes of death in the United States have been linked to diet. At the same time, medical costs are fast approaching $200 billion. He stressed the need to increase the priority of prevention-oriented practices as part of our national health policy. The estimated savings of an effective preventive nutrition program, he said, could be a significant factor in reducing health-care costs. Sen. McGovern said: "Consumers should be made aware that less nutritious, or so-called 'empty calorie' or 'junk' foods which are often high in saturated fat, refined and processed sugars, and salt, may involve a health risk." He said that "it is time we turn our sights toward a goal of better nutrition, not just medical care."

Sen. McGovern explains that 'the purpose of the Dietary Goals report is to point out that our diets have changed significantly during this century and represent a critical public concern." And he added that it is important that we recognize that the public is confused about what to eat to improve health.

# DIFFERENCES OF OPINION

According to Sen. McGovern, "Clearly, some, or all, of the dietary goals may be subject to honest scientific differences of opinion. Nonetheless, these recommendatins, based on current evidence, represent a consensus which offers guidance for making prudent decisions about one's diet. They are not a legislative initiative. Rather, they provide nutrition knowledge with which most Americans can begin to take responsibility for maintaining their health and reducing their risk of illness."

The goals should be viewed "in an outgoing context as part of the evolution of a national nutrition policy," Sen. McGovern explained. In that respect, he adds, they are similar to the Recommended Dietary Allowances of the National Academy of Sciences, which are updated every five years.

Evolution of a national nutritional policy—other opinions

The ranking Republican on the Select Committee, Sen. Charles H. Percy (Ill.) said that the report "fails to adequately represent the scientific and medical controversies which exist with respect to the setting of dietary guidelines and to the substance of the goals themselves."

Specific reservations of Sen. Percy were:

(1) The accuracy of some of the goals and recommendations given the adequacy of current food-intake data;

(2) The question of what would be the demonstrable benefits to the individual and the general public, especially in regard to coronary heart disease, by implementing the dietary practices recommended in the report; and

(3) The question of whether advocating a specific restriction of dietary cholesterol intake to the general public is warranted at this time.

The National Live Stock and Meat Board and others have continued to challenge the politicians where they promote "fad" diets as matters of public health, and their efforts deserve the help of all in this industry, the National Independent Meat Packers Association has told its members.

The President of the National Cattlemen's Association called the report "a bit more balanced" than the first edition. However, Richard A. McDougal added, "the report still treats meat and other animal products in a way that is not justified by valid scientific evidence." Mr. McDougal said: "The report still reflects too much the view of just one segment of the scientific community. It appears to us that there is equally, if not more, compelling evidence suggesting that recommended dietary changes would make little or no difference in the incidence and severity of cardiovascular disease or cancer."

# A "DISSERVICE"

Food processors' recommendations ignored

Dr. Ira I. Somers, Executive Vice President of the National Food Processors Association (formerly the National Canners Association), said that "the purpose of dietary goals may be admirable, but ignoring or disstating the facts about one of the largest segments of the food industry is a disservice to consumers."

The latest report ignored many NFPA recommendations. It includes a quote which NFPA protested in the first report, which indicated that the decline in certain nutrients in the diet was the result of a shift from fresh products to canned, frozen, and dried produce. NFPA had asked a revision to show that the nutrients remained high when the canning process is completed.

Another NFPA recommendation not incorporated in the final report was that it would be advisable to "at least create a balance in the diet between fresh and processed products."

NFPA also took issue with the reports conclusions that to maximize micro-nutrient availability for those on reduced diets and to ensure adequate nutrition availability to those who do not widely vary their diet, "it would seem prudent not only to increase use of fresh foods but those undergoing the least processing."

The future of the goals is difficult to determine. As a Congressional statement, it will receive (and has received) considerable publicity. Members of the public will follow the goals as people follow any "fad," and some food manufacturers will promote products based on parts of the goals.

Too controversial to be good politics

The second edition of the goals will likely be the last we hear from Congress in this area for some time. As Sen. McGovern and his fellow Senators found, they are too controversial to be good politics.

There will be follow-up studies sponsored by government agencies on implementation of the goals. The Food and Nutrition Board of the National Academy of Sciences has a contract with the US Department of Health, Education and Welfare to identify research needs in connection with the dietary goals, and the Agriculture Department has contracted with the Board to study such subjects as ranges of nutrients, public health problems, and fabricated foods.

USDA's Agriculture Research Service is considering the Senate group recommendations as part of research on Recommended Daily Allowances. USDA hopes to use this information on RDA's and the recommendations from the Food and Nutrition Board as the basis for nutritional specifications for revising the USDA food selection guides.

# SOURCES FOR ADDITIONAL INFORMATION

Select Committee on Nutrition and Human Needs, U.S. Senate, Dietary Goals for the United States—Second Edition, December 1977, GPO Stock No. 052-070-04376-8. $2.30.

Select Committee on Nutrition and Human Needs, U.S. Senate, Dietary Goals for the United States—Supplemental Views, November 1977. GPO Stock No. 052-070-03987. $5.75.

These publications are available from: Superintendent of Documents, Government Printing Office, Washington, D.C. 20402.

# THE WHITE HOUSE

Responding to a strong public interest in human nutrition, the federal government is working on the development of a national nutritional policy and a unified mechanism for implementing such a policy.

A national nutritional policy

The natural food business has a major stake in the outcome of this policy and the way it is implemented. The outcome of this increased attention to nutrition might well mean added government regulations on food processing and marketing, including requirements for fuller food labeling and added restrictions on the use of chemicals in and the advertising of foods.

Among the significant activities focused in Washington, DC are:

● Efforts by the White House to coordinate and reorganize the federal nutritional structure.

● Increased attention to nutrition policy by Senate and House Committees.

● Activities within the federal agencies themselves to sharpen their focus on nutrition.

# NATIONAL POLICY NEEDED

The importance of developing a national food-nutrition policy has been stressed by Esther Peterson, Special Assistant to the President for Consumer Affairs. She said that nutrition, or food policy, relates to the food system as a whole — "which means it relates to the need of the farmer for an adequate income to stay productive, as well as to the need for policy makers and program planners for current, reliable information on the nutritional status of people."

Peterson supported developing a system of research independent from production research within the food system policy structure. She said: "Nutritional science is too important to be left to scientists."

Who can be trusted?

She stresses the importance of giving consumers adequate and complete information on additives and what they can do about them. Consumers want complete information about what they buy and are not aware of the benefits of additives, she said. "Frankly, the American public is frightened by recent scientific research on possible carcinogens in our food." "They are," she added, "in a quandary about who they should trust."

# REORGANIZATION

Under the Reorganization Act of 1977, the President has the authority to submit reorganization plans to Congress over the next three years. The organizational plans will go into effect unless disapproved by Congress within 60 days.

The objective of an Office of Management and Budget review was "to improve the government's capability to address the nation's needs for adequate supplies of reasonably priced, safe, and nutritious foods." The President's memo to federal agencies identified several factors which he believes will increase the need for a comprehensive food and nutrition policy mechanism. These include:

"— the increased use of pesticides, preservatives, artificial flavorings, and other chemicals in the production and processing of food;

"— changes in the availability of energy and land resources;

"— increased reliance on the packaged food supply;

"— environmental concerns and regulations; and

"— changes in the international situation which affect the demand for American farm products."

**Interagency Human Nutrition Research Group**

An Interagency Human Nutrition Research Group, organized by the White House Office of Science and Technology Policy (OSTP) is working on ways to get better agency coordination. The OSTP Working Group has representatives of the Department of Agriculture, The National Institutes of Health, the Food and Drug Administration, Department of Defense, Agency for International Development, and has occasional participation by the staff of the Office of Management and Budget.

OSTP Associate Director Gilbert A. Omenn explained that the objectives of the Working Group are:

(1) to define the domain of human nutrition research;

(2) to describe and assess existing programs;

(3) to draw major agencies together to identify jointly priority research areas among current programs and proposed new areas;

(4) to build mechanisms to enhance coordination of research activities and the sharing of nutrition research information throughout the federal government.

# MORE RESEARCH

**Areas for expanded research**

Six priority areas have been identified where continued and expanded research efforts "appear needed."

(1) Normal development and prevention of disease — including research on preventing obesity, vitamin dependencies, and arteriosclerosis.

(2) Treatment of disease.

(3) Human nutrition requirements and physiology.

(4) Nutrient composition of processed and unprocessed foods. Extensive research, Dr. Omenn said, seems necessary to determine the effects that food processing — cooking, canning, freezing, preserving — have on the nutrient content of foods.

(5) Nutritional status monitoring.

(6) Nutritional education.

The interagency group is particularly concerned about coordination of research among federal agencies. It does not suggest that it is appropriate to try to define the research responsibilities of the agencies "so precisely that there is no overlap in coverage of these six areas," so long as research planning and research information is coordinated.

There is a growing attention to human nutrition within various federal agencies. This increased activity is being spurred by a Congress very interested in the subject.

Secretary of Agriculture Robert Bergland told a Senate committee last year that "this country must develop a policy around human nutrition, around which we build a food policy for this country . . . And in that framework we have to fashion a more rational farm policy. We've been going at it from the wrong end in the past."

# 16

## Anatomy of a Health Food Fraud Case

### by David Armstrong

When Lester Lowe walked into the small warehouse in downtown Los Angeles in the spring of 1977, it seemed like a routine inspection, the kind Lowe, a California State Food and Drug Specialist, had made many times before. Instead, it was the beginning of a complex fraud case that would shake the natural foods industry, raising questions about accuracy in labeling and the ability of the industry to guarantee the integrity of its products.

What Lowe found were workers taking jars of standard Derby House mayonnaise, dipping them in vats of warm, dirty water to loosen their labels, and replacing the Derby House label with the label of their employer Jack Patton's "Lecinaise," a popular mayonnaise substitute.

A case of fraud

Lowe and his supervisor Howard Ratsky snapped photos of the procedure. Shortly thereafter, the Department of Health slapped a recall order on Lecinaise. In December of 1977, Jack Patton plead no contest to 30 criminal counts. On March 22, 1978, he was sentenced in Los Angeles Municipal Court to 30 days in jail and an $18,500 fine. An appeal is pending on the sentence, though not on Patton's guilt, in the Appellate Department of Los Angeles Superior Court.

Those are the bare bones of the story. But to flesh it out, we must go back 40 years to the late 1930s, when Patton says he began marketing Lecinaise. For years, the need for a low-fat replacement for mayonnaise had been evident. Lecinaise appeared to be that product.

According to Patton—and to the labels his Lecinaise jars were carrying when they were recalled in 1977—Lecinaise contained "multiple mixes of vegetable oils, lemon juice, apple cider vinegar and three percent lecithin," the enzyme that helps break down fatty substances in the digestive process. Nowhere on the label did it say that Lecinaise contained eggs, sugar, salt and the preservative EDTA. But it did contain them, at least in recent years, and this labeling omission—which Patton unsuccessfully argued was justified—was to prove the major bone of contention when his product became the subject of a legal battle.

Unlabeled ingredients

Patton's product was not an immediate success—Patton, early on, had trouble getting glass and standardsized jars, among other things—but its popularity grew steadily. Established distributors like Kahan and Lessin (K&L) in Los Angeles carried it for 20 years all told, as did San Francisco's Landstrom Foods. When the natural foods industry began its remarkable growth in the 1970s, respected new firms like Westbrae Natural Foods in Berkeley picked it up. Lecinaise was eventually sold in Oregon, Colorado and California.

Everywhere it was introduced, Lecinaise sold well. Michael Besancon, the proprietor of Follow Your Heart, a restaurant and retail outlet near Los Angeles, figures he sold $50,000 worth of Lecinaise in his kitchen in just a few years. Many people in the industry used Lecinaise themselves. "I was buying the damn stuff because I liked it," admits Ernie Miehle, now K&L's national sales manager. "It was a good mayonnaise product."

# NAGGING DOUBTS

Even as the popularity of Lecinaise grew, however, there were nagging doubts about its authenticity. These doubts would have been confirmed had a series of letters to Patton from Early California Foods, the Los Angeles company that made Lecinaise for Patton in the mid-1970s, been public knowledge. Copies of the letters were obtained by **Whole Foods**.

In six letters between September 4, 1974 and February 5, 1976, officials of Early California Foods warned Patton that they would no longer make his product if he did not bring his label into compliance with the actual formula used to make Lecinaise, as required by federal law.

In the first letter, dated September 4, 1974, assistant plant manager Ben Lee wrote: "I am very surprised to read the ingredient panel of your label, because I formulated your Jack Patton Mayonnaise Spread and Dressing according to the original formula that you furnished." Lee advised Patton that his label was "misleading and deceptive" because: "multiple mixed vegetable oil . . . is a collective name and is not allowed to be used" under federal law; because there was no apple cider vinegar or lecithin in Lecinaise; and because the "water, eggs, sugar, spice or mustard flour" that then were in the product were not listed.

In spite of intensifying pressure from Early California Foods, Patton refused to change his label. On February 4 of the following year, the company notified Patton that they would no longer make his product. Later requests by Patton to reopen his account caused the company to reply that they would do so only if they could proofread the Lecinaise label before and after it was printed. Patton went looking for another supplier.

At about the same time, friends in the industry were warning Michael Besancon that Lecinaise was not what it appeared to be. " 'Hey, Mike,' they said to me, 'the guy (Patton) isn't straight. He's not doing you right,' " Besancon remembers. Every time, I went to him and said, 'Jack, this is the situation and this is what I've been told.' And every time, he swore that that was not the case, that his product was pure and as labeled. We probably had 10 or 15 confrontations."

# CUSTOMER COMPLAINTS

Consumer complaints reached distributors like Westbrae and Landstrom, but their accuracy, the distributors say, could not be established. Ken Krich, general manager of Westbrae, recalls that Good Food People, a Westbrae customer in Austin, Texas which is part of a religious community that does not eat eggs, claimed that Leciniaise contained eggs. "So we called Patton," Krich remembers, "and he said, 'Oh, it isn't true.' "

"We had some suspicion, but it was a very popular item. And, oh, I don't know, it was kind of a combination of no firm evidence and a little bit of greed, and a little bit of a feeling that the customer must be right. If everybody buys this stuff, it must be what it is supposed to be. It had been around for years. So I didn't want to believe what I was suspecting."

Formulator protests mislabeling, refuses to make product

Ernie Miehle, who was director of sales for Landstrom at the time of the state action, recalls that his firm, too, had had consumer complaints. "But you get that all the time anyway. People who frequent health food stores are a suspicious lot. If you change the color of a label, they assume that the product has been changed. And they will tell you that the product doesn't taste the same. And for that reason you don't put too much credence in these reports."

Nevertheless, Westbrae and Follow Your Heart were sufficiently unsettled to commission separate laboratory analyses of Lecinaise. These proved inconclusive, however, so despite growing unease, distributors and retailers continued to handle Lecinaise. Proof that the product did indeed contain the eggs, sugar, salt and preservatives that had been feared came not from consumer complaints or lab reports, but from a letter to Patton's customers from the State Department of Health in May 1977, advising them that Lecinaise was in violation of California law.

Patton was charged with a misdemeanor in Los Angeles Municipal Court. State and city officials testified that Patton simply bought standard mayonnaise from CHB Foods, Inc. of nearby Pico Rivera, and Pfeiffer Foods of Los Angeles (makers of Derby House mayonnaise), which he marketed as a health food product. According to the court ruling, the list of ingredients on the relabeled mayonnaise should have read "vegetable oil, water, whole eggs, egg yolk, vinegar, salt, citric acid, sugar, spices and EDTA, a preservative."

The response from distributors and retailers who had handled Lecinaise was mixed— part anger and part embarrassment. Embarrassment that the industry had not been able to detect and police violations of its own standards. Anger that one of their own would knowingly violate those standards.

# INDUSTRY REACTIONS

"The guy's a rip-off artist and we've lived with him for years," groans Miehle. "The story was so bad, I was hoping it was in the closet and would never come out. It's a thing that tests the credibility of our industry, because we let this guy exist and bought his product. We all did it with the best of intentions, only to find out he'd been screwing us for years."

Krich was even sharper in his judgement of Patton. "The guy was putting another label on mayonnaise! There's just no question in my mind that that's totally dishonest and fraudulent. There are many people that have allergies to eggs that were eating his product—and were getting sick and couldn't figure out why. He was endangering people's health to make a profit. I think that was really low."

Although they generally perceive state and federal health bureaucracies as uncomprehending at best when it comes to natural foods, industry people polled by **Whole Foods** unanimously backed the authorities on this one. Jan Stoll, merchandising manager at K&L, spoke for everyone when she said flatly, "The fellow just abrogated all responsibility in relabeling a commercial product."

Jack Patton, although he did not formally deny the charges against him, did offer an explanation in the sentencing hearings early this year. Patton went through several defense attorneys before settling on Robert Leff of Beverly Hills shortly after he entered his plea of no contest. When **Whole Foods** contacted Leff, he claimed not to have heard from Patton in several months and said he did not know how to reach his client.

Patton "took a vacation" right after the sentencing, according to Leff, then went back to work—but not in the health foods business. "He's a musician, an entertainer initially," Leff said, "so he was entertaining this summer with a musical combination. I think he was on the road back East with them." Leff said he doesn't think Patton is in the health food business any longer. A telephone call to the Los Angeles number of Patton Natural Products turned up a disconnected phone with no new listing.

Nevertheless, Patton is said to be concerned about the effects that the Lecinaise case has had on his reputation, asserting through Leff that his sentence was harsh and his representation of the product was misunderstood. Leff concedes that there were some "minor technicalities in the labeling," but says that Patton did not claim that the product was eggless, as irate customers claim.

# A CHANGED FORMULA

According to Leff, Patton did indeed market a mayonnaise substitute—eggless, and free of salt, sugar and preservatives— until 1966, when he changed the product's formula. At that time, says Leff, Patton sent a letter to his customers, advising them that Lecinaise would comply with the legal standard of identity for mayonnaise—meaning that it would contain eggs, sugar and salt, as mayonnaise is required to do.

Since the word mayonnaise appeared on the Lecinaise label, Leff continues, the presence of eggs, sugar and salt was implicitly understood by buyers—or should have been—even though these ingredients were not listed individually. "What I found out," says Leff, "is that the witnesses the prosecution produced that sold this stuff in the health food stores don't understand the standard of identity. They say they do. But if they do, then they know it contains eggs."

Leff also maintains that federal law—as distinguished from California law—did not require full ingredients labeling when Lecinaise was on the market. "Our position is and has been that when you're engaged in interstate commerce, as Patton was, you comply with federal law. So he was complying with federal law, he was being supervised by federal law, his label was in compliance with federal law."

**Whole Foods** asked Leff why Lecinaise, if it met federal regulations, was not being sold in Oregon or Colorado, where no state charges were lodged. He replied:

"Well, the fact is that there were some minor technicalities in the labeling—which under the law became a technical violation, as I see it. So they were right in requesting him to take it off the market because it did not carry an accurate label. It didn't in my opinion carry the charges that the people contended was the result of all this—that he was selling a product that was allegedly eggless and salt-free."

Continues Leff, "Somebody at some point in time believed that it wasn't the same product, and it turned out that it wasn't. But I don't think it had the heinous qualities that the court determined on all the multiple charges." Leff adds that the legal battle over Lecinaise has had an adverse effect on Patton's business. (He was a purveyor of about 30 products.) "Oh, he took a substantial loss."

Patton's former customers, as well as his prosecutors, are less than impressed with his defense, which they dispute on nearly every count.

Some of Patton's early customers—Landstrom and K&L, for example—believe that Patton probably did market a health food mayonnaise substitute at first. "It evidently had to be a legitimate product without all the junk in it, because it had a tendency to go bad at one time," recalls Miehle. "And then he evidently said, 'Oh, the hell with it all, I'm just going to get anybody's mayonnaise, put all the preservatives in the world in it, put my label on it, and who's going to know the difference?'"

Others doubt that Lecinaise was ever legitimate, partly because they believe that the know-how to make a palatable egg-free mayonnaise substitute did not exist 30 years ago, and partly because they simply do not trust Patton.

# VERBAL ASSURANCES

There is evidence, however, that contrary to Patton's claims, he continued to represent Lecinaise as a natural product to some customers and consumers long after 1966. Follow Your Heart's Besancon and Westbrae's Krich tell of repeated verbal assurances from Patton that Lecinaise was egg- and sugar-free. Both so testified at Patton's sentencing hearing.

They also introduced into evidence a letter dated March 24, 1976 from Patton to his customers in which Patton wrote, "We put out two products with very similar-looking labels . . . Our multiple mix oils mayonnaise is made with organic, fertile egg yolks. Our Lecinaise formula has no eggs in it."

Even after Patton was caught selling relabeled mayonnaise as Lecinaise, he continued to claim that Lecinaise was free of eggs in explanations that became ever more tortuous.

On June 15, 1977, he again wrote customers. "I've stated before . . . that we have manufactured two very similar products with *very identical labels* [our emphasis] and some people have confused one with other . . ."

"In our mix oil mayonnaise," Patton wrote, "we use organic, fertile eggs. (We discontinued this product to avoid confusion and problems.) In our Lecinaise formula we do not use those eggs."

Tortuous explanations

Even more damaging to Patton's case, however, is a handwritten letter from Patton to a worried consumer assuring the consumer—who had a high cholesterol blood count and wrote Patton asking him to verify the safety of Lecinaise—that Lecinaise was entirely safe. The letter, dated November 14, 1977, reads in part:

"You are the second party in 38 years to write us in this regard. The other party who said . . . Lecinaise was loaded with cholesterol was told Lecinaise had a very, very low cholesterol, if any. Her or his doctor had it tested in a laboratory and apologized. Said all his heart patients will be told to use Lecinaise.

"Finally, I enclose a copy of lab test, the latest one. So you have nothing to worry about."

The laboratory test Patton refers to in his letter was conducted in 1958, according to research done by the Los Angeles City Attorney's office and verified by Patton. This was well before the changeover to standard-of-identity mayonniase in 1966, yet Patton continued to cite the test results as current.

# ALTERED REPORT

Moreover, research by the City Attorney's office revealed that the words "no cholesterol detected" in the lab report were typed in at a later date on another typewriter. During his sentencing hearing in March, Patton told the court that he typed in the words himself. He testified that before doing so, he cleared it with the laboratory chemist who had conducted the test.

According to Deputy City Attorney Lynn Miller, the prosecuting attorney, her side introduced into evidence a signed affidavit by the chemist that said he had never performed a test for cholesterol on Patton's mayonnaise product. "He's not authorized to tell somebody 'no cholesterol detected' if he never performed the test," says Miller. "And even if he had, no chemist calls up somebody and says, 'Uh, by the way, you can type in blah-blah-blah' on his test reports." The defense did not call the chemist as a witness.

A shaky defense

Patton and Leff's claim that Lecinaise was labeled in compliance with federal law also appears to rest on shaky ground. In breaking with Patton in 1975, Early California Foods' Ben Lee pointed out that when the federal Food and Drug Administration (FDA) and State of California reviewed Patton's labels in 1965, "they approved the labels . . . without the ingredients list, not with the ingredient list on it . . . at that time the FDA and state regulations allowed the use of such label if it had federal standards of identity."

However, Lee went on, "this is 1975, and both federal and state require full ingredient lists on the panel in descending order on the label . . . but you continue to reflect to 1965." Lee cited and updated Federal Food, Drug and Cosmetic Act and the Fair Packaging and Labeling Act in deciding to stop manufacturing Lecinaise.

Patton may well, as Leff says, have suffered severe financial losses after the recall of Lecinaise in 1977. But in 1976, by prosecuting attorney Miller's reckoning, he grossed "$150,000 to $200,000" on the relabeled mayonnaise. Miller cites records reportedly showing that Patton bought some $90,000 of CHB and Pfeiffer mayonnaise in 1976, after Early California dropped the product. A quart jar of Lecinaise retailed in Los Angeles area health food stores at an average price of $3.70 early in 1977. The same mayonnaise bearing the Derby House label sold in supermarkets in the area for about a dollar.

Miller allows that Patton's label did have the word mayonnaise on it, but adds "Not everybody knows what that means. What people look at is the list of ingredients. His ingredient list stated multiple mix vegetable oils, apple cider vinegar, lemon juice and three percent lecithin. In terms of the CHB mayonnaise, it was not multiple mix vegetable oil, it was straight soy oil, just one oil. It was not apple cider vinegar, it was just straight distilled vinegar. This is standard brand mayonnaise.''

# THE EGG TESTS

The weight of the evidence, then, confirms Patton's guilt. He bought standard mayonnaise that he relabeled and sold at premium prices, misrepresented a laboratory report that was, in any case, outdated, invoked federal regulations that were also outdated, and assured customers and consumers that Lecinaise was pure.

But Patton not only violated the letter of the law, he violated the spirit of working relationships he had established over a period of years with people who trusted him, and who, despite honest intentions and expertise in the natural foods field, were unable to pinpoint the violations. People with educated palates failed to identify Lecinaise as plain mayonnaise. Others who questioned Lecinaise's authenticity were unable to confirm the presence of eggs, for example, in the product.

**Violating the spirit of working relationships**

This last point is puzzling. Besancon and Krich say that separate laboratory analyses of Lecinaise failed to find eggs. Comments Krich: ''We tried to test for eggs. But you can't test for eggs if it's got lecithin in it, if lecithin is a part of the eggs that passes the test. Except there's a $3,000 test you can do, and we didn't want to spend $3,000 on it.''

**Whole Foods** contacted Melanie Baltezore, the laboratory manager of Unilab Research in Berkeley, with questions about testing procedures for detecting eggs in a mayonnaise product. According to Baltezore, lecithin and eggs can be differentiated by taking ''an amino acid profile of a known mayonnaise product versus a lecithin-type product and comparing a third product to those things.'' Baltezore says such a test at Unilab would cost ''$125 to $150.''

Of course, testing a full range of products can be difficult and costly, even for an established enterprise. Says Landstrom's Robert Merriam, ''We don't have the time to analyze 11,000 items (the number Landstrom holds in stock). And they change back and forth—sizes, packages and everything else.'' Merriam confirms that he had heard that Lecinaise was being tested, ''but that was maybe a week before Patton got caught. As a distributor, we had to trust our manufacturer.''

Trust. The word comes up again and again when Patton's former customers discuss the Lecinaise controversy. Trust is an important ingredient in the natural foods industry, a legacy of the days when the industry was small and everyone knew one another. Certainly, many people knew Jack Patton. K&L and Landstrom worked with him for 20 years, Besancon since about 1970, Westbrae since they picked up Lecinaise in 1975.

To know Patton was not necessarily to trust him completely. As Miehle tells it, ''The guy is a strange businessman. I remember seeing his invoices, and they were written on a piece of paper torn out of a kid's copybook. And you'd never know when you'd get merchandise from Patton. He'd send you a bill sometimes, and sometimes you could read it and sometimes you couldn't.''

# NATURAL BRIGHT ORANGE

Others were put on guard by what they saw as Patton's peculiar history on the periphery of the Hollywood entertainment world, a history they feel left him with a certain glibness. Krich remembers getting a phone call from Patton in early 1977 about a new French dressing that Patton was marketing.

''He said, 'This is all natural, no preservatives, no this, no that.' So I looked at it and it looked just like commercial salad dressing, French dressing. Bright orange, and it said no emulsifiers. I called him up and said, 'Jack, how do you emulsify this?' Because oil and vinegar separate. 'How do you keep it together?' 'Oh, it's all natural.' 'How do you get that bright orange color?' He said, 'Oh, it's all natural.' He obviously didn't know anything about what was in the product.''

Still, industry people gave Patton the benefit of the doubt. Explains Besancon, "I go on the premise that if you make a statement to me I don't know to be false, I have to accept it at face value. There's no way for me as a merchant in Los Angeles to go to, say, New York and find out about a product that's manufactured there and shipped to me here. I have to take the person on his veracity."

When state health inspectors publicized Patton's relabeling procedure, they revealed the limitations of trust and exposed the vunerability of the industry to people who choose to take advantage of its traditional informality.

A vulnerable industry

While emphasizing that they check out new products as thoroughly as possible, industry people concede that there is no rigorous, industry-wide test to ensure that misrepresentation will not occur. "If you come up with the answer, kiddo, tell me," jokes Jan Stoll. Then she adds, more seriously, "We (K&L) go through motions that the average retailer cannot go through. We require signed—with the corporate seal of the company—indemnities for Food and Drug, verifying that the product is unadulterated and is indeed what the label says it is. If a place is doing their own manufacturing, we try to visit that establishment. Granted, that's not always possible. We talk with other distributors around the country. If there are suspicions about somebody, we try to pursue it and look at it further.

"But mostly it's a matter of faith. It's a matter of faith."

"It's hard to really know," concurs Krich. "You can go down and visit the plant. But Westbrae doesn't have that problem any more. We carry very little that doesn't have our label on it. And, since Jack Patton, we have been very cautious. Because we were very embarrassed by it.

"Now your bigger companies, they weren't so embarrassed, because they carry something like 10,000 items. So you can't help but blow one once in awhile. But we carry so few items, we really try to be careful. What we do is quiz people hard on how their product is made. You know, do they understand the questions we're asking about their product? We decide if we trust the person or not. We ask around the industry. There are no secrets. Stories get around pretty fast."

# STANDARDS NEEDED

Such safeguards notwithstanding, it took state authorities to confirm the suspicions about Lecinaise and take action to stop distribution and sale. Government intervention—particularly when it's by governments that are invariably ill-deposed towards natural foods—is not something industry people relish. But it was necessary—this time.

What can be done to make certain it doesn't become a habit? How can the industry apply preventative medicine to itself?

"Well, we hope we'll be able to rely on the standards committee of the National Nutritional Foods Association to do that," says Merriam.

Besancon believes that the industry should go much further. "What I would like to see is something similar to the old Organic Merchants that started in San Francisco in the late sixties that would certify products. Right now, there's no one that has a base-type criterion for certification of any particular product.

How can the industry protect itself?

"We need a certification program and a means to do it. And that's an expensive proposition, because you have to inspect the premises. It can't be done by the government, because, say, we want to certify something 'Code N' for naturally grown. They won't certify it as that because they don't see that there's any difference between one method of cultivation and another."

"A publication could do it," Besancon offers. "A coalition of publications and groups could do it. I think it's an absolute necessity if we're going to exist and keep our credibility. Something that would give customers and store-owners alike confidence in what they buy. And a recognizable logo to go with it."

In the meantime, the industry is left to ponder the lessons of the Lecinaise experience, its self-confidence shaken, its vulnerability to the inside con painfully exposed.

# Section III: Snacks & Sweets

The American sweet-tooth is notorious, and is large enough to support two major industries—the manufacturers of the junk foods, and the enterprises devoted to correcting the excess, including weight-loss programs, a wide array of books and magazines about nutrition, and purveyors of the foods which offer an alternative diet. Kicking the junk-food habit is often the first step on the path to natural foods.

Many consumers begin the transition to more wholesome eating by way of natural food snacks, juices, sodas, or non-sugar sweeteners. Various "munchies" are the items most likely to make their way first from the warehouses of the natural foods industry onto the shelves of major supermarkets. The customer who might curl a lip at kelp or bean curd is often willing to reach for a carob-coated "energy bar" rather than the habitual chocolate candy bar.

A prudent shopper at the natural snacks rack would look closely at the ingredients listed on the labels. The industry offers a wide range of such munchies, some hardly different from the candy-store brands, and some made with carefully chosen components which are processed as little as possible. The label-conscious purchaser who wants to avoid refined sugar will need to know its various guises, recognizing, for example, that "brown sugar" is refined white table-sugar with a light molasses coating added after refining. Some snack foods may include three or four different sweeteners, perhaps with only "Honey" printed large on the front of the package.

At present, the use of fructose as a sweetener is a matter of debate within the natural foods industry. Although generally regarded as healthier than sucrose (refined white sugar), fructose is the product of a highly technological process involving chemical interactions. Fructose is natural in an apple, but many doubt if it is natural in a bottle after being extracted from corn. Many manufacturers are sticking to the reliable old stand-by, honey.

As the first chapter in this section will show, honey is about as reliable a product as can be found, and cannot legally be greatly altered by the supplier. Once the bees' work is done, the honey-packer may heat it up briefly and filter it—and the rest is labeling.

While the word "honey" on labels has strict limits of use established by law, phrases like "natural fruit juice" may be used to describe extremely dissimilar products. The extent to which bottled juices are "natural" is a matter of degree. Some may undergo little more than a squeezing of the fruit and straining, while others may be a blend of concentrates with an emulsifier added to prevent separation in the bottle. The choices and problems faced by juice processors, and a few tips for buyers, are discussed in this section.

Another way to have the benefits of fruits in the diet is to get them in their dehydrated form. The amount of processing that occurs between the tree and the customer depends partly on what a particular fruit requires, and partly on the goals of the packer: Some aim for the brightly-colored product which has more eye-appeal to many customers. Treatment of the fruit with gases is not at all uncommon.

The chapter titled *From Tree to Table* includes several paragraphs on the use of sulfur compounds on dried fruits. That information, from the Institute of Food Technologists (IFT), indicates that such treatment is well within the limits prescribed as "safe" by federal agencies. But some persons concerned with natural foods express three main reasons for viewing the IFT position with scepticism: The addition of any chemicals to our foods is considered undesirable; the limits of safety set by government agencies change under the influence of new research and political pressures; and the Institute of Food Technologists consistently expounds positions which are favorable to the practices of the giant food industries, and unfavorable to organically-grown, natural foods.

One aspect of the political economics of food is illustrated more vividly in the chapter *Recess from Junk Food*, which shows some of the problems involved in bringing more wholesome foods into public school systems. School cafeterias, lunch rooms, and vending machines provide an important part of the nourishment of this nation's young people, and what is offered is shaped to a great extent by the fact that schools are publicly funded, and are therefore subject to influences beyond good nutrition for the students.

The natural foods industry is just starting to make an effort to enter the schools with wholesome alternatives, and has encountered both an entrenched food establishment and a set of consumers who are hard to wean from meals of chocolate bars and colas. Making natural foods highly desirable in school cafeterias is one of the toughest challenges being tackled by people concerned with the diets of young people.

75

# 17

# Honey

## by David Johnston

The honey you buy which is labeled "natural," old fashioned," "country style," "raw," or "organic" may have been heated to 150 degrees Fahrenheit or more, pumped through a fine filter, cut with other kinds of honey, and otherwise processed. This is a far cry from the made-in-the-backyard image projected by much of the labeling.

Honey labeling is a neglected problem in the natural foods industry, made worse by the fact that honey sales through natural foods retailers constitute a significant part of the honey market. Just how significant is not accurately known. The demise of the American Honey Institute eliminated the one nationwide honey trade group in a position to compile national figures.

**Honey production statistics**

Some product statistics are available. The California Crop and Livestock Service estimates that commercial apiaries (those with over 300 colonies) in the 20 major honey-producing states produced more than 101 million pounds of honey last year—down eight percent from 1976. In addition to domestic production, the Foreign Agricultural Service of the US Department of Agriculture said that another 5.5 million pounds—less than 6 percent of the domestic output—was expected to be imported from 32 countries last year. That is a total of 116.5 million pounds, a figure which does not include the honey produced by smaller apiaries and sold directly to the retailer or consumer.

Honey production is down. The amount of honey extracted from each colony of bees has decreased from 59.7 pounds in 1976 to 55.3 pounds last year in the major honey-producing states.

**Legal definition of "Honey"**

The USDA sets standards, which most states follow, for grades of honey, and defines what can legally be labeled "honey." According to the legal definition, honey is limited to "the nectar of the floral exudations of plants gathered and stored in the comb by honeybees." Therefore, such terms as "raw," "natural," or "organic" add no real meaning, since, according to the legal definition, anything that isn't "raw," "natural," or "organic" couldn't be sold as honey. Nevertheless, many honey packers put these terms on their labels. The result, says Marilyn Kiser, assistant manager of the California Honey Advisory Board, is, "It's a mess. Words like 'organic' and 'natural' just don't mean anything." the California board is the only state agency in the USA established solely to promote honey.

Miller's Honey, in Colton, California, is among the many who use the term "organic" on their labels. Jackie Ness, a company spokesperson, said, "We use the term because, if you look it up in the dictionary, it means free from foreign particles. And our honey doesn't have any, so we don't think there is anything wrong with using it." Miller's strains its honey through a fine-mesh cloth, and reportedly never heats it above 125 degrees Fahrenheit.

Confusion also arises over the terminology commonly used to describe how the honey is processed after the beekeeper has extracted the honey from combs and sold it to a packer. These terms, as they frequently appear on labels, are "uncooked," "unheated," "unfiltered," "unbleached" and "undiluted." Here is the real significance of these terms.

# HEATING AND COOKING

No commercial honey is ever cooked if you think of cooking as putting something on the stove and boiling it. Honey packers generally do apply different amounts of heat, for two major reasons: First, heating makes honey thinner, easier to handle. This is significant because commercial packers, dealing in large quantities of honey, are concerned with rate-of-flow. Second, heating honey reduces its tendency to granulate, a factor in consumer acceptance of honey. A less important side-effect is that heating can kill off the natural honey yeasts which could cause fermentation and spoilage.

Nearly all honey will granulate if it isn't heated. That is because honey is a supersaturated sugar solution, which means that its sugar concentration is so high that sugar would crystallize out of the solution if left at room temperature. Heating retards this granulating process.

**Granulated honey**

Heating does not ruin honey as long as the heat is not prolonged and the honey is cooled immediately. Some of the larger packers flash-heat their honey to tempeatures above the boiling point for a few seconds by pumping the honey through heated pipes. "We've found it doesn't do much harm to the honey," says Dr. Eric Mussen, an apiculturist at the University of California at Davis.

But prolonged exposure to heat can cause the enzymes and proteins in honey to deteriorate. "If honey was heated to 160 degrees Fahrenheit for a long time, the enzymes would break down, and proteins would alter in shape, and the color and flavor would change—and not for the better," says Dr. Mussen.

Some honey producers maintain that any heating is harmful to honey. One is Bob Sterling, of Sterling & Son Honey near Little Rock, Arkansas. "When honey is heated," Sterling says, "it loses flavor and some of the oils and esters that give it aroma. I don't heat my honey at all."

The type of honey called "buttered" or "creamed" is nothing more than honey in its granular state. But, just because it is granular does not prove that the honey has not been heated. some packers process their honey using heat, then regranulate it by adding "seed" honey crystals to produce the very fine granulation and creamy texture.

# FILTERING

Despite any label claims to the contrary, any honey that is clear and has a shiny appearance has been filtered, or at least strained to remove particulate matter such as bee parts and pollen. These are always present in honey as it leaves the comb.

**Grades of honey**

The USDA grades honey according to its filtration. The greater the clarity, the higher the grade. US Grade A honey, for example, is the rating given to honey that has been strained through a screen or cloth of at least 90 meshes per square inch. (For comparison, a nylon stocking has about 100 meshes per square inch.)

US Grade A honey is also officially designated as "Fancy." Other USDA grades are B, "Choice," with clarity equivalent to straining through a 57 to 79 mesh sieve; Grade C, "Standard," equivalent to at least an 18 mesh sieve; and Grade D, "Substandard," equivalent to less than an 18 mesh. These grades have no significance beyond the size of particles in the honey, and imply nothing about quality.

The USDA does, however, keep a quality-rating of honeys which is seldom seen by the public. Their rating method includes three factors on a 100-point scale. Flavor can rate a 50-point maximum, absence of defects (particles) can rate 40 points, and clarity, 10 points. Neither these ratings nor the four official grades place any constraints on the marketing of honey. All are legally saleable.

Larger packers may go beyond simple straining. Some firms, according to Dr. Mussen, mix "diatomaceous earth"—the chalky silica skeletons of plankton—into their honey. This chalk-like substance picks up foreign particles and is removed as the honey is pumped through a series of filtration discs. Beekeeper Bob Sterling asserts that these filtering and straining processes "take out the pollen and what the good Lord and the bees put in the honey in the first place." He handles the problem by simply letting the honey settle overnight. On the other hand. Roland vom Dorp, general manager of Western Commerce, a Southern California honey packer, maintains, "filtering removes all the dirt that's in there accidentally. The amount of pollen that's present (which is removed by filtration) is negligible."

Even honey which is sold in the comb may have been filtered and processed. Some packers who sell "comb honey" process the honey and then pour it into a jar along with a clean comb.

# DILUTION

The term "undiluted," as it is generally applied by honey packers, means that no water has been added to the honey. The more moisture in honey, the greater the risk that the honey will ferment. According to Dr. White, that is because the glucose in the honey releases hydrogen peroxide which retards fermentation. As more water is added, the concentration of glucose decreases, reducing the bacteria-fighting qualities of the honey.

However, adding water to honey would constitute an adulteration, which would mean that, according to the legal definition, it could no longer be called honey. So the term "undiluted" has no special significance.

**Moisture in honey**

# BLENDING

A blended honey is one composed of honey from more than a single source. Even honey labeled as the product of a single source—Sage, Orange Blossom, Clover—may in fact be blended. Many states, like California, require only that 51 percent of the honey come from one source in order to use that source-name on the label.

Blended honey is not necessarily inferior to unblended. Blending is used to alter the moisture content and to enhance the flavor of certain strong-tasting honeys. Orange Blossom, for instance, is commonly blended with a milder, lighter honey in order to reduce its bitterness.

**Blending improves flavor**

# PESTICIDES

Pesticide contamination may be a slight danger in honey, but this danger is probably less with honey than with many other foods. The reason, according to Dr. Mussen, is that "pesticides are a lot more likely to kill bees than get into the honey, because a bee that's gotten into a pesticide will probably never make it back to the hive." And a bee affected by insecticide will soon exhibit changes in behavior which will make the colony refuse it admission to the hive.

Pesticides have been so widely used that there is virtually no such thing as a pesticide-free environment. Dr. Mussen points out that traces of pesticide are even found in moss in northern Alaska, where these chemicals have never been used.

The work-habits of bees help to reduce the problem. Worker bees gathering nectar dive deep into the blossoms, where the concentration of pesticides is much lower than on the outer parts of the flowers.

One major question often raised about honey is whether it has any nutritional or medicinal properties. The answer: Honey is marginally superior to refined sugar but is not, by itself, nutritionally significant. Medicinally, however, honey evidently has a distinctly positive value.

Honey is actually a composition of several substances. Ted Hooper, in his book *Guide to Bees and Honey*, breaks down an average honey sample into these component parts: water (18 percent), glucose (35 percent), fructose (40 percent), other sugars (4 percent), and other substances (3 percent).

are found. Vitamins, minerals and proteins are all present, but only in trace amounts. "The problem is that there aren't enough of these things to make any dietary difference. Nutritionally, honey just isn't significant," according to Dr. Jonathan White, a USDA honey researcher in Philadelphia.

Unlike refined white sugar, the two main sugars contained in honey—glucose and fructose—are pre-digested. They are far more easily absorbed into the human bloodstream than refined sugar. Honey can be a quick energy source for athletes under stress and for elderly persons who may have digestive problems, according to Dr. White.

Honey also has some value as an internal medicine for allergies, and as an externally-applied dressing for wounds. Research has shown that honey contains floral substances which operate in the human body as allergy-fighting antibodies. "There was a man in Oregon who made honey from poison oak. It didn't taste very good, but he sold it to people who were allergic to poison oak, and it did help them," Dr. White said.

Honey is useful as a dressing for wounds due to its bacteria-fighting properties, and because it is hygroscopic—that is, it draws water from the air around it. When applied as a dressing, it draws lymph from the blood which further aids in keeping bacteria from infecting the wound. "But I don't use honey for any of these reasons," Dr. White said. "I like it because it's a natural sweetener, and it tastes good."

**Does honey have a medicinal value?**

# 18

## Juices

by Jim Schreiber

Let's start with apple juice. That's simple enough.

Take some apples, squeeze them up, pour the juice in a bottle, cap it, and there it is. Apple juice: the lowest-cost, best-selling juice on the market.

Or buy some apple concentrate and apple peel, add water, add some enzymes, heat it, bottle it, cool it, and there it is: apple juice. The label could say the same thing—apple juice—in both cases. No regulations or standards require anything different.

But it would be a mistake to assume that the difference in these two theoretical bottles is the difference in a "good" and a "bad" juice on the grocery store shelf. Fruit juices all start at the source, a fruit growing on a tree, bush, vine, or shrub, and can be handled in a wide variety of ways at each stage before disappearing into a shopping bag. The only way to get fruit juice which is entirely unprocessed is to pluck and eat the fruit in the field.

Starting at the source, few fruit juices claim to be "organic." If that claim is made outside of the few states which have organic-labeling laws, the concerned shopkeeper is in the usual position of having to find out just what that term means, seeking certification documents and standards from suppliers. Since there are no universally recognized organic standards, decisions about acceptability remain in the hands of the retailer and consumer.

**The apple of your eye**

The fruits which become bottled juices are generally not the fruits which line up in handsome rows in produce bins. The latter are selected for size and cosmetic appeal to the consumer, while fruits for juices can be smaller and have visual imperfections, which in no way lowers the quality of the juice. That eye-appeal may double the price of the fruit, which would be a pointless expense for the juicemaker. The juice processor may buy fruits which remain after the over-the-counter lovelies have been sorted out, or may contract for an entire crop, whichever is most reliable and economical.

# FILTERING SEEDS

Even the most ardent advocate of unprocessed natural foods does not seek a fruit juice which includes stems, seeds, leaves and skins. Choices have to be made to determine how much clarity is desired, and how it is to be achieved. The major methods to clarify a juice are settling, mechanical filtering, centrifuging, and the use of clarifying agents. Overnight settling is a common approach among smaller bottlers, who then simply draw the relatively solid-free liquid from the top part of the settling tank, producing a juice which remains somewhat cloudy and settles out more in the customer's bottle. Pumping the juice through metal screens, cellulose fibers, or cloth is often combined with the settling process, to remove all the particles larger than the mesh of the filter. A similar result is attained by whirling the liquid in a centrifuge, which separates the heavier from the lighter particles.

Screens, whirls, enzymes, and skeletons

To bring about the transparent clarity that so many supermarket shoppers have grown accustomed to, something more must be done to the juice. The addition of diatomaceous earth or of enzymes enhances the settling-out action by making the smaller particles form clusters which drift to the bottom. Diatomaceous earth—the powdered silica skeletons of microscopic sealife—is widely used in various aspects of the natural foods industry, including the filtering of honey and as a pesticide in grain storage. An inert material, it has no known harmful effect on human beings, but to the natural food "purist" it is a processing substance not found in the fruit itself. Unlike diatomaceous earth, enzymes do bring about chemical reactions in the juice, and some processors indicate that some flavor and aroma are taken out along with larger particles when enzymes are used to clarify juices.

The virtues of various degrees of clarity are largely matters of taste. Some buyers will be suspicious of a clear juice, and prefer the "mouth feel" of the less clear product. Nutritional claims are rare among these products, but clarity by itself does not indicate that nutritional value is missing. In fact, the particles which produce cloudiness are largely cellulose, of no nutritional value, so it is even possible for a clearer juice to have a slightly higher proportion of nutrients.

Clouds of cellulose

Making nutritional claims would involve the bottler in the regulations of the Food and Drug Administration, requiring a nutritional analysis to be printed on each bottle. Ironically, this would be easier for the high-volume producer who makes a standardized drink than for the bottler who stays close to what nature provides. Because the fruits themselves vary according to season, weather, locale and other factors, the producer who does the least processing will probably offer juices which vary the most from batch to batch, which may puzzle customers who expect a uniform product behind a uniform label. But to provide such uniformity requires careful control of what is taken out of and added to the juice in its most natural state. Without such control, the bottler would have to analyze the juice made from each load of fruit and print up new labels in order to make any statement about the nutritional value of the product.

# PREVENTING SPOILAGE

A problem faced by the bottler of natural juices is what to do about keeping the product stable while it sits in the grocery store. Bacteria are everywhere, and yeast cells naturally and universally accompany fresh fruit, so quick spoilage, fermentation, and, eventually, vinegar are the result of doing nothing about preserving the juice. The only way to avoid the problem of preservation is to sell all the juice within two or three days of bottling.

Refrigeration always advised

Refrigeration works, and is advised even by bottlers who take other steps to retard spoilage. But refrigeration adds costs to shipping, and few shopkeepers can devote refrigerated space to their complete stock of juices along with all their other perishable items.

To increase shelf life, bottlers use a "hot-pack" technique, which pasteurizes the juice. This is usually done by quickly heating the liquid to about 190° F. for a few seconds just before bottling, so the juice is around 160° F. when it goes into the bottle. Such pasteurizing takes place in a heat exchanger that works a lot like a car radiator: the juice is pumped through a maze of thin tubes or plates which are surrounded by hot water or steam. Immediately after being capped, the hot, bottled juice goes through a spray bath of water which cools it, halting the speeded-up chemical reactions caused by the brief heating. The hot-packed juice has a shelf life of many months, rather than the few days of the unpasteurized product.

Both heat and sunlight can affect a juice in the bottle, triggering chemical reactions. Oxidation inside the bottle can make the juice darken and change in flavor. To forestall oxidation, a bottler may choose to stabilize the juice by adding acid—most commonly ascorbic acid, otherwise known as vitamin C. If the juice comes from a plant that contains natural oils, while the bottle sits on the shelf the oils will separate out—which is not acceptable to many consumers—so it is not unusual to add an emulsifier to hold back the separation. Lecithin and various gums, such as carob gums, can be used as emulsifiers in fruit juices. Again, these are not necessarily unhealthful ingredients, but they are something added to the juice which is not found in the original fruit.

# IT TAKES CONCENTRATION

**From roadside stand to food technology**

Once the juicemaker gets beyond the roadside stand next to the orchard, countless decisions have to be made as to amount and type of processing to engage in to supply a product economically to a larger market. Many choose to use purees, nectars or concentrates. This can lead into the mysterious realm of food technology, where chemists can create concoctions which seem nearly identical to natural ingredients, and can be very difficult to detect. One executive of a natural fruit juice company told, with grim humor, of 50 drums of Concord grape concentrate which entered a Los Angeles flavor fabricating plant and emerged as 500 drums of Concord grape concentrate, which was purchased by an unsuspecting juice bottler.

That true story suggests the difficulty for the consumer, retailer, wholesaler, broker, and even the bottler of knowing exactly what is in fruit juices that do not come straight from the field. Whether or not federal watchdogging is desirable, it is a fact that there are large gaps in legal definitions of fruit juices, and the regulations on the books are not now extensively policed by any government agency. Complete information about all the juices found in natural food stores would involve tracing the entire "life history" of each one through a tricky array of terms. For instance, "100 percent pure strawberry concentrate" is, in theory, nothing but strawberries, while "100 percent natural strawberry concentrate" may contain ingredients other than strawberries.

A pure puree is made by pulping the fruit and forcing the pulp through a screen, to strain out seeds and skins. The puree can be frozen, canned, or otherwise packed under sterile conditions. The major advantages of puree over fresh fruit are easier handling, storage, and shipping, which makes it possible to have papaya juice for Christmas in Nome, Alaska—a far cry from the fleeting seasonal roadside stand.

# MORE THAN FRUIT

A "nectar" is defined by the FDA as a pulpy liquid food prepared from fruit and water and one or more sweeteners and optional acidifiers. The nectar regulations specify different percentages of pulp for different fruits, ranging roughly from 15 to 40 percent. Allowable sweeteners include sugar and corn syrup, but oddly omit honey. Permissible acidifiers include such items as citric acid, ascorbic acid, mallic acid, tartaric acid and lemon juice. With such a range of ingredients allowable within the FDA definition, the buyer's information is far from complete if given only the term "nectar."

Although food technicians can brew up drinks whose chemical profiles are nearly identical to natural fruit juices, it is possible to use refractometry, chromatography and other techniques to find out what's in the bottle. Quality control personnel at fruit juice production facilities may ask something that sounds like, "How many bricks?" and learn a lot from the answer. What they are actually asking is, "How many Brix?" The Brix scale is a standardized measure of the amount of dissolved solids in the liquid. The Brix measurement runs close to the percentage of sugar in a juice, and, since each kind of fruit has a normal sugar level, a departure from the expected Brix number will suggest that the juice has been doctored—perhaps watered down, perhaps dosed with sugar.

The purchaser with scientific inclinations might want to check out fruit juices in such ways, but few have the inclination, the time, or the money to do so. Fortunately, there is a simpler test which can be applied to both juices and sodas. Since sodas are much like fruit juices in their ingredients—with the addition of carbon dioxide — the same criteria generally apply. And so does the same easy, final test. Taste it.

To test it, taste it

"Taste it" is the advice given by people throughout the natural juice and soda industry. To the tongue which is educated to natural flavors, artificial flavors usually simply taste artificial. In addition to the palate, the eye can be useful in judging a drink. If it looks too good to be true, it often is. Extreme clarity indicates the extensive use of enzymes. A too-bright, cosmetic appearance suggests artificial coloring. And complete uniformity of the beverage from one lot to the next is a clue that somewhere along the way someone is taking pains to add to or take away from the variations which nature imposes on fruits.

# THE ACID BITE

Sodas, of course, will be more acidic than non-carbonated drinks, since the acid "bite" is part of the experience of thirst-quenching. It is not unusual to add citric acid to heighten the effect, and at the same time ward off any spoilage problems. Spoilage seldom occurs in sodas, in any case, because their carbon dioxide does not allow oxidation to occur.

Sometimes a completely trustworthy company will have other problems which affect the product. A recent problem is the supply of bottles. For the producer who uses fresh fruit, it is important that the ripe fruit and an adequate supply of bottles be on hand at the same time. But, due to bottle-makers' strikes, juice and soda bottlers have had some problems meeting the growing demand. Larger companies get the bottles first; some sizes are being phased out as an economy move; some glassworks are switching to beer bottles only; and the supply is sometimes short. In at least one case, operations were suspended because there were no bottles available. The use of plastics and metal cans is one way to outflank the shortage, but many of the people who sell natural beverages doubt that such containers would be acceptable to their customers. And bio-degradable plastics cannot hold carbonated drinks.

Breaking the bottle barrier

Bottles cause a pang of worry for yet another reason: the ecological concern. Glass is practically indestructible and litters the highways, city streets, and parklands. Yet for people in the natural foods industry who are sincerely concerned about the environment, the re-useable, returnable bottle is often too costly a venture. Bottles weigh nearly as much empty as full, which would create a high shipping cost. Added to that would be the cost of cleaning and sterilization, which is more difficult and expensive with returned bottles than it is with new bottles. Unless the bottles become standardized, so they need not be returned to their source, this problem will remain.

# 19

# From Tree to Table

## by Janice Fillip

The story of dried fruit begins in the orchard. With the exception of dwarf apple trees which bear fruit after one year, most trees do not bear for their first six years, and are not considered profitable until their tenth season. Trees continue to bear fruit for a relatively long time: peach trees for 25-30 years, prune-plum trees for 65 years, and pear trees for as long as 100 years. Yield per acre varies dramatically with the type of fruit being grown. For example, Timber Crest Farms realizes 3-4 tons of apricots per acre, but as much as 20 tons of pears per acre.

**Originating in the orchard**

Fruit is hand-harvested from May to October. With the exception of pears, fruit is allowed to ripen as long as possible on the trees. The longer the fruit is on the tree, the more natural sugar it contains since sugar development occurs during the last ten days the fruit is on the tree. The relationship between potassium and calcium in the soil plays an important part in determining a fruit's content. At Timber Crest, periodic soil/leaf analyses are taken to monitor this balance. Although trace minerals are routinely added to compensate for a calcium or potassium imbalance, Ron Waltenspiel remarked, "the best fertilizer is the farmer's foot."

If pears are allowed to ripen fully on the tree, they become too mushy to dry successfully. When pears reach a certain sugar-content level—determined by a pressure gauge—the pears are picked and put into cold storage at a core temperature of 35° F to ripen for seven days. Ruth Waltenspiel described a shortcut for ripening pears: Pears emit ethylene gas which causes them to ripen. If a box of rotting pears is placed under boxes of good pears, the ethylene gas given off by the rotting fruit can hasten ripening of the good fruit by about two days.

The day after the fruit is harvested, it is pitted and dried. Apricots are generally pitted by machine. Peaches, nectarines and pears are hand-cut. Pits are a saleable by-product of the drying process. Among other applications, apricot hulls are used as an industrial abrasive to clean jet engines and are also processed into apricot oil. Charcoal briquettes are made from peach pits, and pear cuttings are used for fodder. Cutters at Timber Crest are paid 50 cents for every box of fruit they pit (for pears it is slightly higher) and average from nine to twelve boxes an hour.

# DRYING TUNNELS

Reaching an average temperature of 120°F, the propane-fueled drying tunnels at Timber Crest dry up to 25 tons of fruit a day. Although each fruit dries at a different rate, the average drying time is twenty-four hours. Drying reduces the fruit's weight by removing moisture. Ten pounds of fresh apples dry away to one pound of dried fruit. The dry-away ratio is seven to one for peaches, six to one for apricots, three to one for prunes, and two to one for cherries. After drying, fruit is placed in cold storage until it is needed to fill an order.

Prior to packaging, the fruit goes along a shaker belt and is churned in a "dry wash" tunnel to remove loose pieces. Timber Crest packages over 65 percent of their fruit under their Fruit Pac label. These fruits are honey-dipped. A conveyor belt propels the fruit through a honey-and-water spray solution. The ratio of honey to water varies with each fruit. The greatest amount of honey—65 percent—is sprayed on peaches because water causes peaches to mold, and honey has a preservative effect.

The most commonly used figure for per-capita daily intake of sulfites from solid foods and non-alcoholic beverages in the US in approximately 2 mg. The Acceptable Daily Intake of sulfites for adults, as established by the United Nations FAO/WHO is 0.70 mg of $SO_2$ per kg of body weight.

Sulfites are normally formed in the body and converted through sulfite oxidase into sulfate for excretion in the urine. Presumably, sulfites added to food materials are metabolized in the same way and, in the amounts normally consumed, contributed less than one millimole (96 mg) to the normal daily sulfate production and excretion. Sulfites are considered Generally Recognized As Safe by the Food and Drug Administration.

*Dried, weighed and packaged*

# DRIED PINEAPPLE

Most of the dried pineapple sold in the US comes from Taiwan. There the pineapple is hand peeled, cored, sliced by machine and dried. Plain dried pineapple has a high acid content and is reported to taste like sour shoe leather. Sugar—Taiwan's major export crop—is usually used to sweeten dried pineapple. Pineapple slices are placed in small tubs filled with a sugar and water mixture. The water is gradually evaporated off, leaving a glasse' fruit which contains around 80 percent sugar. Most importers agree that "honey dipped" pineapple is actually sweetened with sugar. One importer has located a source in Taiwan which offers an alternative to sugar-cured fruit. Pineapple concentrate—the type used to make pineapple juice—is substituted for sugar-water. Analysis shows that the resultant fruit contains 45-50 percent fructose, 20 percent glucose and less than 5 percent sucrose.

*Sour and sweet*

# SULFITE SAFETY

Sulfites have long been added to food as a preservative: the ancient Romans and Egyptians used sulfur dioxide to treat their wine. Sulfites prevent browning during processing of light-colored fruits and vegetables. Their general preservative effect also conserves the carotene and vitamin C content of foods.

Sulfites come in many chemical forms including sodium and potassium (and occasionally calcium) sulfites, bisulfites, metabisulfites and gaseous sulfur dioxide. The particular chemical agent used for sulfite treatment is primarily a matter of convenience. In drying fruit, sulfur dioxide gas—$SO_2$—is generally used.

*A dried fruit preservative*

# 20

# *Recess from Junk Food*

## by Janice Fillip

The school cafeteria line used to be an auditioning spot for budding comedians. Some wag would inevitably cut up over the green hamburgers or hum a tune about marinated monkey meat. Few kids knew what "nutrition" meant. Health class was a place to doze to rhythmic incantations of the four basic food groups: one from column A, one from column B.....zzzzz. Food was just something to eat.

There is at least one woman in the American school system today who is working to change that picture. Her name is Thelma Dalman. She is Food Service Supervisor for the Santa Cruz City Schools in California. Food is no joke to Thelma. She takes it seriously enough to have spent the past six years introducing natural foods into school lunch programs. Thelma's pioneering efforts may change the eating habits of a future generation.

**JANICE: What are the requirements you must meet to have the cost of your school lunch program reimbursed by the federal government?**

**THELMA:** To receive reimbursement, we must adhere very closely to regulations set by the US Department of Agriculture. We are required to serve two ounces of protein—meat or meat alternatives—all the way through the 12th grade. Soy products are not acceptable. We can use 30 percent reconstituted TVP as part of the protein requirement, but it must be in combination with 70 percent animal protein.

We provide either ¾ or 1 cup of fruit and/or vegetable, one slice of enriched bread, one teaspoon of table fat (that requirement has been reduced from two teaspoons), and one 8-ounce serving of fluid milk. Whole fluid milk was required until about two years ago, but now we can use two percent nonfat or buttermilk. The regulations also allow eight ounces of chocolate milk. In our district, we do not serve that.

We serve vitamin A- and C-enriched foods as often as possible. For the cost of handling, USDA offers a lot of surplus commodity foods.

**USDA lunch program requirements**

86

**JANICE: How did you become involved in serving natural foods in the school lunch program?**

**THELMA:** I got involved with natural foods in 1972 when I heard Dr. Ben Feingold speak on his theory that artificial colors, flavors and certain preservatives could add to a child's problems if he was suffering from an adverse reaction. The more I listened, the more I realized that he was absolutely right. I recognized that more and more chemicals were being added to foods, and it certainly could have some bearing on the fact that we were experiencing more hyperactivity among our school-age children.

I proposed to study Dr. Feingold's theory in our school district and attempted to sell the program to my School Board. Their objection was that we were exploiting the children by publicly branding them as social misfits.

The State Superintendent of Public Instruction gave us permission and funds for a forty-day study. We came up with 35 students, ages 6 to 11, who were on behavior modification drugs to treat behavior problems caused by hyperactivity. We got permission from their parents to put the kids on a special diet. We eliminated all salicylates from the lunches, including all natural salicylates found in some fruits and vegetables.

# FOOD AFFECTS CHILDREN

**JANICE: What were the results of your study?**

**THELMA:** We did not have a cross-over double blind study. From a scientific standpoint, our study was extremely inconclusive. But during our study, four children were taken off their drugs and stayed off successfully.

We did not prove on a purely scientific basis that we were on the right track by removing artificial colors and flavors from the diet. I was angry that people did not see how much better off our children were without those chemicals in their bodies. A hungry child cannot learn. What a child eats affects his ability to learn. What a child eats affects his social behavior, his social acceptance. Until scientists can measure the cumulative effect of the 4,000 approved additives, I feel, as a person responsible for feeding 8,000 people a day, that I must eliminate these things.

**JANICE: Have you encountered any resistance to serving natural foods?**

**THELMA:** Our parent support is tremendous. The silent majority are parents who do not really know or care, or have not yet educated themselves to the fact that our food supply may not be as pure as they expect it to be.

When I pleaded to eliminate carbonated beverages and sugar-laden snacks from the high schools, my School Board said, "We understand and agree that we should be providing more nutritious products. But these are young adults and are certainly old enough to make the proper choices when it comes to purchasing the food they eat."

My contention is that, until these young people have been educated to make proper choices, there's no way they can make proper choices. At that point, the Board allowed me to hire a nutrition education specialist to work with our parents and teachers.

**JANICE: How do you decide what items to remove from the lunch menu?**

**THELMA:** I have to find a product that meets our standards—or build a product that meets our standards. It's been a long, slow process because products without additional chemicals are difficult to find.

We have to find out what students will eat. School lunch programs have had some bad publicity related to plate-waste. If children don't like the lunches, they won't eat them.

Our competition is fast food operations like McDonalds and A & W. If children could choose where they would like to eat every day, it would be one of those places. We have to find a way to provide a similar product. In our high schools we serve french fries cooked in safflower oil. I would like to be rid of that product, but it brings the students in and takes them away from snack bars. It's been a struggle finding burritos, tacos, and pizzas that are free of artificial flavors, colors and unnecessary preservatives.

*Food additives may cause hyperactivity*

*What a child eats affects his ability to learn*

*Without education, children cannot make proper choices*

*Competition from fast food operations*

# PLATE-WASTE

**JANICE: Have you noticed any difference in the amount of plate-waste since you have been serving natural foods?**

**THELMA:** No. There is plate-waste because children do not have time to eat their meals. They come flying out of the classroom, free at last, and need to get out and run. For five months we experimented in one school with having recess before lunch. There was no plate-waste. The children were hungry because they had gone out and relieved their pent-up energy.

Another reason for plate-waste is that many of our children are being raised eating at fast food operations which do not provide fruit and vegetables. Children are not learning to eat fresh fruit and vegetables. They don't want to take the time to bite into a crisp apple. We have little ones coming into school who don't know how to peel an orange!

**JANICE: What natural foods do you serve in your lunch program? Do the students like them?**

**THELMA:** We could eliminate unnecessary preservatives from entrees and the students would never know. The flavor essentially doesn't change because our fine cooks use herbs for seasoning. But when you get into salads, desserts and snacks, the kids recognize the difference.

We offer dried fruit as an alternative to sugared desserts. We're also giving unsalted mixed nuts and trail mixes. If we add carob stars to the trail mix, the kids think they're getting a candy. We also offer fresh fruit.

When we serve carrot and celery sticks with a dip, they're much more acceptable. We use buttermilk dressing as a dip, and the kids really like it.

Since we started vegetarian entrees, we're experiencing increasing participation. We're on the lacto-ova system, which is mostly eggs, cheese, peanut butter and legumes. I'm very much interested in exploring the use of soy protein and have requested permission to experiment using nuts and grains for protein in school lunches.

**JANICE: Are there any products you are required to use, but would like to change?**

**THELMA:** I have a few products I'm not able to change. The most controversial product is the hot dog. Right now, I'm using a turkey product. If I could be certain the products had been handled the way they should be all along the line, I would ask for a product without nitrites. But right now I still do not feel comfortable avoiding nitrites.

I have a real quarrel with leather fruit rolls, which are offered in a lot of health food stores. They are artificially flavored and artificially colored. Some local people developed a product called "Fruit Cloud" just for us, to replace commercial fruit rolls. It's naturally sweet, made from 100 percent low-moisture fruit such as banana, pineapple, apple and cranberry. It's made by Mrs. Schleff, a retired nutritionist who wanted to help our cause along. She went through all the necessary FDA and USDA inspections to provide us with this product.

# LOCAL HELP

**JANICE: Do you serve any other products made by local processors?**

**THELMA:** Most of our California-based people are able to provide a product for us. Hirschfelder's and Harmony Foods provide some of the quality things we need.

I have recently put in a new product, Yonique, that I'm very pleased with. It is an absolutely pure frozen yogurt. The enzymes have not been killed in it before our students get it.

The Lundberg brothers provide us with a beautiful brown rice. The commodity rice we get is polished white rice which has little or no nutritional value.

Children do not learn to eat fruit and vegetables

Increased participation with vegetarian entrees

The controversial hot dog

With a little help from friends

I'm attempting to develop a system to raise our own vegetables or have them raised for us. We already grow our own alfalfa sprouts. But unless we can get into hydroponics, there is a problem because most vegetables ripen in the summer when our need is lowest.

**JANICE: You mentioned to me that you run your own bakery. Tell us about it.**

**THELMA:** Right now our bakery is under two roofs, in small, inadequate kitchens. It's difficult to operate efficiently at a reasonable cost because of double deliveries, double staff, double equipment. I'm hoping to build a full-line bakery under one roof.

We produce all the breads and most of the pastries used in our schools. I'm trying to get legal permission to provide products to other districts to help defer our costs. Until local purveyors provide a quality product, I personally see no reason why we shouldn't vend that product ourselves.

School bakery defers lunch program costs

**JANICE: Does it cost you more to serve natural foods? How do you handle increased costs?**

**THELMA:** It's about 15¢ a meal more expensive to have natural foods. We are required to operate in the black, and it's much cheaper to serve a chocolate brownie than trail mix.

When we serve carbonated beverages, we also serve Mount Madonna pure fruit juices. We raise the price of the carbonated beverage and sell the fruit juice for less than it costs us. We aren't providing any candy now, but during the time we were, we raised the cost to a point where it was almost out of reach.

We contract meals to five other school districts and the county hospital. This helps subsidize our costs. We have been paying our own way.

Natural foods 15¢ a meal more expensive

# NEEDS OF SCHOOLS

**JANICE: How can members of the natural and health food industry help food service people introduce natural foods into the school system?**

**THELMA:** Several companies have sent me their catalogues, and I always have managed to buy from those companies. I appreciate being on mailing lists for new products. Most school districts prefer to purchase locally, and will do so whenever it's possible.

School lunch people need to be more aware that natural foods advocates are not food faddists. This is one of the major problems I've encountered. I'm considered some kind of kook or food faddist because I'm requiring purer food.

Natural foods advocates are not food faddists

Health and natural food people should contact their local food service directors and learn about the school district's goals in the area of nutritious and quality meals. If purveyors of natural and health foods learn the needs of the local schools, they may find opportunities to provide products to meet those needs. We have financial limitations, but we're forever looking for a new product that's acceptable.

Food service buyers attend shows sponsored by the American School Food Service Association. Food products are displayed at these shows. That's where I found Yonique and Funky Foods. The conferences are held in every state during spring vacation, which is essentially Easter week. It's necessary to make booth reservations early. Anyone interested in displaying their products at an ASFSA show can get further information by contacting the Food Service office of their State Department of Education, by writing to ASFSA, 4101 E. Iliff, Denver, CO 80222, or by contacting me at Santa Cruz City Schools, 133 Mission Street, Santa Cruz, CA 95060.

# Consumer's Guide

## HONEY

A combination of predigested glucose and fructose, honey is more easily absorbed into the human bloodstream than refined sugars. At room temperature, the sugars in unprocessed honey will crystallize, forming a granulated texture. Buttered or creamed honey is simply granulated honey.

- Flash heating is often done to make honey flow more readily through packaging machinery. Prolonged heating at temperatures over 160° F can kill naturally occurring honey yeasts which cause fermentation and spoilage. It can also affect the flavor and aroma of honey, and may destroy some of its natural nutrients.

- Clear, shiny honey has been filtered either with diatomacous earth or through a cloth or mechanical strainer. (An inert material, diatomaceous earth is the powdered silica skeletons of microscopic sealife.)

- Honey grades—A, B, C, D—are based on particle size and indicate the degree of filtration the honey has undergone. Grades are not a quality rating for the honey.

- Although raw, natural, organic, uncooked honey is, by implication, direct from the bee to thee, there is no legal definition for these terms and they may be used without discretion on labels.

- Comb honey may be heated and filtered, then put into a jar with a clean comb.

- The term *undiluted* means that no water has been added to the honey. (Water helps honey to ferment.) Under federal law, it is illegal to sell diluted honey, so the term undiluted really applies to all honey on the market.

- When *Whole Foods* surveyed apiaries across the country asking, "What kind of honey do you sell," one pragmatic Texan responded, "Whatever kind the bees bring in." Bees gather honey from a variety of plants in a given area. In most states, only 51 percent of the honey must come from a single source in order to use that source-name on the label.

# JUICES

Juices may be merely squeezed and bottled or can be highly processed. Unprocessed juices from the same manufacturer may not always taste the same, since the fruit varies with season, weather and general growing conditions.

- Yeast cells and bacteria which naturally accompany fresh fruit can work their way into juices, causing them to spoil or ferment. Pasteurization eliminates these yeasts and bacteria. Since pasteurization may also affect nutrients in the juice, some natural and health food manufacturers prefer not to pasteurize their juices. Unpasteurized juices should be kept refrigerated, and will spoil faster than pasteurized juices.

- Ascorbic acid, vitamin C, is often added to juice to slow down oxidation from heat and light which causes the juice to darken and change flavor.

- If a juice contains natural oils, they will separate into layers unless an emulsifier is added. Lecithin and vegetable gums are often used as emulsifiers in juices.

- Purees and concentrates are manufactured by mechanical processes. Nectars are a combination of fruit pulp (from 15-40 percent), water, sweetener and acidifier. Sweeteners used in nectars may include sugar and corn syrup. Acidifiers include citric acid, ascorbic acid, mallic acid, tartaric acid and lemon juice.

# DRIED FRUIT

The natural sugar content of dried fruit is determined by how long the fruit is allowed to mature on the tree and by the potassium/calcium balance in the soil.

- With honey-dipped fruit, the ratio of honey to water varies with the type of fruit. Peaches have the highest amount of honey added because they are most susceptible to mold from moisture.

- Dried pineapple is described as tasting like sour shoe leather due to its high acid content. Most importers agree that honey-dipped pineapple is actually sweetened with sugar.

- The bright orange color of some dried fruit is due to sulfur dioxide gas applied to prevent light colored fruit such as pears, apples, apricots and peaches from browning.

- Federal law requires that imported fruit be fumigated.

- Dates and figs may be hydrated—moisture added back through a steam process.

- The preservative potassium sorbate is sometimes added to figs and prunes.

# Section IV: Grains & Beans

Grains, the substance of our Staff of Life, have been hammered to death by this nation's large mills in order to offer the consumer puffs of bland white bread with all the substance of a balloon. Current trends, however, show an increasing consumption of non-white breads, and major mass-market bakers are now wrapping their loaves in words that sound like a return to traditional methods like Granny's mom might have used at home. Fortunately, amid all this old-fashioned verbiage, the natural foods industry still provides grain products which offer something more than words.

Direct from the fields, grains are largely indigestable by human beings. They require some processing, even if only hulling and steaming, to become food for people. The processor is free to decide how to handle the grains during their transformation into flours, breads, mixes, breakfast cereals and other familiar products. At the two extremes of production are the highly-skilled craft of slow milling with buhr stones to keep the nutrients intact, and automated high-speed pounding followed by squirts of manufactured nutrients to replace some of the ones annihilated by the hot pulverizing process.

Similar choices are made in the manufacture of grain products other than flour. Breakfast cereals, for example, can be kept fairly close to the original grains, or can be processed beyond recognition, resulting in an artificially fortified product which might best be described as a sugared vitamin-concentrate sponge.

The chapters in this section of the *Guide* examine the options open to millers and bakers, and highlight the contrast between the products found in mass-market stores and natural foods stores. For the shopper, an examination of labels will usually reveal which grain products have been manufactured with added vitamins. From natural foods bakers, it is possible to find breads which contain only sprouted wheat and water, requiring no "enrichment."

Another staple in the whole foods diet is the unglamorous dried bean, whose merits were first made known to many people in Frances Moore Lappe's *Diet for a Small Planet*. Since then, the nutritional, economic and ecological benefits of beans have been extolled in many publications, but these legumes continue to sit modestly in their bins and bags, largely ignored by the creators of promotional fireworks. To reflect this lackluster image, we have titled the chapter on this subject *Bored with Beans*.

The soybean, unlike its cousins, holds an honored position in the natural foods industry, and is the basis of a growing array of tasty, nutritious products. Soybeans are the special topic of the entire next section of this book.

# 21

# Milling for Quality

## by Jim Schreiber

Despite differences in emphasis, prime millers of whole grains for the natural foods market agree firmly about at least one thing: Top quality can only be obtained from slow, cool grinding by authentic old-fashioned millstones. The only present source of such stones in the United States is a firm in North Carolina. All other real millstones were cut in Europe, where the supply from Paris ended in the 1920's.

Having a burrstone for milling is not enough. Not just anybody off the streets can be turned loose at the wheel to crank out quality flour. Stanley Roy, vice-president and general manager of Elam's in Illinois, expressed concern that the true artisans of stone milling seem to be a vanishing breed. An increased or long-term demand for stone-ground flour will require millers showing skills, care and experience not needed in modernized, metalized high-speed mills. The reawakened interest in stone-ground whole flour began only some ten years ago.

One such artisan, acknowledged as a master miller in the proven tradition, is Al Gunther, manager and miller at Henderson Mills in Colorado. "Modern milling extracts the 'goodies'—that's what we say around here," Gunther explained. "At 119°F. all the enzymes are gone." He carries a thermometer to insert in the flour at the exit spout, and adjusts the flow to keep the temperature below 90°F.

**Low temperature milling**

"A roller mill pulls off the bran, and then mid-way along takes out the germ," Gunther said. "When I grind, you get the entire vitamins and minerals, the full value of the grain, and keep the protein and vitamin E." To assure that nothing is lost, grains milled on the big 30-inch stone at Henderson pass through a sifter that extracts the larger particles. These are routed to an 8-inch stone which regrinds them before they are returned to the main flow, ensuring that the flour particles will be uniform in size, for best quality.

At Manna Milling in Seattle, company president Edward Hyatt begins the quest for quality at the source: "We look for grain that is organically grown, from soil that has

94

preferably not ever been chemically treated—or at least for three or four years. And, of course, we want grain that hasn't been treated with pesticides. That's a top priority.

"Next, we look for a high level of protein. There's a simple test, and the farmer determines it. This is different from a grain's being organic. We've found no correlation between protein content and the organically grown nature of the grain."

Al Gunther pointed out that protein content does correlate with latitude. Protein content is higher in wheat grown toward the north. "In northern Montana, right up near the Canadian border, it runs about 16 percent. Here at the level of Colorado it's around 12 percent. At least that's better than places south of here, where it's 11 percent. I'm told that the hard winter is good for the wheat." Henderson Mills was also concerned with using organic grains. "For a retailer," Gunther said, "the number-one thing should be to get a copy of the organic certification to post in the store."

Protein content and organic grains

At Elam's, Stanley Roy expressed skepticism about easy claims of organic quality, because of the inherent difficulties of controlling organic production. Drift from a neighboring farm's spray, or runoff from rains, above or below ground, can reach an organic farmer's fields undetected, he said. "I don't believe there is any nutritional difference in organic and non-organic, but organic production probably does reduce carcinogenic pesticides. If I could press a button, I'd stop the use of pesticides 100 percent."

# DESTROYING PESTS

Modern, high-speed milling of white flour results in a product so low in flavor, aroma, and nutrients that it has little appeal even to the taste-buds of bugs and rodents. But infestation is an ongoing concern to the old-style millers of rich, tasty whole grains. Mr. Roy asserts, "I wouldn't put a flour on the shelf, as a retailer, if it didn't go through an infestation destroyer."

The infestation destroyer at Elam's is an Entoleter: a pair of parallel steel disks about two feet in diameter spin at 3500 RPM. The outer rims of the disks are connected by many thin, steel rods. It is rather like a merry-go-round bordered with a cage of close-set, narrow bars. The milled flour pours into a hole at the center of the top disk and is hurled into and through the rods. The impact smashes any tiny insects, larvae or eggs that might be present in the flour.

The infestation destroyer

An alternative to such a machine—and an advisable practice in any case, both to control infestation and to preserve the nutritional and flavor qualities of the flour—is to keep the temperature down. Even in mid-summer in Seattle, the storage area at Manna Milling stays at a continuous 60-65°F. cool level, which keeps bugs in check. Manna president Hyatt recommends that packaged whole grain flours be kept refrigerated by retailers and by consumers. In the natural foods industry, he noted, no preservatives are used, so refrigeration is the best way to maintain the many nutrients and flavor while preventing infestation.

In addition to keeping whole grain products cool, millers advise a fast turnover of inventory, both at the mill and in the retail shop. For the retailer, this means ordering amounts that can be sold within about 60 days. "Health food stores should be selling only the best, cleanest, freshest products," Elam's general manager said. "I've sometimes felt ashamed and embarrassed by what I've seen. The whole industry needs some cleaning up. I've visited stores where on the shelves I've found our products that are *years old*. I think a store like that should go out of business." Each package at Elam's is code-dated by month, but Stanley Roy said he would like to see the retailer put a delivery date-stamp on such products, and put them on sale before two months pass. "If it won't sell that fast, the retailer should reduce the order or discontinue it," he said.

# THE ENEMY OF GRAIN

Problems with packaging

"Polyethylene bags create the illusion of freshness," Edward Hyatt said, "and grain products packaged that way may feel good to the touch of the consumer. But poly-bags sweat on the inside, and the moisture and the heat it creates is the biggest enemy of grain. That's where you lose nutrition and can get new infestation. Our coated cellophane bags show the product, avoid the oiliness you can get on paper bags, and still allow the product to breathe."

The possible disadvantages of paper bags have not been an actual problem for Henderson Mills. "We've never had any complaints," Al Gunther said. There may be no problem at all if the turnover is sufficiently rapid at the retail level. For the Colorado firm, a large portion of their swift sales are through the King Super Store chain.

The packaging done by Elam's has an eye on the supermarkets, and is designed for the benefit of the consumer and the retailer. The cardboard boxes handle well on shelves, and can be re-sealed at home with their tongue-and-slot top. The boxes depict what can be done with the product, and give recipes. An added advantage emphasized by Elam's general manager is the durability of the package. A dented box still retains a quality product intact in the inner bag, but a plastic, cellophane or paper bag is much more easily broken open, leading not only to a likely mess, but also to easier spoilage and infestation.

The words *Stone Ground* are not subject to control. Their presence in advertising or on packages does not assure that the product was ground only on a slow-turning old-fashioned burrstone at cool temperatures. A story murmured in the industry portrays a milling firm executive saying, "Stone ground? Well, sure, I suppose it passes over a stone somewhere in the process." Large, high-volume milling plants simply don't use the traditional stone-grinding techniques. The smaller mills which do use them are not evasive about it, and sound proud to describe their milling procedures in detail.

# NEIGHBORHOOD MILLS

Mill-it-yourself

Regardless of the care taken by the most expert of millers, it is unavoidable that grain, the instant it is ground, begins to lose its nutrients and starts a decline toward rancidity. When asked about home or in-store milling, Hyatt and Gunther applauded the practice. Done with skill and care, using a good quality of grain, and prepared for eating right away, on-the-spot stone-ground milling is more than a match for commercial milling in flavor, freshness, and nutrition. Al Gunther said, "I think there should be small mills all over the country, stone grinding the old-fashioned way in towns and neighborhoods." But he voiced a concern about artificially fabricated millstones, and raised the unanswered question of possible harmful effects from the constituents of such man-made millstones.

The natural foods milling business is not threatened by the current interest in home milling. "Most people are looking for convenience foods," Edward Hyatt said. "They can't take two or three hours to prepare each meal from scratch. What we're trying to do is provide products which are both natural and convenient." While demand for whole grain products in general is showing a steady increase, most companies are considering expanding lines of mixes to suit the wants of the contemporary natural foods consumer.

To help make sure that the art of stone grinding stays contemporary, master miller Al Gunther is now compiling a scrapbook on all the steps in traditional milling. He has picked up a few tricks during his own experience as a miller, but the book will also include what he first learned at the elbow of an 86-year-old man using a water-driven millwheel.

# 22

# *Flour from Stones & Hammers*

## by Jacques de Langre

Producing flour in high-volume, high-speed commercial mills always destroys essential nutrients of grains. For people seeking natural foods with nothing added or taken away, this gives a decided advantage to the miller and baker who works at home or as an artisan in a small, local shop. Many bakers are surprised to discover that dough made from carefully milled flour will rise without the addition of yeast.

The use of traditional millstones declined in the technological nations after the industrial revolution. In stone grinding, as originally done, wheat berries are dropped at the center of two natural stones, and a slow, progressive crushing action mills the grain without tearing the wheat germ. Properly done, stone grinding still allows the grain to germinate, and retains the normal acidity and oxidation level of whole grain.

High temperature is the enemy of grain. Heat oxidizes not only the vitamins originally present in the grain, but also the oils which give flour its taste and smell—its "bloom." Heat also destroys the enzymes required for the proper working of bread dough.

The friction of stone grinding by the householder or the local "cottage industry" baker does produce some heat, and therefore requires care. If the flour is allowed to stack up in the mill, it can heat up beyond 150° F., which begins to be harmful to the nutrients. As a rule of thumb, if it gets too hot to handle bare-handed, it is too hot for the grain. Even when ground by traditional, cool methods, flour should be used without much delay: the vitamin E is gone five days after wheat is ground.

In the cylinder mills used in commercial production, pairs of smooth-ground or ridged cylinders rotate at different speeds in order to create a better tearing action in the narrow gap between them. While cylinder mills greatly increase the pace of production, they generate temperatures that oxidize the constituents of the grain and cause immediate rancidity of the oils. Such flour instantly becomes deficient in structure, nutrients, enzymes, bloom, and freshness.

Faster and hotter yet are hammer mills, which are the most popular among industrial milling operations. In these mills, many hammers with extremely high linear velocity whirl around a central axis, pounding the grain kernels at top speed. The shock and heat

**Grain goes immediately rancid**

produced by hammer milling result in an endosperm that is incapable of germinating, and in the greatest loss of nutrients.

After such milling, flours may then be subjected to a process called "aging"—a term which conceals a deception. The "aging" process can include the use of methyl bromide, organic mercurials, nitrogen trichloride, chlorine dioxide, alum, chalk, ammonium carbonate and nitrogen peroxide, as preservatives, bleaches and whiteners. What remains after such "aging" is a substance in which only calories remain.

This destruction of the food values of grains is no secret to chemists, commercial millers, or governments. The laws of the United States and several other countries require millers to enrich their flour. What is this enrichment? Commercial milling removes about ninety nutrients: The law requires millers to return four of them!

The typical nutritional profiles of whole wheat, refined flour, and enriched white flour are shown here in the Wheat Nutrient Table.

| Nutrients | Whole Wheat | Refined 70% | White Enriched |
|---|---|---|---|
| Protein % | 12 to 15 | 10 | 10 |
| Oils % | 2.26 | 1.1 | 1.3 |
| Carbohydrates % (as starches) | 66 | 73 | 75 |
| Thiamin mg. | 3.6 | 0.7 | 6.4 |
| Riboflavin mg. | 1.87 | 0.61 | 4.0 |
| Niacin mg. | 52.45 | 9.35 | 53 |
| Iron mg. | 34 | 11 | 89 |

**Consumer is guinea pig**

Only thiamin, riboflavin, niacin and iron are part of the currently enforceable enrichment program, and in such a chemicalized, non-food form, these are probably useless and may be harmful. Commenting on the high level of iron enrichment, Dr. C.N. Stil of the W.S. Hall Psychiatric Institute said, ". . . considering how little we know of the intricacies of iron absorption . . . iron fortification above that found in grain constitutes nutritional experimentation on an unprecedented scale." The American consumer is the guinea pig.

Once this battered, oxidized, chemically-treated material reaches the baker, the only recognized way to make it seem alive and workable is to add yeast. This practice has been condemned for thousands of years—to the extent that the offering of leavened bread during Passover was punishable by death under ancient Hebrew law. The action of yeast in dough was seen as the same as the putrefaction of vegetables and meat.

Modern European nutritional researchers such as Dr. E. Lenglet in France and Dr. J. Kuhl in Germany also suggest that eating yeast can be dangerous to health. Certainly it is unnecessary in baking, since dough from carefully milled flour will rise without it. And alternative leavening agents can be discovered by bakers. I have been having good results with miso, which works well and creates no problem with flavor.

In order to assure the best and safest nutrition in baking, it is advisable to find a source of unadulterated grain. Dr. E. Pfeiffer, the mainstay of the biodynamic gardening movement, points out that "wheat grown on good soils is almost twice as high in protein as average commercial wheat." Sources of valuable information are the Society for the Preservation of Old Mills, P.O. Box 435, Wiscasset, ME 04578; and Millstream: A Natural Food Baking Journal, P.O. Box 8584, Parkville, MD 21234.

# 23

# *Sprouts Are Sprouting*

## by Robert C. Carey
## & Machmud D. Rowe

Imagine a food so nutritionally complete that people could live on it, and little else, and be healthier than they are right now. A food that can be grown in the kitchen in less than a week, using no soil, no fertilizer, nothing at all except air, a small amount of water, and a container. A food so economical that an entire family could eat a nutritionally complete meal for only pennies. A food so versatile that people could bake, dry or fry it, blend, steam or stew it, or simply eat it uncooked.

What you have just imagined is sprouts, which are being offered in growing numbers of natural food stores and restaurants.

Sprouts represent an immense, untapped food resource for all mankind. Sprouts could feed the world. Until recently, sprouts have been a potential, not an actual, food resource in the USA.

In Asia, sprouts have been a food source for over 5,000 years. Western cultures have known about them for the last couple of centuries. As people become more nutrition conscious, the benefits of the ancient practice of growing sprouts have become more well known. People are becoming familiar with sprouts in Chinese foods, in sprouted grain bread, and as a tasty addition to sandwiches. Sprouts may soon be as American as apple pie and frozen yogurt.

It took awhile for word to get around about sprouts. People were not exposed to them and had not developed a taste for them. The process of sprouting seemed complicated, messy and tricky. Agribusiness seemed to provide an unending, year-round source of fresh produce. But rising food prices and increased interest in nutrition have led to rediscovery of sprouts. The demand for more varieties is on the increase.

Pound for pound, penny for penny, sprouts are the most nutritious and economical food known. In days of dollar-a-head lettuce, it makes sense to raise sprouts at home for 12¢ per quart. Most varieties of seeds will yield six to eight times their volume in sprouts. Like everything else, seed prices will increase with inflation, but it will always

**Living vegetables—a nutritionally complete food**

be cheaper to buy the seed than the produce grown from it. Sprouts offer the greatest food value per dollar in the world today.

Offering the greatest food value per dollar

What are sprouts? Sprouts come from seeds. Almost any seed will sprout, although some (tomato and potato) are considered toxic. "Seed quality" seeds have a quick germination rate, low (10-12 percent) moisture content, and are untreated with chemicals. Seeds with low germination periods germinate slowly and partially. Partial-germination seeds rot easily and create a mold problem. While low moisture content is important, a seed without moisture—a "hard seed"—will not germinate. Most garden seeds are chemically-treated to combat certain pests, neutralize soil conditions and prevent mold. Using chemically treated seeds for sprouting presents a potential health hazard.

# AN EYE ON SEEDS

Seeds may be purchased from seed associations or farmers. Two problems in seed purchasing are getting undesirable seeds with low germination periods or which have been chemically treated. Bima is one of the sources which guarantees high germination, no chemical treatment and no weeds.

How to buy seeds

To be sure of what they are getting, buyers should request a seed analysis report. Analysis reports contain the date seeds were tested, the lot number, germination percentages (total germination and hard seed germination) and weed counts.

Shelf life of seeds varies with the seed and its storage conditions. Seeds should be stored in cool, dry areas out of direct sunlight. It is not necessary to refrigerate seeds. Refrigeration adds moisture which could cause premature germination.

Although the English firm of Thompson & Morgan is currently marketing seeds in colorful paper bags, polyethylene bags insure a longer shelf life. Seeds will not germinate in poly-bags unless the bags are punctured and moisture gets in. Unopened bags of seeds will last from one to two years; opened bags will last up to one year.

The most common varieties of sprouting seeds include alfalfa, black-eyed peas, cabbage, corn, garbanzo beans, lentils, mung beans, peanuts, radish, soybeans, sunflower seeds and wheat. Alfalfa, mung beans and wheat are now the most popular varieties, although lentils are rapidly gaining popularity.

One of the few known complete foods, sprouts are in a class by themselves. Sprouts go directly from their growing medium into your mouth. They are still alive and growing when eaten. For this reason, they are sometimes called "living vegetables."

A factory of nutrients

Sprouts are a tenacious factory of nutrients containing vitamins, minerals, protein and enzymes. These nutrients multiply during sprouting. For example, the B-complex content in germinated wheat increases 600 percent in the first 72 hours. Vitamin E content is tripled and Vitamin C increases six-fold.

The protein content of sprouts in quality and quantity is comparable to that of many meats. Either individually or in combinations, sprouts can provide a complete protein, containing all the essential amino acids. Enzymes necessary for proper digestion and assimilation of food nutrients (especially protein) are abundant. Vitamins A, B, C, E, G and K are readily available in well-balanced quantities. Essential minerals—such as calcium, zinc, iron and magnesium—are generously provided. Sprouts are also one of the highest sources of natural fiber. A dieter's delight, sprouts are low in carbohydrates and calories, but rich in essential food nutrients.

# EASY TO GROW

Sprouts are easy to grow—and fun. The first step is to soak the seeds, beans or grains overnight according to a varying recommended time. Soaking starts the process of germination. Seeds expand as they absorb and store moisture which is necessary to begin their life cycle. The soak water of most seeds (not soybeans) is full of valuable nutrients which can be used for making soup, tea or for watering plants.

How to sprout seeds

After soaking is completed, the seeds should be drained and put into a sprouting medium. An European company imports Bio-Snacky, a three-tier tray for sprouting. Bima has developed simple sprouting utensils: the Sprout-Ease Tube Sprouter, the Econo-Sprouter and the Stainless Sprouter.

Sprouting is made easier by these utensils, but they are not necessary. Sprouts will grow in a colander. A jar covered with cheesecloth or nylon mesh held in place by a rubber band also works as a sprouting medium. The blotter method grows sprouts between moist cloths or paper towels. Although these methods work, they tend to be messier than specially-designed sprouting utensils.

Sprouts should be rinsed twice a day with fresh, tepid water. In two or three days, the sprouts will burst their surrounding seed hulls. The seed hulls should be rinsed away. Seed hulls are not harmful, but their removal minimizes mold problems and ensures fresher-tasting sprouts.

After hulls have been rinsed away, continue to rinse sprouts twice daily, morning and evening, for one or two more days. Growing time will vary with temperature and water conditions.

For all seeds, soak water should be warm and rinse water should be tepid. Final rinse should be cold. Ideal sprouting temperature is 65-75°F. When rinsed more than twice a day in 80°F water, sprouts will grow much longer and faster. However, this forced-growth method reduces nutritional content of sprouts and is not recommended.

Sprouts should be stored under refrigeration in containers which allow ventilation (since the sprouts are still alive). To freshen stored sprouts, rinse with cold water and drain well. Sprouts store successfully for days without nutritional loss.

# DARK OR LIGHT?

A controversy exists over whether or not to grow sprouts in the dark. It is time to take sprouting out of the closet. Seeds should not be grown in direct sunlight: it kills them. It is advisable to sprout seeds in indirect light, not in darkness. While growing in darkness may cause certain seeds to have a higher content of one or two vitamins, growing in indirect sunlight gives higher quantities of balanced vitamins. Certain sprouting seeds, notably alfalfa and cabbage, green-up as they grow in indirect sunlight, providing the added nutrient chlorophyll. Sprouts grown in the dark do not contain chlorophyll.

Although many books on the subject make sprouting seem more complicated than it actually is, there are numerous guides which provide good nutritional information and recipes. Three of our favorites are *The Jar Garden*, a children's book by Dorothy Weeks, *The Bean Sprout Book*, by Gay Courter, and *Complete Sprouting Cookbook*, by Karen Cross Whyte.

**Time to take sprouts out of the closet**

# 24

# Making Grains into Breakfast

## by Jim Schreiber

After decades of publication, *The Northwestern Miller* went out of business in 1973. Many of its pages over the years had been about breakfast cereals. In a farewell editorial, the publisher wrote of the growth of giant, diversified "milling" companies which made many products in no way related to grains. "In fact," the publisher said, "the flour milling industry *The Northwestern Miller* was founded for and designed to serve, no longer exists."

**Fortified "candy"**

In the hands of corporate giants, breakfast cereals have in recent years been the subject of much public controversy. Attention at present is focused most sharply on the sugary products sometimes called "candy breakfasts." It is no secret that most breakfast cereals consumed in the USA are so highly processed that they require fortification with laboratory-made vitamins to replace those destroyed during manufacturing.

Despite the growth of the milling conglomerates, the industry which "no longer exists" appears to be alive and well—on a smaller scale—on the shelves of natural food stores. Although the steps in the manufacture of these breakfast foods are similar to the steps employed in making fortified, sugared cereals, there are usually important differences in what is and is not done to the products.

## THE RIGHTEOUS OAT

**Oats have a fat problem**

Many people in the natural foods industry have been in pursuit of what Nathen Hunt of Magnificent Munchies calls "the righteous rolled oat." This quest, which has been unsuccessful so far, is especially significant because oat flakes are a major component of the granolas, in addition to their solo role as an uncooked breakfast cereal.

Fortunately, high-quality rolled oats are already widely marketed. The one factor that makes the best of them less than perfectly "righteous" is that no present label can certify the product as 100 percent organically grown. When one company recently tried to produce an organically-grown rolled oats product, the result was judged to be a failure.

102

At first glance, the process of flattening oat kernels into flakes for the breakfast bowl would seem to be easy, but the nature of the oat grain makes it troublesome. Oat flakes for human consumption must always be a compromise, carefully balancing traits during processing to turn out a product which is palatable to the consumer. The trouble with oat kernels is that, compared to other grains, they are fat.

# A TASTE LIKE SOAP

Oats contain up to five times as much fat as wheat—mostly oleic, linoleic, and palmitic fatty acids. This might not be a problem, except that the outer part of the kernel contains the enzyme lipase which, when moist, interacts with these fatty acids if it comes in contact with them. The result of this enzyme action is free fatty acids which are considered unhealthy, give rise to bitter flavors, and are associated with rancidity. Simply rolling the oat kernel brings the enzyme and the fats into contact, with all the undesired results. If such a product is used for baking in the kitchen, the use of baking soda or of some oils will turn out breads or cookies that taste like soap.

To prevent these disasters, the enzyme can be inactivated by treating the oats with heat, a processed called "stabilization." In this operation, the oats are quickly steam heated to slightly over 200° F. for about three minutes. The stabilized oats have improved flavor and resist going rancid—but if the steaming is overdone, going past the point of inactivating the unwanted enzyme, the oats will tend to go quickly rancid because the steaming also begins to destroy the natural antioxidants in the grain.

Once the oats are stabilized, they are kiln dried to a moisture content of around six percent. In the kiln, the oats take on their familiar nutty flavor, become dry enough for safe storage, and the husks become more brittle for easier separation from the kernel. Some kilns send the oats down through a vertical series of pans in which the grain is stirred and dried uniformly. A lack of uniformity here can ruin the batch, because underheated grains are flavorless and overheated grains taste terrible. Under the best known circumstances, the temperature is held below 175° F until the grains reach an eight percent level of moisture, and are then toasted at around 300° F for about 20 minutes.

The next step after cooling is the separation of the kernels—the groats—from the hulls. In the usual process, the oats are passed between a horizontal pair of large, circular milling stones. Only the top stone spins. The gap between the stones is set to be narrower than the length of the grains but wider than the width of the grains. As the grains roll between the stones, they stand on end, and the husks pop loose in the cramped space. The hulls and oat groats are then separated by various devices which may blow air, use static electricity, vibrate, brush and screen the components.

Oat husks are considered to be inedible by human beings, and usually become a part of cattle feed. Oat dust has recently become viewed as a special problem, which will be discussed below. The dust is kept out of the final product because it becomes an unacceptable gummy paste in the consumer's bowl.

# THIN CONVENIENCE

Prior to rolling, the kernels may be cut into smaller pieces or may be left intact as uncut, whole groats. Smaller pieces produce thinner flakes, which provide a shorter cooking time for the consumer than whole groat flakes.

Just before rolling, the oat groats or pieces are usually steamed, making them moist, hot, and easier to shape. The steamed oats pass between rollers which commonly produce flakes slightly more than 1/100 inch thick. The flakes are immediately air-cooled and sifted to remove small particles, and are then ready for packaging—or for further processing in granolas.

In each step of processing, changes occur in the oats which include both advantages and disadvantages. A manufacturer may choose to omit any step, with mixed results. While controlled heating does stabilize the oats, it is well known that any heating also

Care important in steaming

destroys some nutrients in grains. Steaming eliminates some nutrients, but at the same time it breaks down starch chains in the oats, making the product much more digestible, which is of special importance in granolas which may be eaten without further cooking in the home. Thick-rolled whole oat flakes suffer less physical damage than the cut, thin-rolled flakes, and have added eye-appeal to the natural foods consumer, but especially in granolas may be a mouthful that is a challenge to chew.

Organic oats on horizon

Although nobody can produce the imaginary breakfast oats that include all the advantages and none of the disadvantages, there are now oat cereals on the market which are high quality within the real and reasonable limits. And we may yet see the "righteous" rolled oat—a carefully processed product made entirely of organically grown oats from the northern plains states.

New Life Foods, according to Larry Eggen, is investing half a million dollars in a facility to produce rolled oats which meet their strict requirements for organic certification. The project came about after approaches to Quaker and ConAgra elicited "laughs and snickers," as Eggen put it. To these milling giants, the interrupting their operations to process a mere 10,000 pounds of organically-grown oats was out of the question.

When Triangle Milling in Oregon recently tried to produce organically-grown rolled oats, the product did not meet their standards. In Eggen's view, the basic problem was regional differences in field oats: Oats grown in South Dakota and parts of Minnesota yield 39 to 41 pounds per bushel, but the Northwestern oats usually yield less. The minimum needed for a top-quality, economically sensible product is about 38 pounds per bushel. New Life Foods is in Minnesota.

# BURYING DUST

One cost involved in the processing is known by few consumers or dealers in natural foods: the bag house. To handle the dust created in the oat flakes production, New Life Foods spent $60,000 on a dust-collection facility required by the Environmental Protection Agency. This bag-house is a two-story structure which contains stacks of plastic bags, rather like vacuum cleaner bags, in which the oat dust is accumulated. Federal rules concerning occupational health and safety require that the filled bags be buried at least four feet deep, or be deposited in land-fill areas. This regulation is enforced because some bag-house residues have been found to contain harmful substances—although the New Life Foods dust will be from harmless organically-grown oats which could be used for fertilizer. The cost of this dubious application of the rule will, of course, ultimately be borne by the consumer.

The bag house

# POP GUNS

Puffed cereals

Among the more charming of breakfast foods are the puffed whole-grain cereals. The basic puffing process is quite simple: moist grains are heated and then subject to a sudden drop in pressure; the steam inside the grains instantly expands, puffing up the grains from the inside. This procedure is so straightforward that it can easily be done on a small scale at home.

Rice, wheat, oats, corn and millet are the grains most commonly puffed whole, using the same basic process. According to the manufacturer for El Molino Mills, it is best to process whole-grain puffed cereals as quickly as possible—in 20 seconds or less—avoiding high temperatures in order to retain the desired flavors and the maximum nutritive value. As with other cereals, the starch chains must be broken to accomodate human digestion, and some nutrients are lost whenever cooking occurs. Texts on cereal technology indicate that puffing destroys nearly all the vitamin B1, but does not affect the niacin and riboflavin.

A rather different sort of puffing process is used to make the varied shapes, formulas and flavors of breakfast cereals which line supermarket shelves under trademarks like Cheerios, Kix, and Coco-Puffs. Rather than using whole grains, such products are based on mixtures.

Such mixtures may contain a wide variety of grains, flours, dyes, sugars, flavorings, vitamins, salt, or preservatives. The mix, moistened with water, is forced under pressure by a screw mechanism into a cooker. The pressure squeezes the dough through a die, where a blade chops off the individual die-shaped pieces. Next, the pieces are tumbled in a cooker. At about 12 percent moisture, they are loaded into a pressure chamber, heated by steam injection to over 500° F until compressed at about 200 pounds of pressure per square inch. The end of the chamber then pops open, instantly reducing the pressure, and the grains explode into a drying chamber. At three percent moisture, the product is cooled and packaged.

Another puffing device resembles a multi-barreled Gatling gun—the early machine gun which often shows up in movies about the early US Cavalry or the Bengal Lancers. Called a "cooker-extruder," this machine forces dough under intense heat and pressure (up to 350° F and 500 psi) through a narrowing passage. Several such parallel passages are arranged to exit past whirling blades at the point where the dough reaches the normal atmosphere of the room. As the dough emerges from these portals it is shaped by dies and explodes into the room as it is sliced into pieces by the spinning blades. Then the product is dried, screened, cooled and packaged.

**Mixes of grains and chemicals**

# OTHER FLAKES

Wheat, corn and rice are often used to make the familiar flaked breakfast cereals which, in appearance, lie somewhere between rolled oat flakes and the dough-formed products. Each type of grain has its own special characteristics, so details of processing such as cooking time and added moisture may vary, but the steps in manufacturing these flakes are quite similar.

In making flakes, whole grains may be used or they may be milled to yield smaller pieces. Hulls are separated out for use as animal feed, and the germ separated out to become, for instance, wheat germ or wheat germ oil. The remaining kernel parts intended for flaking may be put into large, warm chambers for tempering before further processing.

The first stage of cooking is inside a large vessel which moistens the pieces and heats them under slight pressure for an hour or two. The vessel rotates or agitates the pieces to prevent clumping and promote even cooking.

After the initial cooking, the pieces move along a conveyer to a drying facility where they reach moisture levels of 20 to 30 percent, depending on the kind of grain being processed. Driers are of various designs: some tumble the kernels down through a current of hot air, some pass the kernels next to steam pipes, and some blow air up past the kernels through rotating, perforated discs. Temperatures may range from 150 to 300° F.

The grain particles at this point are quite shapeable, and the starch in them has become gelatinized. They may be tempered just before going to the flaking rolls, to assure an even distribution of moisture.

When the pieces pass between the steel flaking rolls, they are subject to tens of tons of pressure, and take on the familiar flake shape. The flakes go immediately to the toaster oven, where they remain from one to three minutes, until they blister and reach the desired color.

In the large commercial operations, sugar, salt, malt, flavoring and coloring agents, and some vitamins may be added to the cooker at the start of the process. Sprays of various B vitamins are usually applied just prior to flaking or after toasting.

**Cooked, rolled, sprayed, and toasted**

# SHREDDED CEREALS

No sweeteners or flavoring

Among the breakfast cereals manufactured by the giant mills, none comes closer to a natural product than various types of shredded wheat biscuits. These are often made without sweeteners or flavorings, and include the bran and germ along with the rest of the kernel.

In the production of this kind of breakfast cereal, the wheat is cooked and then tempered to a moisture content of about 50 percent. This soft grain is run through a pair of rollers. One of the rollers has parallel indentations around its circumference, so the cooked wheat comes out of the rollers in unbroken strands. A long series of such roller pairs stands over a conveyer belt, and as the strands move along, each pair of rollers adds a new layer on top of the preceding one. Rectangular biscuits are formed when the belt passes under a wheel which has dull blades on it, resembling the paddles of a water wheel. The blades crimp and separate the strands into single biscuits.

The doughy biscuits then move to a hot oven which toasts and dries the outer part but leaves the interior damp. In a further oven heating, the inside of the biscuit is baked until the moisture level drops to near 10 percent. Because this product is subjected to much less heating than most flaked cereals, its inner structure undergoes less change.

# GRANULA WAS FIRST

These days, many of the oat flakes produced in the USA end up in bags of ready-to-eat granola. The history of breakfast foods bearing that name has gone full-circle more than once in the last century.

Breakfast was a health food

The first ready-to-eat breakfast cereal on record was called "Granula." Introduced during the middle of the Civil War, it was made from baked whole-meal dough, and was considered to be a health food. The first "Granola" was made at Battle Creek by J.H. Kellogg from baked oatmeal, wheatmeal and cornmeal dough, reportedly as an addition to vegetarian diets. C.W. Post shifted the marketing techniques for such cereals away from vegetarianism and health, toward convenience and flavor, setting the direction the breakfast cereals industry would take until the present time.

Granolas as health foods were recently "rediscovered" for the mass market while grocery shelves abounded with highly-processed, fortified, sugary cereals. Giant mills were quick to see a trend, and got back into the granola business in its new form, again emphasising alleged natural and healthful aspects of their products.

Contemporary granolas generally consist of oat flakes toasted along with an assortment of other ingredients. As described above, the quality of this basic ingredient can vary with its regional source, and the type and extent of processing used in producing the flakes. Products may differ in stabilization, kiln drying, steaming, toasting, and thickness, all of which can affect the taste, feel, chewability and digestability experienced by the consumer.

In addition to the final quality of the oat flakes in the granola, quality is often considered to vary with the ratio of oats to other ingredients. Some manufacturers express scorn for what they describe as bags of nearly 100 percent oat flakes sweetened with brown sugar.

Other sweeteners used in granolas include honey, ribbon cane syrup, and maple syrup. Buyers can make choices among these on the basis of their individual viewpoints. The other major variables among granolas is the proportion and quality of the other parts of the mix, such as nuts and raisins.

# UNCOOKED CEREALS

Uncooked cereals have one outstanding advantage over the ready-to-eat varieties. They are generally the result of much less processing and therefore remain closer to the food found in nature. This advantage, of course, goes hand in hand with the relative inconvenience of having to cook them at home.

Basically, uncooked cereals are grains which are taken out of the milling process at a stage prior to being ground to the fineness of flour. In determining the quality of these products, all the considerations about good milling procedures must be taken into account. Excessive heat will destroy nutrients and can help induce rancidity by eliminating natural antioxidants. And, compared to the national scope of steel-roller milling, stone grinding is found on only a limited scale.

The size of the grain particles has an obvious bearing on the cooking time required in the kitchen, and consumers have come to expect their cooked cereals to have certain textures. With convenience as a factor in marketing, major milling companies have looked for ways to create "instant" uncooked cereals. Trade secrets are involved in this aspect of processing, but some of the literature suggests that chemicals such as disodium phosphate and proteolytic enzymes have been used to shorten cooking time while maintaining a usual particle size.

**Made instant by disodium phosphate**

This brief sketch of the breakfast manufacturing industry shows that the products called breakfast cereals cover a broad range, from additive-laced doughs to carefully-milled, untreated grains. Ongoing scientific studies are repeatedly showing that organically-grown grains are nutritionally and economically on a par with those grown by chemical agriculture, without the ecological destruction or apprehension about pesticide residues which attend chemical-intensive farming. High-quality breakfast cereals are already available, and as the natural foods industry continues to grow, it is likely that organically grown grains will become more widely available.

With proper packaging and turnover of stock, the happy lack of preservative compounds in our breakfast cereals is not a real disadvantage. There is no reason to expect a real food to last on the shelf forever.

As the mass-market "candy breakfasts" continue to be questioned, consumers are becoming more aware of the differences, and of the choices open to them. With this growing awareness, we can expect to see a rebirth of what the Kellogg brothers started behind their barn a century ago.

# 25

# Class Action vs General Foods

$L$egal history of importance to the food industry is being made in California. A class action suit has been brought charging General Foods and Safeway with unfair and deceitful business practices against children, false and misleading advertising practices, misbranding, fraud, and breach of their public.

The charges are brought by a coalition including the Committee on Children's Television, Inc., the California Society of Dentistry for Children, the American G.I. Forum of California, the Mexican-American Political Association, the Director of the California State Office of Narcotics and Drug Abuse, and numerous individuals in their professional capacities as educators and members of the medical profession and in their private capacities as guardians of their children. They are represented by Public Advocates, Inc. of San Francisco.

The primary defendant is the largest food advertiser in America: General Foods Corporation. Another defendant is the largest supermarket chain (by sales) in America: Safeway Stores, Inc. The prestigious Los Angeles law firm of Gibson, Dunn & Crutcher represents the defendants.

## INTRODUCTION

This case involves issues of great importance to the natural food industry, to advertisers and to consumers. The Introduction to the class-action complaint filed in court is printed below:

GENERAL FOODS and POST CEREALS are engaged in one of the most sophisticated, damaging and cleverly calculated anti-children schemes ever perpetrated by a major corporation in America. During the last five years, through the expenditure of approximately one billion dollars in television advertising and marketing, they have induced the formation of lasting poor nutrition habits and tooth decay in millions of children, particularly youngsters from low-income families.

1. GENERAL FOODS and POST CEREALS are using a high-pressure multi-media campaign which exploits trusting children in order to sell sugar concoctions as nutritious breakfast cereals. GENERAL FOODS sells five of these so-called "cereals." Marketed as "POST CEREALS," these are:
"COCOA PEBBLES" (over 46% sugar);
"SUPER SUGAR CRISP" (over 43% sugar);
"FRUITY PEBBLES" (over 47% sugar);
"HONEYCOMB" (over 42% sugar); and
"ALPHA BITS" (over 38% sugar).
A parent concerned about a child's sugar consumption might just as well serve a candy bar for breakfast as one of these "cereals." Because each of these products is adulterated with at least 38% sugar, they should more accurately be labeled "candy." In this Complaint they are collectively called "candy breakfast." (Unless otherwise indicated, all Defendants are hereafter collectively designated as "GENERAL FOODS.")

Selling sugar concoctions as cereal

2. Breakfast is the single most important meal of the day. Nevertheless, using deceptive advertising, GENERAL FOODS falsely markets candy breakfasts such as SUPER SUGAR CRISP and COCOA PEBBLES as a nourishing "part of a balanced breakfast." Aside from small amounts of some vitamins, none is any more healthful nor any more a "part of a balanced breakfast" than a bottle of soda pop (Coca-Cola - 4.2% sugar [sucrose]), a piece of cake (pound cake - 30.6%), or a chocolate bar (Milky Way - 26.8%, Tootsie Roll - 21.1%). In short, GENERAL FOODS has built a lucrative business upon knowingly (1) giving misleading and injurious nutritional advice to innocent children and (2) selling sugar as "cereal."

3. The irresponsibility of GENERAL FOODS has even greater impact because GENERAL FOODS is the most aggressive pusher of fabricated foods in the country. It spends millions of dollars extolling the virtues of chemicals and additives in our foods.

GENERAL FOODS is the largest American food advertiser and one of the two largest American advertisers of any product, spending $219 million annually in advertising. It spends a higher amount for advertising as a percentage of sales than any other "cereal" manufacturer. GENERAL FOODS has assets in excess of $2 billion.

GENERAL FOODS has also actively and skillfully opposed governmental attempts to regulate the safety and healthfulness of our food supply. In effect, GENERAL FOODS has sought, under the guise of free enterprise, to be free of governmental regulation so that it may give small children misleading information.

Opposing government attempts to regulate safety and healthfulness of the food supply

4. The sales of candy breakfasts are the object of a multimillion-dollar advertising campaign carefully geared toward persuading our children of a falsehood—that eating such sugar products for breakfast is good for them, will help them feel "full of vitality" and will make them strong, happy, growing people. See advertisement labeled Exhibit A which is attached hereto and incorporated herein by reference. In fact, consumption of sugar in large quantities is known to have frequent serious adverse medical consequences, including a substantially increased incidence of tooth decay — a fact which has been deliberately omitted from GENERAL FOODS' advertising and packaging.

5. Moreover, the detrimental impact of the POST CEREALS scheme falls most heavily on poor, disadvantaged and minority children, whose families must spend a higher proportion of their incomes on food. As a result of the sort of irresponsible and incomplete nutritional information provided by GENERAL FOODS in its advertising and marketing campaign, such families frequently end up purchasing a higher proportion of "junk" and empty-calorie food than nutritious food. Studies show a clear association between malnourishment and the amount of unhealthful and starchy "junk" food on hand at home. GENERAL FOODS perpetuates the cycle of malnourishment, since there appears to be an inverse relationship between percentage of "junk" food consumed and performance in school: a poor diet impedes learning, and underachievement in school will limit income for a lifetime.

# USE OF CARTOONS

6. Promotion of POST CEREALS is aimed at children and occurs primarily on television, deliberately planned during children's hours. Through the calculated use of cartoon characters and fast-paced and seductive dialogue, GENERAL FOODS engages in the massive deception of children. Television advertising has reached such a sophisticated level that children actually increase their attention spans during the commercials. By the time they reach age 18, most American children will have viewed 350,000 commercials, the overwhelming majority of which advertise for foods containing added sugar. The candy breakfast industry, which spent over $80 million in 1970 for advertising, employs a legion of market researchers, child psychologists, and the most manipulative of advertising trickery. Children are the most vulnerable prey for such tactics, and they are the victims: they receive an adulterated product, are subject to a higher incidence of tooth decay and, at the deliberately misleading suggestion of GENERAL FOODS, will establish a lifetime of poor eating habits, including near addiction to excessive sugar in their diets.

7. Americans today consume nearly 23% more refined sugar than we did in 1947 and children in particular are now consuming an unhealthful amount of sugar.

There are many other adverse health conditions known to be associated with excessive sugar consumption, none of which has ever been mentioned in POST CEREALS' advertising. Having known of these dangers for years, GENERAL FOODS deliberately advertises a falsehood to children: it affirmatively portrays its candy breakfasts as cereal products central to a good diet.

8. To sell sugar as cereal is deceit. POST CEREALS suggests that its product is one thing when it is in fact another. Despite the fact that every major dictionary defines "cereal" as a plant product made from grain, POST'S grossly adulterated candy breakfasts are falsely labeled and advertised as "cereals," "wheat puffs," "rice cereal," and "corn cereal." In fact, several contain more sugar than any grain product, and others contain a larger quantity of sugar than of all other ingredients put together. To sell a Tootsie Roll (23% sugar) as "nutritious" or "part of a balanced diet" would be grossly fraudulent. Yet GENERAL FOODS' products, advertised as "cereal," contain a higher percentage of sugar than is contained in most commercially marketed cookies, most candy bars, and from nine to eleven times the percentage of sugar (sucrose) contained in Coca-Cola. In short, children, their parents, and the general public are not being told the truth by GENERAL FOODS and BENTON AND BOWLES. To allow this subterfuge to continue would suggest that any product may be sold to the public as cereal, even if only a fraction of the product is, in fact, cereal.

# IS IT CEREAL?

9. A multiple deception is involved. This includes, but is not limited to, First, parents and the public are being induced to buy something labeled "cereal" which is in fact candy, and which does not fit the commonly-accepted definition of the word "cereal." Many parents would not buy these products if they were correctly labelled as "candies," and if the packages disclosed the high percentages of sugar contained in the product. Second, GENERAL FOODS and POST CEREALS deliberately obscure and fail to warn child and adult consumers of the possible unhealthful consequences of ingesting large quantities of sugar, including the risk of tooth decay. Third, GENERAL FOODS and POST CEREALS routinely sell their candy breakfasts to children by means of gross appeals to the fantasy world and imagination of the child and obscure the products' deficiencies and high cost. Said appeals are developed by child psychologists and sophisticated ad agencies, and are totally unrelated to the merits or actual characteristics of the products advertised. Fourth, small amounts of vitamins are added to persuade parents and children that candy breakfasts are nutritious and essential for them, when in fact (a) the additives do little more than replace vitamins previously removed by GENERAL FOODS' own processing, (b) many children derive little benefit from the

additives, (c) children are incapable of evaluating their own needs for such vitamins additives, and (d) such additives fail to compensate for the harmful effects of eating foods, such as GENERAL FOODS' candy breakfasts, which contain excessive amounts of sugar and inadequate amounts of protein. Thus, the representation that, because they contain added vitamins, the products are "good for you" and will contribute to health and strength, are clearly misleading. Fifth, the actual percentage of sugar in the candy breakfasts is deliberately concealed by GENERAL FOODS and POST CEREALS. Sixth, the message actually conveyed to children by GENERAL FOODS is that candy breakfasts are just as nutritious as milk, toast and juice. Seventh, POST CEREALS bombards children with advertisements which correlate the amount of sugar in a product with "good taste." By extolling the merits of "chocolatey good taste" (COCOA PEBBLES) and "golden sugar" (SUPER SUGAR CRISP), GENERAL FOODS and POST CEREALS are deliberately advocating overconsumption of sugar and indoctrinating children in a false conception of nutrition. Eighth, the candy breakfasts are portrayed as "part of a balanced breakfast" by ads which emphasize the GENERAL FOODS products by showing closeups of them, while portraying other foods only in the background. In fact, candy breakfasts, even with added milk, lack over 86% of the daily requirement of protein, and contain percentages of sugar that are high even for candy bars. Thus, they are junk foods containing mostly "empty calories," and are not "part of a balanced breakfast," as that concept is commonly understood.

Indoctrinating a false
conception of nutrition

(Note: Sugar percentages used in the complaint were based on a conservative estimate of figures determined by the University of Texas Dental Branch in a three year nutritional study. Results of these tests are available in *Brand Name Guide to Sugar*, Ira L. Shannon, D.M.D., M.D.S.: Nelson-Hall Inc., 325 W. Jackson Blvd., Chicago, Illinois 60606.)

# GENERAL FOODS REPLIES

**Whole Foods** contacted General Foods Corporation and their attorneys to ask for their responses to the charges in this case. Neither General Foods nor their attorneys would comment on the issues involved, because the case is still in litigation. Rhoda Kaufman at General Foods provided us with the position statement which is printed below.

When asked if General Foods disputed the sugar percentage figures used in this case, Kaufman responded that "we do not consider percentages meaningful" because, she said, percentages sound like there is more sugar in the cereal than there really is. General Foods finds sugar gram content more relevant than sugar percentages, she said, and they intend to print sugar gram content on their product labels in the near future.

Here is the General Foods statement:

**General Foods takes sharp exception to the attack against its Post presweetened cereals.**

**The attack seems based on a fundamental belief that even modest amounts of sugar are bad for you — an assumption not supported by scientific facts.**

**The groups filing suit link the consumption of five presweetened cereals — which each contain less sugar in a one ounce serving than you would find in a medium sized apple or orange and less than half the sugar in a 12 fluid ounce can of cola — with widespread nutritional deficiencies, excessive sugar consumption and broadscale dental disease.**

**The groups fail to point out that since the turn of the century, when the first ready to eat cereals were developed, some people have added sugar to their breakfast cereals. The first presweetened cereals were developed with that thought in mind. The amount of sugar in one ounce of any one of our presweetened cereals is less than two rounded flatware teaspoons — the kind of teaspoon you would use at the table.**

General Foods'
policy statement

As to dental caries, most scientists recognize that tooth decay is a function of many factors relating to carbohydrate usage; for example, quantity ingested, stickiness of the food, and whether the food is eaten at or between meals, or consumed with other foods which will remove it from dental surfaces. Several major, well-respected studies — at the Forsyth Dental Center, the University of Michigan and the University of Alabama — found no correlation between consumption of either regular or presweetened cereals at breakfast with tooth decay.

Our cereal products are good, wholesome foods, fortified to meet 25% of the U.S. Recommended Daily Allowance of several important vitamins. A glance at the nutritional labelling on any of these products so indicates.

We think it is time that groups working in the public interest abandon food scare tactics which abuse reputable products and only serve to confuse and mislead the very consumers they want to help.

# IN SUMMARY

**Attempting a media gag**

Publicity about this case is apparently unwelcome by General Foods. They attempted to impose a gag order on Public Advocates, Inc. and their clients. The court denied their petition. A gag order is customarily used in criminal cases to insure that reports in the media will not influence the judicial process. Lois Salisbury, attorney for Public Advocates, knows of no precedent for imposing a gag order in a civil case.

Why would General Foods avoid publicity? The Federal Trade Commission recently announced its intention to study television advertising and its effects upon children. A variety of proposals being weighed by the FTC ranged from the establishment of sales guidelines on children's advertising to counter-commercials of an educational nature. The most stringent proposals being considered would ban TV advertising of products considered harmful to children's health.

Previous attempts to regulate on these questions have been forestalled by the food industry lobby. Salisbury says she believes that the publicity surrounding this case "was instrumental in focussing the FTC's attention in this area."

Salisbury emphasizes, "This case does not attack sugar. It attacks deceptive advertising to the most vulnerable audience, children." Children are not a mature audience capable of telling the difference between cartoon programming and commercial advertising. Nor are they able to make knowledgeable nutritional decisions. Cartoon advertising can create fantasy expectations which the reality of the product cannot meet. That these fantasy expectations could be harmful has already been recognized: Spider-Man brand vitamins were barred from advertising on children's television and in comic books because these advertisements could induce children to take excessive amounts of vitamins.

**Whose responsibility is it to protect the children?**

Few would dispute the idea that children need to be protected from injury which they are incapable of perceiving. But whose responsibility is that? Children are in the care of their parents, adults who presumably are able to read nutritional labeling, to determine what products their children will eat, and to insure the healthfulness of their children's diet. Mature parents realize that massive amounts of a vitamin won't make anyone as strong as Spider Man, and that eating presweetened cereal confers no superhuman abilities. Since the parents are guardians of their children's health, doesn't the "fiduciary obligation" rest with them? Aren't they, rather than the advertisers, the responsible parties?

The notion that parents actually decide what their children eat is questionable. General Foods spends $23 million for advertising their cereals to children. They wouldn't do it if they didn't expect it to pay off. The very nature and scope of this advertising campaign assumes that children influence what their parents buy.

Attorney Salisbury maintains that, although parents are the guardians of their children's well-being, they are unable to overcome the false message of advertising. Parents do not possess the resources to respond on an equal basis to highly sophistocated, multi-million dollar advertising.

Many parents do not possess the knowledge to make intelligent consumer decisions. The US Senate's Select Committee on Nutrition and Human Needs reported in its "Dietary Goals for the United States" that *"about 34.7 million adults 'function with difficulty' within consumer economics and an additional 39 million 'are functional (but not proficient)' . . . the level of general competency decreases as levels of education and income decline."* Salisbury points out that, when parents are incapable of exercising this responsibility, they rely upon corporate reputations to guide their buying.

If parents are not always able to assume the responsibility for what they or their children consume, it can be argued that manufacturers have a duty to insure that their advertising not be misleading, that it convey a realistic image of what the product is and does, and that the consumer be protected from possible harm from the product.

**A manufacturer's duty not to engage in misleading advertising**

Such responsibility is shared by the distributors of these products. Case law dating to the 1920-30's provides a legal basis for holding distributors as well as manufacturers accountable for the products they sell. For this reason, Safeway Stores was named as a defendant in this lawsuit. As the largest distributor of General Foods products, Safeway is a direct beneficiary of the allegedly fraudulent General Foods advertising.

Safeway reportedly displays presweetened cereals at children's eye-levels. In contrast, Salisbury points to such marketing practices as those of the Berkeley Co-op. While the Co-op still carries presweetened cereals on their shelves, they also post nutritional information which states the percentage of sugar in the product. This practice helps consumers make an informed choice.

Aside from the usual astronomical request for damages—over $40 million right off the bat—this lawsuit seeks that restrictions be placed on fraudulent advertising practices, especially those involving children. Since General Foods has allegedly not regulated itself in these matters, the suit further asks that the Board of Directors of General Foods be expanded to include two court- or state-appointed members to safeguard public interest and to investigate questionable practices within the corporation. Also, General Foods would be required to label the percentage of sugar in children's foods, to contribute to research into the effects of sugar consumption, and to institute an educational campaign to repair the damage allegedly done by false advertising. The courts will decide which, if any, of these actions will be required of the defendants.

**Proposals to safeguard public interest**

This lawsuit is likely to focus public and corporate attention on the issues of power and responsibility involved in advertising and marketing. The concerns of this case apply to the natural food industry as well as to the mainline food industry. Manufacturers are held to be responsible for the impact of their products upon the health of their consumers, just as they are responsible for the impact of their manufacturing processes upon the environment. By becoming a self-regulating industry dedicated to truthful, full-disclosure labeling and advertising of unadulterated products, the natural food industry can avoid abuses like those alleged in this lawsuit.

# 26

# *Bored with Beans*

## by Janice Fillip

One of the earliest cultivated crops, beans have been grown for centuries in Africa, Asia and the Americas. In the 1800s, Gregor Mendel discovered the fundamental principles of inherited genetic traits through experiments with beans. Beans nourished early pioneers and sustained countless cowboys on their traildrives into American song and legend. Yet, despite their colorful and historic past, the subject of beans elicits a yawn from most folks in the natural and health food industry. Beans, they say, are boring.

Ironically, people are bored to indifference about one of the best, most inexpensive sources of protein available. Containing no cholesterol, beans are an important source of vitamins and minerals. A normal serving of beans can supply as much as 40 percent of the minimum requirement for thiamin (B1) and pyrodoxine (B6), plus niacin, iron, calcium, phosphorus, potassium and folic acid, according to the Idaho Bean Commission. Although lacking methionine, one of the eight essential amino acids, this deficiency is easily corrected by serving beans with small amounts of meat, dairy products, or cereal grains such as rice or corn. The problem with beans is not their nutritional value— it's their image.

**An excellent, inexpensive protein source**

During the 1930's Depression, many people lived on beans, which became a symbol of poverty. Since beans remain a staple food in many lesser-developed countries—largely due to their nutritional value—they have retained the image of a poverty food. No one in the natural or health food industry seems particularly interested in glorifying beans. No one seems to give a hill of beans about beans—expect farmers.

**Nitrogen-fixing properties**

Farmers, both commercial and organic, value beans for their nitrogen-fixing properties. Plants require nitrogen to live. Although approximately 30 percent of the atmosphere is nitrogen, most plants cannot use nitrogen in its gaseous form from the air and must depend on the relatively small quantity of nitrogen in the soil to help them survive. Beans are a legume, one of the few plants with the capacity to take nitrogen from the air and transfer it into the soil. Legumes have parasitic bacteria, *Rhizobium*, which form

114

nitrogen nodules on the plant roots. The nodules release nitrogen from the plant into the soil for use by other plants which cannot draw their nitrogen from the atmosphere. Because of this nitrogen-fixing ability, beans are often cultivated as a rotation crop or as green manure to help nourish the soil.

The distinction between commercial and organic is not as clear cut with beans as it is with other crops. Commercially-grown legumes are seldom sprayed with pesticides or treated with chemical fertilizers. They are, however, generally grown in rotation with heavily sprayed and fertilized crops. This raises the question of whether beans grown without chemicals, but on chemical-ladened land, should be sold as "organic," as they often are.

Farmers are not completely bored with soybeans because they are a profitable crop. The largest cash crop grown in the United States, soybeans outdistance second-place wheat in both planted acreage and dollar volume. The US currently grows about two-thirds of the world's soybeans, mostly for export. Domestic use of soybeans is primarily for livestock feed and for processing edible oil.

Oil soybeans are edible soybeans which have been genetically hybridized to produce a higher oil content. While only an estimated 5,000 acres of vegetable soybeans are grown in this country at present, there is a growing demand for this sweeter-tasting soybean. This demand has been directly linked to the tremendous growth of the tofu industry in the past few years. Although vegetable soybeans cost more to produce than oil soybeans due to their lower yield per acre—oil soybeans produce approximately 40 bushels per acre, while vegetable soybeans produce around 25 bushels per acre—many growers are switching to vegetable soybeans.

Edible beans—lima, blackeye, kidney, garbanzo, pinto, white, navy, mung, lentil and adzuki—are harder to harvest than soybeans. While soybeans are cut above ground, other edible beans require a special machine to cut the plants off below the soil. Combines must be specially equipped to prevent soil harvested along with the beans from getting into the machinery.

Cultivating edible beans can be a financially risky business. According to Larry Eggen at New Life Food, one bean crop is lost every five years due to weather. Early rain at harvest causes beans to sprout in the fields or to discolor, making them cosmetically unacceptable. Eggen estimates that 40-60 percent of last year's organic edible bean crop in Michigan was lost to rain during harvest.

After harvesting, beans are cleaned and bagged, an operation costing from 75 cents to $1.00 per bushel. In the cleaning process, farmers often have a 10-15 percent dockage (loss) of beans due to damaging and cracking. Damaged beans, or screenings, are sold for fodder at one cent a pound.

Soybeans are cleaned in a fanning mill or spiral which takes out anything not shaped like a soybean. They are not washed, since moisture shrivels the hull and lessens the bean's keeping ability. Edible beans go through a fanning mill, and then proceed to a gravity table and an electric-eye system which remove misshapen and light-colored beans. Although shape and color have little to do with the bean's nutritional value, Ardel Anderson at Living Farms points out that "most people aren't going to buy discolored, misshapen beans."

Organic beans often do not look as good as commercial beans, because most organic farmers cannot afford the $10,000 worth of equipment necessary for a gravity table and an electric-eye monitor. The relatively small size of their bean crop cannot justify the expense. Larry Eggen reports that farmers experimenting with cooperative ownership of cleaning equipment have found it to be a successful alternative to paying the high cost demanded by commercial cleaners.

Cleaning costs are not the only reason that organic beans are more expensive than their commercial competition. There is widespread feeling among distributors that organic farmers are asking too much for their products. According to Ardel Anderson, "In most cases, people buy nonorganic because organic is too expensive. A 100-200 percent premium is too much."

Not susceptible to bugs and rodents, edible beans have an excellent shelf life and are only somewhat seasonal. Taking these factors into consideration, Lester Karplus of

Vegetarian Inc. feels that retail markup on edible beans should only be 25-30 percent. Instead he finds natural and health food stores "selling the same beans that are in supermarkets at twice the price." In view of an approximate 50 percent drop in commercial prices for this year's bumper soybean crop, Karplus remarked, "I don't believe that consumers are getting that much better a product from the organic market."

Another factor in high organic prices is the lack of a well-developed distribution network within the organic industry. Deliveries may take as long as six weeks. An order of 10,000-20,000 pounds of assorted beans per month is considered a large order by the industry, but not by freight companies. "How do you get two to four bags of beans to the West Coast from Michigan?" asks Ardel Anderson. "It isn't practical." Anderson suggests that distribution costs might be reduced if regional entrepreneurs with large warehouses ordered in bulk from suppliers and sold smaller orders to local markets. Looking ahead, Anderson says, "We need a lot more growth in the organic industry to justify larger shipments and lower freight rates."

Specialty beans

That growth may come in the area of specialty beans—lentil, mung, adzuki and garbanzo—which are becoming a lucrative alternative crop. While the small edible bean crop supplies a small demand, the demand for specialty beans is much greater than current domestic production.

Its nut-like flavor and ability to mix with other vegetables have made the garbanzo bean (chick peas) fashionable as an appetizer and salad ingredient. Burgeoning interest in Middle Eastern foods, such as falafel and hummus, has created another market for garbanzo beans. The domestic crop, grown primarily in southern California's arid climate, is not sufficient to supply current demand. Most of the garbanzo beans on the market are imported from Mexico.

Lentils and mung beans owe their popularity to sprouting. Cultivated in the cool, humid climate of Washington, Oregon and Idaho, domestic lentil crops fall short of meeting current demand. The difference between domestic supply and demand is made up with lentils imported from Mexico. Mung beans are beginning to catch on with organic farmers in Texas and Oklahoma where they adapt well to the long, arid growing season. Secondary regions of cultivation included southern California, northern Kansas, and Nebraska.

Adzuki beans are extremely popular in Japan where they are used as the base for a sugary pastry filling. Only about five percent of Japan's demand for adzuki beans can be met by their domestic production. Recent experiments indicate that Minnesota's sandy soil may provide an ideal location for growing adzuki beans, which could easily become a competitive cash crop for export to Japan.

Perhaps beans will become less boring as they move further into the international marketplace, acquiring an exotic allure to brighten their image. With a bit of luck, beans might just become worth a hill of.

# SEEDS OF FUTURE PAST

End of a genetic heritage?

"Up to the present time we have been able to return to areas of genetic diversity to collect germplasm for further breeding programs. Suddenly in the 1970's we are discovering Mexican farmers are planting hybrid seed from a midwestern seed firm, that Tibetan farmers are planting barley from a Scandinavian plant breeding station, and that Turkish farmers are planting wheat from the Mexican wheat program. Each of these classic areas of genetic diversity is rapidly becoming an area of seed uniformity.

"The reason for alarm and concern about the loss of native strains is the irreplaceable nature of the genetic weath. The only place genes can be stored is in living systems, either living branches, such as the bud wood of apple trees, or the living embryos of grain or vegetable seed. The nature varieties become extinct once they are dropped in favor of introduced seed. The extinction can take place in a single year if the seeds are cooked and eaten instead of saved as seed stock. Quite literally, the genetic heritage of a millennium in a particular valley can disappear in a single bowl of porridge."

*From a report by the National Academy of Sciences.*

# Consumer's Guide

## GRAINS

Immediately after a grain is milled, the oil in the grain begins to go rancid and the nutrients begin to deteriorate. Vitamin E, for example, is generally gone five days after wheat has been ground. Grains milled with the stone ground, low-heat method deteriorate less rapidly than those milled under high-heat. There are, however, no controls over use of the term *stone ground*. Before paying extra for stone ground products, investigate how the product was milled. Stone grinding idealling reaches a friction temperature of less than 120° F.

- To ensure freshness, purchase flour ground in the store or buy grains and a flour mill to grind your own.
- After high-heat milling, flours are usually aged with preservatives, bleaches and whiteners. These include methyl bromide, organic mercurials, nitrogen trichloride, chlorine dioxide, alum, chalk, ammonium carbonate and nitrogen peroxide.
- Commercial milling removes about 90 nutrients from flour. Law requires that processed flour be enriched by adding back four nutrients: thiamin, riboflavin, niacin and iron. These are added in a chemical, non-food form.
- There is no evidence that organically grown grains have a higher protein content than those grown under chemical methods.
- Storing grains and flour at a low temperature guards against infestation.
- Polyethylene bags may sweat on the inside, and the resuiting moisture and heat can lead to loss of nutrients in the products and can increase the chances of infestation. Cellophane bags, paper bags and cardboard boxes do not tend to sweat.

## BREAKFAST CEREALS

Higher quality granola has a good portion of ingredients such as nuts, seeds and raisins, as well as oat flakes. Be aware of the sweeteners used in granola, which may include brown sugar, cane syrup or even refined white sugar. Artificial flavors and colors may also be used. Check the label.

- Uncooked cereals are generally less-processed than ready-to-eat cereals.
- Instant, uncooked cereals may have been processed with such chemicals as disodium phosphate, or with proteolytic enzymes, to shorten cooking time.

## BEANS

Although they are one of the best, most inexpensive sources of protein available, beans lack methionine, an essential amino acid. This deficiency can be easily corrected by serving beans with small amounts of meat, dairy products or cereal grains such as rice and corn.

- Commercial beans are seldom sprayed with pesticides or chemical fertilizers, although they are rotated with heavily sprayed and fertilized crops.
- Vegetable soybeans used in soyfoods have a lower oil content and sweeter taste than soybeans used to make oil.
- Displays of organic beans may include misshapen and light-colored beans because organic farming operations are generally too small to afford the sophisticated gravity tables and electric-eye monitors used to select only standardized beans. The misshapen, discolored beans are not nutritionally inferior—they just do not look as pretty.
- Beans store well and are not susceptible to bugs or rodents.

## SPROUTS

- Before buying sprouting seeds, ask to see a seed analysis report. The best seeds have a high germination rate and a low (10-12 percent) moisture content.
- Seeds for garden planting are chemically treated and should not be used for sprouting. They are a potential health hazard.

## IN BULK

- When buying from bulk bins, use the scooping utensils to prevent contamination.

# Section V: Soyfoods

In a world where hunger is a daily reality for millions of people, and even the beef-fed American public is feeling the squeeze of the ever-rising price of meat, foods made from soybeans have an important and unique place as a source of high-quality protein. Soyfoods, according to many commentators, make the most economic and ecological sense as the foundation of human nutrition on a planetary scale.

Long a staple in the Asian diet, soybeans are swiftly becoming an important source of protein in the United States, often as a highly-processed ingredient added to other prefabricated foods, and unnoticed by the purchaser. In the natural foods industry, the major new use of soybeans began as a direct "import" of Asian cottage-industry methods for the production of soybean curd, most commonly known as tofu.

Knowing that the American consumer would have a limited appetite for squares of bean cake floating in broth, the small-scale non-Asian producers of tofu in the United States began experimenting with soyfoods more acceptable to Western tastes. The result is already a wide variety of appealing soyfoods which provide the consumer with a protein-rich alternative to meat. Many foods now made from soybeans have a resemblance to familiar products, ranging from ice cream, through mayonnaise and sauces, to breakfast sausage—and the manufacturers of these products say that they have many more in the works.

This section of the *Natural Foods Guide* highlights individual soyfoods manufacturers to show the swift development of the industry from its hesitant beginnings a few years ago to the present day. Chapters in this *Soyfoods* section also show the contrast between the production of soyfoods by this industry and the soy products which are concentrated, spun and textured by major food industries to add to other foods.

Soyfoods are likely to take a larger place in the diets of customers at natural foods stores. Usually, soyfoods first appear on the shelves in the forms used in the Orient, and are later adapted to the American styles of eating. When they arrive on our shores, these foods are likely to have unfamiliar names. (As soon as we knew what tofu was, the soycrafters started talking about tempeh . . . whatever that is.) This section of the guide includes explanations of these imported words, tells how the various soyfoods are processed, and sorts out the differences in such items as shoyu, tamari, and supermarket soysauce.

119

# Food of the Future

## by Jim Schreiber

Why devote so many pages of this book to the subject of soyfoods?

- Soyfoods are a rapidly growing part of the natural foods industry.
- A wide variety of soyfoods can be made in local shops with minimal processing, providing fresh, nutritious, low-cost natural foods to customers.
- Foods from soybeans are a complete-protein alternative to meat, with strong economic, dietary, and ecological advantages.
- Soybean products are already an important and expanding part of the mainstream American diet.
- Soyfoods offer a way to cut food costs at home and to combat hunger on a worldwide scale.

Soybeans are the number-one cash crop in the United States, and are the number-one source of protein and fat in the national food economy. In recent years, Americans have been eating about 13 billion pounds of protein annually which originated as soybeans in the field. The USA produces about 75 percent of the world's soybeans, and exports about half its yearly crop.

**A soyfood revolution**

Although soybeans have long been a major part of the diet in East Asia—to such an extent that one researcher has said that the Chinese civilization could not have existed without them—soybeans have had a hard time becoming accepted as a visible food in the USA. Part of this aversion dates from the Second World War, when soybean products were used as an austerity source of protein, substituting for other foods which were in scarcity. Soybean foods were not only associated with hard times but, to the American palate, tasted funny—oily or beany or fishy.

Food technologists have now spent decades trying to remove or alter the odor and taste of soybean products, and soybean product merchandisers have successfully guided soybeans out of consumer awareness but into their stomachs. As recently as September 1978, *Food Product Development* magazine was saying, ". . . the products are simply a lot better than they were in 1973-74. Advances in processing technology of the vegetable products have introduced a blander, more functional product. Steam introduced into the system at various points during extrusion is used to 'blast off' undesirable flavor notes or to form fibrous structures in the products.''

Through texturization, concentration and isolation, soy products find their way into countless highly processed foods, often under a vague labeling term such as "vegetable protein." Americans usually don't know it, but they are eating technologized soyfoods by the ton, and liking them. What the manufacturers do know is that soy protein is highly nutritious, and cheap. The consumer, of course, pays for the high level of technology.

At the other end of the technical spectrum is the small natural foods shop making its own soyfoods for local sale, drawing on the centuries of experience of soyfoods-makers in Japan, China, and Indonesia.

# CONSUMER ACCEPTANCE

These small shops are in a good position to make use of information developed by the automated soy industry, such as this statement in the same issue of *Food Product Development*. "According to recent surveys, many consumers believe soy protein improves over-all quality, nutrition, and economic value of meats" Such surveys suggest that the expected dislike of soy products may be misleading, and that the public at large is beginning to see the inherent value of this food. The step from commercial turkey-salami-textured-soy-protein-and-heaven-knows-what-else loaf to a natural, store-made "Soyage" may now be easy for the average consumer to take.

Although the soycrafters in the natural foods industry start with the low-level, appropriate technology of East Asia, and enter the market with traditional Oriental foods, they soon begin to think about inventing new natural recipes with direct appeal to the standard American taste-buds. Many consumers find the traditional Oriental soyfoods acceptable and even delightful, but the larger market demands products that don't "taste funny" the first time they're tried. This is one of the major ways in which the Soyfoods Revolution is growing in the USA right now.

Soyfoods provide a model of the small, local cottage industry using appropriate technology and fitting well into desirable ecological patterns. Because the current natural soyfoods tend to be quite perishable, the local soycrafter is at an advantage, and can avoid concern about vast fleets of refrigerated vehicles. These products allow the natural foods business to operate in good conscience, knowing that the bean plant itself is adding nitrogen to the soil where it grows, and that their products are giving the consumer a complete protein, comparable to that of meat. Any soybeans produce about 508 pounds of protein per acre; beef, about 58 pounds.

Complete protein does not mean complete food. Soybeans lack vitamin B-12 entirely, and are not a good source of minerals. In a joint study by the US Department of Health, Education, and Welfare and the Food and Agricultural Division of the United Nations, researchers shopped in East Asia and then studied 100-gram samples of various products. Their analysis of 100-gram tofu samples showed these results: 63 calories, 86.7% moisture, 7.9 g. protein, 4.1 g. fat, 0.3 g. carbohydrate, 0.1 g. fiber, 0.9 g. ash, 150 mg. (milligrams) calcium, 104 mg. phosphorus, 2.2 mg. iron, 12 mg. sodium, 151 mg. potassium, .04 mg. thiamine, .02 mg. riboflavin, 0.4 mg. niacin, 27 mg. magnesium, .6 mg. zinc, .3 ug. (micrograms) selenium, 3.3 ug. iodine.

# THE B-12 DRAWBACK

The matter of vitamin B-12 seems to be the only serious drawback of soyfoods. Raw soybeans contain a substance which increases the body's need for B-12, but is destroyed by heat. Philip S. Chen, in his *Soybeans for Health, Longevity, and Economy*, says, "Swenseid and co-workers have shown that the liver stores considerable amounts of this vitamin, enough to last 3 to 24 years depending on its capacity, the daily requirements of the body, and other factors." Chen suggests the occasional use of brewers yeast to guard against B-12 deficiency in a soyfoods diet.

Soycrafters use low-level technology

A complete protein, not a complete food

Chen also lists nutrients in 100 grams of soymilk as compared to cow's milk. (The soymilk figure is given first in this list: soymilk/cowmilk.) Water 92.5 g./97.0 g.; protein 3.4 g./3.5 g.; fat 1.5 g./3.9 g.; carbohydrate 2.1 g./4.9 g.; ash .5 g./.7 g.; calcium 21 mg./118 mg.; phosphorus 47 mg./93 mg.; iron .7 mg./.1 mg.; thiamine .09 mg./.04 mg.; riboflavin .04 mg./.17 mg..; niacin .3 mg./.1 mg.

Soyfood pioneers

*The Book of Tofu* by William Shurtleff and Akiko Aoyagi contains 500 recipes and basic instructions for making tofu, soymilk, tempeh and other soyfoods. A companion volume, *Tofu & Soymilk Production*, is a technical manual for small shops. Soymilk production is also described by Smith and Circle and S.S. De in the books listed at the end of this article. A wide variety of soyfoods recipes are found in *The Farm Vegetarian Cookbook* (The Book Publishing Co., 156 Drakes Lane, Summertown, TN 38483). Other recipes of interest appear in *Soybean Diet* by Herman & Cornellia Aihara and in *The Chico-San Cookbook* by C. Aihara (both published by the George Ohsawa Macrobiotic Foundation, 1554 Oak St., Oroville, CA 95965).

Although the soybean lends itself to simple transformation into a variety of tasty, wholesome foods, the amazing bean alone cannot bring about a dietary change in America. The bringing of the "Soyfoods Revolution" to the natural foods industry is the work of individuals, toiling and playing with new recipes in their own kitchens and shops. No person deserves more credit for this revolution than William Shurtleff who, along with Akiko Aoyagi, wrote *The Book of Tofu*, and told us all how to do it. (An updated pocket-size version of *The Book of Tofu* has been published by Ballantine Press.) Shurtleff travels the globe, sharing his expertise on soyfoods, covering topics as specific as chip-dip recipes and as broad as the role of soybean production in future patterns of world protein hunger.

# SOYCRAFTERS ASSOCIATION

Backbone of the revolution

Other individuals, most of them with small soyfoods shops of their own, met recently to form the Soycrafters Association of North America (SANA), which is likely to serve as the backbone of the Soyfoods Revolution in the natural foods industry. SANA selected Larry Needleman as its first president. Needleman, whose Bean Machines, Inc. imports the prime line of Takai tofu and soymilk equipment from Japan, has been a major source of information about soyfoods equipment for our industry.

Needleman wrote about the spirit of the new organization at its first gathering in Ann Arbor:

"Imagine a group of seventy people representing enthusiastic dedication (almost to the point of craziness) to the production and distribution of tofu and other soyfoods, gathered in an informal setting in a university town in the Midwest, with meetings scheduled from nine in the morning till eleven at night—and you've got a good idea of what went on . . .

"Sharing began immediately. Groups of people gathered here and there and began asking each other about their shop or organization. Those passing by would hear a familiar word such as 'yield' or 'pressure-cooker' and just stopped to join the conversation. It was apparent that here was a gathering destined to be stimulating and mutually beneficial . . .

"The first evening, Bill Shurtleff set up a slide show about tofu and miso production in Japan. The presentation ran the gamut from small, traditional shops built over their own well, to large, fully-automated factories turning out tens of thousands of pounds per day. Bill answered questions and added a personal touch to the showing because he had shot the photos himself over a period of years, and was familiar with the language, traditions and production of the Japanese . . .

"On Saturday morning, The Soy Plant showed us their method of producing tofu and soymilk. Those with less experience absorbed information and asked questions, and those with more experience volunteered information, clarified points and offered suggestions. Then Wataru Takai, the overseas sales manager for Takai Tofu and Soymilk Equipment Co., Japan's largest manufacturer of this equipment, explained principles behind each step of production, and the uses of the equipment . . .

# LABOR INTENSIVE

"At a later session, it was remarked that many soyfoods producers are operating on an inefficient labor intensive basis. Some felt this was a good way to begin, first becoming intimate with the steps of production and developing a market 'track record,' and then using that base to upgrade production by purchasing more sophisticated equipment. Others felt that the time and energy involved in putting together a makeshift shop which was outgrown in about six months would be better spent in raising the capital to start at a higher technological level . . .

"In one of the most popular and exciting discussions of the conference the consensus of the group was that tofu and soymilk were the foods that Americans have been waiting for. A list of related products that have been marketed with incredible success includes tofu burgers, no-egg salad, honey soymilk ice cream, tofu chip-dips and dressings, flavored soymilk, tofu 'mayonnaise,' and pressed, marinated tofu. There was unanimous agreement that it was these new soyfoods that would capture the interest and palate of middle America, people who had turned up their noses at that tasteless white cake of tofu floating in water . . .

**Tofu and soymilk—foods that America has been waiting for**

"Later we discussed the problems of proper storage and display of our products. In US food markets, tofu has usually been sold with Oriental foods in the vegetable section. Getting it moved to a cooler, more appropriate cheese display case, where it will stay fresh longer and compete favorably with dairy products, has met with resistance . . .

"In the evening, another slide show by Bill Shurtleff showed us how tempeh, a key protein source for millions of people in Indonesia, is quickly and simply produced as a cottage industry in their homes. Having sampled this unusual food at lunch, we were eager to learn about it because it was delectable. Somewhere between a deep-fried fish cake and Kentucky fried chicken in flavor and texture, it lent itself to use in a seemingly endless variety of ways . . ."

Toward the end of the conference, discussion turned to marketing and finance. It was found that some firms lacked capital for growth, while others had enough capital but needed greater management skills to keep up with the growing demand for soyfoods. That demand is not uniform nationwide. Different regions show various levels of consumer awareness, interest in, and acceptance of soyfoods.

Before leaving Ann Arbor, the participants formed the Soycrafters Association of North America as a trade association to promote soyfoods and exchange information among the members. With the founding of SANA, the Soyfoods Revolution took its longest recent stride. Soycrafters were no longer isolated persons, groups and shops, but had become a nationwide network devoted to the same purposes, sharing their experience for mutual benefit, and the ultimate benefit of the American consumer.

**Forming a nationwide network**

When S. S. De wrote his 1971 report on soybean foods, published by the United Nations, he did not have this new natural food industry in mind, but his words are nevertheless prophetic: "Research and development in the field of soybean processing and utilization have been very remarkable in recent times and one could predict a new era in the use of soybean as a human food."

Listed below are some of the major sources we have used for information presented in this section:

*Technology of production of edible flours and protein products from soybean.* (Agricultural Services Bulletin 11). S.S. De. Agricultural Services Division, Food and Agricultural Organization of the United Nations. Rome, 1971.

*Soybeans and Soybean Products.* Klare S. Markley (ed.). Interscience Publishers, Inc., New York, 1950.

*Soybeans: Chemistry and Technology: Volume I — Proteins* (Revised Second Printing), Allan K. Smith and Sidney J. Circle (eds.), AVI Publishing Co., Inc., Westport, CT, 1978.
*Soybeans as a Food Source.* W.J. Wolf and J.C. Cowan (eds.). CRC Press. Cleveland, 1975.

# Refabricated Soy Protein

## by Janice Fillip

**Textured vegetable protein products introduce consumers to health and natural foods**

The experience of retailers across the country suggests that textured vegetable protein products may be the single most useful item on the shelf for introducing health and natural foods to the average American shopper.

Wedged between a pizza parlor and a candy store in a Reading, PA, shopping mall, Nature's Garden offers a vegetarian barbecue sandwich on their juice bar menu. Store manager Susanne Clofine recalls, "When we first opened, no one knew what it was. Seeing us prepare the barbeque gives customers encouragement. They realize their children would eat it."

Mrs. Pat Robertson, owner/manager of Breads for Life in Springfield, MO, agrees. Her store carries vegetable protein granules for making "meat" loaves and roasts, but the biggest-selling vegetable protein products are canned and frozen products. Robertson suggests that these products, especially luncheon slices, offer a convenient alternative to processed luncheon meats.

When Marion's Health Foods in Boston added tacos made with textured vegetable protein to their selection of prepared sandwiches, the response was remarkable. "People love them. "We can't make enough," says owner Marion Lennihan.

Why are textured vegetable protein products so popular? Jim Burrus, manager of Potomac Health Foods in Takoma Park, MD, thinks the main reason is that people are "getting away from meat and the chemicals that are put into meat." Meat analogs (substitutes), made primarily from textured vegetable protein, are bringing new customers into health and natural food stores. According to Clofine, textured vegetable protein products are "the first place customers start, because they can relate to their appearance and flavor. They come into the store for TVP and look around." Lennihan also credits textured vegetable protein products with bringing in new customers, "Our store is not in a health food neighborhood, but if we have something that looks familiar, customers will relate to it."

An increase in the number of vegetarians is contributing to the popularity of textured vegetable protein products. Robertson observed, "A major portion of the people (who buy these products) are vegetarians or in the process of becoming vegetarians. They look on it as a protein food." These products have another reason for appealing to vegetarians. According to Lennihan, "Some of the vegetarians, especially the guys, miss the old hot dog and hamburger stuff." With meat analog products, they can have their burger and eat it too.

Explorers who venture into the world of natural and health foods though the door marked "TVP" usually come back for more. Earthereal Trade Company Health Food Store and Restaurant in Shreveport, LA, found that diners who taste textured vegetable protein entrees in the restaurant often become store customers. Manager Jackie McCann explained, "A lot of customers who haven't eaten health foods before don't know it's not meat. They're surprised at how good it tastes. Sales in the store have increased because of the restaurant."

Feedback from *Whole Foods'* readers shows that 58 percent of the retail stores surveyed in the natural and health food industry sell textured vegetable protein products. Burris summarizes the important role these products are playing: "People enjoy these products and will come back and buy other natural foods. It keeps increasing their knowledge and taste for natural foods."

Textured vegetable protein comes from soybeans. With a protein concentration of approximately 35 percent, soybeans can be considered a naturally-occurring protein concentrate. Working since the turn of the century, food chemists have developed a technology to increase soybean's protein concentration and form textured soy protein products, commonly known as TVP.

*Textured vegetable proteins developed by food chemists*

Actually, "TVP" is a trademark owned by Archer Daniels Midland Co., which is used to describe their textured soy products. There are three types of textured soy products commonly referred to as TVP: textured soyflour containing 50 percent protein, soy protein concentrates with a protein content of 70 percent, and soy protein isolates with a whopping 90 percent protein content.

Dr. John Harvey Kellogg, a Seventh Day Adventist, is credited with developing the first textured soy analog in the early 1900's. The first textured soy protein fiber product to be marketed is thought to be a chicken analog made by Worthington Foods Inc., a division of Miles Laboratories.

In the late 1930s, Loma Linda Foods, an outgrowth of Loma Linda Sanitarium and Hospital established by the Seventh Day Adventist Church, began extensive marketing of meat analogs as a transition product for people adopting the Adventist's dietary philosophy and switching from a flesh to a nonflesh diet.

By 1968, texturized soy protein products had gained such widespread acceptance that the New York State Department of Mental Hygiene was adding General Mills' beef, ham and chicken analogs to meals for institutionalized patients. In 1971, textured soy protein was approved for school lunch programs.

# THE PRICE OF BEEF

Rising beef prices in the mid-70s spurred the meat industry on to using textured vegetable protein as a meat substitute and as an extender and fortifier in frankfurters, bologna, meat loaves, meat balls, meat patties, salisbury steak, chili con carne, and luncheon meats. According to Richard Mergeheen, director of products and marketing for Central Soy Company, the textured vegetable protein market "experienced a phenomenal growth in the mid-70s, with the shortage of beef. When meat prices decreased, the volume of soy protein sales decreased. Now meat prices are on the upswing again."

However it is used, textured vegetable protein is a big money-maker. Industry trade journals report that annual sales from vegetable protein in 1973 totaled $83 million, and predict sales as high as $1.5 billion by 1980, projecting that half the processed meats consumed in the 1980's will be vegetable protein analogs. The frozen food industry alone foresees $100 million in sales by 1980 for frozen soy extenders and analogs. These great expectations all stem from the simple soybean.

*A big money-maker*

# FROM SOY TO FLOUR

Textured soyflour, soy protein concentrates and soy protein isolates all originate with soyflour.

One of the first companies to introduce soyflour in the United States was Fearn Soya Foods. Fearn's president Louis Richards remembers that, when Dr. Charles Fearn started the company in 1925, no one knew what soyflour was. Now a large majority of the retail stores in the natural and health food industry sell soyflour.

The chemical and functional properties of soyflour are different from those of grain flours, which is why Richards prefers to call it "soy powder," a term often heard in our industry. Soyflour is used in baking to increase protein content, to improve digestibility by balancing wheat flour's acidity, to enhance browning characteristics, and to extend shelf life. It is also used in confections, snacks, carob coating, soup mixes (especially cream style), K rations, as a breakfast food combined with cornflakes, and to improve the body and flavor of beer. While cookbooks recommend that 25 percent of the wheat flour in most recipes can be replaced with soyflour before the recipe has to be reformulated, Richards says that in commercial formulations the percentage of soyflour substitution is considerably lower.

**Processing soyflour**

In processing soyflour, soybeans are cleaned in conventional grain cleaners to remove over- and under-sized beans and foreign material. Next the beans are conditioned with humidity to soften the outer hull before they are mechanically cracked into six or eight pieces and dehulled. Cracking allows the hulls to be separated from the cotyledon (meat) and hypocotyl (germ) by screening, aspiration or centrifuge. Since 85 percent of the hull is made up of carbohydrates, dehulling eliminates much of the bean's carbohydrate components. After being flaked by a large blade, dehulled soybeans are rendered into flour either by grinding/pulverizing or by solvent extraction.

Typically, beans are steam heated at approximately 270°F. for 20 minutes before being mechanically ground or pulverized. This method involves no chemical processing and produces a full-fat flour containing all the oil originally in the soybean (18-20 percent).

In the solvent extraction method, oil is removed from the soyflakes through the use of a solvent, usually food grade hexane, a flammable, colorless liquid derived from petroleum. Soymeal remaining after the oil has been removed is desolventized by flash heating. Highly volatile, hexane will "flash" out of meal which is exposed to high temperatures. This heat application serves the additional function of inactivating or destroying a variety of anti-nutritional factors present in raw soybeans, such as trypsin inhibitors, hemagglutinins, saponins, isoflavone glycosides and anti-vitamin factors. (For a complete discussion on methods of solvent extraction, see the chapter on Edible Oils.)

**Defatted soyflakes**

The defatted soyflakes produced by extraction are ground or pulverized into soyflour. If the soyflakes have been processed with low heat, the soyflour will have a whitish color. A darker, toasted look indicates that the soyflakes were processed under high heat.

Defatted soyflour contains 53-55 percent protein and less than 2 percent oil. Degummed raw soybean oil or refined bleached soybean oil is added to defatted soyflour to produce lowfat soyflour (5-6 percent oil content) and highfat soyflour (up to 15 percent oil content). Lecithinated soyflour is produced by adding up to 15 percent lecithin to lowfat or highfat soyflour.

# ISOLATING THE ISOLATE

**Obtaining protein isolates**

Although industrial use of soy protein isolates began in Chicago in 1935, the first edible grade soy protein isolate was not developed until 1959. Today soy protein isolate is widely used in protein supplement drinks and products. as a binder in processed meat products, and in the manufacture of ersatz dairy products.

Protein isolates are obtained simply by readjusting soyflour's pH balance. When alkalized with a sodium hydroxide solution to a pH of 10, protein and carbohydrate materials in the soyflour dissolve. Undissolved fiber and carbohydrates with high molecular weights are removed by a centrifuge, leaving a solution of sugars and protein. This solution is then acidified in a hydrochloric acid solution to its "isoelectric point." At this point, the protein separates from the acidic solution. A centrifuge removes sugars from the protein.

Both sodium hydroxide and hydrochloric acid are precipitated out of the protein isolate at each stage of the pH adjustment. The sodium ions do, however, react to form a sodium salt which remains in the isolate in a small quantity.

pH adjustment—from acidic to alkaline and back again

The protein precipitate is again alkalized, this time to a 7.0 or neutral pH. The next step is spray drying: in the presence of heat, the isolate solution is atomized into fine particles in the same way that perfume is sprayed out of an atomizer. The spray dries instantly into a protein isolate consisting of not less than 90 percent protein. Isolates are used directly as food ingredients or are spun (much the same as textiles are spun) into protein fibers.

Adjusting the pH has an effect on the protein molecule in soyflour. According to Dr. William Barone, director of textured protein research for Central Soya Company, adjustment of pH changes the molecular weight of the protein through a reaction called "association." Barone explained that association does not change the nutrient value of the protein or alter the amount of protein that can be effectively used in the body. As the protein molecule gets heavier, viscosity and solubility characteristics of the molecule are affected. These characteristics influence how the molecule will combine with other ingredients to form the various textured protein products.

Under high alkaline conditions at temperatures over 40°C. (105°F.), two amino acids present in the soyflour—lysine and cystine—can react to produce an amino acid derivative, lysinoalanine. One study has shown that lysinoalanine has a detrimental effect on the kidneys of test rats. Barone observed that "subsequent works failed to duplicate the test results of that study and were highly inconclusive." When questioned about lysinoalanine, Dr. Oliver Miller, vice president in charge of research and development for Loma Linda Foods, replied, "We haven't seen enough evidence to warrant discontinuing the use of isolates or fibers."

# EXTRUDING TEXTURES

The extrusion process is a method for making textured vegetable protein from protein concentrates or soyflour. A protein concentrate is formed by dissolving soyflour in water or aqueous alcohol and extracting the soluble sugars. Concentrates are not pH adjusted. Because they retain their textural integrity when "retorted" or heated for canning, concentrates are most often used in canned textured vegetable products.

According to Dr. Barone, extrusion is synonymous with texturizing. The most popular extrusion method uses the Wenger thermo-plastic extruder. Defatted soyflour or protein concentrate is mixed with water and put into the extruder under a high pressure, at temperatures exceeding 132° C. (270° F.) for about 20 seconds. Screws and blades inside the extruder convert the liquid mixture into a more plastic, gummy state. The extruder then forces the protein mixture through a die—a mechanized cookie cutter— that determines the size and shape of the texturized product being made.

The mechanized cookie cutter

# IF IT'S FAB, IS IT FOOD?

Isolated, concentrated, extruded, spun, texturized: vegetable protein has come a long way from the simple soybean. Nutritionists point out that vitamins and minerals present in raw soybeans are removed or rendered less available for use in the body by these fabrication processes.

Texturized vegetable protein is not a complete food. It is a complete protein, containing all the essential amino acids, and is often added to foods to increase fortification and to balance the amino acid profile of other foods. Dr. Miller expressed the opinion of many textured protein processors: "We're steering away from the concept of having a perfect food where everything has to be in everything. We don't purport any one product is the ideal food. We're not really making manna here."

**Protein supplements—more is not always better**

Since protein requirements vary with each individual's physiological construction, it is difficult to answer the question, "How much protein is enough?" Hypnotized by speed, the automobile industry engaged in a horsepower race geared to make the standard American automobile the fastest machine on wheels. But the national 55 m.p.h. speed limit has hobbled Mustangs, declawed Cougars and left Cobras coiled.

More is not always better. While highly concentrated proteins can serve a nutritional function, Louis Richards cautions, "Good nutrition is not just a matter of high protein. Too much protein can actually put a strain on the body."

If dietary protein is not accompanied by carbohydrate in the same meal, some nutritionists maintain that the protein will not be used efficiently in the body. This phenomenon is referred to as the "protein sparing action" of carbohydrates. Protein is used as a "building block" in the body for cellular construction and repair. Carbohydrate is the fuel which enables protein to do its work. If there is not enough carbohydrate consumed, the body will manufacture it from protein, reducing the amount of protein available for structural work. Reflecting this consideration, Richards sees a "trend to lower protein supplements because people realize that real nutrition depends on the right balance of protein, carbohydrates and fat."

Economic considerations will probably influence this trend. While protein isolates wholesale for 70 cents to 80 cents a pound, soyflour, with its lower protein concentration, sells for only 25 cents a pound. There is an additional cost to producing highly concentrated vegetable protein: the cost of energy.

Production of textured protein products does require more energy than production of other soyfoods, such as tofu, miso, soy milk or tempeh. But textured protein products are not designed to replace these products; they are designed to replace meat. Dr. Barone emphasizes that, to properly gauge the comparative energy cost of textured protein products, "Look at the energy expense of putting one pound of meat on the shelf."

# A SMALL STEP FOR SOY

With protein concentrates accompanying astronauts into space, it seems clear that fabricated proteins are here to stay. Frank Posten, manager of product marketing for Worthington Foods, considers the textured protein market to be "on the threshold compared to what it will be. The general population is more health conscious, and texturized soy products contain no cholesterol, no preservatives."

The food-industry-at-large has finally realized that vegetarians exist and offer new opportunities for product development, especially in the areas of textured protein products. The Loma Linda experience may, however, dampen that enthusiasm. Dr. Miller reports that Loma Linda's sales have not increased proportionately to the increase of vegetarians. "Many people who are interested in leaving flesh out of their diet today are not interested in eating something that looks like flesh," he said.

The textured vegetable protein consumed by the natural and health food industry is produced by major food corporations such as Archer Daniels, Ralston-Purina, and Central Soya. But the technology for production is not beyond the reach of the local entrepreneur.

**Texturize-it-yourself**

The Meals for Millions Foundation has recently published *The Village Texturizer: A Low-Cost Machine For Preparing Texturized Food Products At The Village Level.* This pamphlet contains a schematic for a small texturizing machine capable of producing animal and vegetable protein products on a community level. The pamphlet includes a complete construction diagram, cost breakdown, and an operating and experimentation manual. It also details the uses of a texturizer in a small business, including a cost analysis for producing soy patties from defatted soyflour on a daily basis and a realistic feasibility worksheet. The pamphlet is available from Meals for Millions Foundation, 1800 Olympic Blvd., P.O. Box 680, Santa Monica, CA 90406.

# The Fermentation Transformation

## by Janice Fillip

When told that the French populace was rioting for lack of bread, Marie Antoinette offered, "Let them eat cake." She paid with her head for failing to recognize an historic reality: revolutions in the body politic begin in the stomach. Judging from holiday television commercials that caroled "deck the halls with plopp plopp, fizz fizz," American stomachs are ripe for a revolution. Fermented soyfoods—miso, shoyu and tempeh—may be in the forefront of that revolution.

Although virtually unknown in America before 1960, miso has been used for centuries in Japan as a flavoring for food. Miso was introduced to Japan by Chinese Buddhist priests who revolutionized Japanese spiritual thought in the 7th Century. Miso came to America as a part of another revolution, the soyfoods revolution.

Until recently, miso sold in the US was manufactured in Japan. Three years ago, Mutual Trading Company in Los Angeles began the first commercial production of miso in America, under their Cold Mountain brand. Sheguru Mori, Mutual's director of sales, explained that it was no longer economical to import miso from Japan, since the demand had grown so considerably in this country. Although the majority of miso produced by Mutual is consumed by the American-Oriental community, Mutual is also the major supplier of miso to the natural and health food industry.

Over 80 percent of the retailers we surveyed indicated that they sell miso. The Food For Thought Natural Food Store, Restaurant and Bakery in Stowe, Vermont has been serving miso soup in their restaurant for three years. Collective member Suzanne Smith says miso is a good product to carry, "if people working in the store know what it is and know how to explain it. There still are a lot of people who come in and say, 'What's miso?'"

Miso is a fermented soybean paste traditionally used as a seasoning, a digestive aid and a health tonic. Making miso is incredibly simple: a koji starter is mixed with cooked soybeans or grains and salt. The mixture is put into vats—traditionally cedar, but now usually stainless steel—to ferment. The ratio of soybeans to grain, the amount of salt and the length of fermentation can all be altered to form the various types of miso available commercially.

Koji is made by inoculating polished white rice with spores of *Aspergillus oryzae* fungi which incubate under controlled temperature and humidity conditions. As the mold grows on the rice, it produces the enzyme amylase which converts rice starch to fermentable sugars. When koji is added to soybeans or grains, this sugar feeds the microorganisms—yeast and bacteria—which cause the mixture to ferment. Koji is used the same way that malt is used in fermenting alcoholic beverages:

Koji begins the
fermentation process

# SPORES IN THE USA

It is not necessary to start from scratch to make koji. Dried koji spores are available commercially from Mutual Trading Company in Los Angeles.

Now that all the raw materials for making miso—soybeans, koji and salt—are readily available in the US, it is just a matter of time before members of the natural and health food industry realize that the miso they are importing from Japan can be made in their cellars for a lot less money. It is not necessary to be a miso master or a microbiologist to make miso. In their wonderfully comprehensive *The Book of Miso*, William Shurtleff and Akiko Aoyagi give explicit directions for making miso at home and on a community scale. The book compares traditional manufacturing techniques with modern technological processes and gives complete nutritional and microbiological information on miso. *The Book of Miso* is available from Autumn Press, 7 Littell Road, Brookline, MA 02146.

Guidebook for making
miso at home and on the
community level

Armed with *The Book of Miso*, The Soy Plant in Ann Arbor decided to give miso-making a try. With their first batch of sweet miso finished and almost sold out, Steve Fiering enthusiastically said, "It's very simple to do, as long as you can get koji. Soybeans are cheap and can be cooked easily on a restaurant-type stove. We put the miso on top of our walk-in cooler to ferment, and it takes almost no labor after that. It's real easy. I'd encourage people to get into it." Fiering estimates that it cost the Soy Plant 75 cents a pound to produce their miso, including packaging costs. Based on the tremendous response they have received from consumers, Fiering indicated that The Soy Plant plans to open a miso shop in the near future.

# MISO MASTER

For those who prefer to learn the craft from a miso master, the Asunaro Institute teaches classes in traditional methods of making fermented foods, including miso, shoyu and sake. People from different parts of the US and Europe gather at Asunaro to study under the tutelage of miso master Noboru Muramoto. In keeping with his macrobiotic philosophy and his desire to see miso become an American food, Muramoto has successfully experimented with using indigenous American grains and legumes to produce chick pea, peanut and green pea miso. Muramoto is available for consultation to any organization wishing to learn how to make fermented foods. He may be contacted through Asunaro Institute, 4600 Cavedale Road, Glen Ellen, CA. Phone: (707) 938-9846.

Americanization of miso

There are a number of instructive publications available which deal with all aspects of miso making. The Northern Regional Research Laboratory of USDA (NRRL/USDA) offers excellent literature on miso production and research, as well as koji starter cultures, free of charge. Both literature and starter can be obtained from Dr. Hwa L. Wang, NRRL/USDA, 1815 North University St., Peoria, IL 61604. The pamphlets "Traditional Fermented Foods" by C. W. Hesseltine and Dr. Wang, and "Miso Fermentation" by K. Shibasaki and C. W. Hesseltine, both contain a detailed explanation of the fermentation process and microbial activity during fermentation.

"Miso: Preparation of Soybeans for Fermentation," also by Shibasaki and Hesseltine, examines and evaluates the miso-making characteristics of twenty-two varieties of soybeans available in the US.

# SHOYU, TAMARI AND SOYSAUCE

While miso is a comparative newcomer to the American marketplace, soysauce has appeared on supermarket shelves for years. Over 90 percent of the retail stores we surveyed reported that they sell shoyu, tamari or soysauce. A number of retailers said they did not know there was any difference in these three products. But there is.

A qualitative difference

The word "tamari" comes from the word tamaru, meaning "to accumulate." This is an apt description of the liquid formed on top of miso as it ferments. Tamari is made only from fermented soybeans. In Japan, tamari is 25 percent more expensive than a comparable grade of shoyu, according to Bill Shurtleff, and accounts for less than ½ of 1 percent of the total soysauce output in that country. Almost all the products labeled as tamari in this country are not tamari, but shoyu or natural shoyu.

Shoyu is produced in a similar manner to miso, except that more water is used and the mixture is pressed and filtered to create a liquid, rather than a paste, product. Natural shoyu is made from equal parts of roasted, cracked wheat and soybeans, and is fermented under natural temperature conditions. Commercial shoyu is made from defatted soymeal, is force fermented in temperature-controlled rooms and may contain preservatives and additives. Using whole wheat, defatted soybean meal, water and rock salt, Kikkoman International in San Francisco, CA, is the only domestic producer of commercial shoyu.

Soysauce is a general term used to describe the unfermented synthetic or chemically-produced shoyu which accounts for about 2/3 of the shoyu sold in America. Soysauce is produced by hydrolysis. Defatted soybean products or other proteinous materials are mixed with an 18 percent hydrochloric acid solution and heated for 8-10 hours. The mixture is then neutralized with sodium carbonate and filtered. Caramel coloring, corn syrup, salt and water are added, along with a preservative such as sodium benzoate. Often chemical soysauce is blended with fermented shoyu before it is sold, to enhance its weak flavor.

When George Ohsawa introduced natural shoyu to the Western macrobiotic movement, he sought a term that would differentiate this natural product from other shoyu and from soysauce. The term Ohsawa chose for his natural shoyu was "tamari." Now that traditional tamari is being made available in the American marketplace, distributors who label their natural shoyu as "tamari" are faced with a big headache.

Since Japanese laws will not permit natural shoyu to be labeled "tamari," companies that have their products bottled in Japan—such as Eden Foods and Chico-San—are spared the headache. While distributors such as Erewhon Inc., Soken Trading Company and Westbrae Natural Foods appear willing—and in some cases even eager—to alter their labeling to reflect the true nature of their product, they are encountering opposition from an unexpected quarter.

A labeling headache

The Federal Trade Commission, watchdog of accuracy in advertising, has recently proposed regulations governing what products can be advertised as "natural." There is some question as to whether a naturally-fermented product will be allowed to be labeled "natural" under these proposed regulations. It is likely that much natural shoyu will continue to be labeled "tamari" for some time.

Consumers interested in buying a true tamari product should be certain that the product is made from whole soybeans rather than defatted soymeal, is fermented naturally rather than under forced temperature conditions, and contains no additives or preservatives.

The George Ohsawa Macrobiotic Foundation (GOMF) Inc. at 1544 Oak Street, Oroville, CA 95965, publishes two excellent books on soyfoods which include sections on miso and shoyu. *Soybean Diet* by Herman and Cornellia Aihara has chapters on production of miso and tamari, and recipes for their use. *The Chico-San Cookbook* by Cornellia Aihara is a fine collection of macrobiotic recipes and cooking tips.

# TEMPEH

**A salt-free fermented soyfood from Indonesia**

While tempeh—pronounced "tem-pay"—is a fermented soyfood, it differs from miso and shoyu in that it originated in Indonesia rather than Japan, it contains no salt, it is used as a main dish rather than a flavoring, and it ferments quickly.

Tempeh requires only a few hours of work to prepare, and is often ready to serve the day after it is started. Soybeans, grains or other legumes are inoculated with *Rhizopus oligosporus* mold spores to form tempeh. Similiar to koji, the spores are available in powdered form from Farm Foods, 156 Drakes Lane, Summertown, TN 38483. Tempeh starter spores are also available from NRRL/USDA, along with a free pamphlet, "Mass Production of *Rhizopus oligosporus* spores."

The Farm, a spiritual community in Tennessee, has included tempeh as a mainstay in their vegetarian diet for the past six years, marking the first time in Western history that tempeh was produced by indigenous craftspeople for local consumption. In addition to the tempeh starter, Farm Foods also market a tempeh kit, containing starter, soybeans and instructions. Farm Foods has begun marketing frozen tempeh throughout the Southeastern US and on the West Coast.

Robert Pepper, president of Farm Foods, said that the sterile conditions required in tempeh production make it more suitable for small-scale operations. "It's pretty easy to make at home in a warm corner for your family. It's much more difficult when you get into larger scale production," he said. Steve Fiering at The Soy Plant agrees, "It's deceptively hard. The incubation box is of utmost importance. Even with a good batch, we have to throw away some of the tempeh."

Although Country Store Health Foods in Sun Valley, California sold over 50 pounds of homemade tempeh a week, owner/director Joan Harriman discontinued their tempeh production. "It got too busy," she said, "There is really no money in it. It has to be done as a community service. A retailer will not make money making [their own] tempeh, but will make money overall because of greater customer interest."

Surata Soyfoods in Eugene, Oregon sells over 200 ten-ounce bags of frozen tempeh and 25 ten-ounce bags of fresh tempeh a week. Collective member Martha Murry reports, "It is a little early to tell how much we're making on it. Judging from the reponse, there is no way we can lose. People are trying it and really like it. The potential is wide open." Murry thinks that tempeh production should not be undertaken at a retail store level: "It's better to buy from a manufacturer. Incubation variables and keeping other bacteria down need a clean, stable environment."

**Soyfood cookbooks**

Since revolutions start in the stomach, it is no coincidence that most of the publications spawned by the soyfood revolution are cookbooks. *The Farm Vegetarian Cookbook* is among the best resource books available on tempeh production and recipes. The book explains how to grow tempeh starter, how to make tempeh, and how to tell when tempeh is ready or ruined. In addition, *The Book of Tempeh* by William Shurtleff and Akiko Aoyagi was published by Harper & Row this year.

Two textbooks which offer technical information on production of a variety of soyfoods, including fermented foods, are *Soybeans and Soybean Products* by Klare S. Markley, Interscience Publishers, Inc., New York; and *Soybeans: Chemistry and Technology* by Allen K. Smith and Sidney J. Circle, AVI Publishing Company Inc., Westport, CN.

# 30

## Do Soybeans Stunt Your Growth?

### by Jim Schreiber

In her valuable book titled *The Great Nutrition Robbery*, Beatrice Trum Hunter raises some important questions about the nutritional values of soybean products: "Admittedly, the soybean is of better biological quality than other vegetable proteins, but its drawbacks are overlooked by many of its enthusiastic supporters." She mentions "several antinutritional elements," including trypsin inhibitors and hemagglutinins.

Trypsin is a vital digestive enzyme produced by the pancreas. All the scientific studies agree that raw soybeans contain substances which stop trypsin from doing its necessary work of digestion. These substances are called trypsin inhibitors (TI). Due to the presence of TI, "Raw [soybean] meal causes growth inhibition, depresses metabolizable energy of the diet, reduces fat absorption, enlarges the pancreas, and stimulates hypersecretion of pancreatic enzymes in chicks, mice, and rats," according to J.J. Rackis in the authoritative text, *Soybeans: Chemistry and Technology*.

Hemagglutinins are substances which cause red blood cells to clump together. Rackis observes that, "According to Liener (1953), hemagglutinin is responsible for about 50% of the growth inhibition of rats fed raw soybean meal."

Fortunately, the normal processing of soyfoods involves moderate amounts of heating, and that heat destroys both trypsin inhibitors and hemagglutinins.

"From a practical standpoint, trypsin inhibitors do not appear to be a serious problem in feeds and foods since they are largely inactivated by moist heat," according to W.J. Wolf and J.C. Cowan in *Soybeans as a Food Source*. These researchers report that temperature, time, particle size, and moisture content affect the rate and extent of TI inactivation. They state the TI is adequately inactivated by steaming (212°F.) whole soybeans for 15 minutes, if the beans start with 20% moisture; or by steaming for 5 minutes if the beans start at 60% moisture due to overnight soaking.

Hemagglutinins apparently pose even less of a threat to nutrition than TI. According to Wolf and Cowan, "The ability of hemagglutinins to cause clumping of red blood cells

**Trypsin inhibitors and hemagglutinins**

in a test tube serves as a useful assay procedure, but there is no evidence the agglutination [clumping] of red cells occurs when hemagglutinins are ingested. Hemagglutinin is readily inactivated by pepsin; thus it probably does not survive passage through the stomach. Furthermore, undigested hemagglutinin would have to be absorbed from the intestine to come into contact with red blood cells, an occurrence which seems unlikely because of the high molecular weight of the hemagglutinin." That is, the molecule is probably too big to pass through the wall of the intestine. To be a problem, hemagglutinin would have to survive heating, and stomach juices, and then pass through a membrane where it won't fit.

# DENATURED PROTEIN

Beatrice Trum Hunter acknowledges that "these undesirable features are largely deactivated by heat, "but, with her usual concern and caution in matters of nutrition, says that "this [heat] treatment denatures the soybean's protein."

**Heat improves digestibility of soy protein**

What is "denaturation?" Broadly, it is the modification of the protein, making it to some extent different from the way it was in nature. A recognized scientific definition is that denaturation is a major change from the native structure without alteration of the amino acid sequence. (*Soybeans: Chemistry and Technology*, p. 128).

Sidney J. Circle, writing in *Soybeans and Soybean Products*, says that "Protein is a complex and sensitive material, easily alterable by various agents which may be *physical*, including heat, freezing, pressure, irradiation, sound (including ultrasonic waves), and surface forces; *chemical*, including hydrogen and hydroxyl ions, other cations and anions, organic solvents and solutions, and oxidizing and reducing agents; and *biological* (enzymes)."

In their 1975 book, Wolf and Cowan say, "Since most foods are heated during one or more stages of processing, this form of denaturation is most commonly encountered but is also least understood." They state that the literature on soybean denaturation is "often confusing and contradictory."

Beatrice Trum Hunter is correct. Soybean protein is denatured when heated. And scientific research has not yet revealed just how this takes place. But a more fundamental question remains: What does denaturation do to the nutritive value of the soybean product?

"The experimental information concerning the effect of heat treatment on the digestibility of the proteins of the soybeans shows that, in contrast to its action on other food proteins, heat improves the digestibility of soybean proteins, as well as the proteins of other beans," writes H.H. Mitchell in *Soybeans and Soybean Products*. All the information we examined agrees that, while excessive heat can reduce or destroy the nutritive value of soyfoods, the heat normally used in processing increases the nutritive value of the product.

# HOW THEY GROW

One major way to determine the actual nutritive value of the protein in a food is to give a controlled diet to young test subjects—usually animals—and see how well they grow. Such studies result in a number called the PER, the Protein Efficiency Ratio. The PER is the number of grams gained in body weight for each gram of protein consumed. PER for various foods ranges from zero, for proteins which promote no growth, to about 4, for whole eggs. Wolf and Cowan list the PER of tofu at 1.93, of soymilk at 2.11, and of tempeh at 2.48.

**Remarkably nutritious and safe**

Using other measures, Mitchell gives the "true digestibility" of eggs and beef as 100%, of whole milk as 95%, and of optimally heated soybeans as 96%.

It is always appropriate to raise questions about the foods we eat. In the case of soyfoods, all the evidence indicates that properly processed products are both remarkably nutritious and safe. The poetic Asian phrase for tofu—"meat without a bone"—seems to be quite correct.

# 31

# *Making Money Making Tofu*

## by Ellin Stein

Tofu? What's a tofu?'' A surprisingly large number of people still say that, and then nod with vague recollection when reminded of the little square of soybean curd that puzzled them at the Asian restaurant. But not for long.

Tofu, a staple in the diet of millions of people in the Orient for over 1,000 years, is an ethnic food that seems destined to duplicate the pizza boom in America after World War II. While the sale of health foods is expected to double by 1980, the consumption of soy protein in the USA is predicted to increase twelve times in the same interval. If recent years are any index, tofu will be among the leaders in that increase.

When *The Book of Tofu* was published in 1975, there were 65 tofu shops in the United States, all Oriental-owned. Early in 1978 there were over 100. Most of the new ones are started by non-Asians. Since their book appeared, authors William Shurtleff and Akiko Aoyagi have received hundreds of letters, asking for more information on setting up tofu shops. Perhaps this growth is partly due to an increased awareness that soy products are the most economically efficient source of protein. And the introduction of tofu into the mainstream American diet may be aided by its diversity: You can chill it, freeze it, grill it, deep-fry it, powder it, crumble it, spread it and—counting its by-products—drink it.

**A versatile and economical protein source**

## A LABOR OF LOVE

Traditionally, in the Orient, the production of tofu has been labor-intensive, employing only a minimal technology. This labor-intensive pattern has so far been repeated in the USA, where small-scale commercial tofu shops have tended to be collective operations, in which the workers agree to pay themselves low wages, making tofu as "a labor of love." Asian-American tofu firms often show a reluctance to talk about their operations, apparently from a concern that a market which has been firmly in their grasp might be invaded by the occidental newcomers. The two largest tofu manufacturers in north California did, however, report increased sales. In the past two years, the production at Quong Hop is reportedly up one-third; at Azumaya, up by one-fifth.

Larry Needleman, a former food consultant to the State of California, started Bean Machines, Inc. in order to distribute quality Japanese tofu-making equipment in the USA. Needlemen—who has an M.A. in Hotel Administration—says that tofu consumption in this country has been doubling every six months for the past two years. In his view, the few large tofu manufacturers cannot keep up with the growing demand, and there is plenty of room for the smaller tofu shops on everything from the community to the regional level. He suggests that the prospective community-level tofu producer first consider (1) production goals, (2) cost of raw materials, (3) the kind of equipment to be used and (4) the corresponding labor costs, (5) packaging expenses, (6) competition from established tofu firms, (7) the amount of capital inventment, and (8) how to raise the capital.

The operators of the new tofu shops—none of which is more than four years old—agree that it is best to start small, producing about 30 or 40 pounds per week. They advise learning how to make tofu at home, developing skills and "paying your dues."

# OUT OF THE KITCHEN

The size of the step from home-kitchen to commercial production varies. Steve Fiering of The Soy Plant, a small tofu collective in Ann Arbor, Michigan, suggests a minimum output of 100 pounds per day. The Farm, a large Bay Area collective places the minimum at 250 pounds per day. A new tofu plant in Berkeley, California produces up to 300 pounds daily, sold about 80 pounds through Berkeley Bowl, their market on the premises, and the rest to five other stores. The two Berkeley Bowl owners, working 14-hour days, found that the small scale of operations was not worth the effort, so they planned to expand.

**Evolution of American tofu shops**

A problem shared by all the shop-owners I talked with was how to strike a balance between, on the one hand, investing too much in equipment which will not be operating at capacity for a long time and, on the other hand, investing too little, with the result that workers must labor sixty hours each week just to fill the demand. All agreed to one thing: Plan Ahead Carefully.

The successful tofu shop generally starts with traditional hand-labor equipment in a space large enough to accomodate expanded operations, and suitable for meeting health codes. As tofu-making skills are being perfected, and money is set aside for new equipment, sales increase, and the original equipment begins to operate near its full capacity. When the demand is greater than the shop's current output, labor-saving machinery can be introduced. According to The Book of Tofu, Volume II, a manual for commercial production, the cost of starting a traditional tofu shop with a daily output of 330 pounds ranges from $2,500 to $7,500, with the equipment costing from $1,500 to $4,000.

Basic business skills predictably prove to be necessary for the success of tofu shops. Benjamin Hills at Surata Soyfoods in Eugene, Oregon said that their growth sometimes outstripped their administrative abilities, and he recommended taking business courses, such as bookkeeping. The owners of Laughing Grasshopper in Massachusetts credit their success partly to a good financial advisor, and suggest thorough research of the business aspects before starting a shop.

Tom Timmins at Laughing Grasshopper suggested "figuring out neat production systems," and mentioned Crystal Hill, a New Hampshire tofu shop, which created a soybean grinder from an industrial garbage disposal unit. More usual for grinding is the Hobart Vertical Cutting Mixer.

Despite a concern for tofu making as an ancient "art," the traditional Japanese wooden settling boxes were universally condemned. Stainless steel cuts down considerably on clean-up time, which easily won first prize as the most tiresome part of the process.

# TOFU OLYMPICS

Labor-saving plans and devices are welcome throughout this industry, both to cut costs for larger operations and to reduce the physical burden on the workers. "Tofu-makers must be in Olympic physical condition," Timmins remarked. Tofu-making equipment has not been manufactured in the United States, and the complexities of obtaining it from Japan are immense. Producers have their eye on Bean Machines, Inc., Larry Needleman's company, as a possible source of reasonably priced, good quality equipment.

While the small tofu shops continue to grow across the country, the corporate giants of the food industry are doing other things with their soybeans. High-technology soy products include pet food, shortening, salad oil, meat analogs, margarine, and lecithin. Central Soya, an Illinois firm subcontracted to General Foods, produced 30 million pounds of soy products per year, primarily textured vegetable protein and spun protein fibers for meat extenders. Other major corporations involved in manufacturing such products include Lever Bros., Procter & Gamble, and Hunt-Wesson.

Jim Yancey of the American Soybean Association—a lobbying group for soybean growers—described tofu as "too foreign," requiring a major change in American eating habits. He said it would probably be at least five years before a large corporation started marketing it.

The Food Protein Council commissioned a Gallup Poll which was published in April 1977. They reported that 33 percent of the people polled believe that soybeans will be the most important source of protein in the future—ahead of fish at 24 percent and meat at 21 percent. Fifty-five percent said that soy products provide adequate or superior food value. Younger age-groups living in large cities were the most favorable to soy protein, indicating that support for soy products is likely to grow in the future.

Whatever the corporate response or the polls might suggest, small-shop tofu production is on the increase, responding to a real demand, with a focus on offering a quality product. They often take an artisan's pride in their work, and aim to run profitable businesses without being overwhelmed by hard labor, and without exploiting the consumer. "Tofu-eaters have high food-consciousness," Steve Fiering says. "A good product at a good price will withstand corporate competition."

William Shurtleff, co-author of the book that started it all, alludes to a "Soy: Food of the Future" movement. Every indication is that he is correct when he says, "That movement is stronger than ever."

*Megacorporations and soy products*

# MIDWEST SOY PLANT EXPECTS TO GROW

When The Soy Plant started serving the Ann Arbor, Michigan area in January 1977, they were producing 50 pounds of tofu per week. By the spring of 1978 they manufactured 1,000 pounds per week at a rate of 350 pounds per day. To maintain that output, four people worked a 40-hour week—which includes about ten hours of clean-up. They began to pay themselves $2.25 per hour.

Initial capital at The Soy Plant was $2,500. That figure does not include their boiler and steam kettle, which they obtained free of charge. Their main expense was a $1,200 soybean grinder from Japan.

The most troublesome piece of equipment was their home-built press. Soy Plant worker Steve Fiering estimates that they could produce 500 pounds of tofu per day with a better press. In addition to this upcoming expense, they expect to spend $1,000 to install a new drain.

The Soy Plant produces 2.5 pounds of tofu for each pound of soybeans. Their wholesale price, 65¢-per-pound, breaks down to 8¢ for supplies, 10¢ for overhead, 10¢ for packaging, 30¢ for labor, and 7¢ for capitalization. Retail prices are generally in the 70¢-85¢ range.

*The Soy Plant*

When The Soy Plant started distributing 100 pounds of tofu per week to Ann Arbor's two co-op stores, they were not meeting the existing demand. Although they "haven't had time to turn people on to tofu," says Fiering, they are still not able to keep pace with the growing demand.

Their local distribution of one-pound and 24-pound tubs includes two restaurants, the co-ops, and eight other retail stores. Their market doubled since fall 1977, when Midwest Natural Foods began distributing one-third of their output to shops in Pittsburgh, Milwaukee and other cities.

# A BUSY GRASSHOPPER WAITS FOR PROFITS

Laughing Grasshopper

The Laughing Grasshopper, located at Miller's Falls in western Massachusetts, was so busy meeting the existing demand for tofu that they had no time to do any merchandising—except giving out free samples.

Their initial output of 1,000 pounds per week was a larger beginning than most of the new tofu shops, but it grew to 4,000 pounds during the summer and reached 6,000 pounds in the fall of 1977. They distribute to over 100 small shops, supermarkets and restaurants in Boston and the western part of the state.

Members of the Laughing Grasshopper collective bolstered the $8,000 investment of their own money with a $10,000 nine-month loan. Since their beginning, they have invested no more in the business, except for leasehold improvements such as sinks and drains.

Ten people worked 40 hours per week in crews of four, using one member of the crew just for clean-up. Most of their equipment was found locally. They use four cauldrons, but worker Tom Timmins estimates that the addition of a pressure cooker would more than double their production of tofu with no increase in labor. He stresses the importance of experimenting with production techniques in order to reduce the considerable physical labor.

The wholesale price of their tofu is 44¢ per pound—about 15¢ for production, 15¢ for labor, 7¢ for distribution, 5¢ for overhead, and 2¢ for supplies. Workers are paid $2.75 per hour.

Laughing Grasshopper tofu retails for 52¢-79¢ per pound, with one-fourth of their output marketed through a distributor. Their product is sold in tubs which hold 50 eight-ounce pieces, or in recyclable five-gallon cans, for which the customer pays a refundable deposit.

Timmins says he does not believe that Laughing Grasshopper is in direct competition with New England Soy Dairy, another local tofu producer which also offers soy milk and ice bean. The market, says Timmins, seems large enough to support both firms at a consumption rate of 10,000 pounds per week.

# DOWN ON THE FARM

The Farm

The Farm, Steven Gaskin's Tennessee commune, opened a soy dairy branch in San Rafael, California in the fall of 1976. For one year they sold their tempeh, soy-"mayonaise," ice bean, soy milk and tofu in their downtown Farm Food Company store.

Economically, things were fine. Individuals worked four hours per day—unpaid—to produce 250 pounds of tofu daily at a cost of 50¢ per pound. And they could not keep up with the demand.

Although most small tofu operations mention lack of space as a major problem, The Farm is probably the only successful one to shut down because of it. They plan to go into large-scale wholesale production. At this writing, The Farm was looking for an old milk dairy as an ideal site for their new soy dairy.

People at The Farm recommend starting small and graduating first to a semi-automatic batch method, and then to a vacuum-pressure method. They indicate that one important matter to consider when expanding to a major, commercial level is compliance with USDA and local inspection standards.

# HOPE IN ROCHESTER

In May 1977, The Rochester Tofu shop started making 150 pounds of tofu per week. By 1978 that upstate New York plant was producing 1,000 pounds per week, but reported discouragement about supporting the shop solely by the local market.

"We underestimated the costs and overestimated the market," according to Rochester Tofu partner Andy Schechter. "The demand here is climbing steadily—but not rapidly." Some Oriental restaurants which were seen as potential customers continue to buy their tofu from a large manufacturer in New York City.

Compared to most shops its size, the Rochester plant began with a higher capital investment—$8,000—but fewer people. The two partners usually worked a grueling 60-hour week, using a lever press and a steam cooker backed by a home boiler. But despite the investment of time, money and effort, and an unusually high yield of around 2.9 pounds of tofu per pound of soybeans, the cost analysis did not look good.

Of their 50¢-per-pound wholesale price, 10¢ is for materials, a high 40¢ is for overhead and packaging, and for labor—nothing. The Rochester Tofu experience has been fewer people working longer hours for less money.

Their twice-weekly distribution in four-gallon buckets to 22 stores, one Oriental restaurant, two university dormitories and two natural foods restaurants did not bring in the income to meet their costs.

# TOFU RECIPE DOUBLES IN OREGON

Benjamin Hills and the other members of the Surata Soyfoods collective in Eugene, Oregon worked without pay for six months while they put their tofu shop together. Distribution had already been established by their cooperative bakery.

Their initial investment in the tofu plant was $2,000. By early 1978 they had put another $2,000 into remodeling, in addition to 30 percent of the gross, which was used for equipment changes. Hills recommends starting larger than you think you need. Surata, he says, would start with $3,000 if they could begin again.

At first, the collective worked two days per week to make 300 pounds of tofu. Later they worked five days per week to make 1,000 pounds. Operating at full capacity with their present system, they can produce 1,200 pounds per week.

Their open-cauldron method is slower than pressure cooking but, Hills says, makes better tofu. He wants to replace their present rigged-up hydraulic press, because it is plagued with engineering problems and a high bacteria count. The next step for Surata is to buy another cauldron for $350 and a small motor-driven hydraulic press for $1,600. That equipment could double their production.

The yield at Surata is 2.5 pounds of tofu per one pound of soybeans. Their tofu costs 50¢ per pound to produce. That is 8¢ for supplies, 12¢ for overhead, and 30¢ for labor. Members of the collective are now paying themselves $3.00 per hour for their work.

Their tofu, packaged in one-pound plastic bags or 20-pound tubs, sells wholesale for 58¢ per pound and retails for 68¢ to 81¢ per pound. Demand has doubled over the last year. This increase is apparently not due to a doubling of customers, but to twice the consumption by the same people.

The Surata enterprise helped create a market for their tofu by giving it away at county fairs and open markets, and by promoting new recipes and uses for tofu. Hills indicates that Surata replaced the existing commercial tofu market because their product was of better quality and fresher.

**Tofu information**

Sources of more information on Tofu:

*The Book of Tofu, Volume I*, William Shurtleff and Akiko Aoyagi, Autumn Press, Inc., 7 Littel Road, Brookline, MA 02146.
The basic book, giving nutritional information, descriptions of tofu making on various scales, uses of byproducts, 500 recipes, lists of tofu shops, restaurants and resources.

*Tofu and Soymlk Production*, William Shurtleff and Akiko Aoyagi, New Age Foods Study Center, P.O. Box 234, Lafayette, CA 94549.
A technical manual for commercial tofu and soymilk production, ranging from the local shop to automated tofu factories.

Bean Machines, Inc., P.O. Box 881, San Rafael, CA 94901. Larry Needleman's firm, importing good-quality Japanese equipment and promoting the development of American-made equipment.

*Soybean Digest Blue Book*, American Soybean Association, P.O. Box 158, Hudson, IA 50643.
Lists soybean growers, crop analysts, large-scale equipment, restaurants, etc., in all phases of soybean use, with an agribusiness orientation.

*The Farm Vegetarian Cookbook*, The Book Publishing Company, The Farm, Summertown, TN 38483.
Recipes for the use of soybeans, tofu, tempeh, soymilk, gluten, and soy flour, with an introduction by Stephen Gaskin.

# 32

# *Soyship Enterprises*

## by Richard Leviton

Every day the New England Soy Dairy in Greenfield, Massachusetts manufactures three thousand pounds of tofu. Through a network of distributors, supermarkets, and their own refrigerated truck, they ship this product all across New England, New York, New Jersey, and Pennsylvania. Established over three years ago as the Laughing Grasshopper Tofu Shop, the company has experienced enormous and exhilarating growth, and started two major expansions in one year. This shop was one of the first to open, and is today the largest of this new breed.

For the New England Soy Dairy, the matter of appropriate technology for tofu-making has been a formidable yet stimulating challenge. In Japan, the homeland of tofu, there are some thirty-eight thousand shops, ranging from small household enterprises to automated factories. Understandably, there is a well-established tofu-making equipment industry as well, and every production contingency is covered by the appropriate item or machine from this efficient network. This is simply not the case here in the US: Prospective entrepreneurs must scratch their chins and take one of the following options—adapt available technologies, design and fabricate, or import equipment from Japan.

In mid-1976 when the company began to organize its first shop, there were no import channels open, nor any Japanese equipment catalogs to pore over—only rumors of marvelous tofu-making machines locked away in Japan. The three partners purchased a hefty commercial blender, an apple cider press, cast iron candy cookers, and large stainless steel pots. Smaller items were made from scratch or done without. With cramped quarters, inadequate drainage, long days of grueling work, and sympathetic but strict guidelines from the health officials, the partners soon began to dream of better days, better equipment, and a new shop. The company was soon running at full capacity, seven days a week, ten hours a day, with an expanding market and a growing reputation. While threeman crews labored through hours of heavy lifting on wet floors, ill-suited equipment and a process they barely understood, the business found its footing.

**New England Soy Dairy**

# RAPID GROWTH

Studying its mistakes, the company found it easy to plan its new shop. Midway in that hectic first year, 1977, they began what was to be a six month search for suitable quarters. Important trade contacts were established and the labor-saving machines from Japan were swiftly imported. By February 1978, the New England Soy Dairy (as it became called) settled down in its new shop, several rungs up the ladder in sophistication and efficiency. In the new shop was a thirty-seven gallon pressure cooker, a stone grinder with continuous feed, an hydraulic press, ratchet presses, stainless steel settling boxes, capacious sinks, light, drains, a smooth cement floor, and a walk-in cooler the size of their entire first shop. This set-up promised a three-fold increase in production abilities with less physical exertion.

Within the next eight months, full operating capacity came within sight, and certain key machines were suddenly perceived as inadequate for a burgeoning tofu factory. Sales projections placed the demand for New England Soy Dairy tofu beyond the capacities of the physical plant. The company is again planning a major expansion that would quadruple its output. But this time they are less harried and rushed; there is the leisure for thorough planning and research. Tandem pressure cookers run off an electronic control panel, several grain silos for dry soybeans, automatic bean soaking tanks, highly efficient soymilk extraction machines—these are a few of the innovations slated to simplify, accelerate, and refine the tofu-making process, so that the optimum nutritional yield can be obtained from the soybeans.

New England Soy Dairy planners have learned that it is practical to adapt existing American technologies, especially the food-processing division, to suit unusual needs. One foray into this field was the installation of a complete soymilk plant. Standard dairy items, such as bulk holding-tanks, ice-builder, plate-cooler, homogenizer, steam kettle, pumps, and packaging machine, have been transplanted from the world of the cow to the world of the soybean, to process soymilk.

Company directors have scheduled the purchase of a mayonnaise production system, with machines for blending, cooking, packaging, labeling, in a manner very similar to conventional commercial mayonnaise production. In spring 1978 the company began packaging tofu in heat-sealed plastic tubs, using a machine imported from Japan. Company members began considering applying vacuum-packing, a process used to package meats and cheese, for hermetically sealing fresh tofu.

In each of the above cases, the company has fallen back on old-fashioned "Yankee ingenuity" in assembling the appropriate technology to fit their special needs. Often it has been possible to re-vitalize discarded American technologies (from the diary and food-processing industries), locating inexpensive used machines, and adapting them. As their shop has grown in complexity, so too, has their mechanical expertise, so that today they employ a full-time engineer-maintenance-designer (formerly a tofu-maker) to plan, install, and direct the assembly of machines.

**Adapting American technologies to produce traditional Oriental foods**

# LARGER MARKETPLACE

The New England Soy Dairy was fortunate to be located in a densely populated area of the US, which was, even then, well saturated in natural foods awareness. The company found immediate outlets in Amherst and Boston for their organic tofu, and soon the refrigerator shelves in many stores throughout the region were stocked with New England Soy Dairy tofu. But it was easy to be represented in the health foods market and this fell somewhat short of the company's initial mobilizing goals.

Company directors, vegetarians themselves, believe firmly in the value of meatless diets and have wanted to make tofu available to the millions of consumers in the Northeast. Since the general public does not deal through natural foods stores, The New England Soy Dairy turned its attention to opening up the market for tofu in that basic American marketplace, the Supermarket. The supermarket is perceived as the conduit to

**Tofu in supermarkets**

the American mainstream. Tofu correctly packaged and presented in these mass food centers can have an enormous impact on the American diet.

The company reached the stage in its growth where the self-evident sale of tofu in natural foods outlets reached a plateau, and continued sales growth became dependent on soliciting a wider market. With this in mind, company marketing directors initiated sales campaigns in several large regional chains, emphasising tofu's versatility through recipes, on labels and in hand-outs, through articles and coverage in the media, and in-store demonstrations. Tofu's exceptional low-cost coupled with its culinary versatility will undoubtedly contribute to its explosive popularity in the coming years.

# NEW SOY PRODUCTS

The New England Soy Dairy uses the term "dairy" to indicate its ambitious intentions to develop and market a full line of new soyprotein products, called soyfoods. Many are quite similar in use and appearance to conventional dairy items yet all are derived entirely from soybeans and, consequently, are low in calories and fats, high in protein, and free of cholesterol. To complement its two styles of tofu, the dairy developed an eggless mayonnaise, called "Soymayo," made from soymilk, tofu, vegetable oil, vinegar and spices, and packaged in glass pint jars. "Soymayo" can be used exactly like conventional mayonnaise but with the comforting assurance of being free of any animal ingredients.

**Soymayo**

Soymilk is the next item on the company's list of "dairy" products. After a year's research through scientific literature, consultations with food scientists, soybean and dairy experts, experimentation, and hours at the drawing table, the company assembled a complete soymilk processing facility at their Wells Street location. Plain and flavored soy-milks are produced here and packaged in cardboard ½ pint and 1 quart cartons. For a procedure nearly identical to the standard cow's milk operation, the company found it necessary to employ a retired dairy mechanic to supervise the installation of the various stainless steel machines. Soymilk, not easily obtainable in New England, is rich and creamy white, high in protein, free of cholesterol; it can be used just like cow's milk and sold at competitive prices.

**Soymilk**

Company researchers are working on a variety of new soyfoods including soy sausage, made from soybeans and spices, and tempeh, a fermented soy cake. Other items planned include soy ice cream, soy yogurt, deep-fried spicy tofu, creamy tofu puddings and dressings, and soy cheeses.

**On the drawing board**

In the US today, there is very little of this kind of experimentation with soybeans; although it is generally recognized that soybeans are the protein source of the future, it is only on the West Coast that one can easily find a delightful array of soyfoods such as the New England Soy Dairy envisions. Soymilk ice cream, yogurt and cheese are also not well known and relatively unavailable at present.

Often on a quiet afternoon at the company, someone might be found dreaming of the day when the New England Soy Dairy maintains a fleet of milktrucks, making the deliveries in local neighborhoods of tofu, soymilk, ice cream and butter, leaving them in a small box in the garage, retrieving the empty bottles and next week's order—just like years ago. What people see on this quiet back street in Greenfield is just the infancy of the new American Soyfood Industry.

# MIDWESTERN INTEREST

The Soy Plant was an outgrowth of the relatively well-developed natural foods consciousness in Ann Arbor, Michigan. With the help of three nearby natural foods distributors—Midwest, Eden, and Peoples, a large co-op warehouse—and the support of seven local natural foods retailers and restaurants, The Soy Plant made its start in August 1977.

The company's aim has always been to be an experimentally structured "workers cooperative." The Soy Plant is incorporated as a nonprofit corporation. Its by-laws state that control of the company is in the hands of the workers, or any body that the workers empower. The experiment is a success in that business is thriving, but the dedication and involvement that was first hoped for only partly materialized.

During the first six months, The Soy Plant grew from producing 300 pounds a week of the main product, nigari firm tofu, to a production of 1200 pounds a week. In this period the work was long and hard, and the pay was barely at a survival level, but the workers developed lasting skills as soycrafters and as business people.

By January 1978, it became clear that the operation had already outgrown its first home, a small room in the basement of a restaurant. The group decided that the best location would have to include retail facilities. That would offer not only a business advantage, but would also keep the workers in touch with the people using the soyfood products, would provide a center for educational activities, and would serve as a test market for new products.

When a suitable building was found in the market area of Ann Arbor, plans were drawn up for the production and retail facilities. For the first time, capital was needed in order to renovate the new space. Previous capitalization had been minimal, about $4000 derived from the workers' own savings and personal loans.

Cooperative members provide capital for growth

To raise new capital, the group conceived a novel approach: They decided that the best source of capital would be the people who use The Soy Plant products, similar to the way in which a co-op gets loans from its members. It was determined that the main cost of the product was labor, and the company could afford to give people tofu in exchange for the capital they provided. With the fresh capital, the firm could move to the new location, renovate the equipment, and reduce the amount of labor needed to produce each pound of the product.

# RAISING CAPITAL

Printed flyers announced that The Soy Shop would give one pound of tofu free-of-charge each week as "interest" for every $100 loaned to the company. At the retail price of 70¢ per pound, that was equivalent to more than 35 percent interest per year—an excellent deal for regular users of tofu.

The Soy Plant received over $10,000 in loans with this method. In addition to capital, it generates a sense of involvement and support on the part of the people who participate. Connected with the community in this way, the company still remains independent of outside control.

Soyproduct expansion

After moving to the new shop in June 1978, the firm's workforce grew to nine people, producing about 2200 pounds of tofu each week. The retail store has shown steady growth, and new products made in the shop are showing increasing popularity in the store's soy-based natural foods delicatessen—which does about $700 of business each week.

The new products include soymilk, tempeh, spiced tofu, spreads, ice bean, tofu pies, okara peanut butter balls, and soy sausage.

"Soy sausage is one of our most promising products," says one company member. "We use, basically, the recipe from The Farm in Tennessee, and retail the product for 95 cents a pound. If the response that soy sausage has received in New England is any indication, this will be an important product. It's easy to package and distribute because it's dry and has a good shelf life compared to many soyfoods."

The Soy Plant's experience is that, unlike the East, the Midwest has been unreceptive to selling tofu in bulk. They are encouraging bulk sales in order to reduce the cost to the customer and to decrease the packaging labor and materials in production. Bulk sales have not yet become widely accepted in their area.

Soymilk sales have been slow to grow. Soy Plant workers have observed that, for most consumers, soymilk is an acquired taste. Customers usually begin by drinking it flavored with honey and vanilla, and switch to the plain variety after they become used to the taste. Of the 100 gallons sold each week, about two-thirds of it is flavored.

Their two spreads—one with eggless soy mayo and tumeric, and one with tofu, sweet miso and tahini—are apparently appreciated by natural foods consumers for their convenience. Distribution of these spreads is limited by their rather short shelf life.

The Soy Plant plans to expand again, moving the main production facility out of town and increasing its capacity. This plan stems from the company's view that soyfoods will grow rapidly in the next few years, and that Ann Arbor is a favorable location to serve as a natural foods distribution center for the Midwest.

# FROM THE CRYSTAL HILLS

On a hillside in the White Mountains of New Hampshire is a small town named Bethlehem. In a modest building just off Main Street is a small soyfoods business named the Crystal Hills Tofu Shop. The local native Americans call the nearby mountains the crystal hills.

Crystal Hills Tofu began in the kitchen of Pat and Jay Gibbons, and grew into a bustling, small-scale soyfoods factory, beginning commercial production in September 1977. The shop is now run by three full-time and two part-time people, who make up to 1500 pounds of tofu and several hundred pounds of "Soysage" each week. These products are delivered throughout New Hampshire and Vermont.

**Crystal Hills Tofu Shop**

Their "Soysage" uses okara, a shredded soy fiber which is a byproduct of the tofu-making process. Combined with whole wheat flour, wheat germ, nutritional yeast, oil, soy sauce, honey, herbs and spices, it results in a product which is far different from the flavor and texture of tofu. They recommend "Soysage" sliced and fried for use in sandwiches or pizza, or used as-is for a vegetable pate, or cooked for breakfast along with scrambled tofu.

Crystal Hills Tofu Shop has plans to add miso, tempeh, tofu pudding and, eventually, soymilk to their product line. To the Gibbons, it is more than a business: "Dedicated to the ideal of serving people by serving soybeans, we hope to promote a compassionate distribution of the world's food supply and aid in the healing of our Earth. We also hope to contribute to the development of a sane technology to serve these ends."

# THE BEANING OF MOTOWN

The soyfoods revolution has come quietly to the mechanical heartland of the nation, Motor City, Detroit, USA. Yellow Bean Trading Co., a small distributing company, is bringing in tofu, soymilk, and tempeh produced at The Soy Plant in Ann Arbor. Yellow Bean's refrigerated van takes the products to health and natural food stores, restaurants, fruit markets, and Oriental grocery stores in Detroit.

**Yellow Bean Trading Company**

The business is operated by Carol Ann and Timothy Huang, who made soyfoods a major part of their diet while living on The Farm in Tennessee. They were married on a branch of The Farm in Wisconsin, where their son was born.

Yellow Bean Trading Company first started trucking in Detroit in January 1978, shortly after their arrival in the city. The original 100 pounds of tofu distributed per week grew to 400 pounds. They also carry nutritional yeast, sprouts, textured vegetable protein, soybeans, soy flour, and *The Farm Vegetarian Cookbook*, which includes outstanding soyfoods recipes. In addition to distributing, they give demonstrations on how to cook with tofu and other soyfoods.

As the wholesale business grows, the Huang family is now setting up a store and restaurant, Yellow Bean Vegetarian Foods. At first, the restaurant is planned as a carryout, including a deli case. Their long-term vision is to move later to a larger location, open a sit-down restaurant, and begin producing their own tofu and soymilk.

"We have great faith and inspiration that this thing will take off and grow," says Carol Ann Huang. "It all takes time, but there's so much energy in soybeans, and people are looking for a better, simpler way to live and eat. We see it all the time. And we feel really glad to be part of this 'revolution,' and offer what we've learned."

# Section VI: Herbs

Herbs are the fastest growing category of products in the natural foods industry. Interest in herbs has been increasing rapidly in recent years as more people cast a critical eye on the powerful (and costly) drugs administered by physicians. Concerned with maintaining their own health, people in large numbers are including herbs in a holistic approach to healthful living. Rather then relying on the M.D.'s usual chemicals—with their unpredictable side-effects—many users of natural foods are finding valuable lessons in the centuries-old folk traditions about the uses of botanicals.

A predictable side-effect of this growing consumer interest is an equally growing scrutiny by regulatory agencies. When people outside the medical profession start to talk about the treatment of ailments, the regulators worry about the unlicensed practice of medicine, about claims which are not scientifically proven, and about consumers unwittingly harming themselves. As the section on Rules and Regulations has indicated, enforcement tends to be haphazard.

The problems of regulation have become an immediate, top-priority concern of the herb industry, and will directly affect the availability and restrict the labeling of many herb products. Several chapters in this section are devoted to discussions of the special legal difficulties which pertain to the buying and selling of herbs.

Many observers of trends in the natural foods industry attribute the sudden renewed interest in herbs partly to the publicity received a few years ago by ginseng. Popular accounts made the ginseng root seem to be almost a cure-all, a botanical miracle.

While it is true that ginseng is highly regarded in Asia as a tonic, and scientific studies have shown ginseng to have definite beneficial effects, the marketing of some of the products bearing the banner of ginseng has been a hotly controversial issue within the industry. No studies have included all the available ginseng products, but some product samples have recently undergone laboratory analysis. Those few dozen samples exhibited a wide range in the amounts of active ginseng substances, and some of the samples apparently contained no ginseng at all. Legitimate dealers in good-quality ginseng products express concern that the entire trade might be destroyed because some of the products have been mislabled.

Without laboratory analysis, the consumer is not in a position to be absolutely certain of the amount of active ginseng in a product, but these chapters—which cover the production of ginseng in Korea and in the United States—include information which can help the ginseng purchaser to know what to look for in order to obtain the best value. Since many high-quality ginseng products are available, a knowledgeable shopkeeper may be able to offer sound advice.

Setting standards for ginseng and other botanicals is one of the main concerns of the Herb Trade Association, which sponsors symposiums on a broad range of subjects related to herbs. A report on one of these sessions, showing recent efforts at self-regulation, is included in this section.

Apart from the problems and debates in the herb trade, these botanical products can offer the consumer an interesting, valuable and flavorful spectrum of nutrients, along with a pleased palate. This section of the *Guide* contains chapters on the varied ways to make herbal preparations, and on the uses of herbs to maintain the health of animals.

147

# 33

# *A Growing Herb Trade*

## by Jim Schreiber

As the herb trade grows swiftly in America, problems grow to keep apace. Some figures show herb sales as second only to vitamins in health food stores, with herbs on the increase while vitamins are evidently leveling off—but at the same time, herb company executives talk as if haunted by a ghost that could put the herb business in ruins. That ghost is the Food and Drug Administration, which often seems as difficult to grapple with as a spectre.

**Herbal information-gap**

More basic than encounters with the FDA is the scarcity of solid information about herbs. While many companies handle several hundred kinds of herbs, only a small portion of them appear on any FDA list, and both retailers and consumers face difficulties in selecting from among so many unknown items. This problem is compounded by the fact that an herb may have a half a dozen different common names.

This information-gap is now being narrowed by the media. Householders' magazines, books, radio talk-shows, and chamber-of-commerce publications are paying increasing attention to herbs. These sources, added to information available from suppliers and the lecture tours of noted herbalists, can provide the buyer with a good grounding in herbs.

**A growing demand for herbs**

Herb tea blends and herb capsules are among the fastest growing items. Major corporations, including Lipton, Campbell, Standard Brands, and large vitamin firms are eyeing the herb tea market, according to Ben Zaricor, a board member of the Herb Trade Association. The HTA projects a heavy demand for herbs for the next several years. Although no real shortage is expected on shop shelves, keen competition for herbs from fields throughout the world is likely, while prices at the sources of supply go up.

Consumers are becoming more knowledgeable about herbs, and are now buying herb products which sold poorly a few years ago. As this knowledge increases, herb processors give more attention to the value of their products, seeking the right combination of quality, price, and service. This works to the benefit of the retailer who is concerned with passing on value to customers.

148

# GETTING INFORMATION

The natural food store's buyer can get more information than is available in books, magazines, and catalogs. The product can be directly examined for freshness, appearance, taste, aroma, and cleanliness. Buying from companies which offer a wide range of herb products can cut down on paperwork and may offer the advantage of discounts for large orders.

Point-of-purchase reading materials are available from many herb companies (don't use any which make medicinal claims) and the larger firms have botanical specialists on staff who can answer detailed questions, and can explain how the herbs are processed. When and if the herb industry makes it a standard practice to use botanical names on its labels, the confusion generated by the multiplicity of common names will be greatly reduced.

**Herb Trade Association**

The Herb Trade Association, in cooperation with industry companies, concerns itself with quality standards. Much of its effort is directed toward coming to terms with the FDA. Studies by the HTA played a key role in the creation of standardized Good Manufacturing Practices for the herb industry, submitted by the FDA. It may be the HTA's efforts which have helped bring about a change in the FDA attitude toward herbs, which is less like gangbusters now than it was a year or two ago.

Hope is widely expressed that the Food and Drug Administration, with the help of the HTA, will sort out its own confusions about herbs. At present the FDA is applying to herbs the 1958 laws which Congress enacted to protect the public from toxic and cancer-producing additives—even for herbs which have been used for hundreds or thousands of years without complaint. "It's as if they took a can of carrots and peas, called the peas a food additive, and banned it because no one had proved it safe," one herb executive said.

The Herb Trade Association can be reached at 4302 Airport Blvd., Austin, TX 78722.

# 34

# The Essence of Herb Flavor

## by Fern R. Kozer

Downstairs, seated in her burgundy velvet chair, my grandmother would sip petals of jasmine and orange blossoms. On her tea table, she kept tea caddies full of rose or violet petals, clove, pieces of vanilla beans and cinnamon sticks, which she would drop into the cups. "A good tea can stand on its own—no need for sugar, whether served in glasses from a samovar in my Russia or from an Australian billy can," she would affirm.

Herbal tea drinking didn't become popular in Europe until the early 1600's. It was the first hot stimulant to reach Europe, and was greeted as an exciting luxury item. Around 1650, this new beverage reached the American colonies. It was no drink for the common man, since it cost between thirty and fifty dollars per pound.

**Growth of herb tea popularity**

During the twentieth century, interest in herbs increased in a dramatic and unforeseen manner, due to the outbreak of the two World Wars. Britain and Europe twice found themselves squeezed out of their Oriental and American drug supplies, and were forced to fall back on their own lands' resources: herbs. During World War II, the Soviet Union and Italy took up large-scale herb farming. Germany and France had always had plentiful herbs of their own, growing wild. In Britain the Ministry of Supply began to organize methodical herb cultivation. Children were induced to go on forays for medicinal herbs and vitamin C-rich rose hips. Gardeners were urged to reserve a patch in their yards for useful drug-producing plants as well as for vegetables.

In the last ten years, American interest in herbs has been boosted partly by the publication of such books as Aldous Huxley's *Doors of Perception* and Carlos Castaneda's series about his experiences with a yaqui *brujo*. But the wave of interest in herbs is not limited to those who are exploring the plant world for its potential psychoactive properties. The interest is far more general. Today, many people are disenchanted with technology, and are following the path of men like Thoreau, who a century ago advocated a return to nature.

Herbs are seen by many people as an affirmation of life itself amid a world of artifice. Herbs are now being rediscovered due to the spread of health food and natural food stores, mail order firms, and a growing understanding of the special value of herbs. Two major attitudes toward herbs account for much of the growing public interest: Herbs apparently help people stay healthy to a greater degree than commercial tonics and vitamins; and herbs are regarded as just as effective for common complaints as many of the patent pills on the pharmacy counter, and are generally less expensive.

This does not mean that the lay herbalist can ever replace the competent doctor when it comes to a serious ailment—although there are some people who swear that herbal medicine has produced good results for them where orthodox treatment has failed. Herbalists assert that an herb in its unprocessed, natural state contains—in addition to its active principle or alkaloid—organic and non-counterfeitable food which provides both a nourishment and a stimulus for the cells of the human body. This food consists of a highly complex, integrated natural synthesis of organically-derived salts, vitamins and nutrients, which in commercial drug products are usually considered extraneous and are therefore omitted.

*Herb alkaloids give nourishment and stimulation*

# MAKING HERB PREPARATIONS

Chemists argue that the amount of alkaloid contained in an herbal dose cannot be accurately predicted, owing to regional variations in soil, weather and other factors. This is true, but practiced herbalists are not unaware of it, and can take such differences into consideration. Balance in the composition of herb blends is a technical skill which can be acquired after much study and practice.

The way herbs are prepared is not a haphazard matter. Such preparations as decoctions, tinctures, capsules and infusions may be appropriate for some herbs and not for others. Sometimes it is necessary to start with fresh, undried herbs in making preparations, but usually it is sufficient to start with the dried material.

If an herb has an active ingredient that evaporates easily or is quickly destroyed when exposed to light or air, it is usually imperative that the freshly picked herb be used. The active principle in an herb will be retained if the herb is administered as a tablet or capsule made up of the powdered herb, or if the herb is chewed and swallowed in its original form—provided, of course, that the active principle has not evaporated.

But the active principle is not always present in a tea or extract. If the active ingredient is not soluble in water, but is soluble in alcohol, it will be of no use to make an herb tea. In such an instance, the benefit of the herb will be preserved in an alcohol extract. Some active principles are not soluble in either alcohol or water. Then the herb must be taken whole, or as a tablet or capsule.

*Water and alcohol soluble alkaloids*

The solubility of herbal ingredients is seldom stated on labels, and is not always mentioned in books on herbs. If other sources do not provide this information, it can nearly always be found in the *Merck Index* or in the *United States Dispensatory*. The following paragraphs will give a brief discussion of the basic ways of making herbal preparations.

# Decoctions

If the active principles of an herb are soluble in water and cannot be destroyed by flame heat, then a decoction can be made. A decoction is especially useful for hard materials such as roots, barks, and seeds. The usual practice is to use one ounce of the herb per pint of cold water, placed in a flame-proof glass or porcelain container. The container is covered and the substance boiled until a dark, rich color is visible in the liquid. The decoction is then strained and allowed to cool.

*Basic herbal preparations*

A decoction should generally be prepared fresh for each use. It can be kept a little longer if refrigerated or a quantity of food-grade alcohol is used to help preserve it.

# Essences

An essence is prepared by dissolving about one part of an essential oil in ten parts of alcohol.

# Fomentations

A fomentation results from dipping a cloth or towel into a heated infusion or decoction. The cloth is wrung out and applied locally to the body.

# Infusions

A hot infusion is essentially the same thing as a tea. The usual preparation involves taking an ounce of herb, pouring about a pint of boiling water over it, allowing it to steep, and drinking it hot or cool after straining. An infusion can also be made cold by placing the ounce of herbs in a pint of cold or tepid water, closing the container and leaving it for a few hours or overnight. Shaking the mixture occasionally helps the cold infusion process. The liquid is ready for straining and use when it has taken on a dark, rich color.

# Ointments and Salves

These are prepared by mixing two parts of a powdered herb with about eight parts of a base. Common bases are lard, vaseline, wool fat, hydrated wool fat or lanolin. Bases can also be made by emulsifying paraffin or beeswax with cetyl alcohol or pectin.

# Poultices

A poultice is made by mixing herbs with just enough water to moisten them. The mixture is heated in a double boiler, placed between two pieces of cloth, and applied to the affected area while hot. Poultices are replaced when they cool, and application is repeated until some relief is felt.

# Tinctures

A tincture is prepared by placing the herbs in a tightly closed container along with alcohol for two weeks. The container is shaken vigorously daily. After two weeks, the liquid is strained or filtered.

# Tablets and Gelatin Capsules

Some people enjoy the effects of a particular herb but dislike its taste, and sometimes a busy schedule allows little time for preparing an herb tea. Herbs in tablet or capsule form can bypass these limitations.

The relatively high cost of herb tablets and capsules is a reflection of the expense of manufacturing them. Some purchasers may prefer to invest time rather than money. An alternative for them is to buy empty gelatin capsules and the herb in powdered form, and to capsulate the powder by hand.

Herbs, teas and spices are best stored in air-tight containers, ideally made of opaque material such as dark-colored glass or ceramic, to protect them from sunlight. Ground glass stoppers, screw tops or tight corks help keep moisture from entering. Shelves for herbs should not be in direct sunlight, especially if clear containers are being used.

Plastic containers are less favored than glass, because gases can diffuse through plastic. Aromas can penetrate the plastic in both directions. Although many herbs do not lose their potency with age, some, such as mint, decline in both potency and aroma, and are best preserved in glass.

Refrigeration of herbs should be avoided because it is moist, and herbs should be kept dry. A cabinet with doors is an excellent storage area. Regardless of the kind of storage, herb containers must be clearly labeled, because one dried herb often looks like another.

Traditionally, herbs and spices have been used in whole or ground form for most food preparation. Modern food manufacturers, however, often decide that the herbs' natural color is not appetizing. Meat processors shudder at the implications of green shades in their fresh sausage. Canners fear that herb pieces will be regarded as contamination. Cheese-makers like the flavor of caraway, but consider the seeds unsightly. So the spice industry has devised ways to provide the flavor without the substance.

Current chemical engineering techniques can separate the flavor constituents from the vegetable base, by distillation or by solvent extraction. The distillation technique is the older of the two, and is more widely used. The crude herb is boiled in water in a closed metal cauldron. Steam emerges and is condensed. Little by little, the volatile flavor constituents come out along with the steam. The flavors, usually colorless, separate from the steam as an oily liquid. In the trade these are called "essential oils."

In many applications, essential oils closely resemble their parent material. But some herbs lose character in the process because not all of the flavor will distill, for not all of it is volatile.

The grassy, woody, and bitter roots have to be coaxed out of their shells by another technique, solvent extraction. By this method, the herbs are steeped in a low-boiling-point organic compound such as hexane or acetone. These solvents dissolve all the flavor constituents, both volatile and non-volatile. The spent herbs are filtered out and the solvent is evaporated. What is left behind is a heavy, dark-colored substance—the oleoresin. The oleoresin contains a very complete flavor spectrum which closely resembles the flavor of the original herb.

Essential oils and oleoresins are highly concentrated, sometimes as much as a hundred times more than the parent herb flavor. This concentration makes it difficult to disperse minute quantities evenly throughout a food product. The normal practice is to disperse the concentrate evenly in salt or sugar to a strength equivalent to the original raw herb. Most food products contain salt or sugar, and when the flavoring is introduced in this way, the "dry soluble" or extracted herb flavors disperse readily through the product. With this process, flavor quality and strength can be standardized and maintained from year to year, eliminating variations which occur in field-grown herbs.

These modern processes are a far cry from the 5000-year-old herbals carved in stone by the Sumerians. The herb garden my grandmother planted may have withered and gone, but the flavors and traditions she carried on in America now bloom stronger than ever in a growing variety of forms.

# 35

# Herbs for Animals

## by Scott Fickes

M_y friend Enrico, a shepherd and farmer, would sometimes tell me of his joy in grazing his animals in the high meadows of the Sierra Nevada. Enrico loved his simple life. His summers were spent deep in the mountains with several pack horses, a few sheep dogs, and his partner. When the snows of winter came, they would move to a small farm on lower ground, where grain and hay could be stored and supplied during the cold season.

The animals were generally in good health when enjoying the fresh air and virgin grasslands of the highlands, but in winter they were confined to a corral and fed commercial feed in bales and bags. When springtime came, it was often found that many of the animals had contracted intestinal worm parasites.

**A humane way to restore animal health**

In such confined conditions, where movement is restricted and natural foraging is retarded, livestock often become weak and prone to disease. Commercial feedgrain, by FDA standards, can include five parts per million of organophosphate pesticides. It is only when the animal's body is in such a weak and toxic condition that the worms can enter and take hold. Once inside, the worms debilitate the whole system, taking first choice of the most important nutrients, leaving the host animal to starve to death unless some change occurs. In this weakened, undernourished condition, bacterial infections of the lungs, skin and internal organs can easily develop, adding complications to an already sad case.

## STUPIFIED SHEEP

Such ailments in animals, whether livestock or pets, can be reduced or prevented by an intelligent organic approach, including mineral and herbal preparations specifically designed to maintain optimum health. While diet is the most important single factor in disease prevention, when diseases such as worms do appear, specific herbal formulas have been proven effective as a humane means to restore animal health.

154

When such diseases broke out, Enrico—like so many small farmers who are just meeting their bills—was repeatedly faced with a crisis that could mean the loss of his herd. For him, the only answer was to call a veterinarian. He felt he had no choice, although he knew that his beloved animals would spend several days stumbling and bleating, stupified while their metabolisms recoiled from the toxic effects of the massive chemical assault.

The deworming treatment for Enrico's sheep—and for other ruminants such as goats, cows, and horses—involves inserting a tube down the nose or throat so a selective poisonous compound can be pumped directly into the gullet, while the sheep squirm and fight the entire process. Apparently many of the toxic anthelmintics—dewormers—cannot be made palatable to the animals, whether added to the feed or in the form of a chewable tablet. Their instinctive reaction is to not eat the stuff. One of the common deworming agents used is DDVP, which is closely related to World War II nerve gases, and is in the pest-strips sold to hang in human rooms.

Chemical deworming

The veterinarian, with his tubes and toxins, is simply doing what he has learned as the best, most effective methods. His education includes the literature from the major chemical companies. And he has a difficult task—using just enough poison to kill the worms but not enough to kill the sheep. Whatever might be said against such measures, one thing must be said in their favor: They work. The worms do die.

But it was the initial toxic condition and low tone-level that made these animals so susceptible to illness in the beginning. More toxicity, in the long run, can only lead to more illness and a shorter life span. And the next cure for another illness down the line might well include more toxic chemicals.

Enrico's face showed disbelief when I told him there was an herbal formula that would let him deworm his herd and keep them well without those side effects. He took some convincing, but today springtime is a happy occasion for Enrico and his family, and, of course, his sheep.

# HERBS FOR HEALTH

Chemicals do work, and may sometimes be useful in extreme cases. But more natural, and humane, animal rearing methods are available. If their effectiveness is understood, people can choose an alternative way of relating to the well being of their animals. Beyond an immediate crisis, it can be seen that the general health of an animal is the single most important factor in disease. This is where herbs become most useful.

When an animal is healthy, its body is fully functional at a high level of energy, and its natural resistance prevents disease. Herbal toners can help to maintain this strong, thriving state, and can help cleanse and neutralize toxins. Often, when an animal is ill, an herbal formula can replace common, but debilitating, toxic chemical treatments. While much more research can be done in the area of optimizing animal health, we can meanwhile employ the herbal formulas which have proven their usefulness. A look at the shelves of natural food stores will show that herbal products currently available for animals include flea and tick remedies, intestinal tonics and dewormers, shampoos, and various products for livestock.

Herbs for prevention and treatment

Anyone who has lived around a cat or dog is familiar with the problem of fleas or other skin parasites such as lice and ticks. It is worst when not only the pet but the house becomes infested—which may be why so many landlords object to pets in rental units. It often spells fumigation.

To counteract the onset of fleas without resorting to toxins, herbal flea collars are gaining in popularity. The two types being marketed at present are an oil-impregnated rope collar and a eucalyptus-button necklace. Both are designed to release aromatic oils slowly and act as a fumigant/repellant to chase the fleas away. One outstanding limitation to this method is that the collar is only repellant. The fleas live on, and can lay eggs in the carpet, the animal's sleeping area, and elsewhere. When the collar wears out, or another animal walks by, the same fleas can thrive again. Such collars are most useful when both the animal and its living areas are already de-flead. Then the collars create a "protective

Herbs vs. fleas

barrier" to prevent new infestations. People who have tried herbal flea collars generally agree that they work well for about three weeks, and then the active principles just fade away.

An alternative approach is flea/tick oil for dogs and cats, made from an assortment of aromatic oils, and applied by rubbing into the fur. A stronger herbal dusting powder which includes natural insecticidal as well as repellant properties is made by my company, Herbalanimal. Consumer response confirms that it is an effective, long-lasting formula, most effective if the animal's bedding, as well as the animal, is thoroughly dusted.

# HERBS PLUS

Various herbal tonics for animals now appearing on the market are designed to improve the general condition of the intestines, providing a preventative measure against worms as well as toning the internal organs. Worms are second only to fleas in the numbers of cases of parasitic infection. Some products are designed to be similar to the popular "one-shot" (piperazine citrate) dewormers sold commonly in grocery stores and pet shops for deworming purposes, but a close look at the label is advisable. Some contain herbs only. Others display themselves as "herbal" but include piperazine, the conventional chemical deworming agent, along with some herbs.

NR Products of New Mexico makes several tonics for pets and farm animals, including two kinds which are intended to be given daily along with the animal's food. Healthways also offers a daily herbal tonic for pets, available by mail order. Garlic, widely regarded as an excellent tonic for general health, is found as a major constituent of these formulas, in combination with such ingredients as wormwood, kelp and thyme.

Herbal pet shampoos are often made by the same companies that manufacture shampoos for the human head. These products usually contain a castile soap and biodegradable detergent base. Aromatic oils are added for flea repelling, and emollient oils are added for coat shine. These formulas appear to be quite adequate for pet bathing and de-fleaing.

For farm animals, herbal products are abundant, especially tonics designed to act on the over-all system. Hoegger's makes several botanical products for the worming and general health of goats. Salves for goats' and cows' udders have reportedly yielded good results.

As the use of herbal products for animals grows, it is important to remember that the most vital factor in the responsible concern for pets and farm animals is just plain good feeding and attentive care. The books listed below can help to broaden a reader's understanding of the natural care of animals.

*Healing Animals with Herbs*, John Heinerman: Biworld Publishers.

*Herbal Handbook for Farm & Stable*, Juliette de Bairacevi: Rodale Press.

*The Healthy Cat & Dog Book*, Joan Harper.

*Bone Appetit! Natural Foods for Pets*, Frances Sheridan Goulart.

*Folk Medicine*, D.C. Jarvis, M.D.: Fawcett World Library.

**Check labels for hidden chemicals**

# 36

# *Dealing Herbs: Food or Drug?*

## by Janice Fillip

Herbs were humanity's first form of medicine. With the invention of scientific procedures and the development of technology, medicine in the Western world moved away from the use of herbal healers. Active ingredients of many herbs have been synthesized and used in "modern" chemical medicines. Such major drugs as morphine, quinine, atropine and reserpine were discovered through the study of traditional remedies.

Recently, many people have become less eager to pop synthetic pills and more aware of health care as a holistic, rather than a symptomatic, process. The search for gentler, more natural ways of dealing with health problems and health maintenance has created a revival of interest in herbal medicine. As this interest increases, so do the problems for people who buy and sell herbs, because claims about healing are the legal monopoly of the licensed medical profession.

**Worldwide trend toward herbal healing**

The director of the World Health Organization (WHO), Dr. Halfdan Mahler, announced that organization's decision to include traditional healers, village midwives and herbalists in its world-wide health programs. WHO's 1977 Seminar on the Use of Medicinal Plants in Health Care urged international cooperation for standardizing medicinal plants and other drugs of natural origin, advocated further clinical research into the efficiency of herbs, and encouraged the continued use of medicinal plants of proven effectiveness. The seminar reported that "in some countries, the use of medicinal plants has been merged successfully into the national health care system, with both economic and therapeutic advantages."

The United States was not represented at this WHO seminar. Nevertheless, local herbalists in the USA are coming out of the woods and into their communities as educators, consultants and healers. Rosemary Gladstar, an herbalist of considerable repute in Northern California, exemplifies this group. She is active in educating the public in the traditional uses of herbs through individual study groups, seminars, nature walks, and classes at local colleges. Rosemary also works on a consultation basis with local physicians who seek to integrate alternative healing methods with Westernized medical techniques.

Within the medical profession there is evidence of a growing openness to alternative treatments which have a less radical effect on the human organism that is often produced by chemically-synthesized drugs. Across the country, herb wholesalers and distributors report a surprising quantity of herbs being sold to physicians and medical clinics.

# HERB RESEARCH

Herbal research is currently being conducted by pharmacognosy facilities at major universities, including the University of Illinois Medical Center. (Pharmacognosy is descriptive pharmacology dealing with crude drugs and medicinal plants.) The American Society of Pharmacognosy, in conjunction with the Herb Trade Association, plans to conduct studies to determine the safety and efficacy of herbs. At a community level, studies are being conducted by the Berkeley Free Clinic, where herbal remedies are combined with more usual medical practices. For example, while throat cultures are being analyzed—often a delay of several days—herbal remedies, such as herb teas containing slippery elm, are given to patients as an interim treatment. When analysis is completed, the patient may be treated with the appropriate drugs.

Determining safety and efficacy of herbs

Public demand for herbs and information about their medicinal properties creates serious problems for the herb industry. Pharmaceutical companies and medical associations, apparently fearing the loss of authority and profits, are exerting pressure to curtail the availability of herbs, and to hinder the use of herbs as an alternative healing resource. As a result of this pressure and the increased public interest, the Food and Drug Administration is focusing its attention on herbs. Empowered to protect the public from consumer fraud, quackery and potential health dangers, the FDA is enforcing laws which are seen by many people in the herb industry as outdated, prejudicial, and arbitrary.

The FDA does not test herbs in advance. If an herb is reported to have a harmful effect, the FDA will conduct analyses to determine the existence or nature of the toxicity. The FDA has compiled a list of herbs called "Generally Recognized as Safe" (GRAS), but the list is incomplete and inconsistent.

# DANGEROUSLY SAFE

Many herbs, such as senna and psyllium, considered valuable by herbalists for their medicinal properties—and often found, for just that reason, in popular patent medicines—do not appear on the GRAS list. On the other hand, an addendum to the GRAS list states that "a number of fatal cases of nutmeg poisoning have been reported in human beings." That memo, from the FDA Division of Toxicology to the FDA Division of Regulatory Guidance, also states that rue, "taken internally in large doses causes violent gastric pains and vomiting, prostration, confusion of mind, convulsive twitching and in pregnant women, abortion." Both nutmeg and rue are on the Generally Recognized as Safe list. Although yohimbe is listed as unsafe, one herb tea company reports that the FDA does not require that they remove yohimbe from their products, but that they label them "FDA determined unsafe."

No clearly defined national policy for herb regulation

Other inconsistencies arise because the FDA has no clearly defined national policy on the interpretation and enforcement of laws relating to herbs. For instance, lobelia, considered unsafe and a cause of death in human beings, cannot be brought in through California ports. Yet one importer states that it is being imported through New York under the common name "dog grass."

Although the FDA clearly states that its GRAS list is incomplete, the down-to-earth fact is that, if an herb does not appear on the list, the burden of proving it safe falls upon anyone wishing to use or market the herb. There are no restrictions on growing or harvesting herbs. They become subject to scrutiny only when they are labeled and marketed. When an herb is represented, either verbally or on a label, as having curative properties, it becomes subject to federal laws regulating drug standards and use. Section 201 (b)(1)(B) of the Federal Food, Drug & Cosmetic Act defines drugs as "articles intended for use in the diagnosis, cure, mitigation, treatment, or prevention of disease in man or other animals . . ." A company making any medicinal claim for its product is required to prove the effectiveness of that product or face "misbranding" charges by the FDA. Under this regulation, Traditional Medicinal Tea was required to delete the word "Medicinal" from its brand name, or prove that their products had medicinal value. Other tea companies report similar difficulties with their tea names.

# THE COST OF PROOF

The requirements for proving safety and efficacy are sketchily presented in Section 505 of the Act. A new drug application requires "adequate and well-controlled investigations, including clinical investigations, by experts qualified by scientific training and experience to evaluate the effectiveness of the drug involved." Leonilla Strelkoff, president of Imedex International, has considerable experience in herbal research. She estimates that the tests prescribed by the FDA take three to five years to complete, and cost from $3 million to $5 million. These huge figures were verified by Bob Howe of the Herbal Research Labs. It is no surprise that many herb and tea companies prefer to be indirect about the qualities of their products.

If a medicinal claim is made for an herb despite this costly testing obstacle, the herb must be proven effective against specific symptoms of the ailment it alleges to affect. The FDA will not accept tests made outside the USA, regardless of how well-documented those tests are. According to one member of the herb industry, "They don't even want to hear about it!"

The FDA's efficacy requirement illuminates the underlying differences in the drug-medical viewpoint and the herbalist viewpoint. Drugs are designed to attack and remove specific symptoms instantaneously. Usually they neither treat the cause of the illness nor aid in prevention. Herbs, in contrast, are considered by herbalists, researchers, and physicians practicing herbal therapies to be whole, complex substances which act as nutrients to bring about broad biochemical changes. Herbs are seen as gradually affecting the total organism, rather than providing instant symptomatic relief.

Herbal researchers maintain that the FDA criteria for testing safety and efficacy are unclear, and are not applicable to the special nature of herbs. Although herbs are often useful because of the combined properties of their various components, the FDA requires that one active ingredient at a time be isolated and tested against a specific symptom. While a whole herb may be demonstrated to have beneficial effects upon an organism, its individual components might be ineffective against a particular symptom.

**Two different philosophies behind herb and drug therapies**

# MIXED RESULTS

People in the herb industry report a wide range of experiences while attempting to work with the FDA. Enforcement and interpretation of regulations varies among regional and district offices, and can even vary from day to day. Wisconsin ginseng farmers report that the FDA has been extremely helpful in providing them with specifications for establishing their farming operations, and in inspecting and certifying their crops every year. Yet a national tea company which obtained pre-publication FDA approval of their yearly catalog discovered, after their catalog had been printed, that the FDA had changed its mind. Major revisions were required, which was both expensive and a defacement of the catalog's graphic design.

Retailers face a different problem. A merchant who mentions a curative value of an herb may be vulnerable to a charge of practicing medicine without a license. These restrictions vary from state to state. In California, Section 2141 of the Business & Professional Code states: "Any person, who practices or attempts to practice, or who advertises or holds himself out as practicing, any system or mode of treating the sick or afflicted . . . or who diagnoses, treats, operates for, or prescribes for any ailment, blemish, deformity, disease, disfigurement, disorder, injury, or other mental or physical condition of any person, without having at the time of so doing a valid, unrevoked certificate . . . is guilty of a misdemeanor." As a person speaking for the California Board of Medical Examiners pointed out, anyone who has consoled an ailing friend with a bowl of chicken soup has technically violated this Code.

Section 2141 has been tested recently in California. A charge of violating this Code was dismissed when Dana Ullman, the homeopathic healer involved, established a contractual agreement with his clients, clearly stating that he was not performing a medical function. This disclaimer of treatment suggests a possible way to comply with state and federal laws.

# DON'T RECOMMEND IT

When an herb is represented as a "cure" or "treatment" for a disease, the recommendation to use it is unlawful, but it is possible to distinguish clearly between educating the public about qualities attributed to an herb, and recommending the use of that herb for a specific ailment. If a customer comes into a natural food store asking for a cough remedy, it is illegal to recommend the use of eucalyptus. But it is perfectly legal to state that eucalyptus oil is considered by some authorities to be an effective expectorant (promoting discharge of mucus from the respiratory tract), and that it is found in many over-the-counter cough remedies, such as Listerine throat lozenges.

As long as no recommendation has been made that the customer take eucalyptus to cure a cough, no diagnosis or treatment has been offered. Attorney Jerry Green, counsel for Dana Ullman, emphasized that, if no direct recommendation is made, the Code has not been violated. A spokesperson for the Board of Medical Examiners agreed that the procedure given in this example would not be in violation of Section 2141.

Nutritional information is not diagnosis. Health education does not require a license. Representing herbs as foods with certain nutritional qualities, rather than as drugs to be used for the treatment of illness, can alleviate problems with the FDA and state agencies. Stating the nutrient components of an herb does not involve misbranding. This is specifically stated in Section 105.60(B) of the Federal Food, Drug & Cosmetic Act: "A food which purports or is represented to be a food for special dietary use shall be deemed misbranded . . . if its labeling bears any statement, vignette, or other printed or graphic matter that represents, suggests or implies: (1) That the food . . . is adequate or effective in the prevention, cure, mitigation, or treatment of any disease or sympton *except that* the label may state that the food is a source of an essential nutrient and that this nutrient is important for good nutrition and health . . ."

As people become aware of the importance of nutrition and the detrimental effects of chemical additives and preservatives in food, the natural food industry is experiencing increasing growth and support. Gradually the drug-oriented, Westernized approach to medicine is being modified by rediscovery of the validity of time-honored techniques and the international recognition of alternative medical practices. Realization that good health is within an individual's control has led to a growing emphasis on preventative and maintenance health care. Herbal therapy is being explored as a gentler, more integrative approach to health. As people become more involved in directing and maintaining their own health, concepts about "medicine" and "drugs" can be expected to change.

Meanwhile it is possible for members of the herb industry and store owners to avoid legal entanglements. Medicinal claims cannot be made for herbs, but the public can be educated to their beneficial properties. The Herb Trade Association and organizations interested in alternative health methods are active in such education. Customers can be given information about herbs and allowed to draw their own conclusions. The herb industry is now in a delicate legal position regarding the medicinal properties of herbs. Many trends indicate that these laws will change. Until that time, conflict with entrenched attitudes can be minimized by considering herbs not as drugs, but as holistic food.

# 37

## *Herbs and the Law*

## by Dennis M. Warren

It is no secret that the nation's food industry has long considered the more specialized field of health foods as a somewhat separate world inhabited by fanatics. The Bank of America staff, in a report in the *Small Business Reporter*, described pre-1968 health food customers as "aging arthritics, would be Tarzans and all manner of food faddists." That was before the industry broke the billion dollar sales mark in 1975, establishing itself as one of the fastest growing industries and markets in the economy. That was also before Aunt Tilly's.

"Aunt Tilly's" is the name of a new health food "emporium" in Los Angeles. Walk in and you find photos of customers like Dyan Cannon and Barbara Streisand, and seventy employees stocking shelves. The owners of Aunt Tilly's claim a daily gross of $10,000, although competitors hotly dispute those figures. Cut that figure in half and you still have a remarkable story about the growth of public interest in health foods and the acceptance of alternative eating habits. We have moved into an era when the large discount grocery chains are suddenly "experimenting" with health foods lines. You now can even find soybeans at Safeway.

But the health foods industry has had its own stepchild—herbs. Sold to a largely exclusive and limited market, and hampered by a lack of generally recognized nutritional usefulness, the herb industry continued through the sixties at a slow growth pace. While the number of distributors and managers of several midwestern companies continued to make steady gains, the sale of herbs and herbal products remained small in relationship to the food industry as a whole.

The '70s, however, seem to have transformed the herb industry. Sales of herbal products and books about herbs have skyrocketed in the last five years. Favorable articles and press comments on herbs regularly appear in magazines such as *Prevention, Let's Live, East West Journal* and various trade journals. Even the publishers of *Playboy* have uncovered interest in herbs by running a full-length article about the medicinal uses of herbs in their

**Would-be Tarzans**

subsidiary publication *Oui.* The sale of herbs for use as legitimate pharmacological raw materials by chemical distributors continues unabated.

Growing public interest and enthusiasm is reflected in the dramatic growth of relative newcomers to the industry like Celestial Seasonings. After a quick start in the industry through sales in health food stores and cooperatives, that company is actively courting large supermarket chain clients and experimenting with radio advertising. The market has expanded to include herb teas, formulas, creams, salves, deodorants, essential oils and herbal cigarettes. The national cosmetic industry is giving careful scrutiny to the herb market, based on earlier and encouraging marketing programs in herbal bath oils, cosmetics and hair care products.

And now, celebrities are getting involved. I noticed a photograph in a national magazine showing Carol Burnett and the editors of the *Herbalist* smiling arm in arm extolling the value of herbs. The *Herbalist* now claims a grass-roots circulation of nearly 50,000.

# HERB SALES UP

**Dynamic growth**

One recent study conservatively estimated the 1977 volume of herbs sold at the retail level at $50 million, moving herbs into the number-two catagory of health foods based on dollar sales. All this activity has prompted one journal to call the herb business the "most dynamic, exciting and fastest growing" component of the health foods industry. The potential for profit in herbs has resulted in the appearance of a host of new companies manned by youthful, aggressive and largely inexperienced management.

It was inevitable that, in such an explosive market, government scrutiny would increase — and increase it has. Major FDA inspections of herb manufacturers and recalls of herbal products have taken place. In 1977, the federal government issued its ginseng import alert and took action against several ginseng capsule manufacturers and importers. It also gave industry notice of its list of twenty-seven restricted and "dangerous" herbs as part of Compliance Policy Guide 7117.05. The herbs contained on the list—including lobelia, mandrake, morning glory, and deadly nightshade—were classified as unsafe for human consumption and are now classified as "Adulterated foods" when used in herbal teas, formulas or other foods.

On the state level, investigatory and legal actions have taken place across the country. The subjects of these state actions have not been limited to local dealers, but have included out-of-state manufacturers, distributors, lecturers, and authors. California has taken actions against California, Utah, and Idaho companies among others. In one California case, Dr. John R. Christopher, a nationally-recognized lecturer and distributor, agreed to pay $5,000 in civil penalties, revise product labeling, and edit the contents of various publications as a compromise settlement to a consumer protection action filed against his company.

I met with a number of representatives of the Federal Food and Drug Administration and the California Food and Drug Section to explore the current attitudes in government about the herb industry and potential areas of conflict between government and private industry in this field. Uniformly, it was the opinion of these men that the major problem confronting the industry is one of developing credibility.

# CREDIBILITY GAP

Time and again, these regulatory officials would point to a long history of industry members failing to comply with rules and regulations concerning advertising, labeling, quality control, and purity. Equally disturbing was the reference to the intentional attempts by manufacturers to circumvent state and federal laws through various illegal practices. Of equal importance, in terms of credibility of the industry to these officials, was the absence of effective industry self-policing of practices injurious to the industry image and growth. The conclusions drawn by these men was that the violations they constantly see are either purely intentional or the result of "a gross lack of knowledge about the legal limitations" in the herb field.

Unfortunately for the herb industry, the regulatory history of herb manufacturers and sellers is the story of the boy caught with his hand in the cookie jar. FTC, federal, and state cases are replete with examples of defendants relying on the good-faith of their customers in "natural" and "organic" foods and herbs. These are the stories of the worthless formulas, "Indian" herbs, special blends by Asian doctors and herbalists, and unqualified persons dispensing medicinal or curative advice for financial profit. Some of these products were even distributed in pharmacies before the investigation of their effectiveness led to their downfall.

The names of the defendants range from the sounds of credibility—Illinois Herb Co., Master Herb Co., Gardner's Herb Foods—to the less than credible sounding—Pow-A-Tan Herb Tonic, T.B. Compound and my favorite, Daddy Rango's Laxative Herb Tablets.

While it is unfair to equate the mainstream of the herb industry with these latter-day patent medicine schemes, the tendency of manufacturers of herbs to make inflated, exaggerated and unprovable claims for their products was alive and well in 1978.

In preparation for this article, I reviewed the commercial catalogs and advertising literature of a number of herb companies for the compliance with current state and federal rules and regulations. Fortunately for the companies in question, I am no longer a regulatory attorney—because I found repeated illustrations of the grossest violations.

**Selling snake oil**

# WONDER HERBS

As I searched through the commercial literature, I discovered the secrets of Sarsaparilla Tablets—the wonder remedy that stimulates hair growth; Damiana Suprema—the potent aphrodisiac herb; Golden Seal Capsules—the Indian "cure all" herb; Female Formula X—the proven formula to relieve "all those female complaints"; and, finally, Formula 8—the natural alternative to Preparation H. One of the companies whose advertising fell into this category informed its readers that all of its advertising was in compliance with state and federal law! This type of creative advertising copy walks along a sure road to regulatory hell.

But the clear violations were not limited to the smaller companies selling aphrodisiacs, "exorcist pillows" filled with special herbs to cure nightmares, and unsanctioned hemorrhoid formulas. A number of larger companies appeared to be engaging in more sophisticated attempts to circumvent existing laws against commercial therapeutic claims for unapproved formulas and compounds by labeling their products with codes and numbers. I found labeling such as "NF" meaning nerve formula and "LB" meaning lower bowel formula. Another version of this same apparent scheme is to give the formula a number which is explained in the manufacturer's literature as a remedy for a variety of human maladies, illnesses, and diseases.

**Circumventing the laws**

# HISTORY OF USE

In the course of prosecuting a number of cases in the herb field as a government attorney, I had retailers explain to me that a number of the companies using this type of labeling give the retailer a booklet or leaflet explaining the medical implications of each of the specially-labeled formulas or compounds. Interestingly, most of these companies had omitted their names from any literature which contained any medicinal or therapeutic representations. The reason is simple: the manufacturer wants the retailer to take the legal risk of making illegal therapeutic claims for the product, but disclaims any connection with the illegal conduct of the retailer. Several California prosecutions have covered just such questionable labeling techniques.

While I find little support for these types of marketing and advertising techniques among reputable members of the industry, there remains a deep bitterness and frustration

HERBS **163**

in the herb industry over the refusal of the FDA to allow commercial therapeutic claims for herbs in direct connection with their sale. Supporters of relaxing these current regulations stress that "herbs have been used for centuries and have proven safe and effective in many human conditions." This history of use, they argue, should exempt herbs from the testing requirements for over-the-counter drugs as well as the regulations which apply to vitamins and food additives.

**Efficacy provisions**

This is a question of the continuing role of the "efficacy" provisions of both state and federal law. In brief, these provisions require that a substance must be thoroughly tested for its alleged beneficial qualities as well as its protential toxicity prior to its release on the market and the distribution of therapeutic claims. The process required to comply with the GRAS (generally recognized as safe and effective) standard is, admittedly, exhaustive, complex and costly.

These laws aim at protecting the public who rely on the therapeutic claims made by manufacturers at face value. The law used to read "caveat emptor"—the buyer beware. But the law regarding health considerations, products liability and other fields now places the responsibility for product safety and efficacy where it belongs—with the seller.

And the law is not aimed only at the potentially harmful product. It is aimed at the worthless or ineffective product for which medicinal or therapeutic claims are made. The fact that a manufacturer distributed a harmful product with all good intentions is little consolation to the injured consumer. The consumer who forgoes one proven remedy for another product that proves ineffective, becomes sicker and increases his chance of injury because of the misleading claims of the distributor.

So the law here is simple: before you make a medicinal or therapeutic claim you need to prove the claim is medically accurate. In the case of herbs, the problem is one of providing adequate scienticic and medical documentation.

# UNSCIENTIFIC LORE

Because of the long history of use of herbs by native populations and the absence of their use by the mainstream of medical society, there have been few well-defined scientific or medical studies performed. Instead, the industry has relied on literature which is largely anecdotal—stories passed down from one person to another whose reliability is questionable. Much of the pro-herb literature is now clearly outdated scientifically, although eagerly relied upon by the lay public.

**Stories not studies**

More precisely, the available literature suffers from a general lack of specificity on the part of authors and investigators concerning the identity of the particular variety of herbs used. The sound scientific components of proof that are necessary for an adequate evaluation, such as dosages used, method of preparation and formulation, diagnosis of the subject and medical history, are rarely part of the work.

Dr. Walter Lewis, ethnobotanist as Washington University and author of *Medicinal Botany*, points to this deficiency in the available literature as the major stumbling block for the industry in developing credibility and establishing herbs with GRAS standards. His exhaustive research and work has demonstrated that much of the literature is what he calls "myth and fiction." Ronald K. Siegel, a UCLA psychopharmacognosist, points to surprising levels of toxicity of commonly used herbs when ingested in the form of tea, capsules, and cigarettes.

Another critical problem in developing industry credibility is the absence of effective identification standards of herbs. Morning Glory, which is on the "Dangerous Herb" list, is an example. There are severeal different varieties of Morning Glory containing different internal compounds with one variety having 175 horticultural variants. Norman Farnsworth, Ph.D. of Pharmacognosy at the University of Illinois, advocates the development of a botanical index similar to a pharmacopia, to establish standards for product identification and labeling. This is clearly a first step toward the GRAS standards. Since tremendous variations in effect can occur among different varieties of the same herb, a sufficient data base must be developed before they can be labeled with a relative degree of accuracy and ensure safety of human consumption.

# OFFICIAL CONCERNS

These are certainly several of the major concerns of the governmental officials with whom I spoke. An internal government report on herbs reports that there are "problems in terms of public health" and industry credibility through the types of considerations raised in this article. The report states:

**Illness and death from herbs is well documented. It can be speculated that their fall into relative disuse in the past century or more can be equated with a lack of confidence or credibility by the medical community in the patient benefits versus risk. This in turn appears to hinge on the toxicity/deleterious affect/plant identification problem which still exists in the industry today.**

So it is clear that the herb industry has its work cut out for it in proving itself to government and to the larger consuming public. The government officials I spoke with support these suggestions for industry members:

Government's suggestions

1. Develop lines of communication with government to explore the herb industry and educate government about herbs and their legitimate use.

2. Support research studies on herbs and herbal identification for purposes of product identification, labeling requirements and health safety.

3. Develop industry-wide standards for good manufacturing, marketing and advertising practices through the examination of other industries and an examination of the regulatory actions taken in the last ten years.

4. Encourage responsible industry spokesmen to speak out against conduct on the part of manufacturers, distributors, or retailers which threaten the credibility of the industry and the health of consumers.

5. Promote seminars for industry and government on questions affecting the herb industry and the legal parameters of current practices.

The herb industry has a genuine and valuable product to deliver to the American public. Now is the time for the industry to be more creative than ever before in its approach to the public and government alike. It needs to be secure in its commitment to developing its credibility, and more articulate in support of its cause. The industry is in its embryonic stage, and the key to its future will be determined by the actions taken today.

# REFERENCES

For further reading

See *Oui* magazine, March 1977, for Robert Gover's article entitled, "Herbs, Witch Doctors and the Rosy Future of Pagan Medicine." The caption on the article reads "Is Mother Nature, M.D., the best doctor in town? The author's experience indicates that the answer is yes."

See *Health Foods Business Magazine*, March 1978, for an article by Dennis M. Warren, J.D., entitled, "Preventive Legal Medicine for the Health Industry." The article contains a detailed and concise statement of existing state and federal law concerning the definitions of a "food" and a "drug" for use in developing marketing and advertising programs.

See *Medical Botany*, John Wiley & Sons, Inc., 1977, written by professors Lewis and Elvin-Lewis, a husband and wife team of Washington University. The book contains 515 pages of information on plants that injure, heal and nourish, or alter the conscious mind.

See *Consumers' Research Magazine*, March 1977, for an article containing the typical criticisms of herb teas. See also Ronald K. Siegel's article in *JAMA* (*Journal of the American Medical Association*), August 2, 1976, entitled, "Herbal Intoxication—Psychoactive Effects from Herbal Cigarettes, Tea and Capsules."

I think the Herb Trade Association is certainly a step in the right direction. Headquartered in Austin, Texas, the Association offers a variety of services to growers, processors distributors, manufacturers, retail stores, brokers and agents. You can locate them by writing to: Herb Trade Association, 4302 Airport Blvd., Austin, Texas 78722.

# 38

# The FDA Horrors

## by Jim Schreiber

*"No, no!" said the Queen. "Sentence first—verdict afterwards."*

To many people in the herb trade, the Food and Drug Administration is as sensible as the Queen of Hearts in *Alice's Adventures in Wonderland*, shouting "Off with their heads!" willy-nilly. Tales told coast to coast paint the FDA as an unpredictable despot, applying vague rules and regulations in different whimsical ways in different parts of the country at different times. But, nevertheless, the value of the FDA in protecting the public is acknowledged. The best hope which is repeatedly expressed is that the FDA can be educated about herbs, so it will quit treating them like synthetic substances. Herb companies recognize that, through the misuse of arbitrary power, the FDA could destroy the entire herb industry while "protecting" the public from a purely imaginary threat.

**Educating FDA**

One herb company executive spoke of the futility of trying to compromise with a government agency. "A government is nobody," he said. "Suppose you do reach an understanding with an FDA compliance officer. That person may be promoted, demoted or transferred, so the next time you have to start all over again. I told them we'll take them to court next time." But that means money.

*"Oh, I know" exclaimed Alice, . . . "it's a vegetable. It doesn't look like one, but it is."*

*"I quite agree with you," said the Duchess; "and the moral of that is—'Be what you would seem to be' . . ."*

A distributor of Asian products was ordered to call one line "seaweed." They called the local FDA office and suggested that the term "sea vegetable" would be just as accurate for labeling.

166

The FDA officer was heard to turn from the phone and ask, "Hey, have any of you heard of a sea vegetable?" Then, into the phone: "Nobody here has ever heard of a sea vegetable. It's seaweed."

Faced with this thorough FDA inquiry, the company complied. The alternative was to keep the product off the market for an unknowable time, and thousands in court costs.

The FDA power, the investigator's interpretation and selective enforcement of the law, is dealt as a wild card. The FDA agents in Keokuk may fret over toxins, in Ashtabula over microbes, and in Ojai over labeling. An inspector who pokes cotton swabs in ceiling cracks or finds a bug on a bag of peppermint may threaten the existence of an entire herb company. Unlike the food industry giants which—as in the case of saccharin—can delay action years, herb companies are new and small, and generally must toe the line immediately, no matter how arbitrarily the line is drawn.

*"You might as well say," added the Dormouse, which seemed to be talking in its sleep, "that 'I breathe when I sleep' is the same thing as 'I sleep when I breathe'!"*

*"It is the same thing with you," said the Hatter.*

The FDA is concerned with safety. Ginseng is acceptable to the FDA in a breakable capsule in a package that says it is for making tea. But, in the FDA Wonderland, the same ginseng is an outlaw if the capsule is swallowed whole.

The FDA investigators' view of herbs as drugs or medicines sometimes drives them to cloak-and-dagger extremes. Agents with hidden tape recorders visited Elliott's Natural Food Stores in Sacramento. They asked Mrs. Georgana Elliott questions about "cures" for health problems. She suggested books on nutrition, and recommended that people take potassium, kelp, vitamins and minerals for nutrition. She says she made no claims about cures or treatments for specific ailments.

Mrs. Elliott was arrested for practicing medicine without a license. She was found guilty of one charge of the three made. She describes the experience as "heartbreaking" and "disillusioning," but says that the support she has received "makes this burden easier to bear."

No one in the herb trade expects the FDA to vanish like Alice's dream, but many hope that FDA abuses can be corrected. That can only come as a result of educational efforts in the courts and legislatures, supported by a rising wave of public opinion.

**Selective enforcement**

**Cloaks and daggers**

# 39

## The GRAS List

The list below includes the spices and other natural seasonings and flavorings that are generally recognized as safe by the Food and Drug Administration. In addition to the substances on this list, the FDA Commissioner regards such common ingredients as salt, sugar, vinegar, baking powder, and monosodium glutamate as safe for their intended use. The FDA considers it "impracticable to list all substances that are generally recognized as safe for their intended use."

Alfalfa herb and seed
Allspice
Ambrette seed
Angelica
Angelica root
Angelica seed
Angostura
Anise
Anise, star
Balm (lemon balm)
Basil, bush
Basil, sweet
Bay
Camomile, English, Roman, German or Hungarian
Capers
Caraway
Caraway, black
Cardamom
Cassia, Chinese

Cayenne pepper
Celery seed
Chervil
Chives
Cinnamon, Ceylon,
Cinnamon, Chinese
Cinnamon, Saigon
Clary
Clover
Cloves
Coriander
Cumin
Cumin, black
Elder flowers
Fennel, common
Fenugreek
Galanga
Geranium
Ginger
Glycyrrhiza

Grains of paradise
Horehound
Hyssop
Lavender
Licorice
Linden flowers
Mace
Marigold, pot
Marjoram, pot
Marjoram, sweet
Mustard, black or brown
Mustard, white or yellow
Nutmeg
Oregano
Paprika
Parsley
Pepper, black
Pepper, cayenne

Pepper, red
Pepper, white
Peppermint
Poppy seed
Rosemary
Rue
Saffron
Sage
Sage, Greek
Savory, summer
Savory, winter
Sesame
Spearmint
Tarragon
Thyme
Thyme, wild or creeping
Turmeric
Vanilla
Zedoary

Essential oils, Oleoresins (solvent-free), and natural extractives (including distillates) that are generally recognized as safe for their intended use are listed below.

Alfalfa
Allspice
Almond, bitter (free from prussic acid)
Ambrette (seed)
Angelica root
Angelica seed
Angelica stem
Angostura
Anise
Asafetida
Balm (lemon balm)
Balsam of Peru
Basil
Bay leaves
Bay (myrcia oil)
Bergamot
Bois de rose
Camomile flowers, Roman, English, or Hungarian
Cananga
Capsicum
Caraway
Cardamom seed
Carob bean
Carrot
Cascarilla bark
Cassia bark, Chinese
Cassia bark, Padang or Batavia
Cassia bark, Saigon
Citronella
Citrus peels
Clary

Clove bud
Clove leaf
Clove stem
Clover
Coca (decocainized)
Coffee
Cola nut
Coriander
Corn silk
Cumin
Curacao orange peel
Cusparia bark
Dandelion
Dandelion root
Dog grass
Elder flowers
Estragole
Estragon
Fennel, sweet
Fenugreek
Galanga
Geranium, East Indian
Geranium, rose
Ginger
Glycyrrhiza
Glycyrrhizin, ammoniated
Grapefruit
Guava
Hickory bark
Horehound
Hops
Horsemint

Hyssop
Immortelle
Jasmine
Juniper (berries)
Kola nut
Laurel berries
Laurel leaves
Lavender
Lavender, spike
Lavandin
Lemon
Lemon grass
Lemon peel
Licorice
Lime
Linden flowers
Locust bean
Lupulin
Mace
Malt (extract)
Mandarin
Marjoram, sweet
Mate
Melissa Menthol
Menthyl acetate
Molasses (extract)
Mustard
Naringin
Neroli, bigarade
Nutmeg
Onion
Orange, bitter, flowers
Orange, bitter, peel
Orange leaf
Orange, sweet
Orange, sweet, flowers
Orange, sweet, peel
Origanum
Palmarosa
Paprika
Parsley
Pepper, black or white

Peppermint
Petitgrain lemon
Petitgrain mandarin or tangerine
Pimenta
Pimenta leaf
Pipissewa leaves
Pomegranate
Prickly ash bark
Rose absolute
Rose (attar of roses)
Rose buds
Rose fruit (hips)
Rose leaves
Rosemary
Saffron
Sage
Sage, Greek
Sage, Spanish
St. John's bread
Savory, winter
Schinus molle
Sloe berries
Spearmint
Spike lavender
Tamarind
Tangerine
Tannic acid
Tarragon
Tea
Thyme
Thyme, white
Thyme, wild or creeping
Triticum
Tuberose
Turmeric
Vanilla
Violet flowers
Violet leaves
Violet leaves absolute
Wild cherry bark
Ylang-ylang
Zedoary bark

# 40

# *Herb Traders Meet*

## by Janice Fillip

Spying the Cheshire Cat grinning at her from a nearby tree, Alice asked him which way to go. "That," replied the Cat, "depends entirely upon where you want to be."

The Herb Trade Association is facing a problem similar to Alice's. The Second Annual Symposium on Herbs in mid-September 1978 attempted to determine where the Association—and the industry it represents—wants to be. Ben Zaricor of Fmali Herb Company summarized the problem, "What are herbs, a food or drug?"

The research scientists who spoke at the Symposium all referred to herbs as a drug. Yet the representatives of FDA and USDA pointed out that herbs are regulated as a food or food additive. Within the industry, many herb trading companies are concerned with being allowed to sell herbs as a commodity, while retailers sometimes make medicinal claims for herbs, which exposes them to charges of practicing medicine without a license, and may result in herbs being severely restricted because they are not meeting drug standards. According to Dr. Richard Ronk, a representative of FDA's GRAS Review section, "Eventually those [medicinal] claims will have to be substantiated. The way to do that is well-controlled clinical studies."

## FOOD OR DRUG?

The HTA is in the middle, attempting to represent the industry by sponsoring such scientific studies, by presenting self-regulating industry guidelines and good manufacturing practices to the government agencies, by increasing the number of herbs generally recognized as safe, and by providing a forum for communication among the diverse members of the herb industry. Whether herbs are considered a food or a drug is, however, a question that only time and usage will resolve. The only speaker at the Symposium to propose an answer to that question was HTA's Executive Director, Paul

*Reporting on herbal research*

Lee: "An herb is a plant with life-enhancing properties which can grow in your back yard. A drug is a substance that, when injected into a rat, produces a paper."

A number of papers were presented at the Symposium, dealing with herb toxicity, risks and benefits, herbs and the law, and naturally occurring carcinogens. A great deal of herbal research has been done over the past few years, and the results, especially in the area of ginseng research, are surprising: some "ginseng" products have been found to contain no detectable ginseng, and chronic ginseng use has been demonstrated to have undesirable long-term physical effects.

In the area of herb cultivation, Dr. Arnold Krochmal, principal economic botanist for the Southeastern Forest Experimental Station of the FDA, reported on the government's role in herb production. Krochmal has been involved in programs designed to grow marketable herbs under cultivation as an income source for the Appalacian poor. Krochmal said herbs grown under cultivation are chemically the same as wild herbs, but the yield from cultivated herbs is greater.

Dr. E. J. Staba, from the University of Minnesota's School of Pharmacy, reported that his laboratory research on the active constituents in potent medicinal plants is conducted with plants grown from tissue cultures. Staba speculated that tissue culture may be the cultivation method of the future. He said that the industry may be able to "propagate a uniform quality of plants by such techniques in the not-too-distant future. The scientists will follow the industry lead on what to study."

# SAYS NOTHING SAFE

How herbs are grown in the future is considerably less controversial than how they will be used. According to FDA's Rock, "There are no safe materials, only safe uses of materials." Studies presented by Dr. Leonard Bjeldanes, professor of Food Toxicology in the Department of Nutritional Sciences at UC Berkeley, underscored this point. In a discussion on carcinogens in the food supply, Bjeldanes cited research indicating that glycyrrhizic acid found in licorice root resulted in high blood pressure and an increased heart rate. He discussed naturally occurring carcinogens in spices, and pointed out that myristicin—a component in black pepper, caraway, dill, parsley, celery, and nutmeg—has been shown to have a narcotic effect and may cause liver damage. Bjeldanes also reported that tannin found in tea has been shown to be carcinogenic when injected into test animals.

The question of safety is often a question of dosage

Although a substance may be carcinogenic in laboratory tests, it may not be carcinogenic in real life. "Any substance can be toxic or stimulatory," according to Dr. Memory Elvin-Lewis, head of the Department of Dental Microbiology at Washington University. Sassafras was recently removed from the GRAS list when safrole, a component which makes up 85 percent of the oil of sassafras, was determined to be carcinogenic. Yet Elvin-Lewis' research with human populations in areas where sassafras tea has been drunk for generations as a spring tonic, indicates no detectable toxic effects from the tea. While tannins have a toxic effect on the liver, Elvin-Lewis pointed out that recent cancer research suggests that tannins also have anti-tumor properties, depending on dosage.

# ADVISES CAUTION

Often the difference between poisonous and medicinal effects of plants is a "matter of dosage," said Dr. Ara Der Marderosian, professor of pharmacognosy at Philadelphia's College of Pharmacy and Science. Marderosian's research focuses on isolating the active principles of medicinal plants as a source for drugs. While dosage may determine the relative safety of an herb, Marderosian warns that the herb industry, "cannot tell the public to have a free reign. They may lose their lives on that account."

Many individuals selling herbs know virtually nothing about the herbs they sell, according to Dr. Walter Lewis, senior botanist at Washington University. Lewis said,

"It is totally irresponsible to sell to an unknowing public." He recommended cautionary labeling on packages to alert consumers to the potential hazards of the herbs they purchase. Lewis chose two readily available herbs to illustrate his point: camomile can cause problems for people with an allergy to ragweed, and hawthorne enhances hypertension and may lead to cardiovascular problems. Lewis raised the question, "Why should an herb be sold if it has a potential for being dangerous?" Among the herbs Lewis feels should be made available only through perscription are poke, mistletoe and lobelia.

Cautionary labeling

Attorney Dennis Warren warned that herbs present legal, as well as medical, risks. Warren's summary of laws affecting product advertising indicated that an advertiser is liable for product claims made by an advertising company, that a company president is personally liable for actions of its employees, and that anyone endorsing a product is responsible for the claims they promote. According to Warren, literature accompanying a product is considered part of the product label. Unproven claims made in product literature can expose the product to a charge of misbranding.

# SEEKS FUN DRUG

While some people abuse the laws regarding drugs, many more abuse the drugs themselves. Civilization has a history of non-medicinal, ritual or magical drug usage. Many of these drugs—such as tobacco, marijuana, caffeine, peyote and tequila—come from plant sources. At UCLA's Department of Psychiatry School of Medicine, Center for the Health Sciences, Dr. Ronald Siegel is searching for an ideal recreational intoxicant or drug. His studies have shown some interesting trends: There is evidence that, when taken in quantity over a period of months, mint bidis can cause clinical intoxication. "Hare Rama" brand tobacco cigarettes have been shown to contribute to hypertension and insominia due to their extremely high (8-9 percent) nicotine content.

Dr. Siegel reported on preliminary research conducted on the "Ginseng Abuse Syndrome." An outpatient study was conducted over a period of two years, involving 133 chronic ginseng users. The amount of ginseng used varied from a minimum of 3 grams a day to 75 grams a day. Hypertension developed among 22 of the chronic users after twelve weeks of use, then disappeared. Although there was no discernable changes in blood chemistry, ongoing symptoms from chronic ginseng use included nervousness, skin eruptions, morning diarrhea, decreased appetite, and swelling. It was noted that these effects did not occur in people who merely consumed ginseng tea. Siegel said that these effects may be caused by hormone overproduction by the adrenal cortex. Siegel is currently conducting controlled group studies on the effects of ginseng use.

Ginseng Abuse Syndrome

# GINSENGLESS GINSENG

Ginseng is allegedly being abused by some suppliers, as well as by some users. A recent study conducted by Dr. Ara Der Marderosian on readily-available commercial ginseng products showed that a considerable number of the tablets and capsules contained no detectable ginseng. Research presented by Mark Blumenthal of Sweethardt Herbs indicated that some products being sold as "wild red American ginseng" are, in fact, canaigre (*Rumex hymenosepalus*). The report maintained that, "although [canaigre] has no connection with the genus *Araliaceae* (to which *Panax Ginseng, Panax Quinquefolium* and *Eleutherococcus Senticosus* belong), it is currently being labeled as a type of 'ginseng.'" Blumenthal proposed that the HTA determine clear-cut criteria for which plants could be labeled "ginseng."

Determining what can be labeled "ginseng"

A resolution passed by HTA's Committee on Ethics and Standards and approved by the Board of Directors in July, stated that Rumex, or wild red American ginseng, has "no botanical, pharmacological or environmental relationship to ginseng." This resolution was unanimously approved by the general membership of HTA at the Annual Meeting which followed the Symposium. Blumenthal praised the action of the HTA, saying "This is the first time that the herb industry has scrutinized the product to develop labeling standards. It is important to develop a way to rely on the credibility of a product."

# 41

# *A Taste for Ginseng*

## by Jim Schreiber

The retailer who sees the fast-growing popularity of ginseng and wants to sell it is faced with a confusing array of terms, products, companies, claims and counterclaims. Without the skills of the herbalist or the chemist, it seems impossible to make the judgments necessary to pass the best value on to the customer.

The word "ginseng" now appears on labels of packages which contain various members of a whole family of plants—and on some which are not in that family at all. Universally accepted as "real" are *Panax ginseng* and *Panax quinquefolium*, the latter being the native American variety of the plant. In the same family, and similar in effect, is *Eleutherococcus*, which includes "Siberian ginseng." *Panax* is more active than *Eleutherococcus*, but some Soviet studies indicate that the Siberian plant is better at reducing stress.

**Ginseng terminology**

Claims that red dock or yellow dock are ginseng are misleading. And claims that either of these plants has been cross-bred with ginseng are false: that is not biologically possible.

Once the terminology is sorted out, the retailer will have to sink teeth into the subject, becoming familiar with ginseng by grinding up and tasting the unprocessed root. Suppliers are often glad to offer a sample for this purpose. Once the taste of the root is known, judgments about assorted ginseng products become possible.

Liquid extracts of ginseng are sometimes flavored with honey or lemon, making the product more acceptable to some consumers, but making a taste-test fairly useless. And if it tastes like alum, it is probably alum, not ginseng. A concentrated extract is normally very dark brown, and flows quite slowly. If it flows right out of the bottle, it is probably watered down.

Extracts can contain different amounts of alcohol. If the percentage of alcohol is high enough, any effect of drinking an extract brew could be a result of the alcohol rather than the ginseng. In assessing the over-all dollar value to the customer, the alert retailer will bear in mind that a smaller bottle that is not diluted can be a better buy than a larger bottle that is diluted. Ginseng, not alcohol, is the costly ingredient, and because the demand will be far greater than the supply in the foreseeable future, that cost is likely to remain high.

In sampling ginseng tea, the taste of the root is the standard of judgment. Good ginseng tea is neither too bitter nor too sweet, the latter being accomplished by the addition of a sweetener such as sucrose. A light brown color is usual.

# TASTE THE POWDER

Capsules should be opened and the powder tasted and compared to the root. If the normal bittersweet flavor of ginseng root is obscured by sweetness, it is almost certain that a sweet filler has been added.

Taste test for quality

The purity of Ginseng in capsule form can be checked with a pharmacist's scale. The OO-size capsule of pure ginseng should weigh around 650-700 milligrams. A weight of over 800 milligrams indicates that a filler has been added, perhaps lactose.

Major ginseng firms advise buyers to ask their ginseng suppliers for details about the processing of their products, in addition to samples for testing. In the case of Korean ginseng—still by far the largest-selling kind in the USA—the best quality comes from the Kang-Hwa region, according to Dr. Choong-Gook Jang, a biochemist and the president of Sam Sung Korean Ginseng Co.

A company that responds to such requests with literature about medicinal, healing, or therapeutic qualities of ginseng can be bringing trouble for the retailer. Any such claims transmitted from a shopkeeper to a consumer could lead to the arrest of the shopkeeper— not the supplier. At the present time in the USA, the Food and Drug Administration allows only one "claim" about ginseng in any form: It is for use in making tea. Any other use entangles ginseng in the FDA's legal snare of rules about drugs and food additives.

Apart from difficulties with the FDA, the major problem in America's ginseng trade today is the lack of available information about quality. Those concerned with this problem agree that there is a need for a self-regulating organization which would establish nationwide standards. Many people see the seed of such an organization in the Herb Trade Association, which could serve as a model for the ginseng trade. Such self-control is probably the only alternative to ever-increasing government control.

# 42

# Ginseng Harvest: USA

## by Jim Schreiber

Ginseng—*Panax quinquefolius*—is a plant which is native to the North American continent, growing wild in a broad band of forest land from the midwestern Canadian provinces to the Deep South of the USA. Cultivation of ginseng in this natural range focuses in Wisconsin, where about ninety percent of the native plant is harvested.

Rains delayed the harvest in 1978. As a result, some of the intended harvest remained in the ground for another year. Since most of the crop scheduled for harvest last October was four-year-old root, the 1979 harvest will include some five-year-old root.

**A long range commitment**

Unlike most field crops, which can be grown at least annually, ginseng requires a long-range commitment from the farmer. The 1978 harvest came from seeds which ripened prior to 1974. The farmer may choose to start from seeds, which are less expensive than seedlings, but require about eighteen more months to mature. Starting from seed reduces the chances of disease.

Some firms provide seedlings from one to three years old, at increasing prices. Older seedlings, of course, take less time to reach the harvest stage. Under normal circumstances, ginseng is never harvested before its third year, because that is the first year in which it will produce its valuable seeds.

Ginseng requires shade. Instead of the bamboo shelters used in Asia, the Wisconsin ginseng farmers use wooden lath on seven-foot posts to cover the entire field, allowing direct sunlight only 25 percent of the time during summer.

The seed beds need relatively little cultivation. The US Department of Agriculture estimates that one person can care for about two acres of ginseng. The plant grows best in light, dry, loamy soil. Light mulching to hold some moisture during hot weather and to protect shoots from frost is usually done. Traditionally, any single field is used only once for ginseng.

Excessive water will cause root rot and promote blight. For this reason, a good drainage slope is prized. On flat ground, seed beds are mounded to promote runoff during rain. The problem of blight is prevalent enough that some of the crops may be sprayed with chemicals, although farmers prefer to avoid this. They know that fertilizers and chemicals are frowned on by most buyers.

Some ginseng is grown in the Pacific Northwest. According to a USDA report, the Western root tends to be long and thin, less desirable than the size, weight and shape found in Wisconsin.

The ginseng harvest, as described by Robert Corr of the American Ginseng Co., is not a high-technology enterprise. About fifty hands go into the fields, dig out the roots by hand, and load them onto wagons. The roots are washed by hand.

Low technology harvest

# A CASH CROP

The lath that had been used to provide shade is taken down and converted into slatted trays which hold the roots during about two weeks of drying in a well-ventilated shed. Temperatures used during drying usually range from 90° F. to 110° F. When sufficiently dry, the ginseng is ready for selection by the broker.

Robert Corr indicated that the harvesting of four-year-old root makes the most economic sense. "It's a cash crop," he said, which reaches maturity in that time. He stated that he is not aware of any evidence that six-year-old root has any greater amount of the constituents for which ginseng is valued. At four years, the plant has produced seed and has reached a marketable size and weight.

Corr estimates that the 100-odd Wisconsin farms in 1978 produced about 200,000 pounds of ginseng—worth $20,000,000 in export sales. The USDA report indicates that 95 percent of the US crop is exported. In 1975, federal figures showed $12,600,000 in ginseng exports.

A cash crop

Prices are determined by the Hong Kong international market. According to Corr, a Hong Kong company offered $25,000,000 in cash for the entire Wisconsin crop, but were turned down.

The USDA's Science and Education Administration gives a caution to people interested in entering the ginseng farming business:

"High initial cost of planting stock, susceptibility to disease, long maturing period, and a limited market indicate ginseng farming should be approached conservatively. Since yields of dried root average about 1 ton per acre, 100 to 200 acres of mature ginseng could easily supply the total market for 1 year."

To make matters worse, there was a poor seed crop last year, driving seed prices up to $60 per pound, from $40 per pound in 1977. The economic picture in the ginseng farming trade supports Corr's view that "it's a risky business."

# 43

# On a Korean Ginseng Farm

## by Kurt Paine

In September, 1978, my partner, Jeff Kronick, and I attended the International Ginseng Symposium in Seoul, South Korea. During our visit, we were taken to a ginseng farm where we were able to see, first hand, the actual harvesting of fresh ginseng roots.

The farm is located in the northern part of the Republic of Korea, just a couple of miles from the Demilitarized Zone that separates North Korea from South Korea. About two miles from the farm we had to get off the bus and walk the remaining distance on a narrow path, because the farm was in a rather remote area. Along the way, we ran into several Army tanks, manned by US soldiers who are part of the force that the US still maintains in Korea.

**Bamboo shelter protects ginseng harvest**

Upon arriving at the farm, we were taken to the field that was being harvested. When the ginseng plants are first set out in the field, they are covered with a bamboo shelter which protects the plants from the direct rays of the sun. These shelters are left in place until the plants are harvested. In the case of this particular farm, the plants were said to be six years old. In the fall of each year, the upper growth of the plant dies off until the following spring. For the harvesting, the bamboo shelters are removed and the roots dug up.

**Roots graded and cleaned**

After the roots are dug up, they are taken to a temporary grading and cleaning station set up at the farm. There, most of the dirt is removed and they are graded according to size and quality. Any diseased roots are removed. The quality of a root is determined by shape, size, and appearance. The best roots are held out for sale to the Office of Monopoly, which had an inspector there to supervise the grading. The other roots are then sold on the open market to factories that process the various white ginseng products.

We were told that no fertilizers or pesticides are used during the cultivation of ginseng, and we were shown a wild plant growing nearby whose leaves are used as a combination mulch and soil-builder. We were told that, once the ginseng roots are harvested, the field may be planted with other crops for several years until the soil is once

178

again built up. Another person said that, after harvest, the fields may lie fallow for many years. Most of the farms that we saw were quite small, covering only a few acres, although we did see a couple of fairly large plots.

We were also taken to the Korean Red Ginseng Factory, which is owned by the government's Office of Monopoly. There is where all of the Red Ginseng products are manufactured: Only the Korean government has the right to produce Red Ginseng.

# LATEST TECHNOLOGY

This is a new factory, completed in September 1978. With total floor space of about 475,000 square feet, the factory represents the latest technology in the manufacturing and processing of ginseng products. We were quite impressed by the size of the facility and the obvious care taken to ensure the control of quality.

The ginseng roots start out as fresh, raw white roots when they arrive at the factory. They are then sent through a washing room where the majority of the cleaning is done by machine and the remainder is done by hand. Only six-year-old roots are used to make Red Ginseng. After being washed, the roots are steamed for several hours and then partially dried at low temperatures in a large dryer. At this point, the roots are taken outside where they are dried for approximately 30 days. It is this combination of steaming and drying that causes the roots to turn red. We were quite surprised to learn that nothing is added to the roots, and no other procedures are used in this process.

When the roots reach a moisture content of about 12 percent, they are then ready to be graded. The best roots are left whole and packaged in boxes to be sold as Korean Red Ginseng. These whole roots are first graded into one of three grades: Heaven, Good, and Earth—with Heaven being the best grade. They are also sorted according to size, so that within each grade there are several sizes. The factory has a projected yearly output of 300,000 kilograms (about 3,000 tons) of Red Ginseng roots.

The roots not selected for whole roots are made into the packaged Red Ginseng products. In the case of Red Ginseng powder, the roots are merely pulverized into powder and then packaged in jars. The other roots are cooked in water for 24 hours, producing a very thick paste which is used in making the concentrated extract. Other products are also made from this extract. The spray-dried and freeze-dried powders are both made from the extract, using various processes. Instant ginseng tea is made by drying the extract and mixing it with a fairly large percentage of lactose.

The instant tea is probably the least effective form of ginseng since it contains, at most, 30 percent ginseng, while all the other products have nothing added to them, with the exception of a small amount of water in the concentrated extract.

One of the most impressive features of the factory, aside from its sheer size, was the quality-control methods used. In every section where a finished product was being made or packaged, the entire area was kept sterile. Fortunately, we were able to view these areas through large plate glass windows, although we were not allowed entry. All other areas of the factory were kept extremely clean as well.

It is obvious to me that, while the Koreans don't produce the only good-quality ginseng in the world, they are making important advances in the continuing production of high-quality ginseng products. This was also demonstrated to us by the large amounts of research on ginseng being done in Korea, and by the fact that they have put together the International Ginseng Symposium, which hopefully will continue annually. Probably the best way for ginseng to become accepted by the traditional medical community is if this type of research is continued.

**Manufacturing red ginseng tea, powder and concentrated extracts**

**Quality control in the factory**

# 44

# *Where Ginseng is King*

## by Jeff Kronick

When a customer asks the natural food or herb store retailer for ginseng, chances are that a good Korean ginseng product will be put on the counter. Probably 90 percent of the ginseng sold to customers in the United States is Korean, whether it be capsules, tablets, instant teas, concentrated extract or whole roots. Many American companies market their own ginseng capsules using Korean powder. Over twenty brands of Korean instant ginseng tea can be found in stores throughout the US. Claims of "top quality" abound, prices vary widely, and without a keenly discriminating sense of good quality, the buyer can be easily fooled.

Why do so many people believe that the best ginseng is Korean? How can the buyer tell a high quality packaged product from one that delivers minimal benefit? Why are some brands so incredibly expensive when they look and taste the same as brands costing one-third the price? What can you believe about the lines of distinctively-wrapped items—with gold coloring the packaging?

When the International Ginseng Symposium was scheduled to be held in Seoul, Korea last year, it seemed like the best place to seek answers to these and many other questions concerning Korean ginseng. This article tells some of the things we found out during our journey.

From cultivation and processing to packaging and merchandising, the Koreans take extreme care of and pride in their ginseng. Seeds are systematically planted with the sun striking the ground at limited angles under thatch-roof and wall structures. The soil for planting reportedly may lie fallow for fifteen years after the last harvest, with no chemical fertilizers or pesticides used. Because ginseng is a fragile, temperamental oddity in the botanical kingdom, constant attention must be devoted to keeping the plants hardy and disease-resistant during the six years of growth required to develop its healthful properties to the fullest.

Our visiting party of English-speaking business people was privileged to observe the harvesting of a ginseng field. The roots were carefully dug from the soft ground, carried to

**Ginseng cultivation encouraged by government incentives**

180

a sorting and packing area, and inspected by an Office of Monopoly agents. Many people gather for the harvesting tasks, and we were told of government incentives being offered to encourage more farms to convert to ginseng cultivation. While Korean ginseng seems a family affair at this stage of its distribution, the government maintains a vigorous role in bringing it even this far. To understand Korean ginseng, you must realize just what the Korean government's Office of Monopoly does in the Korean ginseng business.

# GOVERNMENT ROLE

The Republic of Korea is funding the creation of "Ginseng Villages" to increase the supply of high-quality ginseng available for export. The Office of Monopoly administers this program by allocating funds and educating the rural populace to grow more and better ginseng. As the branch of the government which strictly controls all legal ginseng trade and production in South Korea, the Office of Monopoly licenses white ginseng companies (around fifty of them at present) to produce and export Korean ginseng products. They establish quality standards, and inspect production facilities frequently to insure that high-grade white ginseng products are consistently produced. Many Korean white ginseng products available in America have the official "Inspected by Office of Monopoly, Republic of Korea" seal.

Beyond these administrative and regulatory functions, however, the Office of Monopoly also manufactures Korean Red Ginseng products. They are the only source for red ginseng in South Korea. When roots are harvested, the government inspector selects the choicest ones, judged by size and appearance of health, which are later steamed and shade-dried to become red ginseng. (White ginseng is sun-dried without steaming.)

The Office of Monopoly opened its new manufacturing plant only ten days before the symposium, so when we visited the facility, it seemed to be operating only on a token basis. Nevertheless, the fragrance of ginseng filled the air. The new building, a four-hour drive from Seoul, covers eleven acres of a 46-acre site. Its production capacity is said to be 6,300,000 boxes of red ginseng products, in addition to 500,000 catties—about 3,000 tons— (600 grams per catty) of red roots annually. The equipment is sophisticated, with immense, modern steaming, grading, pulverizing, packaging and concentrating machinery. Quality controls appears to be a foremost consideration.

**Office of Monopoly controls all trade and production of ginseng**

# WORLD TRADE

Koreans have cultivated *Panax ginseng* for more than a thousand years. Only in the past twenty have packaged, processed products become significant in the world marketplace. In Asian countries, whole and sliced roots still hold a substantial share of ginseng sales—perhaps more than half, if all the roots we saw in stores there are any indication. Total exports of Korean ginseng were $63 million in 1977. The Hong Kong agent for Korean Red Ginseng products reportedly imported $15 million in red roots alone during 1977.

The American market is largely entrenched in convenience producets, and, since the development of various forms of packaged ginseng for tea use, there has been expanded interest here. But the US still accounts for a small fraction of world consumption— probably between $1.5 million and $2 million at importers' costs. Interestingly enough, we exported $26 million worth of American ginseng roots in 1977, mostly to the Orient. Cultivated American ginseng is considered a valuable botanical in Asia, but seems to be prescribed more for younger people, or those who don't require the vital-organ stimulation ascribed to Chinese and Korean ginseng.

In 1970, total exports of Korean ginseng products were $9.9 million. Korea's target volume for 1980 is $100 million. Although American interest is still limited, imports here have increased tenfold in six years. Why this phenomenal growth in an industry which was recently thought to be merely peripheral to natural foods?

**A booming market for ginseng**

First, of course, is publicity. Books, articles, reports, and the herb boom, of which ginseng was a forerunner, have increased the public awareness. Much information filters down suggesting that ginseng is a rejuvenator, heightens sexual potency, and magnifies concentration.

Next enters marketing. Salespeople suddenly began flooding the herb and natural food stores with new lines, heady claims, and effective merchandising tactics. Outlets which previously stocked a few ginseng items found believers among their customers, and allowed different brands of many items to appear on their shelves. Retailers began selling ginseng products to their customers more effectively. And satisfied customers told their friends.

# SCIENTIFIC STUDIES

But can the claims made in ginseng's behalf be proven? The Korean Ginseng Research Institute invited twenty-three research scientists to report their experimental findings with ginseng. Whether their work is conclusive or not can only be judged by one's interpretation of the evidence. Summarized, some of their findings are these:

- For the elderly: Ginseng clearly increased performance in untrainable physical tests; ginseng activated a 20% increase of some of the body's important synthetic processes such as protein, lipid, and nucleic acid synthesis; ginseng demonstrated an ability to help bring high blood pressure values and high blood sugar to normal levels.

- In experiments performed with mice, rats, or rabbits, the following results were indicated: Ginseng potentiated the adrenal responses to stress, and greatly increased the binding of corticosteroids to certain brain tissues. (Corticosteroids are thought to bind to brain tissues in order to increase alertness in addition to other functions, perhaps explaining ginseng's reported antifatigue action.)

- Mice injected with one type of leukemia cells which were then exposed to a ginseng extract for six hours or longer resulted in the death of about 99% of the leukemia cells.

**Testing ginseng's beneficial effects**

- Mice injected with one type of sarcoma cells (malignant) which were then exposed to ginseng extract survived twice as long as mice injected with sarcoma cells which were not treated at all.

- Mice given ginseng are able to swim significantly longer than mice not given ginseng, other factors being equal. (The Chinese have documented this observation independently.)

- In an experiment performed with rabbit hearts, findings indicated that ginseng accelerated protein synthesis and coronary flow while reducing the cardiac rate.

- Ginseng saponins fed to animals were observed to help effectively dissolve non-polar lipids such as triglycerides and cholesterol, dispersing and bringing them into better contact with enzymes, resulting in better hydrolysis of the lipids. The saponins dissipated considerably in the presence of cholesterol. It was also found that ginseng saponin stimulated the absorption of vitamins A and E, both of which are water insoluble.

- Rats and rabbits administered ginsenosides—physiologically active chemical components of ginseng—recovered from induced liver damage significantly more than the animals not treated with ginsenosides. The experiments involved intoxication and irradiation of the liver. Fifty percent more treated animals than untreated ones survived the induced damages. The treated animals also exhibited higher liver-protective capacities.

**Maintaining a high quality standard**

Besides these findings, there were reports of scientific work toward guaranteeing regular levels of pharmacologically-active components in ginseng products available for consumption by the consumer;

Standardized chemical evaluation of ginseng's components so that scientists will possess a common language for research in the field;

Biological control of ginseng root-rots with the addition of organic matter to the soil;

Analyses of many ginseng products on the world market, with facts presented that a high proportion of these are poor quality, and suggestions made as to how the standard of ginseng preparations can be improved;

Chemical studies of ginseng leaves, flowers, and fruit, indicating that both new and known saponins exist in relatively high yields in the aerial parts of the plants, which render these portions valuable medicinal sources;

The botanical history of ginseng in the world, with emphasis on future work toward hybridization, selection for better quality, higher yield, and more effective chemical contents so that humanity may continue to benefit further from ginseng use. It was suggested that all wild ginseng everywhere be declared an endangered plant group and protected from further uprooting, to create a fuller gene pool for the genus *Panax*.

The implications of most of this research remain unclear. The intention seems directed toward legitimizing ginseng in the eyes of Western science as an herb-food-pharmaceutical with various uses bordering on the medicinal. Perhaps not specifically medicinal in the sense of combatting illnesses characterized by definite symptoms, but, rather, the research could lead us (or the FDA, the pharmaceutical industry, and Western scientists) to believe that ginseng may be taken for a number of less specific reasons.

Despite the taxing difficulty of wading through the often nebulous stream of information about ginseng, one conclusion seems inescapable: that ginseng's pharmacological activities are generally construed as a panacea for numerous physiological problems. This explains why the FDA refuses to accept any labeling for ginseng products beyond "tea." Viewed as a drug, ginseng cannot be sold for consumer use in the USA. In combination with most other substances, ginseng products have been banned from import completely. Such mixtures are designated "New Drugs."

# WESTERN WAYS

The methods of Western science excel in isolating components or characteristics of a substance. Especially in the realm of pharmaceuticals, chemistry separates molecular structures from plants and minerals, attempts to synthesize these in the laboratory, and combine the synthesized ingredients in order to produce drugs beneficial in curing disease. With ginseng, this type of research is in its infancy. If huge pharmaceutical concerns with their modern laboratory capabilities and virtually unlimited funds have conducted experiments with ginseng, such information has not become publicly accessible. In light of revelations indicating the staggering profitability of the major pharmaceutical companies, why would they even be interested in ginseng? As a whole food or herb created by nature, anyone has access to the mysterious "Root of Life" without its passing through the diluting or strengthening apparatus of the laboratory.

Is it possible that efforts to legitimize ginseng in the West through modern scientific methods will backfire? The present ginseng researchers could plod along with little financing and eventually achieve pharmaceutical breakthroughs, only to watch the large conglomerates, who already conduct an estimated $40 billion worldwide business, steal their thunder. And what of the herb and natural food companies like Fmali, San Francisco Herb, and Sweethardt who struggled along, urging the government to allow the trade of whole, natural plants and working to convince them of botany's standing in the scientific tradition? Perhaps they will be resigned to trading in ginseng "tea" while the conglomerates hold reign over the very interesting herbal-based products capable of synergistic effects in the human organisms—products the Chinese already manufacture and sell in large volumes many places in the world, but not here.

Although the effects of Western scientific ginseng research on our industry remain to be seen, these investigations will hopefully enlighten us further regarding holistic health-promoting properties of this king of herbs. For several thousand years, Orientals believed it to be a tonic medicine *par excellence*, exceptionally useful in strengthening the human body against disease of all kinds, and improving the energies of vital organs. The name "Ginseng" appears in many Korean medicine books written as early as 100 B.C. Scientific investigation could well verify, in a Western frame of reference, the valuable properties of ginseng long recognized by Orientals, and could lend credence to ginseng in

**Ginseng cannot be sold as a drug in the US**

the public eye. But unless consistent standards of quality are upheld, the consumer will have the can of worms that presently exists—too many low-grade products incapable of producing the desired effects.

# COMPONENTS

While the symposium did not fulfill all the informational expectations held by the businesspeople present in regard to specific products and their potencies, certain facts and opinions were accessible through questioning Koreans in the ginseng trade. J.C. Lee, trading department manager for the Korean Ginseng Industrial Co., Ltd., the sales agent for packaged Office of Monopoly Red Ginseng products, informed me that Korean Red Ginseng Instant Tea is composed of a glucose-lactose mixture (88%) and concentrated red ginseng extract (12%). As the son of the president of one Korean white ginseng manufacturer, Mr. Lee also stated that company's instant white ginseng tea contained 12% ginseng extract in an identical glucose-lactose mixture.

Instant ginseng tea commands a large share of the ginseng sales in the US. In further discussing the many instant teas available with several knowledgable people in the trade, it became obvious that, for the public, there is no sure method of differentiating between high and low quality instant ginseng. Many Korean manufacturers, based upon their knowledge of the markets they strive to reach, decide how their tea should taste before determining ginseng content. Combinations of dextrose, lactose, and glucose are skillfully blended to taste more or less bitter or sweet, according to the potential customer's idea of quality ginseng taste. Most Americans appraise strong, bitter-tasting ginseng as high potency. In reality, only younger roots from two to four years old taste this way, and testing has repeatedly shown that these roots have considerably less of the active chemical components that six-year-old ginseng is known and prized for.

The consumer's lack of knowledge abets this situation. Instant tea costs the buyer 10-25 percent more than concentrated extract for the same amount of ginseng, and since less than 20 percent of the granules can be ginseng, instant teas cannot reflect true ginseng flavor anyway. One Korean company, which reportedly markets a strong instant costing three times the price of many other brands, claims that around 19 percent of their tea granules are concentrated ginseng extract. This concentration was sharply questioned by several Korean ginseng traders who indicated that other companies, in their experience, have attempted to elevate the ginseng extract levels in their instant granules, but the resulting mixture was too gummy to package.

# STAR ROOTS

Another area of much confusion with instant Korean ginseng is the recently-established four-star rating system. We were told that, effective immediately, there will be only three- and four-star teas exported. For the past year or so, instants could bear from one to four stars, supposedly signifying potency differences. Since there are no particular standards named for measuring the effects of high-potency ginseng in the human body, the system will apparently be rendered meaningless. Instant teas previously rated one-star will soon appear here as three- or four-star, with no change in content. All the claims made for the so-called highest quality four-star instant teas will again give way to the sales pitch ginseng salespeople often deliver.

Whatever the truth of ginseng content and potency in instant teas, the consumer who finds them beneficial would do well to add his own honey or (heaven forbid) sugar to concentrated extract if he wants value for his money.

Korean concentrated ginseng extract tea has always been a favorite of connoisseurs. Usually prepared by cooking the roots until a resinous liquid with 2-10 percent water remains, it offers purity and potency. Quality distinctions are more easily made, with the thicker, smoother-tasting concentrates leading the ranks. No concentrate tastes completely mellow, but sampling several will normally weed out the poor ones. Korean

Instant tea contains more than ginseng

Rating product potency

Red Ginseng Extract seems to set the standard, and many white ginseng companies try to duplicate its taste and quality, with doubtful success.

Clues to quality

Korean ginseng powder, whether in capsules or tablets, can be judged by the quality article's smooth, not-quite-sweet taste. Of course, powder is easily adulterated with fillers, and should be purchased carefully. Many ginseng powders are ground tails of younger roots, because the older bodies remain more valuable when left intact in the Orient. The thicker trunks of ginseng roots contain more potency than the tails. To be certain of receiving good powder, the best path is to purchase whole six-year-old roots and grind them yourself. The loss in convenience will be recovered in guaranteed quality.

If you're more enterprising, you can simmer your own roots for an hour or so to make tea. (Concentrated extract requires more elaborate methods that few people would undertake.) Most herbalists agree that teas can be absorbed by the body more readily than chewing fibrous plants, but if you like to chew roots, you'll still gain all the benefits of ginseng. Some Orientals choose large, man-shaped Korean roots if possible, believing in magical properties of ginseng which has assumed human form.

# PRICES

After establishing the quality of a ginseng product, you must know its value in the marketplace, whether you're buying or selling. Many factors come into play here, and the costs of ginseng products in Korea are noteworthy. For instance, Korean Red Extract sells for ten dollars in Korea. In Sweden, the same product sells for twenty-five dollars. In the US, Irving Enterprises, the importer of Korean Red Ginseng products, suggests a retail price of around fourteen dollars in 1978.

There are white ginseng extracts which sell for three dollars in Korea. Here, you are unlikely to find one under ten dollars, with one company's carrying a twenty-six dollar tag. In Korea, the same company's concentrate sells for about nine dollars.

Product prices vary from country to country

The Office of Monopoly recently announced a 20 percent price increase for all Korean white ginseng products, and is expected to hike red ginseng prices soon. While this many appear somewhat drastic, seeing entire ginseng counters in Korean department stores, and visiting shops there which handle only ginseng products, keeps such an increase more in perspective. Many of these retailers stock more ginseng than health food stores here stock vitamins.

The Chinese are also looking to raise their ginseng prices, but have been convinced such a move would be poorly timed right now. Only a few wholesalers offer Chinese or American ginseng to the natural food market in the US, and, until recently, marginal penetration had been achieved due to the higher costs and more limited product line available in these varieties.

Korea now exports ginseng to more than fifty countries. They are determined to expand their markets and gain the foremost status for their ginseng products—a place Koreans believe their ginseng rightly deserves. Certainly no other land possesses a richer ginseng heritage. And neither China, Japan, nor America has matched the collective drive of Korea's ginseng industry to mount the campaign.

The 1978 International Ginseng Symposium in Seoul was a well-coordinated, almost extravagant gathering dedicated to exchanging information, elucidating Korea's role in the world ginseng trade, and demonstrating the necessity of people involved with ginseng working more closely together. As Jae-Koo Ha, Director General of the Office of Monopoly put it, "Due to the pollution by industrial progress and production of chemicals, our environment is contaminated and our health and proper living are threatened. As a result, we are very anxious to seek after natural foods and medicines that will be universal . . . Now Korean Ginseng is not only Korea's, but the whole world's food and health medicine."

# *Consumer's Guide*

By law, retailers are not allowed to diagnose illness or to suggest treatments or cures. Customers who solicit medicinal advice about herbs are exposing store personnel to criminal prosecution for practicing medicine without a license. To learn more about the properties of an herb, ask for nutritional information or consult source books on herbal lore.

## HERBS

In determing the quality of bulk herbs, trust your senses. If the herb is dried out, has no aroma, and is full of foreign materials, the product is obviously not fresh.

- Whenever taking an item from a bulk bin, be sure to use the utensils provided by the store. Health department codes frown on customers sticking their hands into bulk bins because of possible contamination.

- To ensure optimum freshness, you can grow your own herbs. There is a wide range of herb seeds and plants available commercially.

- Federal law requires that all imported botanicals be fumigated.

- Ingredient lists also reveal hidden sweeteners, such as crystal malt, barley malt and corn syrup.

- Experiment with buying bulk herbs and making your own tea blends—that's how the tea companies got their favorite recipes!

- Herbal cigarettes may have nicotine in them.

- There are pet products on the market which are entirely herbal. To be sure of getting an herbal product, check the label of flea, tick and deworming preparations for chemical ingredients.

- Essential oils are colorless flavor concentrates distilled from volatile herbs through a steam process. Essential oils from grassy, woody and bitter root herbs are obtained through solvent extraction.

- In herbal cosmetics, check the ingredient list to see if the herbs are tacked on to a long list of chemicals or if it is really a major ingredient.

- Herbal cosmetics can be made easily at home. The book section of the local natural or health food store should have recipe books for herbal cosmetics.

- To preserve potency, herbs should be stored out of direct sunlight, in moisture-tight, air-tight containers, preferably in opaque glass or ceramic. Gasses can diffuse through plastic containers and affect the aroma and potency of herbs stored in them. Herbs should be kept dry, not refrigerated.

# GINSENG

Ginseng, the fabeled root from the Orient, is appearing on store shelves in a confusing array of products and forms, with an even more confusing array of claims being made for it. Information on ginseng can be found in *The Complete Book of Ginseng*, by Richard Heffern (Celestial Arts, Millbrae, California) and *The Ginseng Book*, by Louise Veninga (Big Trees Press, Felton, California).

- *Panax ginseng* from China is traditionally regarded as the most potent ginseng, but Chinese ginseng seldom finds its way into Western markets in large amounts. The recent improvement in trade relations with China may change this picture shortly. The elevated reputation of Chinese ginseng does not, however, mean that all ginseng from China is high quality.

- *Panax quinquefolium*, American ginseng, grows primarily in the Wisconsin area. American ginseng roots are generally harvested when they are four years old. On the ginseng market in Hong Kong, where international ginseng prices are set, American ginseng draws premium prices. With knowledgeable buyers setting such a high value on American ginseng, you might want to buy American when you buy ginseng.

- *Eleutherococcus*, or Siberian ginseng, is in the same botanical family as *Panax ginseng*, although some experts do not consider it to be a true ginseng. While *Panax ginseng* is considered a more active ginseng, Russian studies have indicated that *Eleutherococcus* has better stress-reducing properties.

- The Korean government's Office of Monopoly is the sole source of Korean Red Ginseng products, and the remainder of the roots are sold on the open market as Korean white ginseng. The normally-white root is turned red by a simple combination of steaming and drying; no chemicals are added. Reportedly, only six-year-old roots are used in red ginseng products.

- Despite some marketing claims, red dock, yellow dock and "wild red American ginseng" (canaigre) do not belong to the same botanical family as ginseng, cannot be cross-bred with ginseng, and are not considered to be ginseng by the Herb Trade Association.

- Concentrated ginseng extracts may be diluted with alcohol and may be flavored with honey or lemon. A taste test will tell. Undiluted extract is usually a dark brown and pours slowly out of the bottle. If a concentrate pours rapidly, it has probably been diluted with water or alcohol.

- Since ginseng capsules are supposed to contain only powdered ginseng root, they should have a bitter-sweet taste. Sweetener may be added to capsules to improve their taste. Your taste buds will tell the difference.

- Ginseng powder may be made from the "tails" on the ginseng root, rather than from the more potent main portion of the root. To ensure maximum potency, buy a ginseng root and powder it yourself.

- Instant ginseng teas are blended with sweeteners such as lactose, fructose or sucrose. Due to formulation requirements, instant ginseng teas contain, at most, 30 percent ginseng. Instant teas may cost from 10-25 percent more than concentrate extract for the same amount of ginseng.

- The Korean government uses a four-star rating system to differentiate the potency of ginseng teas. Since no strict standards exist for measuring these potencies, the rating system is of questionable value.

# Section VII: Cosmetics

Among the non-foods sold in natural foods stores, the most important are the personal care products loosely known as cosmetics. They are important to the retailer as a potential major source of income—falling just below vitamins and herbs in respect to dollar volume in the industry nationwide—and are important to the consumer as substances which will be used directly on their bodies. Cosmetics-users want the products to be safe as well as effective, especially when they are aware of the dangerous products which have at times been marketed by mainstream manufacturers.

Since the use of the terms "natural" and "herbal" has become popular on the bottles of personal care products sold through supermarkets and drug stores by major manufacturers, the consumer may wonder whether these brands differ from those sold in natural foods stores. A quick comparison of the lists of ingredients—lists now required by law—may not answer the question, because chemical names often occur on the ingredients lists of both kinds of products.

With few exceptions, commercial cosmetics cannot be manufactured and packaged successfully using unaltered natural ingredients alone. Plain vegetable or animal substances tend to spoil, stick, evaporate, feel funny, dry up, separate, or do dozens of other things which consumers find unacceptable—and some substances found in nature can be far more toxic or produce more allergic reactions than some invented chemicals.

The differences in drug store brands and the brands sold in natural foods stores are usually found in the relative amounts of natural ingredients, the types of chemicals included in the product, the use of bright artificial colors for eye-appeal, and the presence of artificial fragrances. The conscientious manufacturer of cosmetics for this industry cannot do impossible feats with natural materials, but does create blends of ingredients which do the intended job while reducing the risk to a minimum. Since adverse reactions to natural and artificial substances is a changeable, individual matter, the cosmetics supplier can aim for an ideal but cannot promise delight in every case. Even the person who makes do-it-yourself vegetable cosmetics in the home kitchen for immediate use may experience troublesome reactions.

Individuals vary so widely in their reactions to different cosmetic ingredients that personal experience is the only final test. This section of the *Guide* offers a discussion of the various kinds of ingredients found in these products, their reasons for being there, and includes a brief dictionary of common ingredients to help the consumer read the labels from an informed standpoint.

189

Henna, clay, and jojoba are now enjoying a special popularity in personal care products, and are among the few cosmetic products most accurately described as "natural." Each of these three products is discussed below its own chapter.

# 45

# *A New Face for Cosmetics*

## by Jim Schreiber

The ad in the cosmetics trade magazine shows a close-up profile of a delicate nose. The ad headline says, "Ah, that bewitching 8 alpha, 12-oxido-13,14,15, tetranorlabdane."

The implications of that advertisement suggest many of the reasons for the growing public interest in natural cosmetics: Consumers are becoming ever more concerned about what they put on their bodies; many sellers of cosmetics share that concern; and companies large and small are responding to that concern by offering products under the appealing "natural" banner.

A person looking into the history of cosmetics in the USA will find ample reasons for concern. The ongoing use of coal-tar dyes and other compounds has resulted in case after case of blinding, disfiguring, baldness, and various other injuries. Despite their pre-testing programs, such noted brands as Revlon, Avon, Richard Hudnut and Helena Rubinstein have sold products which were barred by the Food and Drug Administration because of injurious ingredients.

Only recently, after a delaying courtroom contest, has the FDA required complete listings of ingredients on cosmetics packages. Cosmetics packaged after April 15, 1977 were required to be fully labeled. This complete listing of ingredients is not designed to inspire confidence in the heart of a retailer or consumer looking for a natural product.

The cosmetics customer wants to look good, feel good, perhaps smell good, and certainly feel safe. Life-styles and attitudes toward health are among the factors that lead some consumers toward the "natural" cosmetics rather than the "commercial" cosmetics. But the customer concerned with health and safety can look at the label in a natural food store and find such items as cocamido propyl betaine and 2-bromo-2-nitropropane-1,3-diol among the ingredients of a bottle labeled Aloe Vera Shampoo.

This creates a real, immediate, and difficult problem for the conscientious retailer. Suddenly it seems necessary to be both a chemist and a physician to comprehend and merchandise a "simple," known-reliable product.

**Concern with health and safety of cosmetics**

190

Some cosmetics manufacturers—recognizing that many customers will show wide-eyed apprehension when reading a long chemical name—deliberately seek to change their formulations to avoid the alarming terms, using ingredients which sound less scary but do essentially the same job. That, by itself, does not necessarily make the product any more or less safe, any more or less natural. Even after such substitutions are made, a look at the shelves will show that the large majority of cosmetic products are at least partly the result of chemical processes.

Most cosmetics are invented by chemists

It may at first be embarrassing to the industry, but it is a fact that (1) most cosmetics are the inventions of chemists, (2) some cosmetic ingredients found in nature may be a lot more hazardous to users than some created in the laboratory, and (3) there is no way to tell, simply by examining the label, whether a product will be especially beneficial to a particular user.

# NATURAL ALLERGIES

Coconut oil and lanolin sound good and are straight from nature, but coconut oil gives many people skin rashes, and pure lanolin is notorious for producing skin sensitization, rashes, and allergic reactions. These two basic sources of many cosmetic ingredients are usually put through chemical reactions which greatly reduce their natural tendency to induce skin irritations of various kinds. On the other hand, triethanolamine (TEA) lauryl sulfate, a common, mild ingredient in shampoo and other cosmetics, is strictly a laboratory concoction, but is very much less likely to injure tissues than are coconut oil or lanolin. And while pentaerythritol tetraoctanoate has no record of toxicity, bay oil has been known to trigger allergies and irritations of the skin.

Soap results from the chemical interaction of alkalines and fats

Although the FDA does not define common soap as a cosmetic, soap is usually thought of as a cosmetic and is customarily included among cosmetics in stores. But soap does not occur in nature. The most ordinary soap results from the chemical interaction of alkalines and fats. Other soaps are made with the TEA mentioned above instead of an alkaline (which is usually sodium hydroxide), but even these mild soaps are inventions. Hopefully, even the most ardent devotee of natural products will not, because of this, shun the use of soap.

Consumer protection is the aim of the required listing of cosmetic ingredients, but that goal is not always realized. Because any single chemical compound may have many different names, the terms on the ingredients list have been standardized. As a result, a person with a known allergic reaction to Methyl p-Hydoxybenzoate might not recognize the same substance under the standard listing of Methylparaben. Chemical names are so diverse that dermatologists, reading the labels of suspected sources of their patients' problem, may have to talk with the manufacturer to track down the ingredients in a language dermatologists use. If these terms are a problem for medical doctors, it is no surprise that they are also a problem for retailers and consumers.

The term "fragrance" covers a range of potent, unidentified chemicals

Some people allege that even the extensive labeling now required is far from complete, partly because the word "fragrance" is allowed to cover a broad range of potent, unidentified chemicals. They want to know: Is this simply a successful evasion on the part of perfume makers, hiding behind "trade secrets?"

Fragrances often are carefully guarded trade secrets, but there is more to it than that. A fragrance in a tiny bottle may be a combination of more than 200 different chemical compounds, each of which may have a name as complex as that mentioned in the first paragraph of this chapter. To list them would require a large sheet attached to each bottle, a sheet sometimes as lengthy, and technical, and more obscure than the currently required enclosures with prescription drugs.

Shoppers at natural food stores are often curious about the products they see, and customer education is often an important part of what happends in such stores. It would help both the retailer and the consumer to have realistic expectations of what cosmetics manufacturers can and cannot do. It is possible to limit a store's stock to natural products like almond oil, honey, and henna—but all three have been known to cause allergic reactions. It might be possible, after careful research, to limit the stock to a handful of natural cosmetic items which have never been reported to produce toxic or allergic reactions. But it is not possible to limit the stock to items which will never cause a skin reaction on anyone: Allergies are individual and unpredictable. Toxicity can depend on dosage. Reactions to cosmetics are personal.

Cosmetics are personal in many ways, and this provides an opportunity to work with the customer as a unique person. Individual preferences and individual body chemistry both count in the selection of cosmetic products. A customer looking for "the best" might be interested to know that, for example, the best shampoo for people in their teens to mid-twenties might not be the best for older people, because people's hair tends to be oilier during those younger years. It might be "best" to alternate various types of shampoos; some protein shampoos might induce dryness along with body, so a milder herbal shampoo might be alternated with the protein to help relieve the dryness. Men's skin reacts and ages differently from women's skin. And a woman's chemistry may change during the month, with the result that the "best" cosmetic might change from week to week. These are some of the reasons it makes sense to advise customers to make several initial purchases in small quantities, allowing them to experiment to suit their own needs.

Individual body chemistry determines what cosmetic is best

Information about cosmetics is widely scattered, is often not complete, is sometimes contradictory, and is sometimes a matter of ongoing controversy. Cosmetics suppliers often provide explanatory lists of ingredients, and often do not make doubtful claims on their lists. The book *A Consumer's Dictionary of Cosmetic Ingredients*, written by Ruth Winter, lists compounds from Abietic Acid to Zirconyl Hydroxychloride. This is probably the best popular sourcebook on the subject although many people in the industry find its entries incomplete, often lacking answers to their questions.

Source books on cosmetics ingredients

The most authoritative source is *The Merck Index* of chemicals and drugs, available in most libraries. *Merck* lists the various chemical names, tells how they are made, says what they do, gives their various uses, indicates their toxicity, and much more. To use *Merck*, it's more efficient to consult the cross-reference section toward the back of the book first.

# DON'T SAY NATURAL

An administrator of one custom formulator of cosmetics said she would not want her company's products to be called "natural"—except, perhaps, for a few oils extracted from plants. She would limit the use of the word to materials which have been cleaned and purified by filtering, and nothing more. Very few cosmetic products fall within these limits. To make almost all cosmetics, molecules are taken apart and then put back together in a different arrangement.

Rearranging molecules

The distinction is probably clearest in fragrances. The small bottles of oil scents in the rack at the natural food store are probably completely natural, and the small bottles of perfumes in the rack at the department store are probably completely synthetic. But for most other kinds of cosmetics, the distinction becomes more difficult to make, with the difference being one of degree, direction, and intent.

Holding the bottles side by side shows many identical ingredients in most drug store and health food store shampoos. The most obvious difference is the liberal use of artificial D&C colors in the drug store brands, and a tendency to avoid synthetic coloring agents in health food store brands. In fact, this tendency not to use the gaudy, fake colors is one of the more usual characteristics of the natural-inclined brands. Sythetic colorings have been the source of much-publicized harm to customers in the past, and more D&C colors are being banned by the FDA, with many more under investigation as possible hazards. This is rather ironic, since the D&C colors are specifically listed as approved by the FDA.

D&C colors

The inclination of the concerned segment of the cosmetic industry is to use only ingredients of proven safety and reliability. Some manufacturers who now use some synthetic colors and fragrances are seriously considering ending their use entirely. The bright greens and golds and yellows which giant companies hope will sell their cosmetics to a mass market are a sharp visual contrast to the muted shades usually seen in natural food outlets, and that contrast may become even more thorough.

It is certainly "natural" for a cosmetics supplier to claim to offer a superior product.

Historically, the cosmetics trade in the USA has been willing to foster an image of wonders and miracles in a jar. Sometimes the claims have stretched the truth far enough to result in convictions for false advertising.

# EXOTIC ALLURE

The large companies which dominate the mass market in cosmetics have a way of not talking to inquiring journalists. Medium-sized manufacturers, however, are more willing to talk frankly about their products, and—whatever claims might be generated in promotion—the people closest to the actual production of the cosmetics are often the most modest in their claims. Chemists are not likely to talk about miracles, and middle-sized manufacturers do not have vast testing programs to verify the effectiveness or safety of each ingredient or final product. They rely on the general knowledge within the industry, and are not likely to launch investigations to confirm that cetyl alcohol really acts as an emollient and has a very low toxicity. In talking with people directly involved in making cosmetics, one receives the impression that the differences among brands are not very great, and that most companies are making good, safe products that do the basic job they are intended to do. Real differences will show up in the list of ingredients.

Differences among brands show up in ingredient lists

Consumers seem to be of two minds: they would like to believe that cosmetic ingredients can perform miracles, but they don't really believe it. A survey published by *Consumer Reports* indicated that "women simply expect a hand lotion or cream to prevent or treat dryness and to eliminate chapping or roughness," not to provide eternal youth or flawless beauty.

In keeping with the consumer interest in natural products, it is currently popular among cosmetics suppliers to point out that their products are derived from nature. Of course, a moment's thought will make it obvious that any substance is in some way derived from nature. The question to ask is this: In deriving it from nature, do any chemical reactions take place? If the answer is "No," then most people would be willing to call the product "natural." But this question still remains: How effective is it for its intended use, and does it have a history of toxicity or allergy production?

Questions about "natural" cosmetics

Allergies can take anyone by surprise. An individual can develop an allergic reaction to something which never caused a problem before—which is one reason a patch test is advised every time prior to use of allergenic chemicals like coal-tar derived hair dyes. The use of "hypoallergenic" cosmetics offers no guarantee, but does probably give the user more favorable odds. The FDA has a list of many dozens of substances which have a thick record of producing allergies. It has become a custom in the commercial cosmetics industry to call some products hypoallergenic if their ingredients are not on that list of allergens.

# RICH PRICES

In the past, some companies aiming at highbrow appeal have included such items as mink oil and turtle oil among the ingredients of special products. These cosmetics commanded a rich price, although subsequent tests showed that these oils were no more beneficial than salad oil or mineral oil.

An ongoing parade of exotic ingredients

The consumer quest for exotic ingredients with special properties goes on, even as there is a trend toward greater consumer awareness. Amino acids, vitamins, organic compounds, placenta, herbs, royal jelly, and proteins are among the materials now being given a special, honored place among ingredients. Most of these do have a use and a real effect in various cosmetic products, but there is no conclusive evidence that other materials cannot do essentially the same job. Again, personal preference and individual differences come into play. Some consumers might simply enjoy paying a premium for a special product. There was recently a cold cream that cost 1½ cents to make, and sold for $1.50 under one label and for $5 under another label. On the other hand, in the *Consumer Reports* survey mentioned above, a 7¢-per-ounce lotion was strongly preferred over a 49¢-per-ounce lotion. Users didn't know the price during the test.

Buyers of cosmetics in natural food stores might be especially prone to confusion about the word "organic." Such people are often seeking organic agricultural products. But in the cosmetics industry, the word "organic" can have an entirely different sense—a meaning used by chemists. In the vocabulary of chemistry, an organic compound is simply one containing the element carbon. To the chemist, gasoline, granulated sugar, and coal-tar dyes are all organic compounds. Calling a cosmetic "organic" does not tell whether it is natural, safe, or useful.

Herbs can add fragrance, make suds, lift off oils, soothe the skin, and add color to cosmetics—usually shampoo. The word "herbal" on the label is a currently hot marketing technique, popular among major manufacturers, but does not tell the whole story. The best-selling major brand of "herbal" shampoo contains the typical chemicals, including D&C colors. The ingredients list will show to what extent the product contains herbs, regardless of the words in large type on the front of the package.

A hair shaft is dead tissue. No amount of amino acid, vitamin, PABA or protein will bring it back to life. Hair conditioners of different kinds do, however, variously soften, shine, and add body to the hair. Moisture absorbed and retained by the hair will help keep it soft, but there is no conclusive evidence that proteins are absorbed into the hair and "rebuild" it from the inside. But as a coating outside the hair shaft, proteins can give added body.

# UNDER YOUR SKIN

A number of written sources, expressing scepticism about claims that cosmetics penetrate the skin, emphasize that the skin is a "natural barrier" against such penetration. Modern chemistry has learned to get through the barrier. A flavoring dissolved in the chemical DMSO can be placed on the skin and will be *tasted* a few seconds later. DMSO is barred from commercial use. But it is now known that vitamins and other substances spread on the surface of the skin will eventually show up in excreta. Vitamins do, in fact, penetrate the skin. It has not been established, however, that application to the skin has a direct and immediate effect on the cells they touch, although their benefit as part of the human diet is well known. This question of external application of vitamins is subject to further laboratory study.

Vitamin E is definitely useful as an anti-oxidant in cosmetic formulas, helping to prolong shelf life by retarding discoloration and rancidity.

Although it might have little appeal to vegetarians and many other persons, placenta has been an ingredient in some American cosmetics ever since 1958. The usual claim or implication was that placenta would revitalize tissues and help remove wrinkles. However, no investigations have shown that a cosmetic with placenta has any more benefits to the skin than the same cosmetic without the placenta. Another "exotic" ingredient, royal jelly, is an excellent nutrient when eaten, and has also been touted as a youth restorer, but again, there is no evidence to support the claim. As far as is known at this time, all nourishment of human cells takes place via the usual route, which customarily begins at the mouth.

Almost all cosmetics are variations on common themes. They are not all alike, and there is ample room for significant consumer choices, but the basic work of cosmetic products is almost universally done by a limited range of substances: emollients, surfactants, humectants, detergents, fragrances, preservatives, emulsifiers, and sudsing agents.

The specific types and blends of these substances determine their "feel"—whether they seem to be oily, sticky, creamy, vanishing, long-lasting, and other similar variables. Other ingredients can cool, tingle, or promote healing of injured skin.

While the new ingredients lists spotlight a previously obscure face to the consumer, the knowledgeable retailer can offer an immediate, direct and personalized special service to the curious customer—who probably doesn't expect miracles anyway. Cosmetics labels now certainly give the buyer and seller plenty to talk about.

# 46

# *Henna Heads Up*

## by Jim Schreiber

The popularity of henna today is largely a result of the consumers'
growing caution about applying synthesized chemicals to their bodies. Henna may provide
a safe, natural alternative for people who want to color or condition their hair, but who
have a wary eye on the true-life horror stories told about mass-market hair-care products
sold in drug stores.

Henna does have a track record perhaps 8,000 years long as a safe, effective cosmetic
and hair coloring. Even the federal Food and Drug Administration recognizes this. Taylor
Benson, marketing director at Helix Corporation, quotes an FDA source: "...of the many
plant extracts once used to color hair, only the henna plant is now permitted under FDA's
color additive regulation."

That leads straight to a surprising modern mystery: Just what is "the henna plant" and
that product called "henna" on the retailer's shelf? The surprise is that different
knowledgeable purveyors of henna to the natural foods trade have varying information
about the botanical source, or sources, of henna.

A brochure published by the Rainbow Research Co. says "Natural henna is the dried,
powdered leaves of the Alba Lawsonia, Lawsonia Inermis, or Lawsonia Spinosa. These
are small trees or shrubs native to southern and western Asia and North Africa."

Both the Avigal Henna Company's literature (1978) and Mrs. M. Grieve's *A Modern
Herbal* (1931) mention only *Lawsonia inermis* and *Lawsonia alba* as henna. Other sources refer
to *Lawsonia inermis* only.

Taylor Benson says that Helix, when originally trying to find out what henna is, "was
referred to Dr. J. Mahmoudi, a renowned Iranian botanist, who at that time was visiting
the University of Utah. Dr. Mahmoudi agreed to help us and, after testing the samples, he
determined that they were from three different plants: *Lawsonia inermis* (also *Lawsonia alba*
and *Lawsonia spinoza*) was the red henna, *Lyzifus spina christi*, the neutral, and *Indigofera
tinctora*, the black. All three are generically classified by the FDA and commonly marketed
as henna, and all have a long history of use for hair coloring and conditioning."

*An 8,000-year-long
track record for safety
and effectiveness*

*The botanical sources
of henna*

So, in this quiz, the best answer to date seems to be "All of the above." Apparently no studies have been done to discover whether certain of these plants are better than others as conditioners.

# A COAT OF MANY COLORS

How do they get so many colors? The answer depends on who you ask.

As long as the products sold under the label "henna" are unadulterated botanicals which provide the expected results effectively and safely, the classification of the plants themselves may be of only academic interest. A matter of somewhat greater concern is shown by purchasers who often ask the question, "How do they get so many colors? I thought henna just turns your hair *red*."

Again, the answer you get depends upon where you ask. Various magazine articles published recently state that different parts of the henna plant produce the different colors: red, black, and neutral. That is not the answer given these days by most officers of henna-product companies in the natural and health food industry.

As recently as late 1976, an article in *American Hairdresser/Salon Owner* scratched its head over this question: "How are so many shades possible if the henna bush is basically red? This is one of the many questions that is left to conflicting interpretations. Some say when different parts of the plant are ground, i.e., the flower, top leaves, limbs and roots, the results create somewhat different shades."

A *Modern Herbal* states that various shades can be obtained "by mixing with the leaves of other plants, such as indigo." As mentioned above, some sources include the indigo plant as a dyed-in-the-wool henna.

Biochemist Dennis Sepp, an executive of Trans-India Products, Inc., says that his studies have indicated that there is only one coloring agent in henna—that is, in *Lawsonia inermis*. That color, a "firebrick red," is produced by a specific molecule, which Sepp and other chemists have so far been unable to extract in an isolated form. He noted that the black hair-coloring has traditionally been indigo, at least as far back as the time of King Solomon.

Taylor Benson says, "When we at Helix began blending and packaging henna, we spent several months talking with other manufacturers, chemists and exporters, trying to determine the plant source of the three basic henna types used in all processing. It was explained to us by one manufacturer that these colors came from the root, stem and leaves of the henna plant. Another said they were three varieties of the same plant. None of these answers seemed to hold water.

"One major problem was obtaining samples of the three types in a natural state. No botanist could determine the nature of the plant after it was ground. After striking out several times, we received samples of relatively unprocessed henna from Iran."

It was those samples which Dr. Mahmoudi determined to be three different botanicals—all commonly accepted as henna. By blending powders from these three different plants, the processor can produce as many shades as desired, depending only on the degree of skill and care taken.

# IN THE MARKETPLACE

No standards of identity

In looking for the "real" henna, buyers have wondered about in-store tests of the genuine article. Some people expect all henna powder to be green in color—after all, it is the leaves of a plant—but some of the powders sold are almost black. Is that henna? To the firms which order it and import it from overseas, it certainly is. Since the written literature, the companies in the industry, and the trade organizations have not yet established any specific standards about what counts as henna, the question at this moment remains a technical one. Regardless of their shades, the hennas now sold widely in natural food stores have demonstrated a good record for safety.

"Some manufacturers added minerals to effect color changes," says Benson. "For example, red henna with iron oxide produces browns or blacks. Adding magnesium carbonate, peroxide and ammonia to henna produces the 'white henna' in vogue in the 20's. Too, there are liquid henna color preparations that use henna extract. Because henna extract doesn't impart much color and is usually clear to translucent-amber, and because these preparations are usually dark, opaque browns and purples, some questions have been raised about whether or not the main coloring agent is henna."

Henna extracts

Even before the henna reaches our shores from the Middle East or from the Indian sub-continent, the henna trader is wise to exercise some caution. As Dennis Sepp puts it, "All kinds of garbage can be added in Persia." Or at any other point of origin. ·

According to Sepp, Trans-India has a representative in India who buys their henna as a commodity on the open market, perhaps three tons at a time. Their representative supervises the grinding, making sure that no twigs are included to add bulk, and he sends a sample for inspection to the USA office. In Sepp's view, "the better quality henna comes from India."

Rainbow Research has a buyer go to Iran to inspect the product on site, according to Rainbow co-owner Tony Farish. (The other owner is Michael Hornfeld.) "We found that the best henna is out of the Persian Gulf area," Farish says. "Persian henna is the one supplied in the largest quantities to hair-care salons—at $25 to $35 a head—so you know it has to be good."

Imports from around the world

The Helix Co. also prefers the Persian sources, according to Benson: "Our purchases are contracted and shipped annually. We found the Persian henna was consistently the highest quality and the most reasonable in price."

Henna San is a product of Lambda, Inc., which has been in the henna business for 35 years. William Weiss, executive vice-president of Lambda, says, "We buy almost exclusively from Pakistan and Morocco, because so far we have developed the most reliable sources there. There's really not very much difference in the henna from different countries."

Albert Yusko, president of Le Vison Care products, Inc., points out that there are grades of henna, from AAA on down. "There's good stuff and there's garbage," he says. For persons worried about the possible presence of living organisms in the trans-ocean henna shipments, Yusko notes that it is fumigated before, during, and after it goes on the ship, "a total of four times."

# BACK IN THE USA

Once the henna arrives in the USA, what happens to it depends upon the focus, preferences, and marketing strategies of the firm that bought it. Although the FDA has shown no concern about henna, perhaps because it has no record of toxicity, Tony Farish says that comparative tests have shown "significant differences in bacteria counts among different products."

No record of toxicity

"Rainbow was the first to sterilize its henna," Farish says. "What we're looking for is a cosmetically clean product with a low bacteria count. For that reason, our henna goes through the same process as foods like herbs, grains and spices."

Henna powders apparently have no shelf-life problems, whatever the type of packaging used. On one hand, Rick Roen, president of Helix, remarks that henna will bleach out, and should be kept out of direct sunlight; on the other hand, Al Yusko remarks that 2000-year-old-henna still works if it is kept away from water.

At Lambda, "the main problem is color grading," according to William Weiss. "I'd guess that 99 percent of the companies [including those not in the natural foods trade] pay no attention to color grading. We color-check it very carefully. We take a random sample from the batch, test it on samples of hair, and check the color with a spectrophotometer"—a highly sensitive color-measuring device.

The problem of color grading

Rick Roen says, "Helix was one of the first companies to get into different colors. We found that the batches of henna differ, depending on things like climatic conditions which can affect the consistency of a whole year's batch. Chemist say they don't know how to test [for color] in advance, so we test it on samples of hair."

Quality control is carried out in different ways by different companies, ranging from scientific tests to the personal touch. Al Yusko at Le Vison does both:

"I've done my internship with this. I've been a retailer, and I was a hair colorist in the beauty shop business for 15 years, and I sold henna as a manufacturer's representative. And now I'm a manufacturer, and do private label packaging for other henna companies. I still supervise the mixing, and I have an organic chemist do testing."

**Quality control**

Since henna is a plant product, it is subject to all the local variations of weather, soil, climate, and other factors which affect vegetation. Offering a product which is consistent from one month to the next is a problem faced by all the henna companies. That is why many of the firms watch their colors so closely, and recommend in instructions to the consumer that a strand of hair be used to test the product before its application. A test on a small patch of skin is also advisable. Allergic reactions are rare, but possible.

# DO-IT-YOURSELF

Other variations in products arise not from nature but from the manufacturers' creation of a wide range of henna-based or henna-laced products to appeal to the shopper. Rainbow offers 11 shades of henna, a shampoo containing neutral henna, a neutral hair conditioner, and a cleansing bar containing henna and clay. Le Vison offers nine shades of henna, two different shampoos, two cream rinses, and three henna pre-mixes which the customer does not have to blend with water—and, according to Yusko, is now coming out with six more henna-based hair-care products. These are just two examples of what alert retailers already recognize as a trend; more and more products are being offered each year, often with attention to consumer convenience. As convenience, Helix includes a plastic cap and plastic gloves in every package.

**A trend toward convenience**

Although henna is admittedly a messy product to use at home, many customers prefer self-reliance to convenience. "There's a slow-down in henna in the beauty field," Al Yusko says. "The customer goes to the beauty shop to get a henna hair coloring, and it's a very messy process and she gets her head baked, and ends up saying, 'I should pay $35 to get abused?' It makes more sense to pay $3.75 for three ounces of henna and switch to self-service hair-care at home, maybe recruiting a teen-aged daughter to help out."

Not all companies are providing fine degrees of hues and varied products. For much of its history, Henna San was available in neutral only, and the red, brown and black were added to the line later. The self-service customer can blend their basic colors to attain whatever shade is desired.

Since the word "henna" is now rather magical, there is a chance that a tiny amount of henna may be added to some products for sales effects and little else. "Five percent in a product is not enough," says Dennis Sepp. "Trans-India's Henna Gold shampoo has henna as a *major* ingredient, and no other conditioning agents. We do an extraction of henna, so adulterants don't get in."

According to Rick Roen at Helix, "Henna has been put into a lot of shampoos—and they are mostly bogus. They may contain proteins, but not enough henna to make a difference. Trans-India has the best I've seen, and it's from henna."

The lack of standards for henna products is a point of frustration voiced by the officers of many henna companies in the natural and health food industry. Al Yusko says that some of the firms are trying to start an organization to set standards for the henna trade. With so many companies entering the field—"Everybody and his uncle seem to be in the business now," says William Weiss—the time is ripe to set standards for henna products.

**Clear, complete and cautious instructions for use**

Meanwhile, the purchaser can do little to test the products directly. As usual, the reputation, service, and information offered by the supplier will be the main basis for judgment. And one important item of advice was repeatedly offered by the people we interviewed. For henna hair coloring, the package should include clear, complete, cautious instructions for its use. That is apparently what the customer needs most: Instructions, instructions, instructions.

# Yo Ho Ho Jojoba

## by Janice Fillip

**"...and the desert shall rejoice and blossom like the rose."**

—Isaiah 35:1

The arid deserts of Baja and Sonora in Mexico, in southern California and Arizona, are forbidding lands. Seared to summer temperatures in the mid-hundreds, water is a desert mirage, shade a rare gift cast by wild shrubs. Only the hardy can survive these barren wastes.

The scrubby jojoba bush is among the hardy few. It not only grows, but flourishes, in areas of marginal soil fertility. An extensive tap-root system makes the plant drought-resistant and enables it to survive with less than five inches of rainfall a year for as long as 100—possibly 200—years.

But tenacity and longevity are not what is drawing science and industry into the desert to harvest and study the jojoba plant.

In its third year, the jojoba plant begins to bear fruit. Female flowers are pollinated—probably by the wind—in late summer. The fruit matures throughout the winter and spring. During the heat of the following summer, the green fruit dries, its outer skin shrivels and peels back to expose a wrinkled brown nut, resembling a coffee bean. In July and August, pickers enter the oven-like deserts to arduously hand-harvest these nuts. They are a renewable natural source of one of the finest industrial oils yet discovered.

The first potentially broad-scale agricultural crop to be introduced since soybeans, jojoba plants offer a way to turn wastelands into productive lands. A new industry is being spawned to develop applications for this valuable oil and to adapt it to already existing commercial uses. Jojoba may also contribute to the economic advancement of Native American reservations and to saving the endangered sperm whales.

*A renewable, natural source of high-grade industrial oil*

> # "Two or three years ago, people didn't know how to pronounce or spell 'jojoba.' Usually it takes generations before a crop becomes commercial. This crop is phenomenal."
> ## —Dr. D.M. Yermanos

The phenomenon can be traced to the oil contained in the jojoba nut. From 42 to 60 percent of the nut is an oil with a chemical structure very different from that of other vegetable oils. The "oil" is actually a polyunsaturated liquid wax, composed of straight-chain alcohols and free of the glyceride esters usually found in vegetable oils.

The chemical structure and lubricating properties of jojoba oil lend it to a number of applications, including lubrication of high speed machinery, high pressure gear boxes such as automobile transmissions, and delicate space industry instruments.

**Saving the whales**

Until the discovery of jojoba oil, top grade lubricating oil was derived from sperm whales. A clear, oily liquid called "spermaceti" was removed from a cavity in the front portion of the whale's head. On an average, one whale would yield one to two tons of liquid spermaceti, although yields ranged as high as 5.7 tons. The Marine Mammal Protection Act of 1972 prohibited killing sperm whales, and also prohibited the importation of sperm whale oil and its products.

The chemical structure and lubricating properties of jojoba oil and sperm whale oil were termed "virtual duplicates" by the National Academy of Sciences after a series of tests. Kelley Dwyer, executive vice president of Jojoba International, estimates that 13 barrels of jojoba oil or 6½ tons of jojoba seed would replace the amount of oil formerly obtained from one sperm whale.

Pharmaceutically, jojoba oil may prove to be a suitable coating for drugs. In cosmetics, jojoba oil is used as a chemical base for shampoo, soaps, hair care products, creams, sunscreen and suntan preparations, and lipsticks. According to USDA's Agricultural Research Services, jojoba oil is not toxic to mice, even when force-fed at extremely high levels. No indications of acute toxicity have been observed.

In addition to its chemical properties, jojoba oil is credited with having beneficial effects on skin and scalp conditions.

> # "There is a resistance among enlightened people to the actual facts about the oil. Because of its unique properties, it comes off sounding like snake oil."
> ## —David Noble

Is jojoba just another voguish ingredient being eyedropped into a variety of cosmetics to enhance their consumer appeal? The consensus of industry opinion seems to be that, while jojoba itself is not a shuck, some of the jojoba products *are* a jive.

**Therapeutic claims traced to Native American lore**

Therapeutic effects for jojoba are traced back to Native American lore. "In the literature of the Spanish missionaries, there are statements that the local people used jojoba oil for a variety of purposes, including cosmetics, cooking and medicinal," said Dr. D.M. Yermanos, professor of agronomy at UC Riverside's College of Natural and Agricultural Sciences, and the country's leading authority on jojoba.

Yermanos added, "There is no documented recent research to prove or disprove the claims. Whether it has a beneficial effect is something to establish. This information is not available for any cosmetic. The good things advertised, no one spends time to prove. You can capitalize on the folklore on jojoba without having proven anything. That is the usual business approach if you want to make some money."

In Mexico, Dr. Javier Gomez has spent forty years researching the effects of jojoba oil on hair loss and dandruff, but no double-blind studies have been done in this country. Dr. Thomas Sternberg, professor emeritus of dermatology at UCLA's School of Medicine, points out that jojoba "has been used since pre-Columbian times to stimulate and strengthen the hair. But this is not objective research. It's folk remedy." Dr. Sternberg does, however, recommend jojoba products to patients with scalp ailments, and finds the response to be "favorable in the sense of a non-objective valuation by patients."

The way in which jojoba is supposed to affect hair loss and dandruff is fairly simple. "There's no secret," said David Noble, founder of Noble Oil Company. "With an understanding of basic chemistry of the skin, it's no mystery how it works. The basic premise is that you want to put together something beneficial to the skin, something that behaves like the skin's natural protection.

"Sweat glands remove waste from the skin and work in cooling. Sebaceous glands are oil-based, giving a softness, lubricity, flexibility, acid mantle, and protecting from microbial attack. If you run an analysis on sebum [the fatty lubricant matter secreted by sebaceous glands], you turn up having a substance that is approximately 22 percent wax esters, according to one research paper.

"Jojoba oil in its pure state is over 97 percent pure, unsaturated, liquid wax esters. It's very much like the constituent that human skin makes to protect itself. It can help maintain moisture content, dissolve oxidized natural moisture, and is correlated with acne conditions." Noble said that tests were currently underway at a California university to verify the effects jojoba has on acne.

"I have seen half a dozen people who actually have brought hair growth back," Noble continued. "These are the exceptions, not the rule—when hair loss is directly related to secretions of the sebaceous glands which primarily just affects men.

"For the average person, jojoba gives lubricity to the hair shaft, you don't get the greasy feeling, it helps prevent split ends and other problems related to harsh detergent compounds. It helps prevent the feedback cycle where soap compounds defat the skin, remove the skin's protection, and the skin has to continually replace the protection which is often removed to a greater extent than is necessary."

## "People can take any shampoo put out by Proctor & Gamble and put a bit of jojoba in it. They are using the health food industry as a vehicle to make money."
## —Ernie Terrazas

The amount of jojoba used in a product varies with the type of product, formulation, intended use and cost of production. Products such as moisturing creams and lip balm tend to have more jojoba oil in them than shampoo, according to David Noble.

Gary Scaife, owner of Truly Natural Cosmetics which markets the Jojoba Hair Aid line, reported that there is a limit to the amount of jojoba which can be put into a formulation because of the weight of the wax esters. "When the mixture is too heavy, it goes to the bottom of the shampoo and becomes a big glob. Quality does not necessarily mean quantity. In shampoo, you have water, detergents, and conditioning agents. What goes into the product beyond that is never added in large quantities, but only enough to serve its purpose. With jojoba, a little bit goes a long way."

The oil used in jojoba products is derived from crushing jojoba nuts with an hydraulic or electric screw press. Oil is pressed out of the nuts leaving a jojoba meal residue. Solvent extraction methods similar to those used in producing refined vegetable oils (see the chapter on edible oils) can be used to remove the oil which remains in the meal. Oil obtained through solvent extraction goes primarily to industrial users.

The two major processors of jojoba oil for our industry are American Jojoba/Industry and Jojoba International, both in California. "We are trying to keep it cold pressed as best we can," said Bill Rivers, president of California Farm Management Company, the parent company for American Jojoba Industry. "We use a hydraulic press. We are setting up to take the oil in the meal out with hexane extraction. Most cosmetics buyers prefer pressed rather than solvent extracted oil."

Executive vice president Kelley Dwyer estimated that Jojoba International crushed over 50 tons of seeds in the last two years, producing over 100 55-gallon barrels of oil. Their production in 1979 is expected to double, Dwyer said.

**The crushing and filtering processes**

Dwyer explained that once the oil is pressed from the meal, it is filtered either mechanically, through paper or through diatomaceous earth, "depending on the client, what his requests are." While jojoba oil is virtually tasteless, with only a mild odor, it does have a light golden color. Dwyer said that diatomaceous earth clarifies the oil and is often used to filter oil earmarked for cosmetic purposes. "Our oil is considered totally organic for the health food market, with no chemicals," Dwyer said. "We do have a chemical process for industrial processing," he added.

Smaller processors such as Jojobatex in Arizona offer competition to the larger processors. Having just acquired an electric screw press, Jojobatex president Glen Shipley predicts that last year's 15,000 pound crushing will be greatly expanded this year.

Four-D Marketing Corp. is one of the few manufacturers of a line of personal care jojoba products which also has its own jojoba plantations and presses its own oil. Four-D uses a distillate from jojoba meal—rather than jojoba oil—in its line of Super de Jojoba products, according to Ernie Terrazas, company president and general manager. Terrazas explained that the jojoba meal is fermented for 90 days to produce a "tincture of herb." This tincture is used instead of water in Super de Jojoba products. "We use very little jojoba oil in the shampoos as a lubricant. When we make other products, we use the same fermented water," Terrazas said.

**Solvent extraction**

Jojoba oil processed in Mexico may be solvent extracted. "With Mexican jojoba, the filtering process isn't so good. The oil has to be refiltered," according to Gary Scaife.

Terrazas maintained that Mexican oil may also be cut with cottonseed oil. "A lot of people are buying contaminated oil," he said. "If it has less than a one percent acid level, it is acceptable for facial use. If the acid goes up, it can be harmful to the face. When it is cut with cottonseed oil, the acid goes up six or seven percent."

To ensure he is not using contaminated oil, Terrazas tests oil for iodine value, acidity, peroxide value, moisture, and the presence of solvent. When a manufacturer is not certain of the purity of the oil, Scaife cautions, "It is worth the time to take it through a test, to see if it separates out. That can be found out within an hour of receipt of the product."

It may be worth more than time for manufacturers to ensure the purity of their ingredients. Having spent years researching jojoba at the University of Arizona's department of Arid Land Studies, Dr. Jack Johnson decided, out of curiosity, to have a sampling of jojoba products analyzed. "Some did not contain jojoba," Dr. Johnson discovered. "We are making that information available to the Arizona Attorney General. I'll be darned if I'll sit back and see dishonest crooks benefit."

**Gauging the quality of jojoba products**

How can buyers gauge the quality of jojoba products? "The ingredient listing is your only clue," according to David Noble, "although it's not 100 percent sure-fire. Pick up a book on cosmetic ingredients and get an idea of what emulsifiers are. Some common emulsifiers are glycerine monostearate, stearic acid, and triethanolamine (TEA). Then glimpse the ingredient listing, which gives the order of concentration. Generally, if jojoba oil is listed above the emulsifier in concentration, odds are they're not skimping on the ingredients. If jojoba oil is below the emulsifier, it could be an infinitesimal amount.

## "In some cases, the cost of jojoba exceeds the sum total of everything else in the bottles." —David Noble

With retail prices in 1979 ranging from $3 to $8 an ounce, jojoba is an expensive oil. According to Bill Rivers, it takes about 20 pounds of nuts to produce one gallon of jojoba oil. Working under extreme climatic conditions, pickers average from 4 to 5 pounds an hour, and are paid about $3 an hour. Much of the wild jojoba grows in Mexico. "In Mexico, where labor is traditionally cheaper, we pay 70 to 80 pesoes a kilo for nuts—more than even the Mexican government pays," said Dwyer.

Processors pay from $1.30 to $2 a pound for wild nuts. "Last year the market got wild with the boom coming on," recalled Ernie Terrazas. "Prices went up to $3.50 a pound for seed, which makes it a prohibitive oil. Things have gotten hairy the last year or so because there are so many speculators who don't look at it as a solid business, but see it as a fast buck."

A solid business or a fast buck?

Manufacturers pay processors from $65 to $75 a gallon for pure jojoba oil. Kelley Dwyer estimates that it costs about $40 a gallon to squeeze and filter the oil, before overhead and transportation costs are added. "We're producers and distributors of our own oil," Dwyer said. "The people who we sell our oil to have a markup of 10 percent to 50 percent for their own margins."

Almost all the jojoba oil now used comes from wild bushes. To meet the mushrooming demand for oil and to guarantee a constant, reliable supply, jojoba plantations are being established in desert regions. Since it takes a jojoba plant at least three years to bear fruit, five years to become commercially profitable, and ten to twelve years to reach peak production, supply will probably not equal demand for a number of years.

# "Jojoba bean fever is the only disease that can be transmitted over the telephone." —Kelley Dwyer

Jojoba plantations were first started in 1972, "specifically as an Indian economic development program," according to William Miller, special projects officer for the Office of Tribal Resource Development, Bureau of Indian Affairs. "The tribes went through the council process and passed a resolution to participate. There was no question about the eagerness and enthusiasm of the tribal governments."

An Indian economic development program

Twelve California and three Arizona tribes have begun growing jojoba at the Pauma, Morongo and Cabazon reservations in California and the San Carlos Apache reservation in Arizona. The project has run into some funding problems, Miller explained. Tribes need technical and management assistance programs, and must be educated and trained to an increased level of agricultural expertise, Miller said. Sufficient funds have not been allocated for large-scale reservation development, he added.

Private individuals and groups are investing in jojoba plantations in hopes of supplying the increasing demand for jojoba oil. The plants seem to thrive under cultivation, requiring little care. Experiments are underway to determine what varieties produce the highest yield of nuts, and efforts are being made to adapt tree nut harvesting equipment to jojoba nuts.

After completing a survey of jojoba plantations, Dr. Jack Johnson estimated, "At best, we can guess at a total of 5,000 acres. It is almost impossible to tell their status because they haven't been in the ground long enough to bear seeds."

Stelmon King began an experimental plantation three years ago and now sells seedlings through his nursery in Ceres, California. "I've been a farmer in the area for 30 years and was always looking for a crop that takes less care and gives more return per acre," he said. "The interest in jojoba plantations is quite strong. Private investors are willing to invest on speculation."

Jojoba plantations— investment or speculation?

King estimates the cost of plants and labor to establish a plantation runs about $600 per acre, not including land. Dwyer puts the estimation somewhat higher, at $750. Costs are judged to be similar or equivalent to those for almond, pistachio and nut tree plantations—all of which also require a number of years before they bear fruit.

Jojoba International is selling complete jojoba plantations in Desert City, California, including plants, land, water rights, deeds and easements. "We're taking marginal land and putting it to use," Dwyer said. "In selecting areas where the environment is conducive to jojoba growing, there has been an increase in the price of land. When people flock to an area, prices are going to go up. It's still more reasonable than buying a quarteracre in LA and building a house on it."

According to Dr. Johnson, plantations have risks as well as benefits: "So many people are involved in jojoba that don't know farming. There are failures who have been sold a bill of goods or have an ignorance of farming. This was the coldest winter on record and it wiped out a number of growers. Amateurs usually watered until the freeze, and had a pulpy, water-soaked plant. The professional farmers withdrew the water."

**A booming industry**

Jojoba is a booming industry. Once a sustained supply can be demonstrated, most observers expect large industry to leap into the jojoba market. Meanwhile, in the words of Kelley Dwyer, "There is still room for the little guy. Entrepreneurs are what's making this industry go now."

● Jojoba World Trade Association, c/o Lee Edwards, 332 Kalmia, San Diego, CA 92101. Annual dues: $20.

● *Jojoba Happenings*, a scientific journal with grower information. Published quarterly. $10 year subscription. University of Arizona, 845 North Park Ave., Tucson, AZ 85719.

● *Jojoba Grower Advisor*, 855 Linden Ave., Carpinteria, CA 93103. Published by Jojoba International.

● Free information packets on whales are available from Christine Gonsalves, General Whale, P.O. Box Whales, Alameda, CA 94501.

# Clay: Sister to the Sea

## by Warren Raysor

In recent years, minerals have been spotlighted as necessary elements for healthy living. This interest has brought increasing attention to the number-one mineral—clay.

Clay is a general term used to describe a natural powder composed of very fine particles. There are many kinds of clay and each is a natural blend of minerals. It was with the opening of the China trade to European markets centuries ago that clay became popular as a cosmetic. China supplied European royalty with a pure white clay from Mt. Kaolin in China. The powdered wigs and pale faces of the aristocracy owe this to the white clay of China. Europe was hard pressed to find deposits of white clay of 'kaolin' quality.

It was the discovery of kaolin in the American frontier which supported growth of cosmetic powders geared toward a mass market. The pure white clay takes on color easily with the addition of dyes and pigments, moulds well into cakes, and forms an excellent cream body. These qualities gave birth to many powders, rouges, foundations, shadows, pastes, and creams of primary importance to the cosmetic industry.

The new direction of clay as a healthy or healing body pack is a reflection of the ancient use of clay as a medicine. Many medicinal applications of clay have reportedly shown excellent results. Healing successes lead one to believe that clay offers a frontier of undiscovered benefits to healthy living.

**Clay helped open China trade to Europe**

## THE CREATION OF CLAY

Clay is one of the two end products of the geological evolution of the Earth. The other end product is the mineral-rich sea. The processing of Nature's clay begins with the forming of the Earth. In the remote past, our planet was a fiery mass of molten material. The forces of gravity made the various minerals of our once molten ball seek uniform levels of strata. The lighter elements floated on the top, the heavier ones sank towards the center in the way oil and water separate.

As the Earth cooled, a crust formed, becoming a hard layer of rock between the liquid center and the vaporous atmosphere. Because of the layered arrangement of the minerals, the surface is mostly composed of only a small number of the minerals known to exist. These are the oxides of silica and aluminum, which make up over 50 percent of the surface layer, and the mineral classes of iron, calcium, sodium, magnesium, potassium, and hydrogen. The remainder of the elements make up less than three percent of the top layer.

When the surface of the Earth had cooled sufficiently, the vaporous atmosphere condensed. Science reports that millions of years passed as a torrential rain hammered the cooling planet. This storm actually disintegrated much of the rock-hard surface. The water dissolved most of the soluble minerals and washed them away to form the salty seas.

Great volcanic activity and earth-shifting quakes further added to the grinding of the rock into superfine powders, and developed geographic pockets which captured the small particles. These settled to form the clay deposits of today. The unique histories and mineral origins of the many clay deposits provide a wide assortment of mineral powders. Some deposits are vast, while some are secretive and small, and many are undiscovered. Small deposits of clay can be found in riverbeds and streams where a few shovels full can be mined. This is a unique way of collecting a personal supply.

For commercial purposes, a deposit must be larger. A large deposit will give clean selections of a number of clay grades. These large basins of clay offer a wide selection of types for the clay-using markets; ceramic, cosmetic, and industrial. In addition to these large operations, there are many small mining claims which offer special clays to the health market. These clays are usually of excellent quality. Due to their limited production facilities and usually remote geography, the prices are high, easily $15 to $50 per pound.

The most basic clay is the white mineral called kaolinite. It is composed in total of silica and aluminum oxides. This is a pure form and is rarely found in nature. The term "kaolin," from the Chinese, is used to describe white clays which contain few additional minerals in their makeup.

# ITS GENERAL COMPOSITION

Clay composition reflects the minerals of the Earth's surface. This comparison will demonstrate the general relationship.

| Element | The Earth % | Indian Red Clay % |
|---|---|---|
| silica | 59.14 | 57.02 |
| aluminum | 15.34 | 19.15 |
| iron | 6.88 | 6.70 |
| magnesium | 3.49 | 3.08 |
| calcium | 5.08 | 4.26 |
| sodium | 3.84 | 2.38 |
| potassium | 3.13 | 2.03 |
| hydrogen | 1.15 | 3.45 |
| titanium | 1.05 | .91 |
| combined traces | .90 | 1.02 |

In general, raw clay is removed from a vein of pure clay material, and is without contamination of other earth material. If it is moist, it is allowed to dry. Then it is milled, screened and bagged for the market. Clays which show color are those which are rich in mineral contents. Most clays are rich in minerals and show many colors—red, green, blue, yellow, and all manner of greys and browns.

The physical structure of clay is very interesting. Electron microscopes show the particles to measure as large as 3 microns and as small as .04 microns in size. (A micron is one thousandth of a millimeter.) Particles of this size will pass through a screen which will hold water. The particle shape is dishlike, flat and crystalline. Clay, in fact, is a crystal. The thin, flat particles create a large surface area, and it is this feature that allows the clay to join together with water in a tight hydrobond, much like two wet pieces of paper. As the water separates the particles, the volume increases; as the clay body dries and the water evaporates, the volume decreases. This shrinking action causes a unified contraction. It is this mechanical action which creates the tightening mask of the clay.

# KAOLIN AND BENTONITE

Kaolin and bentonite are the two minerals most widely used in popular cosmetics. Both are usually referred to as clays but, technically, bentonite is not a clay. Their difference only lies in their structure. They are both composed of silica and aluminum. Kaolinite has the silica molecule sandwiched between aluminum molecules.

Bentonite is a volcanic product, and is only rarely found with other mineral companions. It is composed of extremely fine particles, mostly of colloidal sizes ranging in the measurements of millimicrons, the smallest whole earth particles known to exist. It is hard to mix with water will absorb over 20 times its weight in liquid and remain a powder. A small amount of bentonite in water will cause it to gel. The small particles carry an electrical charge which keeps them suspended in solution. This action also keeps waters, oils, pigments, etc., in suspension.

A limited variety of fine earth powders always were available, mostly featured on the bottom shelves of health food stores. In the past few years, clay has been given a place in many feature articles, and advertising has excited a wide audience. Many large, established cosmetic companies now feature a clay line.

Products featuring clay as an ingredient include facial packs, shampoos, toothpastes, and deodorants. Most clay preparations for sale in the ready-to-use 'wet' condition contain many ingredients other than clay. Laws require preservatives and anti-fungus additives. Many products use certified colors to tint the naturally white kaolin. The convenience of the pre-mixes is shadowed by this sensitive problem. Clay powders, on the other hand, are gaining in popularity because of their pureness. They are not spoilable, and mix easily with water. Clays in the powder form are usually not adulterated with other ingredients.

# CLAY USES

The internal use of clay is also getting widespread attention. As a rule of thumb, clay is non-toxic. Bentonite has been used as a food additive, and clays have been used as a filler and binder in oral tablets. The argument that clay can be used as a dietary supplement presents this as a general case: that people should eat from the three kingdoms, animal, vegetable, and mineral. Eating of the mineral kingdom may sound a bit gritty, but the chief source of mineral kingdom eating is water. It comes to many as a surprise that the mineral kingdom suddenly shows itself as a large part of the diet! Unfortunately, city purification plants have thoroughly filtered the natural earth waters of its vital solution—clay. It can be proposed that this could be a source problem for mineral deficiencies. Supplementing the body's need for mineral silt may become a new boon for the vitamin companies. Many surprising and significant results have been reported, but these exist mainly on a grassroots level.

Customers will often want to know how to use a clay mask, and what effects to expect. As with most new products, an understanding of the use of clay will help the customer feel good about trying something new.

Clays have been used for centuries by all peoples. The medicinal properties as well as the cosmetic uses have been extolled by the greatest authorities. Using clay as a body pack is almost a natural instinct. Ask anyone who has bathed in one of nature's hot springs, where colorful moist clay deposits were found, if they used the clay. Stories of mud-pack heaven will undoubtedly be told.

The wonder of clay as a facial or body treatment is that it works on both sides of the skin to promote an intensive revitalization of the tissue. The tight mask of the clay forms a dramatic "suction" action over the skin area. This draws the blood deep into the skin, which stimulates tissue regeneration from the inside out. This effect on the circulation is of primary importance. A few millimeters beneath the skin lies an extensive network of tiny blood vessels which serves to nourish the cell tissue. The problem of skin aging and skin disease is many times due to the sluggish circulation of nourishing blood into the feeding capillaries. The drying clay acts as a deep massage and gently, but firmly, brings the circulation to the surface. The clay mask is ideal for the face because a hand massage firm enough to stimulate the circulation would be too rough for the face tissue. Blood-purifying supplements and teas can be used in conjuntion with clay packs. Since the clay works with the blood from the outside, it is logical to build the blood vitality with good nutrition, especially during medicinal clay treatments.

On the outer surface of the skin, clay acts as a deep cleanser. It absorbs excess oils and dirt particles, and cleans the surface of encrusted dead skin cells. A program of continued use can unclog the skin's natural oil ducts and restore a dull complexion with healthy tissue.

The color therapy effects may have value also, but these effects may require an element of belief. Unknowns aside, what is important are the results, dramatic improvements in skin texture with a glow of healthy tissue. You can feel the difference after the first experience.

# PREPARATIONS

Simple clay preparations are both easy and exciting. Here are a few hints.

To prepare clay powders for use, just add water until a soft cream is made. For foolproof results, follow this method: Put a small amount of clay powder in a bowl or jar. Add one tablespoon of water for every two tablespoons of clay in the bowl. (For larger amounts, keep the ratio of two parts clay to one part water, by volume.) Allow the clay to absorb the water. This will take about 5 to 10 minutes. If the clay is dry on the top after this time, add a little more water. If there is excess water added, it will not be absorbed by the clay and will float on top. Pour this excess off. The perfect cream results from this method. No stirring is required.

This clay will remain in a ready-to-use state for many months if the container is closed tightly. If drying occurs, the clay springs back to consistency with a little water. The clay quality actually improves with age as the water separates the clay particles. After about one month, maximum separation is achieved. On the connoisseur level, aged clay is the most ideal for skin applications.

You should choose your clay on the basis of your skin type. A person with a fair or dry skin should choose a mild, light-colored clay. For a normal complexion, use a tan or darker clay. A person with darker or oily skin should choose a strong-bodied red clay. Remember, the light-colored clays are for mild masks, while the darker clays make strong tightening masks.

The pure water and clay mask works wonderfully, but the clay powders lend themselves to addition of other ingredients by the inventive customer. A spoonful of honey dissolved in the water before mixing the clay provides an excellent moisture mask. Milk, cream, egg, fruit or vegetable juice, and powdered herbs make good additional ingredients. Formulas like these cannot be saved for a long time, because the organic matter will spoil. Working with clay powders is simple, natural, pure — and instant!

Senior skin types should try this simple but amazing formula: Choose a mild clay and blend it into a cream with "fresh strawberry" puree. A little honey can be added as a moisturizing agent. Apply the mask and allow to dry. After it is rinsed off, the user won't believe the mirror!

Very few people will show an adverse reaction to clay. It is simply a non-toxic substance. Adverse effects should not be confused with stimulation. Often a flush will remain on the face after a clay pack. This shows circulation activity. Sometimes the skin will be stimulated to eliminate toxic buildups under the skin. Continued use of clay packs will eliminate the waste quickly and cleanly. A bad reaction to a clay pack would be more likely from a pre-mix where other ingredients come into play. Pure clays will not harm even the most sensitive skin.

**A non-toxic substance**

Owing to the extensive advertising campaigns and reading material focused on clay, the clay business is growing. The well-founded "magic" of the mineral kingdom is gaining a satisfied following, and seems to be supporting commercial expansion. The simple word —clay— is being used more and more as a market tool. Even products which always contained kaolin are giving "clay" bold-type billing on the label.

**An advertising buzz-word**

As clay grows in popularity as a cosmetic and cleanser, an interesting question arises! Are all the naturally-occurring clays just clay, or are there many different purposes for the hundreds of natural formulations and blends? No one has the answer yet, so feel free to experiments on your own with one of nature's oldest, safest cosmetics—clay.

# 49
# Cosmetic Ingredients Dictionary

A

**Acetylated Lanolin Alcohol**   Natural lanolin which has been processed into a hypoallergenic form. Used as a softener of skin or hair. Reports of allergic reactions are rare.

**Acid (or Non-Alkaline)**   A compound producing hydrogen ions in aqueous solution. Acidic refers to a pH below 7.0. The pH of hair and skin is normally between 4.0 and 6.0. Proper pH level is effective in helping control skin bacteria and maintain healthy skin. Harsh alkaline cosmetics or alkaline soaps can upset natural pH balance.

**Alcohol**   Usually liquid such as ethyl alcohol that is made by fermentation of starch, sugar and other carbohydrates. Used in skin lotions and numerous other cosmetics. Since it dissolves fat, strong alcoholic solutions can dry skin or hair.

**Alkaline**   Solutions have a pH above 7.0. Most detergents and soaps are alkaline.

**Allantoin**   Originally extracted from comfrey plant root. Used as skin soothing agent and as treatment to promote healing in minor cuts, burns, sunburns, etc. May be synthetically prepared from uric acid. Non-toxic.

**Almond Oil**   Natural nut oil high in fatty acids. Absorbed more easily than filmforming mineral oil. No toxicity on record. Reports of some allergic reactions.

**Aloe Vera**   Extract from leaves of the Aloe Vera plant is used to soothe and protect skin. Alleged to promote healing in skin. No toxicity on record when used externally.

**Aluminum Allantoinate**   Combines astringency of aluminum with action of allantoin for beneficial effect on acne and skin irritation.

**Ammonium Lauryl Sulfate**   A surfactant. Grease-cutting ability may produce dry skin. Generally nontoxic when used externally.

**Amphoteric (1 through 12)**   Surfactants which can be either synthetic or derived from coconut oil. A nitrogen compound capable of reacting either as an electro-positive (cation) agent or as an electro-negative (anion) agent. Acts to even out the electrical charges of the hair shaft. Reduces surface tension, facilitating contact between surfaces. Used with detergents.

**Anhydrous Lanolin**   Protective and water absorbable base containing much less water than hydrous lanolin (regular lanolin from wool fat).

**Antioxidant**   A material, such as vitamin E, that inhibits the oxidation that can turn a cosmetic rancid.

**Apple Cider Vinegar**   Separates and frees individual hairs to allow a more thorough wash. A solvent in creams and oils. No toxicity on record.

**Apricot Kernel Oil**   Natural oil of the apricot (persic oil) which leaves no oily film on skin. No toxicity on record.

**Argil**   Clay of micro-molecular structure that absorbs impurities.

**Avocado Oil**   Natural oil of the avocado. Skin softener and conditioner which leaves no oily film on skin. No toxicity on record.

**Balm Mint Extract**   Liquid extract of balm mint, a fragrant herb with skin and scalp soothing properties. No toxicity on record.

**Beeswax**   Natural wax useful in preparation of creams and lotions, primarily as an emulsifier. Nontoxic.

**Bentonite**   Naturally occurring clay used for "drawing" ability in facial masks. Generally nontoxic.

**Benzalkonium Chloride (BAK)**   Organic nitrogen detergent compound which acts as a preservative against bacteria and mold. Reports of allergic reactions if in eye lotions.

**Benzophenone (1 through 12)**   Used to prevent color deterioration in cosmetics. Protects against ultra-violet light (from sunlight and fluorescent light). Normal usage is slight, usually less than 0.1% by weight.

**BHA (Butylated Hydroxyanisole)** and **BHT (Butylated Hydroxythluene)**   Synthetic anti-oxidants often used to prevent oxidation of oils in cosmetics. Use limited by FDA. Reports of allergic reactions.

**2-Bromo-2 Nitropropane-1, 3-Diol**   Strong synthetic preservative and solvent used in many cosmetics. Many produce formaldahyde or bromo compounds in solution. Not effective at high pH values. Reports of irritation to mucous membranes and allergic reactions.

**Butyl Paraben**   Preservative used to prevent mold growth and extend shelf life. Low toxicity.

**Camomile Extract**   Used to bring forth natural highlights of hair. No toxicity on record when used externally.

**Candelilla Wax**   Derived from the Candella plant and used as a thickener. No toxicity on record.

**Carbomer 934** and **940**   Resins used to thicken, stabilize, prevent freeze damage and prolong shelf life of cosmetics. No toxicity on record.

**Carnauba Wax**   Derived from the Brazilian wax palm tree. Used for gloss and texture. Reports of allergic reactions rare.

**Carrot Oil**   Natural extract of the carrot, used as a natural coloring agent, high in vitamin A. No toxicity on record.

**Castor Oil**   From the castor bean. Used in some masks, night creams and lipsticks. Soothing to the skin. Found in most lipsticks.

**Cellulose Gums**   From plant fibers. Used as emulsifier in cosmetic creams to help provide uniform viscosity. "Methocel" (methylcellulose). No toxicity on record.

**Ceresin Wax**   Natural earth wax used as an emulsifier and thickener. Reports of allergic reactions.

**Cetearyl Alcohol**   Combination of alcohols distilled from plants. Used as an emulsifier and emollient. No toxicity on record.

**Cetrimonium Bromide**   A salt derived from ammonia used as a detergent and topical antiseptic. Reports of skin and eye irritations.

**Cetyl Alcohol**   A wax-like substance which helps emulsify oils into a water base. Derived from coconut oil or produced synthetically. Very low toxicity externally and internally.

**Cholesterol**   Chemical occurring in skin and essential part of the oil in the skin. Synthetic cholesterol is often used in cosmetics to provide moisturizing effect. Nontoxic when used externally.

**Chlorophyllin**   (Chlorophyll) Derived from plants. Used as a freshener and natural color. Can promote sensitivity to light.

**Cinoxate**   A sun screen. Cinnamate or cinamic acid as in cinnamon. Reports of allergic reaction.

**Citric Acid**   Derived from citrus fruit by fermentation of crude sugar. Employed to prevent color, texture or appearance changes in cosmetics. Helps adjust the pH. No toxicity on record.

**Cocamide DEA**   A coconut oil based lather-builder and thickening base. Reports of skin irritation.

**Cocamido Propyl Betaine**   Derived from the salts in coconut oil and used as a foaming and cleansing agent. Reports of skin irritation.

**Coca Butter**   A solid (fat) obtained from roasted seeds of Theobromer Cacao. Used as an emollient in cosmetics. Melts at body temperature. Reports of allergic reactions.

**Coco Betaine**   Mild surfacant derived from coconut oil.

**Coconut Oil**   An excellent moisturizer which serves as a protective layer retaining the moisture within the skin. Reports of allergic reactions.

**Collagen Protein**   Derived by hydrolyzing animal collagen from the dermal layer of the skin. Protein used for hair and skin. No toxicity on record.

**D**

**D & C Colors**   D & C colors are those approved for use in drugs and cosmetics by the FDA. Some contain coal tar dyes, whose safety is subject to controversy.

**Decyl Oleate**   Naturally based ingredient often derived from coconut, used to help the skin absorb cosmetic oils. No toxicity on record when used externally.

**Dimethicone**   An inert silicone-type fluid used to produce a good "slip" and "feel" in cosmetics. It contributes a degree of water repellancy and leaves soft, smooth feeling without being sticky or oily. Toxicity very low.

**E**

**EDTA**   (Ethylenedinitrilo) Tetraacetic Acid. Synthetic chemical which acts to consume metal or mineral ions in solution. Will remove available iron, copper, calcium, magnesium from the system. Used often as anti-oxidant. (Also used as Disodium or Trisodium EDTA.) Reports of skin irritation and allergic reactions.

**Emollient**   Those substances which moisturize by preventing water loss (drying) of the skin and which often have a softening effect on the skin if absorbed (as in the case of fruit and vegetable oil creams). Examples: lanolin, petrolatum, fatty alcohols such as cetyl alcohol, glyceryl stearate, glycerin. Allergic reactions and irritations depend upon specific ingredients.

**Emulsifier**   A substance which enables natural oils to be dispersed throughout a water base to form a cream or lotion. Allergic reactions and irritations depend upon specific ingredients.

**Emulsion**   A system consisting of an oily substance dispersed throughout a water base. All creams and lotions are emulsions.

**Ext. D&C**   Colors certified by FDA for external use only in drugs and cosmetics, not on lips or mucous membranes.

**Fatty Acids**   All natural oils are composed of fatty acids such as linoleic acid, oleic acid and stearic acid. No toxicity on record.

**Fatty Alcohols**   Organic oils found in animal and vegetable fats. Toxicity very low.

**FDA**   Federal Food and Drug Administration, which is responsible for the regulation of the cosmetic industry and the enforcement of the Cosmetic Ingredient Labeling Act. No cosmetic produced after April 15, 1977 may be filled into containers without full and accurate ingredient labeling, using standardized terms.

**FD&C Colors**   Certified by the FDA for use in foods, drugs, or cosmetics. Some are suspected of possible harmful effects.

**Fennel Extract**   Liquid herb extract alleged to help relieve skin and scalp irritation. Reports of allergic reactions.

**Fletan Oil**   A rare ingredient derived from fish liver which includes lecithin, a complex of iodine and phosphate salts. Rich in vitamins A and D, it is alleged to stimulate healing and protect the health of new skin cells.

**Formaldahyde**   Used often as low-cost preservative. Also used as fungicide, insecticide and embalming fluid. Reports of severe irritation and allergic reactions.

**Formalin**   A bacterial inhibitor that is very effective over a wide range of conditions and on a wide range of microbes.

**Glycerin**   Naturally produced emollient derived from vegetable oil, which can also be prepared synthetically.

**Glyceryl Monostearate**   An emulsifying and dispersing agent. No toxicity on record when used externally.

**Glyceryl Stearate**   Natural based ingredient derived from fatty acids. Used to assist in emulsifying natural oils in a water base.

**Glycols**   Glycerin combined with alcohol to form a syrupy alcohol used as humectant. In makeup they help foundation adhere to the skin. Propylene glycol is considered safe by FDA. Reports of irritations from other glycols. Ethylene glycol, diethylene glycol, and carbitol are dangerous if applied in concentrations greater than 5 percent.

**Hectorite**   Naturally-occuring clay used in facial masks to help draw out oils and tone skin. No toxicity on record when used externally. Powder may irritate lungs.

**Hexylrescorcinol**   Astringent and skin-wound cleanser derived from petroleum. Can burn skin if highly concentrated.

F

G

H

**Homosalate**   Substituted phenolic compound used as a sunscreen. Reports of poisoning through skin absorption.

**Honey**   Used as an emollient. Reports of pollen-allergic reactions.

**Hops Extract**   Liquid extract alleged to soothe skin and stimulate cell growth. Reports of allergic reactions.

**Humectant**   Components of creams and lotions added to prevent water loss and drying of skin, and to provide smooth application of cream or lotion. These compounds draw moisture from the air. Examples: propylene glycol and glycerin. Allergic reactions and irritations depend upon specific ingredients.

**Hybrid Safflower Oil**   Oil derived from safflower seeds of a genetic strain which contains predominantly oleic acid. Used as an emollient. High absorption into the skin. No toxicity on record.

**Hydrolyzed Protein**   Natural protein (animal, vegetable or milk) which has been broken down into more readily usable units or made soluble for use in cosmetics. Animal protein is similar in molecular structure to that of human hair. No toxicity on record.

**I**

**Imidazolindinyl Urea**   Anti-bacterial agent used to preserve cosmetics against bacterial contamination and to prolong shelf life. Does not contain formaldahyde or other irritants. No toxicity on record.

**Iron Oxides**   Iron combined with oxygen to color cosmetics.

**Isopropyl Myristate**   An organic salt which helps avoid greasy feel in products with high oil content. Developed from the distillation of plants and acid coming from trees. No toxicity on record.

**Isopropyl Palmitate** and **Isopropyl Lanolate**   Derived from coconut and lanolin respectively, used to help promote absorption of oils into the skin and to produce a nice "feel" in moisturizing creams. No toxicity on record when used externally.

**K**

**Kaolin**   Clay aiding the absorption of oil secreted by the skin. No toxicity on record when used externally.

**L**

**Laked Organic Color**   Organic pigment prepared by precipitating a soluble color with a form of calcium and/or potassium which then makes the color longer-lasting and unaffected by moisture.

**Lactic Acid**   Naturally occurring acid in milk produced by a natural fermentation process. Used to obtain pH levels near those of normal skin and hair. Caustic in concentrated form.

**Lauramide DEA**   Natural based lather builder and thickener, usually derived from coconut oil. Reports of mild irritation.

**Lecithin**   Vegetable product high in protein, natural fatty acids, and other essential nutrients such as vitamin E. Nontoxic.

**Lemon Oil**   Fragrant oil used as a counter-irritant. Reports of allergic reactions. Unconfirmed evidence of role in carcinogenic reactions.

**Lipoids/Lipids**   Fat and fat-like substances which occur in plants and animals.

**M**

**Magnesium Aluminum Silicate**   A naturally occurring gum, often used as an emulsion thickener, suspension agent, or coloring. Mined in the Nevada Desert and the Death Valley area. No toxicity on record.

**Matricaria Extract**   See **Camomile**.

**Menthol**   Naturally derived product of peppermint oil. Used in many drug products because of its counter-irritant and soothing properties. Also prepared synthetically. Concentrations greater than 1 percent can irritate mucous membrane.

**Menthionine**   An amino acid found in various proteins. An essential component in human nutrition not synthesized by the human body. Used as a texturizer. Nontoxic.

**Methocel**   A stabilizer for emulsions from natural gums and water.

**Methyl Cellulose**   From wood pulp. A thickening agent and stabilizer for emulsions. No toxicity on record.

**Methyl Paraben**   An inhibitor of microbial growth, used to preserve cosmetics and extend shelf life. A combination of petroleum and vegetable derivatives. Reports of dermatitis.

**Methyl Salicylate**   (Oil of Sweet Birch, Oil of Wintergreen) Counter-irritant and disinfectant. Easily absorbed through the skin. Reports of severe irritation.

**Mineral Oil**   A heavy, film-forming oil manufactured from crude oil. A mixture of liquid hydrocarbons separated from petroleum.

**Mink Oil**   Natural oil extracted from the subdermal tissue of mink. A very light, film-forming, rich oil similar to human skin oil. No toxicity on record.

**Mistletoe Extract**   Natural liquid extract alleged to have a soothing effect and antiseptic properties. No toxicity on reocrd when used externally.

**Myristic Acid (Myristate)**   Solid organic acid from butter acids, coconut oil or vegetable fats. A lathering agent. No toxicity on record.

**Natural**   Occurring in nature, whether of animal, vegetable or mineral origin. 100% natural cosmetics must be compounded and used immediately, because spoilage will take place in a very short time, although refrigeration may extend the life of the product for several days. Such products are highly susceptible to bacterial contamination if not used or refrigerated immediately. Term is often used to distinguish ingredients from "synthetic," i.e., materials nowhere found in nature, compounded by chemists.

**Nettles Extract**   Herb alleged to enliven hair roots and used for dandruff control. No toxicity on record.

**Oleyl Betaine**   Mild surfactant with both emollient and anti-static properties. No toxicity on record.

**Olive Oil**   Natural oil used as an emollient. Reports of allergic reactions, irritation to eyes on contact.

**Organic**   As used by chemists, this term means that a compound contains the element carbon. Does not imply a natural origin. Most synthetic chemicals are organic. This correct technical use of the term should not be confused with the use as applied to agriculture.

**Ozokerite**   (Ceresin Wax) Natural wax with emollient-like properties. Helps prevent separation of creams and lipsticks. No toxicity on record.

**Palm Kernelamide DEA**   Cleansing and thickening agent derived from natural palm kernel oil. No toxicity on record.

**Panthenol**   A nutritional factor reported to have excellent properties relating to repair and thickening of normal hair. Provitamin B5. Necessary for the normal metabolism of the body. It benefits the hair by increasing lustre, aiding in moisture retention and increasing elasticity. No toxicity on record.

N

O

P

**Peanut Oil**   Natural oil with emollient properties. Reports of mild irritation only when used in soap.

**Pectin**   Extract of plants used as thickening agent in cosmetics. Soothing to the skin. No toxicity on record when used externally.

**PEG**   Polyethylene Glycol. A softener, binder and solvent widely used as a cosmetic base. No toxicity on record when used externally.

**PEG-8 Dilaurate**   Derived from petroleum and used as a softener. No toxicity on record.

**PEG-8 Stearate** and **PEG-100 Stearate**   Derived from natural fatty acids and used as emulsifiers in cosmetic creams. No toxicity on record.

**PEG-75 Lanolin**   Form of lanolin with increased cosmetic properties for emulsion stabilization. No toxicity on record. The most commonly used oil in ordinary cosmetics. Nontoxic.

**Petrolatum**   Thicker form of mineral oil. Composed of hydrocarbons extracted from crude oil. Very rarely toxic or allergenic when used externally.

**pH**   A scale from 0 to 14 used in measuring the acidity or alkalinity of solutions. pH 7.0 is considered neutral. Acidity increases as the numbers decrease. Alkalinity increases as the numbers increase. The normal pH of skin and hair is between 4.0 and 6.0, slightly acidic.

**Placenta**   Lining of the womb, alleged to retard wrinkles. Its efficacy for this use is subject to controversy.

**Polypeptides**   Amino acid residues.

**Polysorbates**   Derivatives of fatty acids used to help dissolve natural oils in a water base. Polysorbate-20: reports of allergic reactions by hypersensitive persons. Polysorbates 40, 60, 61, 65, 80, 81, and 85: No toxicity on record.

**Potassium Alum**   Naturally occurring mineral with astringent properties. Also known as "alum." No toxicity on record when used externally.

**Potassium Sorbate**   Derivative of sorbitol used as a preservative. Reports of mild skin irritation.

**Propylgallate**   Natural acid (Gallic) derivative used as an anti-oxidant. No toxicity on record.

**Propyl Paraben**   Inhibitor of microbial growth, used to preserve cosmetics and extend shelf life. Reports of dermatitis.

**Propylene Glycol**   A solution stabilizer, or cosmetic emollient. Similar to glycerine, it can be obtained from glycerin and sodium hydroxide, or from a combination of petroleum derivatives and carbon salts. No toxicity on record.

**Propylene Glycol Stearate**   Combination of petroleum derivatives, carbon salts and vegetable alcohol derivatives. Lubricant and emulsifier. No toxicity on record.

**Purified Water**   Deionized water that has been boiled to insure no microbial contamination.

**PVP/VA Copolymer**   A petroleum derivative primarily used as a plasma expander. Gives body or holding character in hair sprays. Unconfirmed evidence suggests possibility that polyvinylpyrrolidone (PVP) may contribute to foreign bodies in lungs of sensitive persons with heavy exposure.

**Quaternium**   Organic nitrogen compound commonly called Quaternary Ammonium Salt or Quaternary Ammonium Compounds. The compound has germicidal action and also is a cationic (positive ion) emulsifier. Widely used in regular cosmetics industry, all these compounds are potentially toxic. Reports of irritation to eyes and mucous membranes.

**Quaternium 15** (Dowcil 200) A strong preservative used in some cosmetics to kill bacteria by release of formaldahyde. Reports of irritation.

**Rosemary Extract** Adds body and helps hair hold its natural shape. Also used as fragrance. No toxicity on record when used externally. Toxic when taken internally.

**Safflower Oil** Natural oil of the safflower. High in linoleic acid and other natural fatty acids. No toxicity on record.

**SD Alcohol-1** A denatured alcohol distilled from plants. "Denatured" alcohol is treated to make it unfit for drinking.

**Sesame Oil** Natural oil with emollient properties. No toxicity on record.

**Soap** Product of fatty acids (oils) such as coconut oil or animal fat, treated with strong alkali such as sodium hydroxide. The finished soap normally has a very high pH value and will cause precipitation (soap scum) in hard water. Soap is not considered a cosmetic by the FDA, and is exempt from the listing of ingredients.

**Sodium Borate** Borax, a naturally occurring mineral with cleansing properties. Reports of irritation and of brittleness of hair.

**Sodium C14-16 Olefin Sulfonate** Mild cleansing and wetting agent derived from petroleum. Reports of dryness of skin.

**Sodium Chloride** Common salt or sea salt. Used to increase viscosity or thickness. No reports of irritation if sufficiently diluted. Reports of irritation from concentrated solutions.

**Sodium Lauryl Sulfate, Sodium Cetyl Sulfate** and **Sodium Laureth Sulfate** Surfactant, detergent, emulsifier. Sodium Lauryl Sulfate usually found in shampoos is prepared by sulfation of lauryl alcohol followed by neutralization with sodium carbonate. Grease-cutting ability may produce dry skin. Generally nontoxic when used externally.

**Sorbitan Stearate** Fatty acid derivative used to aid in emulsification and to solubilize normally water-insoluble materials, such as oils, in a water solution. This allows natural vegetable and fruit oils to be combined with water to produce a rich cream or lotion. No toxicity on record.

**Sorbital** Derived from berries, cherries, plums, pears, apples, seaweed and algae. Works as a stabilizer and gives a lubricant feeling to lotion. No toxicity on record when used externally.

**Soy Bean Oil** Natural oil of the soy bean, high in natural fatty acids. Quickly absorbed by the skin. Reports of allergic reactions.

**Stearalkonium Chloride** Nitrogen based compound with hair conditioning properties. Leaves hair with less static electricity and has detangling properties. See **Quaternium.**

**Stearates** A group of fatty acid derivatives used to help produce emulsions in creams and lotions. Reports of sensitization reactions when used by allergic persons.

**Stearic Acid** A white, waxy natural fatty acid from tallow, butter acids, animal fats or vegetable oils. Used in many creams. Provides pearliness and firmness. Not a strong acid which will affect pH. Reports of sensitization reactions when used by allergic persons.

**Sterols** Solid alcohols from animals or plants. Cholesterol or cholesterin is a sterol used as a lubricant in creams or lotions. No toxicity on record.

**Strawberry** Used as an emollient. The seeds act as a scrub. No reports of harmful effects on record.

**Surfactants**   Surface active agents which aid wetting, dispersing and cleaning properties in hair preparations or cleansers. Can be derived from natural coconut oil or prepared synthetically. Normally used to replace soap products in skin and hair cleaning compounds.

**T**

**TEA**   Triethanolamine. Used to adjust pH. Often used with stearic acid to convert acid to salt (stearate) which then becomes a base for cleanser. Colorless, low-alkaline solid. Not a beverage.

**TEA-Lauryl Sulfate**   A combination of coconut oil extract and petroleum derivatives. Used as a cleansing detergent in shampoos. See **Sodium Lauryl Sulfate.**

**V**

**Vitamin A Palmitate**   Vitamin A when ingested helps maintain healthy skin, stimulate new cell growth, and aids in development of bones and teeth; can be stored in the body. Absorbable through the skin. No toxicity on record when used externally.

**Vitamin D**   Helps the body utilize calcium and phosphorous. Aids in development of bones and teeth. Absorbable through the skin. No toxicity on record when used externally.

**Vitamin E (Acetate)**   Vitamin E. Also known as Tocopheryl Acetate. Used in treatment of heart, liver and muscular disorders. Also used in various other disorders of the body believed to be caused by vitamin E deficiency. An anti-oxidant. Natural vitamin E is of higher cost that the synthetic variety; check the label.

**"Vitamin" F**   Once thought to be a vitamin, is actually a mixture of unsaturated fatty acids.

**W**

**Wheat Germ Oil**   Natural oil obtained from the embryo of the wheat kernel separated in milling. Natural source of vitamins E, A and D.

**Witch Hazel Extract**   Completely natural extract from leaves and twigs of hamamelius plant, which acts as astringent, due to its tannic acid content.

**X**

**Xanthum Gum**   Derived from the locust bean by fermentation, and used as a stabilizer, emulsifier, bodying agent or foam-enhancer. Tests indicate it is nontoxic and nonsensitizing.

**Y**

**Yarrow Extract**   Also known as Achillea. Natural liquid alleged to be an anti-inflammatory and soothing to skin. Has mild astringent properities. Reports of sensitization to light.

**Yogurt**   Source of amino acids and protein. Neutral skin conditioner.

**Z**

**Zinc Oxide**   A compound of zinc and oxygen used as an antiseptic and astringent. Also used to make creams and powders opaque. Astringents are some sometimes alleged to be inappropriate for dry skin.

# Consumer's Guide

Except for a few products like clay and henna, cosmetics do not occur in nature. Even soap is a human invention. Although horror stories of cosmetically-induced disfigurements have lead to full disclosure labeling of cosmetic ingredients and closer regulatory control of substances used in cosmetic formulations, the consumer is often left to wander in confusion through a maze of chemically-defined cosmetic ingredients. The dictionary of cosmetic ingredients in this chapter will help in deciphering cosmetic ingredient lists.

- Beware of buzz-words. There may be miracles, but there are no miracle cosmetic ingredients. When a magic word is used to promote a product—the word *herbal* for example—look closely to see what the product really contains, especially if the magic ingredient appears at the end of the ingredient list.

- Cosmetics are made by chemists. In chemical terms, the word *organic* means that a product contains a carbon compound. The term does not necessarily mean the produce is natural, safe or effective.

- Hypoallergenic describes products which do not contain substances identified as allergy-producing by the Food and Drug Administration.

- Cosmetics with vivid colors probably have D&C colors added to them. While D&C colors are officially considered safe, a number of colors once appearing on the D&C list have subsequently been identified as health hazards. All other ingredients being equal, a vivid purple shampoo is not going to get hair any cleaner than a pale yellow or translucent one.

- There has been no proof that the external application of vitamins to the skin has a beneficial effect.

- Cosmetics may contain ingredients derived from animal sources, including lanolin, placenta, keratin, liver extract, hormones, tallow, mink oil and hydrolized animal protein.

- While a variety of henna colors can be obtained by blending different botanicals, they can also be obtained from mineral additives such as iron oxide, magnesium carbonate, peroxide and ammonia. Since henna extract is a clear or translucent-amber color, products containing henna extract may include coloring agents to form varying hues.

- Federal regulations require that all imported botanicals, including henna, be fumigated.

- Be sure that complete, easy-to-follow instructions are included with do-it-yourself henna products. Before applying the henna, color test it on a strand of hair and on a skin patch for allergy reactions.

- Claims that jojoba oil is therapeutic in treating dandruff, balding and scalp ailments originated in Native American lore, but have not been proven by scientific investigation.

- In jojoba products, *tincture of herb* is a liquid substance produced by fermenting jojoba meal from which the oil has been removed. *Tincture of herb* is not jojoba oil.

- Law requires that preservatives, anti-fungus and anti-bacterial additives be added to clay when it is mixed with other ingredients in a product such as toothpaste, shampoo or deodorant. Methyl propyl paraben is a popular additive for this purpose. In powder form, clays do not need additives.

- The consistency of a clay product varies with its intended use. Finely ground clay is used in masks, coarser clay in packs and poultices.

- Note: A flushed face following a clay facial or mask is due to stimulation from increased circulation flow to the skin. This is not an allergic reaction.

# VIII: Edible Oils

The long rows of golden oils on grocery store shelves offer a series of puzzles to the natural foods buyer. Some oils look clear and others appear somewhat cloudy, but similar words are used on the labels of both kinds. Nutritionists tell us that vegetable oils are a much healthier source of fats needed in our diets than animal fats. The volume of sales of vegetable oils in this industry indicates that they are an important part of the natural foods diet, important enough to sustain one of the industry's largest companies and several smaller ones. But consumers and retailers alike have expressed confusion about the terms used to describe these products.

In preparing its report on edible oils, the staff of *Whole Foods* magazine quickly found itself immersed in highly technical information about manufacturing processes on a huge scale. Nobody was squeezing sunflower seeds inside a cloth sack to extract the oil—because nobody can do that. To produce edible oils in quantities sufficient to meet the demands of even the natural foods consumers alone, a major, highly technological industry is required. The equipment used to produce vegetable oils for the natural foods trade is the same as the equipment used to produce Wesson oil, but there can be some differences in the amount of processing and in the use of additives.

The people who specialize in extracting oils have found nuts, beans and seeds to be stubborn. When squeezed enough to yield their oil, they also give up substances which many consumers consider unhealthy or undesirable for other reasons, such as odor or a tendency to smoke readily when used in cooking. To remove the unwanted constituents, chemists devised ways to extract pure oils through methods of refining.

Customers in natural foods shops include people who want the purest possible oils and people who want the least refined possible oils—so the suppliers to the trade offer both kinds. Since there is no magic in oil processing, both the refined and the unrefined oils offer advantages and disavantages.

This section of the *Natural Foods Guide* does not attempt to decide whether refined or unrefined oils are to be preferred. Such a decision should be left in the hands of the informed consumer. The following detailed examination of the processing of edible oils is intended to give the reader all the facts needed to make an informed choice.

A major focus of this section is on the terms commonly used to describe these products. "Refined," "cold pressed," "solvent extracted," "expeller pressed," "bleached," and the many other words used in the edible oil industry cannot be understood apart from a clear description of the various steps involved in the processing of these products. The description given here is intended to clarify the precise meaning of all these terms, and will also provide the reader with a way to look beyond the labels to make judgements about the oil itself.

Due to its unique characteristics, production methods, and uses, olive oil is discussed in its own separate chapter.

221

# 50

# The Cold Facts
# on Cold Pressed

## by Jim Schreiber and Janice Fillip

Consumers often ask about various words found on labels of bottled oil, wanting to know whether some terms have a reliable meaning or are simply tools in merchandising. Retailers and distributors express similar reasons for concern. In deciding which oils to carry, wholesalers and retailers find that oils with widely different tastes and appearances may carry similar dscriptive words on their labels. The most common and urgent question was about the words "cold pressed."

**What are "cold pressed" oils?**

What are "cold pressed" oils? How do they differ from the commercial edible oils sold in supermarkets? Consumers who seek out "cold pressed" oils pay a premium price, expecting that there is a considerable difference. Is there?

To learn the answers to these and other questions, we talked with dozens of oil processors, packers and wholesalers, examined technical literature, and spent an afternoon at a manufacturing plant of one of the major processors of edible oils for the health food industry, PVO International, Inc. (Pacific Vegetable Oils) in Richmond, California.

**Manufacturers of edible oil**

The manufacturing of edible oil is not a cottage industry. Most of the oils sold in natural food stores are manufactured by giant companies, including General Mills, Hunt-Wesson, Kraft Foods (Humko division), McCormick & Co. (Sesame Products Corp. division), PVO International, Inc., and A.H. Robins Co. (Viobin division). The size of these operations is a simple matter of economics. Setting up an oil-processing facility, even in its simplest form, requires great amounts of capital. The source materials—seeds, nuts and beans—from which edible oil is derived are generally purchased on the commodities market on a contract basis—a highly competitive marketplace.

The corporate name and the scale of operations of oil processors was not, by itself, a totally reliable guide to the characteristics of the various oils they sell. The fact that an oil is manufactured by a large commercial enterprise does not always mean that it is a refined oil. Some manufacturers which provide fully refined, bleached, deodorized oil also offer oil which is simply expressed, filtered, and bottled in its unrefined state. On the other hand, the fact that an oil is marketed through health food stores is no guarantee that it is an unrefined oil. An executive of a major commercial edible oil manufacturer—who asked not to be named—remarked that people would be "surprised if they knew what was really in the oil sold in health food stores." The executive was in a position to know, because his company makes some of that oil.

# COMING TO TERMS

Some of the greatest heat in the edible oil trade is generated over the phrase "cold pressed," which is found on the labels of many major brands of oil in the natural foods industry. More questions have been raised about that wording than about any other matter pertaining to edible oil. The answers depend upon whom one asks.

Frans J. Letschert, Manager of International Sales and Operations at PVO, and William Blodgett, Director of Corporate Relations at Hunt-Wesson, independently called the term "cold pressed" a "misnomer" due to the heat produced by the expeller-pressing of oil. Judy Hitchings, Traffic Manager at Agricom, said the phrase "doesn't mean a thing." Roy Anderson, Vice President and General Manager at Sesame Products Corp. said the phrase is "meaningless."

General Mills publishes a technical information bulletin on the "characteristics of cold-pressed wheat germ oil," which is expeller pressed. The bulletin does not state the temperature reached in the expeller process. Vaughn Ball, their Market Development Manager, described General Mills as "the only domestic producer of cold-pressed wheat germ oil."

Viobin—General Mills' major competitor in wheat germ oil—labels its wheat germ oil "cold processed, unrefined." H.D. Bryan, Scientific Affairs Director at Viobin, described their wheat germ oil as "hexane extracted, using unique batch extractors that are custom built for our process." He said that Viobin's wheat germ oil, sold as such, is not mixed with pressed oils. Bryan responded to our questions by letter and wrote the additional comment, "these are proprietary information and the questions are not appropriate for a journal editor to ask."

We asked Danny Wells, chairman of the Standards Committee of the National Nutritional Foods Associatin, about "cold pressed" oil. Wells said, "There isn't any. There's no such thing as 'cold pressed' oil." He said that the NNFA is not currently trying to establish standards for edible oil. "Rather than setting ourselves up as judges," Wells said, "we're trying to get full disclosure from the companies on how the oil is made, and let the buyers make their own decisions." The NNFA information is intended for publication in a book projected for the summer of 1979, according to Wells. He characterized the words "cold pressed" as "a little deceptive," because vegetable oil sources may be subject to "extreme heat" prior to the expelling process.

In *Food Oils and Their Uses*, chemist-author Theodore J. Weiss makes the following remarks:

**Cold Pressing**—Another process for oil recovery which goes back into antiquity is cold pressing. High oil content seeds, such as sesame and peanut, and the oily pulp of olives yield free oil by the simple application of pressure. Oils of this type require no further processing . . . However, cold pressing is not very efficient..

**Hot Pressing**—The oil meals (seed residues from which oil has been removed) remaining from cold pressing contained an excessive amount of valuable oil. This led to the development of more efficient presses, such as the hydraulic batch press and the continuous screw press or expeller. These presses develop pressures of 1-15 tons per square inch, leaving 2-4 percent oil in the meal.

Unfortunately, such presses also develop excessive heat. This causes darkening of the oil and denaturation of oilseed protein. The prepress-solvent method was introduced to reduce damage to oil seeds during crushing. Here the seed is pressed to remove only part of the available oil. The temperature at this point is not sufficient to degrade the oil or protein to any great degree. Solvent extraction is then used to remove the balance of oil from the meal.

In *Bailey's Industrial Oil and Fat Products*, edited by David Swern, the detailed descriptions of the processing of edible oils contain no discussion or use of the words

Everyone has a different definition

Cold pressing

Hot pressing

"cold pressed." The term does not appear in the index. Throughout the book, we found the phrase used only in one sentence about poppyseed oil: "When cold-pressed, the oil can be used for edible purposes without refining, provided that properly cleaned seed is used."

To find out what "cold pressed" means to the primary users of the phrase, we talked with officers of the Hain Pure Food Co., Landstrom (Healthway brand), and Kahan & Lessin (Health Food Store brand).

Confusion in oil labeling

The phrase "cold pressed" was apparently introduced into health food trade oil-labeling in the early 1950's by the Hain Pure Food Co.—a practice which was followed by other major sellers of edible oils to the same market. According to Hain Vice President Jerry Jacobs, " 'Cold pressed' is a term we picked up out of a textbook." The book, he said, was *Food Products*, by Henry C. Sherman, a professor of chemistry at Columbia University, originally copyrighted in 1933.

# TEXTBOOK TERM

Jacobs read us the germane quote from his copy of the Sherman text: "The so-called *cold-pressed* or expeller oil differs mainly from the *hot-pressed* (hydraulic presses) oil in that the former requires longer agitation." The sentence quoted by Jacobs continues " . . . with caustic soda solution before heating in subsequent refining operations." in our 1948 edition of Sherman's *Food Products*. In the next three paragraphs, the Sherman book goes on to describe subsequent heating in refining at 43 to 49°C. (= 109 to 120°F.) and in deodorizing at 200 to 225°C. (= 392 to 437°F.).

To Hain, Jacobs stated, "cold pressed" is the same thing as "expeller pressed." He went on to say that cold pressed is not equivalent to unrefined, and that an oil which is "cold pressed" can also be refined, bleached, and deodorized. An examination of oils sold in health food stores shows that the latter statement is an accurate reflection of a widespread practice in the industry.

In their cold-pressed line, Hain Pure Food Co. offers both unrefined and refined oils. According to Jacobs, their unrefined oils come in their brown and yellow label which states "unrefined," and their bottle with the familiar yellow, blue and red label depicting a salad bowl contains oil which has been refined, polished and finished. He said that consumers and retailers could rely on that distinction.

Refined oils may be labeled "cold pressed"

Health Food Store brand oil is a private label of Kahan & Lessin, primarily for safflower and soybean oil. According to Art Miller, K&L's Director of Sales and Merchandising, their oils are bottled and labeled "cold pressed" by Sona Food Products. He stated that Sona would determine whether the words "cold pressed" appear on the Health Food Store brand label. Miller said that he was not aware of a working definition of "cold pressed" in the industry, and he suggested that Hain or Sona would be in the best position to give such a definition.

Healthway brand is a private label of Landstrom Co., offering a broad line of edible oils, largely labeled "cold pressed." Advertising Manager Gerry Stratford said that, by a literal definition of "cold pressed"—using hand-cranked presses or squeezing by stones as done historically in Mediterranean areas—he knows of nobody in the industry who makes edible oil that way now. He said that the usual cold-pressing practice in the natural foods industry is the use of expeller presses which do generate some heat because of high pressures. In this industry, Stratford said, "what has been used to define it all these years is the pressing of the seed but not using any heat to extract the oil."

# REFINING CONFUSION

Healthway brand oil, according to Stratford, "hasn't been refined. It has been washed and cleaned—some of it dry steamed—crushed and expeller-pressed under high pressure, and filtered for sediments."

Stratford later added this: "Just to add to the confusion, the term 'refined' is probably as ambiguous a term as some of the other ones are. We do not do anything to bleach, deodorize or add any kind of chemical to the oil, or pass it through any kind of chemical in order to change it in any way. We do filter it. We do strain it. There are those who would say that, because we do that, we are refining—that it isn't the pure squeezing. We do not do any of those, with the exception of cod liver oil, which we do deodorize." He noted that, unlike some other brands, the Healthway avocado oil is green, because chlorophyll is natural in the avocado seed. "That's an example of the fact that ours has not been fiddled with," Stratford said.

George Mateljan, President of Health Valley Natural Foods, said that his firm is not a major supplier of edible oils, but that oils sold by his company are cold pressed. He said that Health Valley oils are not refined, bleached, or anything of that kind. When we asked whether he was aware of any definition of the term "cold pressed," Mateljan said, "No."

**Disclosure of refining, bleaching or deodorizing not required by law**

The Health Valley label, which characterizes the oil as "Natural—Cold Pressed," says, "we squeeze oil from nuts, beans and seeds using the so-called 'Cold Press' (or Expeller Press) Method, a mechanical process which uses no chemical solvents. Our oils are cleared of impurities (which can cause rancidity) by passing through a Fuller's Earth Filtering Process which can leave no harmful residue..." The label also advises the reader, "Be sure to read the fine print on labels. Many commercial oils are extracted from the source with chemical solvents such as Hexane (derived from petroleum) which may leave a residue in the final product. They are often treated with alkali (such as soda ash) in refining and then 'preserved' with such chemical additives as BHA, BHT, POLYSORBATE 80, METHOL SILICONE or many others."

The law does require the listing of preservatives, but does not require mention of refining, bleaching, or deodorizing. Mixing edible oil with fuller's earth and then filtering the mix is the process which oil manufacturers and technologists call "bleaching."

# SWISS REGULATIONS

The Swiss government has no doubts about the limits they set on the use of the words "cold pressed," with the result that Hain's oils in Switzerland are labeled "Pure and Pressed." According to a letter from the Food Control Division of the Swiss Federal Office of Public Health, "Our Office allows the recommendation 'Pure cold pressed' only in the case of mechanical pressing and *when the temperature does not exceed* 50°C (ca. 122°F) and without outside heating or solvent extraction. The manufacturer of Hain Safflower oil (Hain Pure Food Co. Inc. in Los Angeles/USA) has communicated to us that the temperature by pressing does reach about 65°-72°C (150-160°F). That is the only reason why we demanded to change the label from 'pure cold pressed' into 'pure and pressed.' We can assure you that we consider the Hain Safflower oil as a very good edible oil, which is manufactured under best conditions and there are *no other restrictions except the word 'cold'* as mentioned above."

**Stiff label standards in Switzerland**

Arrowhead Mills' president, Frank Ford, said that he favors labeling which states how the oil was removed from the seed and indicates whether the oil is refined. To Ford, four different statements on labels would convey the most relevant information: "Expeller Pressed, Unrefined," "Expeller Pressed, Refined," "Solvent Extracted, Unrefined," or "Solvent Extracted, Refined." About government regulation of oil labeling, he said, "The cures of bureaucrats are often worse than the disease." Instead of federal control, Ford said he would prefer to see possible labeling obscurities cleared up "by education, and honesty."

The labels of Westbrae Natural Foods state what has and what has not been done to the oil. Most of their labels say that the oil is expeller pressed, unrefined, filtered, and has not been bleached, deodorized, or extracted with chemical solvents. To Rico Villa, Westbrae's buyer, the use of "cold pressed" on labels is a "complete lie." He called it a "marketing scam," and wondered aloud whether the purveyors of the term would care to bathe in the "cold" oils at the temperature of expeller processing. He expressed approval of labeling which is explicit about the processes the oil has gone through, and suggested that shelf-talkers be used by retailers to inform their customers about edible oils.

**Cold pressed—a marketing scam?**

Phil Parenti, president of Pure & Simple, said he sees edible oils in the same light as whole grain breads, fertile eggs, raw milk, and organic vegetables—special foods which customers of natural food stores expect to be as good and whole as possible. In his view, the term "cold pressed" is a "misnomer," and "there's no oil that's really cold pressed." The best that the customer can get, Parenti indicated, is an unrefined, expeller-pressed oil removed from the seed without the use of solvents. He suggested that consumer education is the best way to clear up confusions about edible oil.

# TASTE AND COLOR

Many oils labeled as "cold pressed" are bland in flavor—nearly tasteless—and very light in color. According to edible oil manufacturers and all the literature we surveyed, such a lack of taste and color is attained only through the alkali refining, bleaching and deodorizing sequence of processing. According to *Bailey's*, continuous caustic refining usually operates at around 140-160°F., bleaching at 220-240°F., and deodorizing at 440-460°F.

Some oils labeled "cold pressed" have gone through this entire process. Other oils labeled "cold pressed" have been bottled after expeller pressing and simple filtering only. The phrase "cold pressed" does not make this distinction. The eye and the tongue of the buyer can readily identify a refined, bleached, deodorized oil: A pale, clear, bland-tasting oil is the final product of that entire series of processes.

Another phrase found on labels of bottled edible oils is "contains no preservatives." Manufacturers often sell both the regular commercial market and to the health food trade, and customarily add such ingredients as BHA, BHT, TBHQ, citric acid or methyl silicone only to the oils for the commercial market. Different oils have different levels of stability, different tendencies to go rancid, and in all cases should be kept away from direct sunlight, heat, and exposure to air.

Edible-oil label claims about "polyunsaturates" are generally accurate statements about one of the most valued characteristics of vegetable oils of many types. Although climate, region, plant variety, and weather can affect exact percentages, most vegetable oils consumed (other than in confections) have over 50 percent polyunsaturates, with safflower oil naturally highest at about 78 percent.

Some labels say "contains no cholesterol," which is a matter of some concern to many consumers. On bottles of vegetable oil, this statement is always true. Cholesterol is an animal substance. No vegetable oil contains cholesterol.

Within the edible oil trade, terms are used which do not necessarily appear on labels. Some of these terms are very precise; others are less so.

Currently, the words "screw-press" and "expeller" are often used interchangeably, to refer to the continuous-process machinery which crushes oilseeds by applying pressure by means of a worm-shaft device inside a slotted metal barrel. Originally, the "screw-press" was of French design, with a horizontal barrel only, and the "expeller" was of later American design, with both a horizontal and a vertical barrel, but both types of machines work in essentially the same manner. Either can be loosely called a "crusher." At the crushing stage, prior to the use of solvents in the process, the product is referred to as "prepressed."

# SOLVENT EXTRACTION

The term "extraction" technically applies only to the removal of the oil from its source by dissolving it in a solvent—not to a crushing process. The term is often used in the phrase "solvent extraction," and the most commonly used solvent for this purpose in the USA is hexane, a petroleum derivative.

"Crude" is the term applied to edible oil which has been removed from its source by crushing, or by solvent extraction, or by both methods. Expeller pressed and solvent extracted "crude" oil may be recombined prior to bottling. "Crude" oil may only have gone through an expeller, hydraulic, or screw press and then been filtered, or it may have been solvent extracted, and the solvent removed by distillation. Basically, the oil is called "crude" at any point in the process prior to alkali refining.

Lack of taste and color attained only through alkali refining

Polyunsaturates

Screw and expeller pressed

Using a solvent to remove oil

"Refining" is, strictly, the mixing of crude oil with a caustic solution to separate the clear oil from the semisolid impurities, chiefly free fatty acids and phospholipids. Strictly, "refining" does not refer to the subsequent bleaching and deodorizing processes, although the term "refining" is sometimes used loosely to apply to those operations as well, since they, too, remove undesired substances from the oil.

The term "bleaching" refers to the removal of pigments from the oil with the use of fuller's earth, activated clays, or charcoal. "Activated" clay or charcoal is previously treated with sulfuric or hydrochloric acid to increase its absorption capacity. Bleaching also largely removed traces of soap which may remain in the oil as a result of alkali refining.

Although some pigments are removed from the oil in the refining and in the deodorizing stages, as well as in the bleaching stage, the term "deodorizing" applies specifically to the removal of "odiferous constituents from the oil" by treating it with steam in a high vacuum at high temperatures—a process advanced early in this century by David Wesson. Deodorizing removes the last of the free fatty acids from the oil and greatly improves its stability. According to *Bailey's*, "Well-deodorized oils of different kinds, when still fresh, are virtually indistinguishable from one another by odor or taste, and merely give a sensation of oiliness in the mouth."

A special item of vocabulary applies to olive oil. The oil pressed from the fruit of the olive tree—not from the pit—is termed "virgin" olive oil. The oil derived from the remaining pulp or from the pit by solvent extraction is commonly called "pure" olive oil, but cannot be termed "virgin."

Other terms, such as Lovibond Color, AOM, Peroxide Number, GLC, and Iodine Value appear on specifications sheets for various edible oils. The more significant of these terms will be discussed below.

# BEFORE REFINING

The processing of edible oils can be visualized as the out flow of an oil through a series of different vats which are connected in a line by tubes. Each vat does something quite specific to change the characteristics of the oil, usually taking something out of the oil before it goes on to the next vat. Most of the individual vats have two other exit tubes coming out of them. One is for useable by-products; the other is for the oil itself, which has been treated just to the point desired for final sealing in a bottle.

That sealed bottle may contain oil that came from only, say, the third vat in the processing series, or it may contain oil that came only from the last vat in the series, or it may contain oil that came from several different vats in the series. The contents of the bottle depend upon what the customer asks for.

The vats in this analogy correspond, of course, to different specialized pieces of machinery used at edible oil processing plants. The "vats" discussed here will include the major processes which may be involved in the production of unrefined, or "crude," oils The major processes of producing unrefined oil may include cooking, crushing, filtering, solvent extraction, and distillation. Below, we will examine refining and the major processes subsequent to refining.

All vegetable oils begin in the fields as seeds, nuts, or beans. The problem faced by the manufacturer is how to take this source material, which may vary with weather and locale, and change it into something useable and acceptable to consumers. The nature of the vegetable materials themselves imposes limits on what can be done and how it can be done, while still being economically feasible. Manufacturers can be relied on to waste as little as possible, because waste is money lost. Using the most efficient recovery methods, during 1977 the industry produced 533,797,000 pounds of saturated fatty acids and 385,931,000 pounds of unsaturated fatty acids in the USA, according to the Fatty Acid Producers Council. During 1976, the average consumption of salad and cooking oils in the USA was nearly 20 pounds per person.

To get at this vast amount of oil, the seeds must first be cleaned, removing stems, twigs, leaves, stones and other unwanted materials. Then, to get at the oil-bearing part of the seeds, hulls are usually separated away. These things are usually accomplished by various screens, reels, rotating blades and blowers. In preparation for solvent extraction, some seeds are rolled into thin flakes for greater efficiency of extraction. Such flaking is considered less important for expeller or screw-press removal of oil, because the crushing machinery breaks the seeds into fine particles.

# Steps in Oil Processing

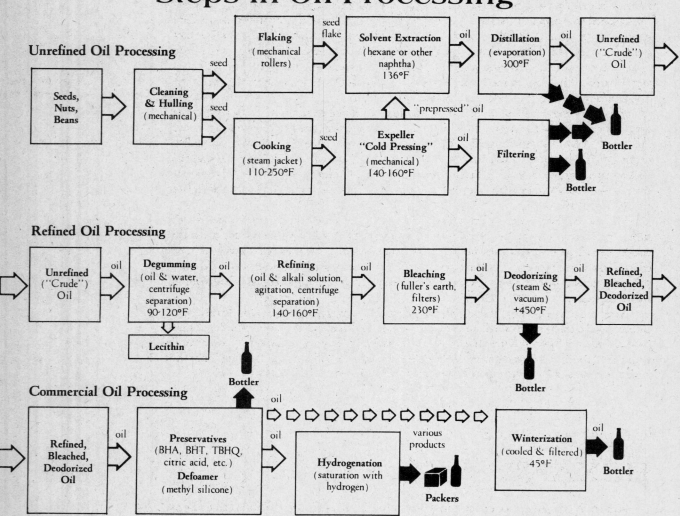

# COOKING THE SEEDS

Before going into the expeller, oilseeds are generally cooked. "It is universally recognized that oil seeds yield their oil more readily to mechanical expression after cooking," according to *Bailey's*. In a typical cooker, large cylindrical kettles are surrounded by a steam jacket, and jet sprays and exhaust vents control the moisture of the seed. The temperature used depends on the source material. Cottonseed is cooked for 30 minutes to two hours at about 250° F. Peanuts are often cooked for less time. According to Richard Schneider, the plant manager at PVO, their safflower seed cooks at about 110-120° F. Although overcooking may darken and harm the nutrients in the product, it is generally acknowledged that the proper cooking of the oilseed aids in the later refining process.

Oilseed moves out of the cooker at a typical rate of 90 tons each 24 hours, depending upon the type of seed and the size of the cooker. PVO presses about 20 tons of seed at a time. The seed is fed into a "cage" at the ingoing end of the expeller mechanism, inside which a continuously revolving worm-shaft presses the seeds against the slotted walls of a metal barrel. The slots in the barrel are gapped at about 0.01 inch, allowing the oil to drain through while retaining most of the solid material.

By controlling the pressure inside the barrel with a choke-nut on the worm shaft, the operator can control the degree to which the oil is expressed, and the temperature inside the barrel. According to Schneider, their expeller presses bring the safflower oilseed to about 140°F., because "if you run it any lower, you can't get any oil out." He said that the back-pressure in the expeller is deliberately kept low in order to keep the heat down, but that some manufacturers might increase the pressure to get more complete—and hotter— expression of the oil.

The Weiss book states that a low temperature during expeller pressing "is not sufficient to degrade the oil or protein to any great degree." To the manufacturer, an added advantage of lower pressure in the expeller is that it reduces wear and tear. The continuous grinding action is very hard on the machinery. At PVO, the entire expeller pressing section is shut down for six or seven weeks each year for a necessary overhaul of the equipment.

After expeller pressing, the oil may be filtered to remove the larger particles and sent directly on to the bottler, with nothing but storage and transportation in between. Since such oil has not been refined, bleached, or deodorized, it will be darker in color, will retain its natural flavor and aroma, will contain no trace of solvents used during other the processing, and may have a greater tendency to go rancid.

Seeds cooked at varying temperatures

How an expeller press works

# HEXANE

Expeller pressing leaves about 2 to 4 percent of the oil in the meal. This is too much to waste. To remove that oil, the oil cake is sent on to the next part of the manufacturing plant for solvent extraction. In many instances, such as at facilities which do not produce unrefined edible oils, all of the seed is "prepressed" by expellers and is then all conveyed to the solvent extraction process.

Hexane is the most widely used chemical for solvent extraction. Hexane is a highly volatile, flammable, colorless liquid derived from petroleum. It is toxic, mildly depressant to the central nervous system, and may irritate the lungs if inhaled. Its use in oil extraction requires extreme care and control of temperature.

Solvent extraction equipment comes in a wide range of designs, all of which are engineered to attain the same result—to bring the seedcake into maximum contact with the solvent for the most efficient removal of the oil. After solvent extraction, only 0.5 to 1.0 percent of the original oil remains in the meal. The meal itself, after removal of the solvent, may be used for animal feed, adhesives, fibers or plastics.

The solvent extraction process

A typical operating temperature during hexane extraction is 136°F. The mixture of solvent and oil during extraction contains about 25 percent oil. The meal itself is commonly separated out through settling tanks and filters.

Recovery of the solvent from the oil, after extraction, is based on the ease with which the solvent evaporates. The oil-solvent mixture usually passes through a series of heated chambers which distil out the solvent from the oil. Since hexane boils at 146-156° F., temperatures higher than that are required for complete removal of the solvent. Temperatures up to 300° F. are not unusual at this stage. The use of superheated solvent vapors in "flash" removal of the solvent can be used "to avoid toasting and to minimize denaturation of the protein," according to *Bailey's*. To make sure that no solvent remains in the product, Schneider said, the PVO plant rules require heating the oil briefly to 260° F. If the product does not flash at that temperature, they can be assured that virtually no hexane remains.

According to *Bailey's*, "The American-produced extraction naphthas [including hexane) are substantially free from nitrogen- or sulfur-containing compounds, and unsaturated hydrocarbons and leave a residue upon evaporation of less than 0.0016%."

All of the processes described above can happen to an edible oil before the operation which is properly called *refining*. In the usual terminology of the industry, oils which have gone through any or all of the processes from cooking to removal of the solvent are correctly called "unrefined" or "crude" oils.

# REFINING AND BEYOND

Unrefined vegetable oils contain many substances other than oil. Although various oils differ in their percentages of saturated, mono- and polyunsaturated fatty acids, these differences are not detectable by the senses of the buyer. It is the other substances in the oil which give it an individual character which is evident to taste, smell, and vision. Oils which have been refined, bleached, and deodorized become so bland in taste and pale in color that it is often difficult to tell one from the other. The American consumer has learned to prefer the fully-processed product overwhelmingly. Customers of the natural food trade include both persons who prefer highly processed oils and persons who prefer the unrefined product. Many health food stores carry both types.

Just before alkali refining, many oils go through a process called "degumming." In this process, the oil is mixed with water, often at 90 to 120°F., which separates various "mucilaginous materials" from the oil. The oil is separated from the gummy substance with centrifuges. This is the source of much commercial lecithin, primarily from soybeans, but also from sunflowerseed, peanuts, corn and other sources.

The refining operation itself consists of making a soapy solution by adding an alkiali, such as lye or caustic soda, to the oil. After agitation, the mixture passes through a heater at 140 to 160°F., at which point the unwanted substances break away from the oil by a chemical reaction. This "break" in the oil is one of the crucial points in oil processing: a product which has not gone through this process is called "non-break" oil.

After the break takes place, the oil is separated out in centrifuges and is sent to a tank where it is washed with hot water at 160 to 180°F. for about 10 minutes. After washing, the oil is again separated out in centrifuges and is then dried by spraying it through a vacuum, reducing its moisture content to 0.05 percent or less. Traces of soap remaining in the oil at this point are removed by the further steps in processing.

Virtually all the edible oil which is alkali refined is also bleached and deodorized. The choices generally available to the bottler are either an unrefined oil or an oil which has been refined and bleached and deodorized. Another option is the addition of preservatives and/or defoamers.

The bleaching of edible oil does not involve the addition of a substance to the oil which remains in the oil and alters its chemistry. The bleaching of oil is not like adding chlorine bleach to one's laundry. It is, instead, similar to the clarifying of fruit juices by treating them with diatomaceous earth, which gathers up the solid particles from the liquid.

# GOAL OF BLEACHING

The goal of bleaching edible oils is simply to remove pigments from the oil. It also eliminates the soaps which may remain after alkali refining.

The basic material used for bleaching oil is fuller's earth, which has the property of effectively clinging to small particles while leaving the oil behind. Charcoal is even more efficient for this purpose, but its cost limits its use in this way, although a small percentage of charcoal is sometimes mixed with the fuller's earth to increase its adsorptive capacity. Further increase in adsorption capacity can be accomplished by "activating" the earth or the charcoal—previously treating it with hydrochloric or sulfuric acid.

In typical bleaching equipment, the refined oil is introduced into a tank where it is mixed with adsorbent material and agitated, under vacuum. This process takes about twenty minutes, during which the temperature is often maintained in the range of 180°-220° F. The reaction inside the tank removes moisture and color from the oil, and removes the soaps produced during refining. During the bleaching operation, the oil passes through filters which remove the fuller's earth and the particles it has picked up in the tank.

After bleaching, the oil is ready for deodorization. This process does not only remove odors from the oil. It also makes the oil yet paler in color, and removes or destroys the peroxides in the oil which could lead to rancidity. During deodorizing, air is excluded from the process and is replaced with nitrogen, which does not interact with the oil.

Deodorization takes place inside a large tank in which trays of oil are bubbled with steam in a high vacuum at high temperature. The oil comes in at the top, trickles down through the series of trays, with steam being blown through it in each tray, and comes out the bottom as finished oil. This usually occurs at the upper end of the 400°F. range. During our tour of the PVO plant, the deodorizer was running at about 470° F. on the read-out graph, which the plant manager confirmed as the usual operating temperature.

When efficiently done, this entire process results in an oil in which little remains except fatty acids. At the end of our tour of the PVO facility, Schneider waved his hand at the building containing the refining, bleaching, and deodorizing equipment and said, "that's what these units do—they take out everything."

What does remain is a food substance which still contains fatty acids which are essential to the human diet. And what does remain can revert in flavor, become darker, and go rancid if it is exposed to heat, light or air. Preservatives can help retard these reactions. In the natural food industry, the alternative to preservatives is extreme care in storage, transportation, bottling, and display on the retailer's shelves.

*Methods used to remove pigments from oil*

# TEST TUBES & TASTE BUDS

During our visit at PVO, we asked Frans Letschert how the buyer can evaluate edible oils, how to distinguish between a refined and an unrefined product. He brought out several bottles and lined them up in a row. In his hand he held a small jar of amber fluid.

The row of bottles on the table were various brands of safflower oil. All looked nearly identical in contents, holding a clear, pale yellow liquid. Letschert pointed at the jar in his hand.

"This is from our own plant," he said. "This is a *pressed* safflower oil, and you see it has a dark color. You can see it's much darker than any of those. To me, that's a clue that those (on the table) are all fully-refined, bleached, deodorized oils. This (in his hand) is not. You see the difference right there.

"If I open any of those bottles, and I open this, I can taste the difference. This one has a very nutty flavor. All that is bland oil. Bland oil is in demand for food application where you want the flavor of the food—not the oil—to dominate. This unrefined oil will, of course, penetrate into whatever food you use it with. It has a special flavor. To my mind, there is room for both."

The usefulness of both refined and unrefined oils, with their significant flavor differences, is also recognized by other members of the industry. For example, at Westbrae Natural Foods, Rico Villa said that none of their oils are refined, but that he

*How to distinguish between refined and unrefined oils*

had no personal objection to refined oils for some uses, such as in some baking and in restaurants when subtle flavors are important. He noted that unrefined safflower oil can be different each time, depending on the crop, and that some people mistake the taste of unrefined safflower oil for rancidity. "Unrefined safflower or sesame oil can be used in deep frying, but I believe that the rate of oxidation would be so great that I'd question its healthfulness if used that way," Villa said.

The test of color and taste

The test of color and taste is something that can easily be made in the warehouse, store, or home. A pale, bland oil can be relied on to be fully refined, bleached, and deodorized.

Unfortunately, it does not work the other way: A darker, tasty oil is not necessarily one which has only gone through expeller pressing. Solvent extracted or even refined oils can be combined with expeller oils in ways which the buyer alone cannot detect. By controlling the process, refined and more-than-refined oils can be kept darker than usual.

The economics of oil manufacture would make such blending an unusual procedure. It costs less—by two or three cents per pound—to produce an unrefined oil than it does to produce a refined one. We know of no instance in which a refined is mixed with an unrefined oil, but it remains a possibility.

The use of hexane or other solvents anywhere in the manufacturing process could probably be detected by running a GLC (Gas-Liquid Chromatography) test on a sample oil. The GLC would also be likely to show whether the oil had been bleached, and could give the fatty-acid profile of the sample. But a basic GLC costs about $75 for one sample, which would be an extraordinary expense for the buyer who is curious about oils.

Earlier, in this article, when talking about terms used in the industry, we mentioned Peroxide number, AOM, and Iodine Value. These are terms which may appear among the specifications used by manufacturers.

Laboratory tests

AOM stands for "Active Oxygen Method," and is a test of the rate of oxidation or rancidity of an oil. In the AOM test, a sample of oil is aerated at 208°F., and is sampled at regular, frequent intervals. The result of the test is a length of time for the oil to go rancid. The test, however, is not standardized as to what level will be called "rancid." The test produces a number called the *peroxide number*, and each laboratory individually determines what peroxide number will be called "rancidity" for a particular kind of oil. The peroxide number itself expresses the amount of reactive oxygen per 1000 grams of oil. Human beings often cannot detect rancidity until 20 percent of the oil has oxidized; peroxide number levels of rancidity are set much lower than the usual human response.

The term Iodine Value will be discussed below. Other terms and tests go beyond the scope of this book, and may be found in the technical literature by anyone interested.

# DISTRIBUTION PUZZLE

Almost all of the oils sold in the health food trade are bought from manufacturers in bulk and are then bottled under familiar industry labels. Our attempt to report who supplies the oils to the various members of the natural food industry was similar to constructing a jigsaw puzzle with missing pieces. A "flow-chart" from the manufacturers through the bottlers to the private-label firms would exhibit many gaps and dead ends. Some executives of companies which sell refined oils to the health food trade spoke off-the-record and declined to have themselves or their corporations named.

Oil sources? Mum's often the word

We talked with major health-food companies which sell oils under their own brand names. Some, like Landstrom Sales Manager Rick Merriam, told us why they preferred not to discuss their sources of oil: "If I tell you, everybody else would be in there trying to buy," he said. Others—especially Arrowhead Mills, Erewhon, Pure & Simple, and Westbrae Natural Foods—were more willing to share such information.

Distributors were not the only companies which sometimes hesitated to talk about their oils. A number of manufacturers declined to answer questions about their processing methods. Other companies answered questions about their processing methods. Other companies answered questions about their manufacturing, but would not state what companies in the health food industry bought their oil. This reaction typically came from firms which produce fully-refined oil. Still other companies, expressing special pride in their unrefined products, were eager to talk about their operations. Our tour of the PVO plant was complete, detailed, and included a straightforward step-by-step explanation of their manufacturing process at every point.

PVO manufactures about 80 percent of the safflower oil sold in the United States. Their customers include Arrowhead Mills, Bingo Distributors, Blooming Prairies, The Bread Shop, Dipsea Inc., Eden Foods, Federation of the Ohio River, Giusto's, Hain, Life Stream, Pavo, United Naturals, Westbrae, Western Massachusetts Cooperative, and many others. Leslie, best known as a salt company, bottles PVO's own Saffola brand and other brands for the health food trade.

PVO—the major
supplier of safflower oil

Five kinds of safflower oil are currently produced by PVO. According to PVO Sales Supervisor David Hoffsten, this is how the ordering works: "A customer calls me and tells me he's interested in safflower oil. I say, 'OK, which grade are you interested in?' I go down the line: I have expeller pressed, I have fully refined, bleached, deodorized without antioxidant, or with antioxidant, and I have high-oleic saff (with or without antioxidant). He'll fit in one of those products with his requirements. We can't do anything better than our product specs, so if a customer comes back with specs we can't meet, I say, 'I'm sorry, that product isn't made.' Our specifications are standard throughout the industry." A comparison of spec sheets from PVO and from Agricom, another processor, shows them to be nearly identical.

At Continental Grain Co., Manager Jerry Knick stated that his company sells prepressed (expeller pressed) oil to D.A.N.C. and to Hain Pure Food Co. "Hain uses prepressed. We do refine it for them," Knick said. He explained that "refined" meant that the oil was processed through alkali wash and deodorized at about 475°F. Continental Grain, he noted, makes a pressed and a refined safflower oil, both of which are sold to the health food industry.

Other sources, other oils

A letter from Marino Garbis at Orland Olive Oil Co. states, "All our olive oil production is sold... to packers such as Hain Pure Foods of Los Angeles, Pure and Simple of San Jose, as well as other packers who need a good, flavorful virgin olive oil for blending with refined olive oil."

Sona Food Products in El Cerrito, Calif. is a major bottler of edible oils sold to the natural foods industry. Sona does not manufacture the oil it bottles. According to Otto Smejkal, their technical director in charge of quality control, Sona bottles oils for Health Valley, Kahan & Lessin (Health Food Store Brand), Lakeridge Farms, Landstrom (Healthway brand), and Norganic. Smejkal said that Sona gets oil from Humko, Hunt-Wesson, Liberty Vegetable Oil Co., PVO, Sesame Products Corp., and Wilsey Foods. Sona bottles safflower, apricot kernel, sweet almond, avocado (imported), peanut, and corn oils, he said.

At Humko, Salesman Alfred Chammel said that all the oils they sell are solvent extracted, bleached, and deodorized. Chammel said that he does not think that Humko sells directoly to the health food industry at this time.

Oils sold by Hunt-Wesson are all caustic refined, according to William Blodgett, Director of Corporate Relations. Blodgett said that Hunt-Wesson buys "crude vegetable oil" which goes to one of their six refineries to be treated with caustic solution, bleached, and deodorized.

The oil produced by Liberty Vegetable Oil Co. is expeller pressed and is refined using sodium hydroxide, according to company Vice President William Adams.

At Wilsey Foods, James Healey, Vice President of Quality Control, Research and Development, said that the company buys finished oil, already processed.

A potpourri of oils

This information provided by Sona's suppliers indicates that PVO and Sesame Products are the only sources from which Sona could obtain unrefined oils. PVO can provide mechanically pressed, unrefined safflower oil, and Sesame Products can provide mechanically pressed, unrefined sesame oil. PVO also manufactures other edible oils, all of which are refined, bleached, and deodorized.

For any particular bottle of oil on the retail shelf, it is often impossible to state with certainty that it came from a certain manufacturer via a certain bottling facility. Any given brand name may include various oils from diverse manufacturing origins.

# 51

# A Survey of Oils

## by Jim Schreiber

**Fatty acids**

A concern for nutrition has made "polyunsaturated" a household word. The desirability of an oil is currently judged to a significant extent by its percentage of polyunsaturates, along with a favorably low level of saturated fatty acids. All edible oils contain some polyunsaturates. The question is: How much?

Precise tests by oil chemists have determined the usual amounts of *saturated*, and of *mono-* and *polyunsaturated* fatty acids in typical samples of each kind of oil. the standard measure of the degree of saturation (including both mono- and polyunsaturates) is called the Iodine Number or Iodine Value.

Iodine Value is determined by a test which uses an iodine compound in the laboratory procedure, and does not indicate that there is any iodine in the oils which people consume. Iodine Values of different edible oils range from about 150 down to almost zero, with the higher numbers indicating a higher degree of unsaturation. There is a loose correspondence between high Iodine Values and a high level of polyunsaturates, which is of some interest to consumers. In the lab test, measured amounts of certain iodine compounds and oil are combined at a standard temperature, and the Iodine Value is the number of grams of iodine absorbed by 100 grams of oil.

Of greater interest to buyers is the percentage of *polyunsaturates*, thought to be of greater health significance than the total percentage of unsaturated fatty acids. Percentages of polyunsaturates are given for each oil in the table below, when we have been able to find that information.

**Linoleic acis**

Without certain unsaturated fatty acids in the diet, human beings develop specific fat-deficiency ailments. Linoleic acid is effective in countering this deficiency, and is one of the major polyunsaturated components of many oils sold in health food stores. Natural oils contain vitamins A, D, E and K, and also aid in the efficient use of the B vitamins. Oils for consumer use in the USA are all more than 92 percent digestible, and are noted as a major source of calories in the American diet.

234

The commercial value of edible oil is also determined in part by such matters as taste, color, odor, onset of rancidity, smoke-point temperature, and clouding or solidifying when refrigerated. The operator of a natural food store faces a special problem in regard to taste, color and odor, because the American consumer has in general learned to prefer a standardized product, refined, bleached, and deodorized to a uniform, bland-tasting, odorless, clear, pale substance, whereas some nutrition-oriented customers prefer an unrefined oil which retains characteristic flavors and aromas, looks darker, and may even contain sediments.

Bland oils—an acquired taste

# UNREFINED NOSES

Unrefined oils seem rancid to some buyers, simply because their noses are accustomed to deodorized oils. Unrefined soybean oil, for example, has so powerful a smell that it makes some people gag. A rationale for extensive refining is that oils may be put to uses for which a strong flavor is not desired by the consumer. Free fatty acids—considered undesirable by many health-conscious customers—are removed by the refining, bleaching, deodorizing process, but remain in the unrefined product. The purchaser of an unrefined oil will, as a rule, have a product which smokes more readily in cooking, becomes cloudy or solid more easily under refrigeration, and goes rancid more rapidly than a fully-refined oil of the same variety. As usual, the refining of a food introduces factors of convenience while eliminating constituents from the original material.

Characteristics of refined and unrefined oils

A low-temperature filtering method called "winterizing" can keep oils clear and liquid in the refrigerator—oils which would otherwise become cloudy or solid. The addition of antioxidants like citirc acid, BHA, BHT, or TBHQ can retard the onset of rancidicty. The addition of a defoamer such as methyl silicone can reduce the foaming action of cooking oils, which is sometimes an important aspect of deep-frying when boil-over could be a problem. Hydrogenation adds convenience in handling, but destroys the polyunsaturated fatty acids. It is unlikely that products with additives, or hydrogenated ("saturated"), would be found in health food stores. If so, the label would tell.

Winterizing and antioxidants

The major sources of information given in the table on particular oils are the Weiss book and *Bailey's*.

Among our written sources of information, we found two of special value. *Bailey's Industrial Oil and Fat Products*, edited by Daniel Swern, is sometimes called a "bible" for the edible oil industry. A volume of over a thousand pages, *Bailey's* describes edible oil processing thoroughly from start to finish. A smaller book, published in 1970, is *Food Oils and Their Uses*, by Theodore J. Weiss, a research chemist with the US Department of Agriculture. Although less technical and comprehensive than *Bailey's*, the Weiss book gives a good general survey of the properties, sources, and processing of various edible oils. And for persons with a strong scientific background and access to a university library, the *Journal of the American Oil Chemists' Society* can provide up-to-date technical information.

For further reading

# 52

# *Oil of the Olive*

## by Janice Fillip

The US produces only 1/3 of one percent of the world's supply of olive oil. Although Star and Bertolli are easily recognized as imported brands, most olive oil sold under familiar labels is bought in bulk from European sources—in Spain, Italy, Greece, Turkey Tunesia and Israel—and repackaged. An estimated 85-90 percent of imported olive oil is refined in the country of origin. Unless the label reads "100% virgin olive oil," it is a safe bet that the oil is refined or blended.

Buying "home grown" is not a simple thing, California is the major—if not the only—source of domestic olive oil on a commercial scale. Over the past forty years, domestic production has steadily declined. In 1936, it is estimated there were over 70 producers of olive oil in California. By 1978, that number had dropped to under 10, many of whom are unable to guarantee continuous production every year. N. Sciabica & Sons is one of the oldest olive-pressing companies in California. How have they managed to survive the decline? Dan Sciabica says, "The only reason we've stayed in business is because we're selling quality."

Selling quality has its drawbacks. For one thing, it costs more. A pint of Sciabica's "Oil of the Olive" sells for $3.69 in a San Francisco natural health food store. Sciabica's oil is expensive not because of its gourmet reputation, but because of the way it is made. N. Sciabica & Sons makes oil the way it used to be made, although Dan Sciabica is the first to admit that there are "faster, more economical ways to make it."

The economics of solvent extraction, caustic washes and deodorization have not influenced Sciabica's operation. At the Sciabica plant, olives are crushed cold and the mash is put into nylon bags which are stacked and compressed by a hydraulic press. When the oil oozes out of the bags, it is at room temperature. A centrifuge then separates the bitter-tasting olive water from the oil. Since it will not combine with the oil, diatomaceous earth is used to filter out sediment which may have escaped from the nylon bags. No heat is applied to the oil during pressing. This prevents the naturally-occurring oxidation inhibitors from being destroyed. Pressed without heat, the oil remains highly stable, and can last up to three years without turning rancid.

**100% pure virgin olive oil—a guarantee of quality**

**The way oil used to be made—and sometimes still is**

236

# TWO SECRETS

Dan Sciabica revealed two secrets of making good olive oil. The first secret is to make the processing operation as sanitary as possible. Sciabica remarked that oil will pick up any odors or flavors around it, "just like a sponge."

The second secret is to start with sound, ripe fruit. Sciabica explained that this is why, in Italy, fruit was allowed to decompose before it was pressed. Color and flavor of the oil are determined by the type of olive crushed and the time of year they are picked. The January-March crush produces a golden oil, while the November-December crush uses greener olives and gives a greenish oil with stronger flavor.

Olives are grown mainly to sell to the canning industry. Generally, the fruit crushed for oil has ripened early, is undersized, or is frost damaged. Although these cosmetic considerations render the fruit unacceptable to the canning industry, they do not affect the quality of the oil. Competition from olive canneries limits the amount of fruit left to mature for crushing. In small-crop years, there may not be enough fruit available for crushers.

N. Sciabica & Sons sells its oil in grocery stores and in natural health food stores. Sales in grocery stores suffer due to the price difference between Sciabica's "Marsala" brand and imported oils. Dan Sciabica feels that customers in grocery stores do not realize what "pure virgin oil" means, so shoppers buy imported, blended oil which is less expensive.

In natural food stores, Sciabica discovered that its business has been steadily increasing. Dan Sciabica credits this to the fact that, when they shop in a natural food store, "People are looking for quality."

**Good oil begins with ripe fruit**

**Quality is worth the price**

# OIL TABLE

| Oil | Fatty Acids Saturated | Polyunsaturated Unsaturated | Polyunsaturated Linoleic* | Average Iodine Value** | General Characteristics Taste | General Characteristics Color | General Characteristics Stability |
|---|---|---|---|---|---|---|---|
| **Almond** | 5% | 95% | 17% | 100 | Usually only available refined. | | |
| **Coconut** | 91% | 9% | 3% | 9 | Usually only available refined. | | |
| **Corn** | 17% | 83% | 59% | 124 | Strong, smells like popcorn. | Golden | Good—high toco-pherol (vitamin E) content. |
| **Olive - 100% Virgin** | 10% | 90% | 15% | 84 | Olive | Golden or green. | Good—contains natural antioxidants. |
| **Palm Kernel** | 85% | 15% | 2% | 18 | Imported from around the world, composition and characteristics of oil vary widely with source. Usually only available refined. | | |
| **Peanut** | 20% | 80% | 31% | 92 | Pea-nutty, Earthy | Amber | Becomes solid when refrigerated. |
| **Safflower** | 6% | 94% | 78% | 143 | Nutty, slightly earthy. | Deep amber to yellow. | Prone to oxidation due to high level of unsaturated fats. |
| **Sesame Seed** | 13% | 87% | 44% | 110 | Nutty, like sesame seeds. | Dark yellow | Good—contains natural antioxidant sesamoline. |
| **Soybean** | 15% | 85% | 50% | 130 | Strong "fishy." | Light amber. | Unstable. |
| **Sunflower Seed** | 8% | 92% | 75% | 130 | Nutty | Dark amber. | Good. |
| **Walnut** | 16% | 84% | 51% | 138 | Nutty | | |
| **Wheat Germ** | 18% | 82% | 55% | 125 | Usually only available refined. | | |

\* Linoleic is the most widespread of the polyunsaturated fatty acids found in vegetable oils, and is essential in the human diet.

\*\* Iodine Value is the standard measure for the degree of fatty acid saturation, including both mono and polyunsaturates. The highest numbers indicate a higher degree of unsaturated fatty acids.

# Consumer's Guide

The tasteless, pale, odorless cooking oil on supermarket shelves is a product of highly technological processes including alkali refining, bleaching and deodorizing. The high temperatures and caustic chemicals used to obtain these oils also removes naturally-occurring nutrients from the oils. Natural and health food stores often offer a range of minimally-refined or unrefined oils for consumers trying to eliminate highly processed, non-nutritious foods from their diets. Just because an oil is sold in a natural food store or health food store does not, however, guarantee that the oil is unrefined.

- Do not rely on the term *cold pressed*. It does not always mean unrefined. The term is sometimes used to describe oils that have been expeller pressed under low-heat conditions, then simply filtered and bottled; it is sometimes used on labels of refined, solvent extracted oils.

- Eyes, nose and tongue can tell the difference between expeller pressed and refined oils. Expeller-pressed oils have a distinctive color, taste and aroma. Refined oils are bland, pale, and odorless.

- The law requires that preservatives used in oils be listed on the label. Common additives to oil include BHA, BHT, TBHQ, polysorbate 80 and methyl silicone.

- Exposure to heat, oxygen and light will cause expeller-pressed oils to go rancid.

- The phrase *contains no cholesterol* is always true of vegetable oils. No vegetable oil contains cholesterol, an animal-derived substance.

- Unrefined oil may be stored under a nitrogen blanket to prevent oxidation. Nitrogen is an inert atmospheric gas which does not mix with the oil.

- Unless olive oil is labeled 100% pure virgin olive oil, it is either a refined oil or a blend of refined and pressed olive oil.

- Olive oil readily picks up flavors and odors of the foods around it. Care should be taken in storing open bottles of olive oil.

# Section IX: Made-up Foods

A large but ill-defined category of products sold in natural foods stores accounts for more money earned by the industry than any other category. In this book, we call this assortment of products "made-up foods" because they would not exist without the intervention of complex machineries and processes invented by human beings. These products are the result of attempts to pare foods down to a selected set of nutrients, to be offered to the purchasers in a highly concentrated, "pure" form not found in nature. The most obvious example of this kind of product is the vitamin pill.

These products are the focus of a heated debate in the industry. There is no doubt that the sale of such concentrated special nutrients is highly profitable, but many retailers doubt whether such items have any place in an industry which claims to sell natural foods. Vitamins, minerals, lecithin, yeasts and all the other nutrients are found in nature, but not in the isolated, high-potency forms which result from chemical processing. What should be called "natural?"

The situation is made more complicated by the policies and activities of the federal Food and Drug Administration, which makes repeated efforts to put vitamins and other supplements under controls resembling those for prescription drugs. Periodically, in response to FDA proposals, members of the industry have had to fight against governmental control of the vitamin trade, arguing that such regulation would limit the public's freedom of choice and ability to look after its own health.

240

Much attention is now being given in the media to the importance of specific nutrients, such as large doses of vitamin C. As these debates go on, great amounts of valuable information about these nutrients become publicly known, to the benefit of the consumer. But what is missing for the natural foods buyer who follows these controversies is an explanation of how these vital substances make their way into little capsules and tablets from. . .where? This section of the *Guide* includes two chapters on vitamin supplements which show that the pills sold in the natural foods trade are the product of elaborate systems of chemical technology, and that they are, nevertheless, different from the drug store brands.

Lecithin, too, is one of the substances receiving a lot of attention in the press these days, as scientists probe its role in the functioning of the nervous system. Whatever the public may learn about its importance or desirability in the diet, the individual who enters the shop to buy lecithin products sees only labels, all of which give the impression that this one is the genuine article. Within the industry, arguments and counter-arguments are exchanged about the authenticity of different brands which have been differently processed. The chapter titled *On the Labels of Lecithin* examines this ongoing debate.

Many people in the natural foods industry express a concern about nutrition on a planetary scale, seeing their work not only as a livelihood, but also as contributing to solutions to problems of world hunger. It is not surprising that major food corporations in the American mainstream express similar concerns—although it may be surprising that one of those corporations is Standard Oil, through its subsidiary Amoco Foods.

Amoco Foods produces yeasts which have an impressive, high-protein nutritional profile, and are sometimes described as one possible way to feed a hungry world. Some of the Amoco yeasts are used in foods sold in natural foods stores. Questions have been raised about the safety of these Amoco products, because earlier attempts to raise edible yeasts on petrochemicals failed, due to the presence of toxins in the final product. The last chapter in this section examines these issues as they were presented in a report by *Mother Jones* magazine.

241

# 53

## The Pill Perplex

### by Jim Schreiber

Within living memory, no one in the world knew anything at all about vitamins. The word "vitamine" was not coined until 1911, to describe a suspected but unknown substance thought to be essential to life. Knowledge about vitamins and minerals is still young and growing, with new discoveries—and new controversies—emerging every year.

**The history of vitamin research**

The history of vitamin research has a rough resemblance to a child's learning about different vehicles. The word "truck" at first seems enough to talk about the ones that haul things along roads, but closer attention shows that there are specialized types such as semi-trailers, flatbeds and pickups. Eventually the child may learn that, in spite of their similarities, a refrigerated truck can do a job that an unrefrigerated one cannot do, and that what had been unseen under the hood has a lot to do with the truck's performance. With each new discovery, new names of things are added to the child's vocabulary. Similarly, the scientist first sees something and labels it, perhaps, vitamin E. As research goes on, more different forms of the substance are discovered, each one able to do certain jobs but not others, each one needing its own name. For a person buying vehicles or vitamins these days, it is important to know a lot more than "truck" or "E." The details make the difference.

**Invisible food additives**

In their short history, vitamins and minerals have been introduced into countless products, as invisible food additives and as the familiar bottled formulations sold in drug stores, supermarkets, and health food stores. A vast literature on the topic has been written by nutritionists, chemists, physicians, publicists, and writers for trade and consumer magazines. Most of these millions of words have focused on the nutritional aspects of the subject, both in the popular media and in scientific journals. Little has been said about their commercial manufacture.

The subject of vitamins and minerals acts as a great watershed in the natural foods industry. On one slope of this Great Divide is a large group of retailers whose business rests mostly or solely on the sale of vitamin and mineral formulations. On the other slope is a large group of retailers whose sales dollars come mostly from food items, with little or no emphasis on these nutrients in capsule, tablet or powder form.

# TWO EXTREMES

At one extreme are such stores as The Good Earth in Fairfax, California, which stripped its shelves of all bottled vitamins and minerals, and refused to stock them despite their profitability. The other extreme is illustrated in a story told by William Shurtleff, co-author of *The Book of Tofu*: Visiting in southern California, he stopped at a large shop under a "Health Food Store" sign to ask if they had any tofu in stock. The entire store was ranks and files of bottled pills. In response to Shurtleff's inquiry at the counter, the clerk looked puzzled at the word "tofu" and explained, "No, this is a health food store."

This division in the industry is reflected in what the stores call themselves. Retail operations with most of their sales dollars in vitamins and minerals almost always describe themselves as *health* food stores. Those with less than half their sales dollars in these products almost always describe themselves as *natural* food stores. A far smaller number of stores in the middle show no particular preference, as a group, for one style of self-description or the other. Most shops tend either to deemphasize these items or to emphasize them strongly; the pattern is what statisticians call a "bi-modal distribution curve."

Various surveys indicate that between 30 and 40 percent of the annual retail sales dollars in the industry as a whole come from trade in vitamins, minerals and other nutritional supplements. Proprietors who reject this potential source of income usually base their decision on a conviction that such pills and powders are simply not natural, and therefore have no place in an authentic natural foods business.

A common argument generally runs like this: The human body is designed to live on foods, not on pills which were not invented until this century. While it is true that the mainstream American food-processing industry depletes the nutrients naturally found in foods, and laces their products with unwanted additives, the way to correct this is to return to an intelligent diet of foods as close to their natural state as it is possible to produce them. Pills are another step away from a natural diet.

A frequent argument on the other side generally runs like this: Ideally, people would and could obtain all their nutrients from foods, but the practical fact is that the American public does not eat that way, and therefore risks a lack of some essential nutrients. In addition, individual needs vary widely and it is often completely impractical to try to get specifically needed nutrients from available foods alone. Pills meet real needs.

# UNANSWERED QUESTIONS

For the many people in the industry who do not stand convinced that vitamin and mineral pills are unacceptable, but who have some doubts about them, the most usual questions are these: Just how "natural" are these products in our industry? How do they differ from the bottled vitamins and minerals usually displayed in supermarkets and drug stores?

In studying the topic of vitamins and minerals, despite all the published materials, we discovered little printed documentation of the manufacturing process. Even authoritative sources of technical information written by experts in their fields, such as the *Encyclopedia of Chemical Technology (ECT)*, contain such statements as, "Industrial concerns manufacturing thiamine have not published the details of their methods . . ." and, "Although the commercial methods [of vitamin E production] have not been described in detail, the processes probably resemble . . ." The literature is filled with reports and diagrams of complex chemical reactions which require some scientific training to comprehend fully, but in order to find out what is involved in the manufacture of these products in our industry, it is necessary to go directly to the manufacturer and ask.

Our research on this topic started early in 1978 when writer Victor Anton Zarley, Jr. began making inquiries of about twenty firms which advertise in this industry's trade publications and in health-oriented consumer magazines. Some of the companies responded with evident candor and in detail which required appreciable time and effort. Some replied briefly. Some sent catalogs. Some stayed mute. No attempt was made to cover the more-than-seventy companies which list themselves as vitamin manufacturers for our industry; the questions being asked were too extensive to survey the entire industry, including tape-recorded interviews, within the available time. Most of the information in this chapter which is attributed to the personnel of specific firms is the result of Mr. Zarley's inquiries and his compiling of the responses.

# WHAT IS "NATURAL"?

Paavo Airola's nutritional definition

Different persons give diverse meanings to the words "natural vitamins." Paavo Airola, in his book *Are You Confused?*, distinguishes between all the isolated and synthetic vitamins in pill form on the one hand, and natural vitamins from such sources as brewer's yeast, lecithin, and wheat germ oil on the other. He indicates that both forms have their uses, depending on the individual circumstances. But Airola's subject is nutrition—not manufacturing processes or marketing practices.

Both natural and synthetic vitamins have chemical names

Chemists in universities and in industry make clear-cut distinctions between natural and synthetic vitamins, giving them different names, and different descriptions of the molecules which comprise the vitamins. For example, a vitamin we call riboflavin or B2 as found in nature is called riboflavin mononucleotide, and a form made in the laboratory is known as 7-methyl-9-(D-1-ribityl)-isoxalloxazine. People who are not scientists tend to be put off by lengthy chemical names, but the reason both these forms are called B2 is that their molecules are similar in structure and they exhibit similar interactions with other molecules. Those formidable names are simply a chemist's way of saying something analogous to "two circles inside of six squares, attached in one place to a row of four triangles." The name alone does not reveal whether the chemical is beneficial or harmful, natural or synthetic. Natural vitamins, too, have imposing chemical names.

In trying to understand the chemical complexities of this subject, we have sometimes found it helpful to imagine vitamin molecules as being rather like housekeys, or as being rather like pairs of gloves. Some small variations in the shape of a housekey will still allow it to do its job, while other variations may make it useless, or might even jam the lock. Some vitamins seem to come in pairs which are mirror images of each other, much as right-hand and left-hand gloves are mirror images of each other. Putting the wrong one into the human body may be similar to trying to put the left hand into a right-hand glove. These mirror image-like twins are called "optical isomers."

Synthetic vitamins lack nutrients which accompany natural vitamins

In discussing the difference in natural and synthetic vitamins, Dr. James Hilbe of the Wm. T. Thompson Co. said, "First, in nature, *all* nutritional materials are accompanied by *other* nutritional materials. E.g., in plants, Vitamin C is accompanied by bioflavonoids, but this is not the situation in animals. When manufactured, Vitamin C is made as the pure, crystalline product with no other nutrients present unless they are added. Second, Vitamin E *can* be manufactured to be identical to the d-alpha tocopherol of nature. However, it can not be manufactured without also making the optical isomer, l-alpha tocopherol. As l-alpha tocopherol does not occur in nature (as far as is known), animals and man do not have the enzymes necessary to process this Vitamin E analog . . ."

# SYNTHETIC DISTINCTION

When asked how much processing can be done to a vitamin derived from natural sources before it should be called synthetic, Dr. Hilbe replied, "This is apparently a subjective decision. For example, d-alpha tocopherol acetate is usually called 'natural E.'

However, there has been a molecular change in the product. My opinion is that if the chemical optical qualities are changed, then it should no longer be called 'natural.' All of our ingredients are 'naturally derived.' We do not use d-l-alpha tocopherol or its derivatives.''

A subjective distinction

A somewhat different view is offered by Harold Kutler, president of NuLife: ''Synthetic vitamins are chemically the same as natural vitamins,'' he said, ''and the difference has always been a nebulous one. Nebulous insofar as it is difficult to demonstrate the difference scientifically, unlike the example of synthetic seawater that will not support life.'' The NuLife Full Disclosure Book makes a distinction between nutrients from natural sources and those which are synthetic. It defines as ''from natural sources . . . any vitamin derived from a food source or any mineral derived from a food or geological source either by processing or synthesis. Thus Vitamin C synthesis from Corn Dextrose is from a natural source while Vitamin A Palmitate synthesized from acetylene or synthetic Beta Ionone would be classified as synthetic . . . so our definition of synthetic in regard to nutrition is any nutrient principally derived from chemicals.''

Natural vitamins from a food or geological source

On the same subject, Alfred Rechberger, president of Essential Organics, said, ''It is believed that a synthetic vitamin is identical to an *isolated, purified* natural vitamin. Vitamins as they occur in nature are complexed with various compounds like synergistic factors, coenzymes, trace elements, etc. Laboratory-made vitamins are devoid of these factors. It is our aim to provide 'whole' supplements . . .

''A substance is not necessarily 'good' because it's 'Natural.' Many plants contain toxic substances or inhibitive factors like phytic acid in grains, oxalic acid in spinach and kale, etc. Special enzyme systems which humans don't have are required to digest these compounds and made them neutral. A genetic defect in humans is responsible for the fact that we do not synthesize Vitamin C like other mammals. Laboratory synthesis, in this case, can provide much good for man. On the other hand, there are also drawbacks with synthetics.''

''Natural'' does not always mean ''good''

# WHAT MANUFACTURERS DO

Over seventy firms list themselves as vitamin manufacturers for the health food trade. The 1978 *Thomas Register* lists ninety companies under its ''Vitamins'' heading. Thirty companies are listed as sources of various vitamins in the 1978 *Chemical Week Buyer's Guide.* The 1977 edition of *Pharmaceutical Manufacturers of the United States* lists sixty firms which mention vitamins among their products. Many duplications appear among these lists, but we are left with more than a hundred vitamin manufacturers listed in the major references. What are all these companies doing?

In general, the companies specialize. An examination of the many lists and catalogs shows that specific components, such as inositol, thiamine hydrochloride, binders, and gelatin capsules each come from a small number of original sources. It is not a literal truth but is a significant metaphor that ''All roads lead to Hoffman-LaRoche.'' The typical company in the health food trade buys its ingredients from these primary sources, purchasing the standardized—not tailor-made—chemicals offered by the primary-source firms. The food-grade chemicals available are of the highest quality of purity.

All roads lead to Hoffman-LaRoche

The vitamin manufacturer in the health food trade takes these raw materials and decides what to do with them—how to combine them, whether to do the tablet-making in-house or farm it out, what quality-control measures will be taken, how the products will be tested and advertised, and how much information about their ingredients and processes to disclose to the public.

As a rule—regardless of arguments over the use of the word ''natural''—the vitamin and mineral supplements offered by manufacturers in the health food industry differ greatly from those usually sold in drug stores and supermarkets. The mainstream commercial trade has no reason to avoid the total synthetics if they are cheaper than the isolates. The drug store brands can, and do, use artificial colors, preservatives, sugar, shellacs, and polyvinyl plastic fillers. Such things are within the laws governing foods. In

Supplements sold in natural and health foods stores are different from those sold in drug stores and supermarkets our industry, the manufacturer, with a prudent eye on the marketplace, will usually exclude some or all such ingredients. Some components are not required on labels.

# LIMITS OF SUPPLY

**Manufacturers' dilemma—what you see may not be what you get**

Ironically, the manufacturers seem to have their own disclosure problems with their suppliers. This is illustrated by a disclaimer in NuLife's Full Disclosure Book: "The information contained here is limited by the data we have. We are not responsible for additives that may be present in raw materials we purchase unbeknown to us." Other limits are imposed by what is actually available from suppliers. Some vitamins are commercially available only in synthetic form because the cost of isolation is immense. Gelatin capsules are made from animal tissues and almost always contain a small amount of a preservative such as methylparaben. The smaller number of capsules without preservatives will, of course, not last as long.

Perhaps the most crucial decisions made by the manufacturer are the components chosen for the products, and the extent of quality control. Nutritional literature indicates that there are required balances among various vitamins, that some are needed in far greater quantities than others, and that some cannot do their job in the body effectively unless other nutrients are present. To make educated choices among the formulations available, the buyer of these products has to keep up-to-date on nutrition. Amid the controversies and unknowns in nutritional information, there are still wide areas of agreement that can help make these choices reasonable.

**Choosing a formulation**

The extent of quality control can vary widely. Like a meal prepared in the kitchen, the ingredients and their combinations at each step can be "tasted"—or the sampling can be left until the serving is complete. The amount of control depends upon the facilities and the inclinations of the manufacturer. On the level of appearance, the tighter the quality control, the more "scientific" and "technological" the company will seem, and thereby may be less appealing to persons who like to keep things natural.

Full disclosure is now being sought by the industry. Some firms have already published their full-disclosure literature. Some report that they are working on it. Others appear uninterested. As yet, there is no complete, final and reliable list of the various companies' positions on this matter.

# DOING THE POSSIBLE

Imagine that you want to go into business as a manufacturer of vitamin and mineral supplements which are as natural as possible. No synthetics. You know that a provitamin A is in carrots, B's are in yeasts, C is in oranges, etc. All you have to do is get the vitamins from the foods into tablets and capsules in concentrations that make it worth doing. But how?

**Isolating vitamins from natural sources requires chemical processing**

A little study shows that many vitamins can be isolated from natural sources. But a little more study shows that the only known methods of isolation involve a complicated series of chemical interactions using a variety of synthetic chemicals in the processing. To produce mineral nutrients which are chelated, as they are in nature, also involves a meticulous, tricky chemical procedure. You find the basic recipes, procedures and standards of purity in such references as the US Pharmacopeia, the National Formulary, and the Food Chemicals Codex. Patents on isolation methods are held by major pharmaceutical houses, and the chain of supply ultimately leads to firms like Hoffman-La Roche, Merck & Co., Pfizer, Inc., and the Eastman—as in Kodak—Chemical Products Co.

In looking at equipment, you realize that, like all machinery, the punches that form the tablets come in standard sizes, so, to keep the dosage the same in each tablet, a filler will usually be needed. Some of the ingredients will not stick together to shape a pill, so a binder must be added, and some are so sticky that they won't pop out of the punch, which calls for a lubricant.

You decide to avoid all the ingredients and processes offered by the chemical industry, and do it yourself, naturally. Very few options are open at this point. Without the complex, high-powered processing, few vitamins and minerals can be extracted in amounts that yield potencies normally called for in a pill. Without using the standardized chemicals and methods of the industry, there is no way to list the amounts of nutrients on the label: carrots and oranges naturally refuse to standardize themselves. The economics of the situation may require charging the consumer a few dollars for a pill that contains as much beta-carotene as a few cents worth of raw carrots—and the FDA may be eyeing your operation with questions about the purity of your non-standardized product.

We may dream about natural vitamins and minerals leaping in significant potencies from organically grown foods into vegetable gelatin capsules with no intervening chemical processes, but at present nobody has the remotest idea how that might be done in reality. In the next chapter are descriptions of how vitamins are produced now.

**Standardization and pricing problems**

# 54

# *Vitamin Alphabet Primer*

## A IS FOR RETINOL

**No vegetable source for natural vitamin A**

Two main types of vitamin A supplements are generally available: synthetic, which is usually vitamin A acetate; and vitamin A from shark or fish liver oils. Natural vitamin A in its complete, finished form is found only in animals, not in vegetable substances.

However, some carotenes—known as provitamins A—readily turn into useable vitamin A in the human body. Beta-carotene, the most bioavailable, is found throughout the plant kingdom. In this slightly indirect way, normal vitamin A requirements can be met within a vegetarian diet. Beta-carotene can be synthesized, but the synthesis procedure starts with vitamin A itself, or else branches off from the synthesis of vitamin A, so that there is no point in synthesizing beta-carotene for the production of nutritional supplements. To the best of our knowledge, there is no current commercial procedure for the isolation of natural beta-carotene from vegetable sources.

Most of the vitamin A and beta-carotene presently marketed is synthetic, created by variations of a laboratory procedure first successful in 1947. In health food store brands, however, the typical source of vitamin A is shark or fish liver oils.

**Concentrating vitamin A from fish oils**

Several processes are available to concentrate the vitamin A from these oils: In one process, the oils are made into a soapy fluid with an alkali and water, and are mixed with a solvent; the water is then separated from the solvent—which then includes the vitamin A—and then the solvent is evaporated, leaving the somewhat concentrated vitamin behind.

A more effective method, molecular distillation, is known to be employed in the processing of some vitamin A for the health food trade. In this method, the fish oil is piped to the center of a heated, rotating disc inside a vacuum still. Some components evaporate more swiftly than others and are drawn off. By using a series of these stills, different components of the oil can be recovered separately. Concentrated vitamin A is distilled out as a specific stage in this series.

A newer process employs propane as a solvent to yield vitamin A which is as much as 35 times as concentrated as it is in fish liver oil.

This vitamin naturally occurs in two forms, A1 and A2. Both forms are known to promote growth, although the exact mechanism is not known. Studies indicate that the vitamin when dispersed in water is more available to the body than when it is suspended in oils. Although vitamin A itself is oxidized easily by ordinary air, capsules and tablets currently marketed have been found to be quite stable.

The latest *Chemical Week Buyer's Guide* lists nine companies as sources of vitamin A.

Solvent extraction gives higher concentration

# B1 IS FOR THIAMINE

Thiamine, vitamin B1, is probably best known as one of the nutrients legally required as an additive to over-milled grain products in order to "enrich" them. Commercial pasta is heavily dosed with B1 because cooking readily destroys this vitamin.

B1, a required additive for over-milled grain products

Synthesis of thiamine was first accomplished in the late 1930's. According to the most recent *Encyclopedia of Chemical Technology*, Hoffman-La Roche, Inc. and Merck & Co., Inc. are the only manufacturers of B1 in the United States. Two forms of this vitamin— thiamine hydrochloride and thiamine mononitrate—find major commercial use. The mononitrate is much less sensitive to heat, and absorbs less moisture from the air than the hydrochloride.

Many nutritionists question the value of any single, isolated B vitamin, and assert that the B vitamins are a complex which work together in specific proportions. Consistent with this viewpoint, vitamin supplement manufacturers for the health food industry typically offer B-complexes of various formulations.

Yeast is a common natural source of B vitamins, including thiamine. In nature, yeasts produce B vitamins as part of their life process, but in concentrations far lower than those found in most nutritional supplements. In commercial production, yeasts are commonly grown under highly controlled conditions, with the manufacturer carefully monitoring the ingredients in the yeast's nutrient broth.

A natural source of B vitamins

According to a medical doctor associated with a vitamin manufacturer, "Yeast is a primary source of B vitamins, but even with the yeast they feed it synthetic B vitamins. They make it available to the yeast and it incorporates a certain amount up to their B-vitamin totals. The yeast actually incorporates the synthetic B vitamins into their metabolism—so is it still synthetic?

"Synthetic B vitamins can be made passively available to the yeast, and the yeast takes up a small amount. But I believe there is a way where the yeast can be forced to take more . . . Then there is another way where they dump it in, and the yeast takes a little, but the rest is just sitting there outside the yeast. So you get both [in the product]."

Published statements by Gides-NuLife acknowledge that high potencies of B vitamins are not available from yeast and other natural sources, and that all high-potency B complexes contain synthesized B vitamins—but that "In this age of stress, we find ourselves in need of generous amounts of the B Vitamins."

High potency B complex formulas contain synthetic B vitamins

*Chemical Week Buyer's Guide* lists six commercial sources of thiamine hydrochloride and four commercial sources of thiamine mononitrate, both synthetics.

# B2 IS FOR RIBOFLAVIN

Generous amounts of riboflavin, vitamin B2, are found in whole grains, cheddar cheese, eggs and other foods. Riboflavin can also be derived through fermentation, and can be produced in pure crystalline form through a process of chemical synthesis.

Various strains of bacteria, fungi, and yeasts have been found suitable for producing riboflavin by fermentation. The growth medium is a sterilized mash of whey, grains or other starches which are kept free from iron, because that metal in minute amounts reduces the yield of the vitamin.

Abundant natural sources for vitamin B2

A major technical problem encountered by the chemical industry was the devising of methods for recovering the B2 from the fermentation brew. A wide variety of techniques have been invented to extract the vitamin, some of them involving petrochemicals, others using primarily heat and agitation to effect the recovery of the B2. Yields of riboflavin in the different processes range roughly from 70 to 1600 micrograms of riboflavin for each milliliter of brew.

Dry vitamin B2, perhaps universally a component of B-complex supplements, is stable in air, heat, and soft light. Patented processes can coat the vitamin inside very small beads of fatty acids, a practice which has no apparent effect on the biological availability of the B2. This coating is used in chewable tablets in order to cover the bitter flavor of this vitamin.

**Fatty acid coating on chewable vitamins**

Eight firms are listed by *Chem. Wk. Buyer's Guide* as suppliers of riboflavin.

# B6 IS FOR PYRIDOXINE

In *The Great Nutrition Robbery*, Beatrice Trum Hunter mentions a study which reported that pyridoxine, vitamin B6, is "not metabolically active as a coenzyme unless in the form of pyridoxal phosphate or pyridoxamine phosphate." A recent article in *Bestways* magazine states, "The only form of B-6 we can utilize in our bodies is called pyridoxal-5-phosphate, also known as codecarboxylase"; the article describes a complex chemical procedure for the derivation of B6.

According to many uncontradicted sources, all the B6 now synthesized commercially is pyridoxine hydrochloride. The McGraw-Hill *Encyclopedia of Science and Technology* states, "The value of pyridoxine and pyridoxamine lies in the ability of the tissues to convert them into pyridoxal."

**No apparent deficiency of B6 in normal human diet**

Although the daily requirements are in dispute, there is no apparent deficiency of B6 in the normal human diet. At least one study does indicate that pregnancy may increase the needed amount. The vitamin occurs in most foods, and is also produced naturally in the human intestine in a manner not yet fully understood. Salmon, calf liver, chicken, bananas, barley meal, and rice are among the many abundant natural sources of B6.

Brewer's yeast may contain as much as 50 micrograms of riboflavin for each gram of yeast. However, the chemical synthesis of B6 has proven to be far less expensive than isolation from any natural source, including yeast.

*Chem. Wk. Buyer's Guide* lists five commercial sources of B6. The latest *Encyclopedia of Chemical Technology* states that only two firms, Hoffmann-La Roche and Merck, produce pyridoxine hydrochloride.

# B12 IS FOR COBALIMIN

Vitamin B12, cobalamin, shows the most biological activity of all the B vitamins. The amount of B12 needed in human nutrition is over a thousand times *less* than the other B vitamins.

Commercial production of B12 is achieved through fermentation. B12 is not produced by yeasts and fungi. It is, rather, a product of the life processes of certain bacilli and streptomyces strains, and is made commercially by methods resembling the production of penicillin for the drug trade. Patents on crystalline B12, on concentrates of B12, and on the use of cobalt and cyanide in the production process are held by Merck & Co., Inc.

**B12 from fermented microbe culture**

The microbe culture is fermented in large tanks at about 80° F. for three to five days, in a sterilized broth which may include yeast, casein, minerals, soybean meal, sucrose, or other nutrients. To attain the largest yields, cobalt is added to the brew.

Introducing cyanide into the process changes all the cobalamins present into the form of B12 known as cyanocobalamin. **There is no indication whatsoever that the poison cyanide ends up in the final product!** Removal of the B12 from the final broth involves a series of steps which commonly employ such substances as fuller's earth, hydrochloric acid, and benzyl alcohol.

*Chem. Wk. Buyer's Guide* lists five companies as sources of vitamin B12.

# C IS FOR ASCORBIC ACID

Vitamin C was the first vitamin to be offered on a commercial scale, in the 1930's. Within a few years of the first synthesis of ascorbic acid, the price of the synthetic was less than 1/100th that of ascorbic acid isolated from natural sources, and the synthetic kept getting cheaper.

Today, all high-potency vitamin C in nutritional supplements is synthesized by an elaborate sequence of chemical processes starting with glucose or corn dextrose. Although this vitamin C is often described as "natural" or "from natural sources," there is no question that it is the highly processed result of a sequence of major molecular changes. The end product is a pure USP Food Grade L-ascorbic acid.

**High-potency vitamin C is chemically processed from glucose or dextrose**

Many studies have indicated that pure ascorbic acid is far less effective—and is perhaps sometimes ineffective—as a nutrient than vitamin C in its natural form. The apparent difference is that, in nature, the vitamin is accompanied by bioflavonoids which evidently play a key role in the utilization of the vitamin by the body. The evidence shows that only minute quantities of bioflavonoids are needed to make large amounts of vitamin C effective.

Taking this into account, vitamin manufacturers for health food trade often include bioflavonoids in their formulations, either as a substance such as rose hips or as a special bioflavonoids component specially produced for this use.

The concentrations of vitamin C found in nature are not sufficient for the manufacturer of high-potency supplements. A Nu-Life booklet illustrates this point by stating, "If a 250 mg. Vitamin C tablet were made from only Rose Hip powder, it would have 8.3 grams of material and would be about the size of a golf ball." The natural rosebud concentrates its vitamin C only to two percent, at most. The main nutritional significance of rose hips, acerola and similar ingredients in vitamin C formulations is as a source of bioflavonoids, not as a source of the ascorbic acid itself.

**Rose hips and acerola— sources of bioflavonoids**

The bioflavonoids rutin, hesperidin, and naringen are commercially available to vitamin pill formulators. No evidence has come to our attention that any particular bioflavonoid is nutritionally more effective than any other.

Six commercial sources of ascorbic acid are listed in the 1978 *Chem. Wk. Buyer's Guide.*

# D IS FOR CALCIFEROL

The general term "vitamin D2" refers to an entire class of vitamins designated D2 through D7. (Due to an error in early research, there is now no D1 in the series.) The only D vitamins of commercial significance are D2 and D3. The others show little biological activity.

Vitamin D3 is the form found in nature. It is present in fish liver oils, and is normally produced in the human skin when radiated with sunlight or other sources of ultra-violet light. Vitamin D3 is known specifically as *cholecalciferol.*

**Vitamin D produced by radiating provitamins with ultraviolet light**

Vitamin D2, a related compound, is known as *ergocalciferol.* It is produced when a specific provitamin is exposed to ultraviolet light during manufacturing.

Although some vitamin D can be derived from fish liver oils by methods like those used to yield vitamin A (see the *A is for Retinol* section), most of the vitamin D in the marketplace is produced by radiating its provitamins with ultraviolet light. The provitamin of D2 is called ergosterol; the provitamin of D3 is called 7-dehydrocholesterol. There is no evidence that these provitamins are, themselves, biologically active.

In the commercial production of D2, common sources of the provitamin ergosterol are baker's and brewer's yeast. To generate the greatest yields, the extraction of the ergosterol from the brew is enhanced by processing it with alkali or compounds derived from ammonia.

The commercial production of D3 generally derives the vitamin initially from a fatty animal substance such as lanolin. The derivation process entails several steps which alter the molecular structure of the materials at each step, resulting in an intermediate product which is about 50 percent the desired provitamin of D3. According to *ECT*, "Although 7-dehydrocholesterol is undoubtedly the major source of mammalian provitamin, the synthetic material is invariably used for the manufacture of vitamin D3."

Once the provitamins have been derived in these ways from yeasts or fats, another process is required to convert them into D2 or D3. To accomplish this change, the provitamin is typically dissolved in ether, filtered, and radiated by ultraviolet lights. Then to recover the vitamin from the other components still in the material, the mixture is combined with methanol (pure wood alcohol) and is refrigerated. Both the ether and the methanol are evaporated away during the processing. The remaining gum is vitamin D in a form used in the subsequent manufacture of vitamin supplements.

Twelve different commercial sources of the D vitamins are listed in the 1978 *Chem. Wk. Buyer's Guide*.

**Ether and methanol used to process vitamin D**

# E IS FOR TOCOPHEROL

Vitamin E is a group of eight different compounds of similar structure, called tocopherols. Four of the tocopherol compounds used commercially are derived from natural sources, probably always from vegetable oils.

The purchaser of various vitamin E products is faced with an unusually wide variety of hyphenated terms on the labels, each term referring to a specific compound of the E group. Fortunately, the differences in these terms characterize some easily understood differences in the compounds.

**Does it start with dl- or with d-?** The first part of the complete name of a specific vitamin E compound will be either *dl-* or *d-*. All the tocopherols that occur in nature are named *d-*. The ones named *dl-* are synthetics. (Other forms, named *l-*, do exist, but are not put into vitamin formulations). The *d-* forms of the vitamin show more biological activity than *dl-* forms.

**Is it alpha, beta, or what?** The second part of the name can, in theory, be alpha, beta, gamma, or delta. These four terms name the four different vitamin E compounds found in nature. The *alpha* form is by far the most active as a nutrient, and, in practice, the alpha form is the only kind we have found on labels of these products listing the specific tocopherols.

**Is it tocopherol or tocopheryl?** On labels, the third part of the name will have a *yl* ending if the alpha compound has been isolated from the beta, gamma and delta by a special procedure. The *ol* ending is used if no such isolation process has taken place, and is commonly found when the vitamin is sold in its liquid form.

**Is it acetate or succinate?** The fourth part of the name, if there is a fourth part, shows that the vitamin has been combined with another compound to improve its stability. The acetate formulation is used for liquids; the succinate form is used for tablets and dry capsules.

Terms like "mixed tocopherols" indicate that the product contains all four—alpha through delta—forms of the compound. The International Units (IU) listed on the labels count only the alpha form, because that is the accepted standard of measurement. Various manufacturing procedures are available for processing mixed tocopherols in concentrated form from vegetable oils. Other chemical methods can be used to change the beta, gamma and delta compounds into the alpha form.

To recover vitamin E from vegetable oils, a typical process employed is alkali refining, as described in the chapter on edible oils. Since the refining process removes many other substances along with the tocopherols, further processing is needed to isolate them. Molecular distillation, involving centrifugal action inside a heated, high-vacuum still, is one of several steps used to separate out the tocopherols. The end result is a substance which is mostly vitamin E.

We found no published information describing details of the processes now in use for the commercial production of the various forms of vitamin E. Many sources state that, in the United States, only Eastman Chemical Products and General Mills manufacture vitamin E. *Chem. Wk. Buyer's Guide* lists eight firms as sources of vitamin E.

**D- tocopherols occur in nature; dl- tocopherols are synthetic**

**Process for recovering vitamin E from vegetable oil**

# H IS FOR BIOTIN

The use of the term "vitamin H" for biotin is obsolete. This vitamin is now listed on labels as *biotin*, and is considered to be one of the B vitamins.

It is unlikely that a deficiency of biotin would occur in a normal diet. Extremely minute quantities of this vitamin are adequate for human nutrition, and it is produced naturally in the intestine. According to *ECT*, "Even in the richest sources the absolute concentration of the vitamin is very low, of the order of one part per million . . . The original 1. 1 mg of biotin methyl ester was obtained from 250 kg of dried egg yolk and Koegl spent five years [ending in 1936] accumulating 70 mg of the crystalline material."

The only reported case of biotin deficiency resulted from diets containing extraordinarily large amounts of egg-white over an extended interval of time. Uncooked egg-white contains a substance which inhibits biotin's nutritional action. (There is no evidence that cooked egg-white has this effect.)

Compared to the isolation of biotin from natural sources, the synthesis of this vitamin is relatively easy and inexpensive. Published descriptions of the synthesis of biotin show about a dozen chemical interactions involved in the production of the vitamin.

**Minute quantities of biotin necessary for human nutrition**

# K IS FOR PHYLLOQUINONE

Vitamin K is another of the vitamins which is found in many vegetables, is also produced in the human intestine, and is rarely deficient in persons on normal diets. A lack of vitamin K results in a decreased ability of the blood to clot.

In nature, this vitamin occurs in two forms, K1 or phylloquinone, and K2. A synthetic form is designated as K3 or menadione.

All three forms, and also vitamin K1 Oxide, are fully effective in promoting the clotting ability. Some studies indicate that the body converts all the K vitamins into K2, which then has the direct physiological effect. Standard tests to determine biological activity indicate that the synthetic, K3 or menadione, is more active than natural forms.

The isolation of K1 from natural sources can be accomplished by a number of different procedures which variously involve solvent extraction, chemical interactions, or molecular distillation. Both the isolated K1 and the synthetic K3/menadione are commercially available.

*Chem. Wk. Buyer's Guide* lists six companies as sources of vitamin K, and five as sources of menadione.

**Vitamin K rarely deficient in human diets**

# XYZ IS FOR ALL THE REST

Inositol, one of the B vitamins, is involved in the regulation of cholesterol and fats, and is commonly included in B-complex and multivitamin formulations. Although inositol can be synthesized, commercial production has been limited to obtaining the vitamin as a byproduct of the milling of corn.

Inositol in corn is in the form of an acid. When corn is milled by a wet process, it is soaked in a milk solution of sulphur dioxide, which removes this acid from the corn. Further processing, including the use of lime, filtering, and washing with water, recovers a salt which can then be converted to crystalline inositol by the use of heat, a solution of sulphuric acid, and cooling.

There are several forms of this compound. The one termed *meso*-inositol is the only one known to have significant biological activity, and is the only one manufactured for use in vitamin supplements.

*Chemical Engineering Catalog 77* lists one company as a source of inositol.

**Inositol regulates cholesterol and fats**

# CHOLINE

Choline is a vitamin found in such diverse foods as soybeans, liver, wheat germ, egg yolk, and brewer's yeast. Lecithin is a prime source of choline among the dietary supplements.

A deficiency of choline usually leads to an accumulation of fats in the liver, and the body also needs choline in order to generate a substance required for the proper functioning of the nervous system.

Choline is synthesized in the form of several compounds, including choline chloride and choline dihydrogen citrate, for use in vitamin supplement forumlations. Several procedures can be used to synthesize choline. One of the most direct involves combining trimethylamine with concentrated hydrochloric acid, adding ethylene oxide and keeping this solution under pressure for several hours, producing choline chloride.

# NICOTINIC ACID

Nicotinic acid is familiarly known as niacin, used in the "enrichment" of grain products. Along with the related compound niacinamide, it is one of the B vitamins, and it occurs in all living things. Yeasts are a natural source of significant amounts of this vitamin.

In the preparation of B-vitamin complexes which include nicotinic acid, yeasts or bacterial extracts can be used as natural sources. For the production of nicotinic acid alone—not as part of a B-complex—chemical synthesis has been found to be more suitable.

The most common procedure for the synthesis of nicotinic acid begins with any one of a variety of compounds called *pyridines*. To obtain nicotinic acid, a pyridine is oxidized at high pressure and temperature by substances such as nitric acid, sulfuric acid, or chlorine.

Several procedures are available for the production of niacinamide from niacin. Usual methods involve heating the niacin at over 200°C along with urea or ammonia gas, followed by a separation process using solvents, ammonia, or resins.

Niacinamide is reported to have the same biological activity as niacin.

# A MENTION OF MINERALS

Our research into *The Pill Perplex* did not include a thorough investigation of mineral supplements. Currently, much is being written in consumer magazines about the special uses of particular minerals such as selenium and chromium, and about chelation. The impression we have received from published reports is that this is an area now in rapid transition, with studies now underway and much more data to be generated and verified.

All minerals are found in nature, and most of the ones used in supplements are mined. Some exceptions used in health food store brands are oyster shell, bone meal, egg shell, and powdered carrot extract. Various procedures are used to isolate different minerals from their natural sources and, if desired, to alter them into compounds which are more compatible with the human digestive system. These procedures range from complicated chemical interactions to simple soaking, mechanical separation and evaporation.

It is generally acknowledged that chelated metals show significantly greater availability as nutrients than those which are not chelated, and several sources indicate that amino acid chelation serves this function best. Several sources state that excessive ingestion of non-chelated metals tends to produce deposits of metallic salts in the body, with harmful effects. A report published in a 1976 issue of the *Journal of Applied Nutrition* asserts that gluconates, fumarates, citrates and EDTA as chelating agents are relatively ineffective in promoting bioavailability, and that only amino acid chelates are effective in this role.

A chemist in the health food vitamin industry stated that his tests showed great differences in the efficacy of chelation in various products. Chelation is not an all-or-none matter, and the extent and usefulness of chelation depends partly upon the technical skills employed in producing the chelated minerals. There is no way to determine this solely by reading labels. Specific chelated products would have to be tested individually.

# ET CETERA

Due to realities of the chemical industry and its economics, many of the vitamin ingredients in formulations for health food stores are identical to those found in the mainstream commercial vitamin marketplace. In order to obtain higher concentrations of these compounds than the concentrations found in natural foods, extensive, standardized processing is necessary.

However, there are often major differences in the other ingredients found in the preparations designed for the health food trade. Our preliminary research indicates that the manufacturers in our industry generally avoid the artificial varieties whenever possible. This does not mean that there is complete agreement as to which of these added ingredients are the most desirable—and this lack of agreement helps to give the buyer a choice.

**A choice for consumers**

The laboratory facilities of the manufacturers can determine whether their products can be expected to disintegrate during digestion, making the nutrients available to the body. These laboratory methods do not claim to take into account the differences in human individuals, nor to be clinical tests comparing the efficacy of the products of various companies. To the best of our knowledge, such clinical comparisons of various brands have not been attempted.

With some formulations, materials are added to tablets to slow their disintegration, to provide "sustained release." Types of cellulose are common in this use, and are excreted with no apparent effect on the body. With other formulations, sugars or starches are included to aid the tablet's disintegration, to assure that the nutrients themselves are not excreted. Some members of the industry allege that others are using polyvinyl fillers—naming no names—and at least one firm suggests that timed-release minerals may be harmful.

**Sustained release**

Chewable tablets usually contain a sweetener and/or added flavor. Natural flavorings are available for this use. Some companies use only fructose as a sweetener; others use only sucrose, asserting that it is not harmful in such small amounts. Some companies use both.

**Chewable tablets**

Although manufacturers do not attempt to produce the bright, shiny, waxed pills found in drug stores, many show some concern for the appearance of their tablets. Some products darken with time, and are often coated with zein, a corn protein, to forestall this change of color. Zein also helps prevent the absorption of moisture by the tablet. Artificial colors are avoided, but coloring is sometimes added from such sources as beets, carrots, or chlorophyll.

**Zein coating**

Depending upon the particular product, shelf life usually ranges from 18 months to five years. A few firms date their labels. Some of the products do contain a preservative such as methylparaben. Most of the soft gelatin capsules supplied to the industry do include this or a similar preservative, but at least two health food vitamin firms state that their gelatin capsules contain no preservatives. According to Dr. Hilbe of Thompson, "After years of research, we have determined that it is safe to convert to preservative-free gelatin. Our capsules are now specified to be free of preservatives."

**Soft gelatin capsules**

The variety of formulations being created and marketed makes a product-by-product study an impossible task, which even the federal government has not ventured into.

There is no requirement that most of the *et ceteras* in the formulations be listed on their labels, and it is the usual practice *not* to list them. The availability of this information depends upon the policy of each firm on the matter of disclosure.

---

Special thanks for the contents of this chapter are extended to the many people who put exceptional time and effort into providing the information published here. These people include Dr. Gregory Hayes; Dr. James Hilbe, Wm. T. Thompson Co; Harold Kutler, NuLife; Alfred Rechberger, Essential Organics; Betty Seroy and Ned Jensen, NF Factors; Scott Treadway, Golden Epoch Co.; and especially writer-researcher Victor Alton Zarley, Jr., who carried the bolus alone for many months.

# 55

# On the Labels of Lecithin

## by Janice Fillip

When Dr. James Hilbe at Wm. T. Thompson Co. was asked to comment on lecithin, he responded by quoting Mark Twain: "It's amazing how much folks know that ain't so."

The term "lecithin" is commonly used to describe a type of fat-like substances, known as lipids, which occur naturally in all living organisms. The chemical name for these substances is "phosphatides" or "phospholipids." The variety of terms used to describe these substances has led to confusion in the minds of consumers, and to labeling controversy among manufacturers of lecithin products.

**Confusion in terms leads to labeling controversy**

Synthesized in the liver, lecithin is essential to the proper function of the human metabolic system. Lecithin comprises an estimated 1/3 of the dry weight of the brain and over 70 percent of the fat in the liver. The myelin sheaths which surround all nerve fibers also contain significant amounts of lecithin. Recent scientific studies have shown that choline—one of the phosphatides in lecithin—is used in the brain to synthesize acetylocholine, a substance that carries messages from one nerve cell to another. Scientists are investigating the possibility that stimulating acetylcholine synthesis by increasing consumption of choline may enable nerves to carry more information with each impulse.

**Oil and water can mix**

Lecithin plays an important role in assimilating nutrients into the body. Oil and water do not mix, but lecithin's molecular structure allows it to unite with both water and oil, solving the problem of absorbing fats and fat soluble vitamins into the water-based human body. One end of the lecithin molecule combines readily with fats while the other end attracts water. This ability to pull fat molecules in a solution enables lecithin to dissolve cholesterol and other fats in the body, preventing them from collecting and attaching to artery walls. In the same manner, lecithin aids the absorption of fat soluble vitamins A and D and the carotene provitamins. Recent arteriosclerosis research has reported some success in reducing high cholesterol levels in patients through the use of lecithin.

Because lecithin can unite oil and water, it has a wide range of industrial uses as a wetting agent or emulsifier in margarine, chocolate, confections and ice cream, milk and milk products, baked goods, macaroni, edible oils and cosmetics. Lecithin is used in these products not for its nutritional qualities, but for its ability to combine oil and water.

A balanced diet should provide all the raw materials necessary for the synthesis of lecithin in the body. Dietary sources of lecithin include unprocessed nuts and seeds, whole grains, unrefined seed oils, organ meats and other fat-containing animal products such as eggs.

# ANOTHER SOY WONDER

Although synthetic phosphatides and ovalecithin are manufactured in limited quantities for pharmaceutical purposes, lecithin used in the natural and health food industry is a by-product of soybean oil manufacturing. Lecithin is produced by removing the phosphatides from soybean oil through a degumming process. Originally the degumming process was introduced not to produce lecithin, but because tanker ships would not carry crude soybean oil unless the lecithin was removed. Since the lecithin in soybean oil attracted moisture, causing tank settlings which had to be removed through costly cleanup operations, the shipping industry required soybean oil to be degummed.

When soybeans are treated with a hexane solvent to remove the oil from the bean, the free phosphatides in the bean are extracted along with the oil. About 2.5 percent of crude soybean oil is crude lecithin. Phosphatides are removed from the soybean oil through a degumming process using steam or water. During this process, about 1¼ pounds of water is mixed with each 100 pounds of crude soybean oil, then passed through a continuous centrifuge. The centrifuge removes around 3.5 pounds of wet gum which is pumped into a continuous vacuum dryer and heated at about 60°C. (140°F.) until the moisture content reaches about .5 percent. The resultant light-brown liquid is around 2/3 phosphatides and 1/3 soybean oil.

Liquid lecithin may be bleached to lighten the color and extend shelf life. Generally hydrogen peroxide is used to remove yellow pigments in the phosphatides, and benzoyl peroxide is used to remove red pigment. Bleaching increases moisture content, causing lecithin to thicken. To offset thickening, lecithin is diluted with oil and fatty acids to the desired consistency. Lecithin with a high fatty acid content is characterized by being fluid or pourable.

The acetone extraction method used to remove phosphatides from soybean oil produces highly concentrated phosphatides used to make lecithin granules. A solvent obtained by fermentation, acetone causes glyceride oils, fatty acids and sterols to separate from phosphatides. The acetone is removed from the phosphatides by drying in a low-heat vacuum system. A mechanical extruder turns the resultant phosphatide concentrate into granules. Because of their low oil content—generally from 2 percent to 3 percent— lecithin granules will emulsify spontaneously in liquid, even in cold water.

The popular yet scientifically unproven belief that lecithin has a positive affect on sexual activity may stem from the fact that stigmasterol, a component removed from lecithin during acetone extraction, is recovered and converted by pharmaceutical companies into progesterone (a female sex hormone) and dehydrolpiandrosterone (a male sex hormone).

# LECITHIN CONTROVERSY

Lack of accepted standards for the labeling of lecithin products has led to a controversy between two major manufacturers over "real" and "imitation" lecithin granules. Ken Herman, manager of the natural products division of American Lecithin Company says, "imitation lecithin granules (are) being labeled, priced and sold as if they really were lecithin granules." Herman maintains that the soy lecithin granules manufactured by Trophic International, Inc. "do not even approach the standards of identity for lecithin." The standards of identity Herman is referring to are set forth in the *Food Chemicals Codex:*

"Food grade lecithin is obtained from soybeans. It is a complex mixture of acetone-insoluble phosphatides which consist chiefly of phosphatidyl choline, phosphatidyl ethanolamine, phosphatidyl serine, and phosphatidyl inositol, combined with various amounts of other substances such as triglycerides, fatty acids, and carbohydrates. Refined grades of lecithin may contain any of these components in varying proportions and combinations depending on the type of fractionating used. In its oil-free form, the preponderance of triglycerides and fatty acids are removed and the product contains 90 percent or more of soy phosphatides representing all or a certain fraction of the total phosphatide complex . . ."

The products made by Trophic are a mixture of lecithin and soy flour, with lecithin making up 40 percent of the total product ingredients, according to Trophic's president Gordon Smith. While the soy and lecithin product does not meet the standard of identity for lecithin—soy flour is not lecithin—the lecithin in the product *does* meet the standards outlined by the *Food Chemicals Codex*, Smith says.

The problem is not one of defining what is lecithin, but in defining how products containing lecithin should be labeled. With lecithin appearing in an increasing number of products, it will become increasingly necessary for some definition to be established or, for example, a drug store brand face cream containing minute quantities of lecithin as an emulsifier may end up being promoted as lecithin cream with the implication that it contains lecithin as a "magic ingredient" rather than simply as a convenient emulsifier.

# FDA GUIDELINES

The Food and Drug Administration has set some guidelines for labeling lecithin products. In the case of Trophic's "Soy Lecithin Granules," FDA ruled that, since low-fat soy flour was the primary ingredient in the product, the label should read "Soy & Lecithin Granules." In complying with this ruling, Gordon Smith observed, "It was never our desire or attempt to suggest this product was a traditional phosphatide fraction of lecithin."

According to Smith, the ingredient blend in Trophic's products—low-fat soyflour, liquid lecithin, dolomite, choline and inositol—offers advantages over traditional lecithin granules which are predominantly phosphatids. Smith said the blend of ingredients is based on a "whole food concept in terms of proper balance of minerals."

Lecithin has a high phosphorus content. When it is taken as a dietary supplement, some nutritionists say that the increase of phosphorus may cause an imbalance in other minerals in the body, especially calcium and magnesium. Smith explained that mined dry-pocket dolomite is added to Trophics products to serve as a source for calcium and magnesium, helping to balance the product's phosphorus content.

The label on Trophic's Soy & Lecithin Granules proclaims the product to be made from an "acetone free process." Smith maintains that the acetone extraction process removes minute fractions of the lecithin system, rendering the lecithin less of a whole food. In their promotion booklet *Lecithin: What You Need To Know*, Trophic states that acetone-derived lecithin granules "are to the soybean what white flour is to wheat—just a fraction of the original product." Smith said that liquid lecithin derived from the degumming process "keeps the lecithin system as produced in the soybean intact."

The acetone extraction method is used specifically to produce a product with a high phosphatide concentrate. NuLife's president Harold Kutler reports that all the suppliers of lecithin granules—Glidden's Central Soya, American Lecithin Company and two European companies—use the acetone extraction process. In the opinion of Ken Herman, "The phosphatide content is the measure of purity of a lecithin product."

Does a significant amount of acetone remain in the lecithin after extraction? While Essential Organic's president Alfred Rechberger accurately points out, "To reach a zero percent level is practically impossible," manufacturers agree that virtually all the acetone used in the extraction process is removed from the lecithin end-product. Herman explains, "Quality control of each batch assures that if there is any detectible residue whatsoever, that the amount is well under the limit set by FDA of 30 parts per million. Acetone has an extremely characteristic taste and smell (the bad taste in one's mouth during a fast), making it very easy to detect even minute quantities."

Acetone does occur naturally in the human body. Dr. James Hilbe points out that acetone is produced in the body as a by-product of carbohydrate metabolism.

# HEXANE OR ACETONE

Which is preferable, the acetone-extracted phosphatides sold by American Lecithin Company as lecithin granules or the Soy & Lecithin Granules made by Trophic International from liquid lecithin and low-fat soy flour, both obtained from hexane-extracted soybeans? The answer remains a matter of opinion: some will agree with Herman, some with Smith, and some with Harold Kutler, who remarked, "I can see no virtue of hexane over acetone."

The controversy over lecithin granules arose because there are no accepted standards of identity for lecithin products. Last year Ken Herman appealed to the National Nutritional Foods Association to help resolve the granule controversy, but Dan Wells, Chairman of the NNFA Standards Committee, says it is not the Committee's function to set standards. "I prefer to educate the people and let them make their own decisions," Wells said. "If someone is mislabeling, we're against that. We're trying to get people to read ingredient labeling, because they'll see the difference (in products) there."

Wells pointed to 19-grain lecithin capsules to illustrate the urgent need for full disclosure labeling on lecithin products. Since soybean oil contains a percentage of phosphatides, Wells speculated that a company could simply put cold-pressed soy oil into capsules and call them "lecithin" capsules. Although Wells stressed that he was not aware of any company doing this, he remarked that some capsules contain primarily soy oil and virtually no lecithin. This problem does not exist with lecithin tablets because regulations require that fillers, binders, and all other ingredients be listed on the label, Wells said.

To ensure the integrity of lecithin products, Wells announced that the Standards Committee is asking manufacturers of lecithin products to support voluntary full disclosure labeling. "We'd like to see percentage of ingredient labeling on bottles," Wells said.

With full disclosure percentage labeling, it will be easier for retailers and consumers to know what ain't so.

**The need for full disclosure and percentage labeling**

# 56

# *Amoco Foods Meets the Press*

## by Jim Schreiber

Standard Oil of Indiana is in the food business. Officers of the oil company talk of feeding a hungry world with their products. "Natural food" made by Standard Oil subsidiary Amoco Food Co. is already winning awards in the United States, where millions of tons of it have been sold. That food, according to an article titled "Eating Oil" in the August 1977 issue of *Mother Jones* magazine, is alleged to be a petroprotein—grown on petroleum products—which may be laced with toxins and cancer-producing chemicals. *Mother Jones*, published in San Francisco with a 1977 circulation of about 10,000, calls itself "A magazine for the rest of us."

Since 1975, Amoco Foods has been marketing Torutein, a torula yeast product, for use in baby foods, gravies, baking mixes, meat substitutes, cereals, and pasta. Some companies, including Loma Linda and Golden California Co., with major sales in health food stores are now including Torutein in their ingredients, or hope to in the future. The extent of sales of Torutein to the health food industry is at present known only to Amoco Foods.

Torula yeast, the tiny edible fungus called *Candida utilis* by botanists, has been accepted as a healthy, high-protein food since its introduction into the American diet. Since its commercial production began in the United States in 1948, yeast grown in woodpulp byproducts has been recognized as a good source of trace minerals and of vitamins in the B-complex group. Torula yeast contains about 50 percent protein and all the essential amino acids. With such a nutritional profile, it is not surprising that torula grown for human consumption finds its way into products sold in health food stores.

But this bright picture of torula yeast as an ideal food becomes dark when we discover that Japanese studies of yeast grown on petroleum products—petroprotein—contain cancer-producing benzopyrene and heavy metals such as mercury, lead, and arsenic in the end product. Attempts to grow yeast on methanol and on paraffin, a low-grade petroleum product, have also been thwarted by the presence of toxic chemicals in the final batch.

*Petroproteins—let them eat oil*

*Torula yeast's nutritional profile*

260

The recipe for Amoco Foods' production of Torutein includes ethanol, magnesium sulfate, potassium iodide, manganese sulfate, calcium chloride, sodium molybdate, cupric sulfate and a dozen other compounds—a list sufficient to raise the eyebrows of any advocate of natural foods. Torutein is the end result of a computer-controlled process that ferments, aerates, separates, and spray-dries the yeast cells, resulting in a tan powder. When used as an ingredient in other foods, Torutein is often listed on the label simply as "dried yeast" or "natural flavoring."

A chemical recipe

Given the alarming history of petroprotein yeasts, and the chemical recipe for the technological production of Torutein, it makes sense to ask whether the Standard Oil Company, through Amoco Foods, is selling cancer-causing, toxic products which reach us wrapped in a Golden California, Loma Linda, or other respected label. It comes down to chemistry.

# TRACE CHEMICALS

A look at the promotional literature of large-scale yeast manufacturers who use more traditional, longer-established approaches reveals that trace chemicals in their yeasts are listed as important to a well-balanced diet. These include magnesium, potassium, manganese, calcium, sodium, sulfur, iodine and many others. Trace amounts of these elements and of the mineral compounds used to culture Amoco's Tuorutein will be found in most foods and soil samples. It is a commonplace among nutritionists that trace amounts of such minerals are essential to the human diet, although excessive amounts can be toxic. In many cases, the complete role of trace minerals and their optimal amounts in nutrition is not yet known.

The mass production of yeast of all kinds, whether torula or the *Saccharomyces cerevisiae* variety which is commonly sold in little packets for leavening, is a highly technological food industry, ordinarily using compounds like potassium hydroxide, phosphoric acid and ammonium hydroxide to provide a nutritious environment in which yeast cells will grow abundantly. The industry emphasis, in descriptions of the yeast manufacturing process, is on bacterial and chemical purity. The use of chemical compounds is a necessary part of the process, because such compounds are the nutrients of yeast cells, whether they grow in stainless steel tanks or on discarded grapes.

Yeast production—a highly technological food industry

Whether it is Boise Cascade's *Candida utilis*, nurtured on wood sugars, or Universal Foods' Red Star *Saccharomyces cerevisiae*, nurtured on purified molasses, large-scaled production of yeast involves the use of chemically-balanced fermentation, centrifugal separation and, for de-activated yeasts, pasteurization. In the competition for chemical "purity," Amoco Foods apparently has the edge, in part because they start with a major nutrient which has flawless chemical credentials.

The torula yeast for Torutein is grown on ethanol. That is not to be confused with methanol (spelled with an *m*). Methanol, used in solvents and anti-freeze, is a toxic poison in small doses. Ethanol, the yeast nutrient, is the kind of alcohol found in liquor, beer and wine. Even if small amounts of ethanol did show up in torutein—for which there is no evidence—it is not a dangerous substance at that dosage.

Torula yeast raised on alcohol

# NOT A PETROPROTEIN

What Amoco puts into the yeast tank is US Pharmacopoeia Grade ethanol, the purest grain alcohol available. According to Dan Murray, Marketing Director for Amoco Foods in Chicago, the source of 80 percent of their ethanol is natural gas, and the rest is derived from ethylene gas. But, regardless of the original source, the ethanol is chemically pure USP Food Grade alcohol when it goes into the fermentation vats.

Chemical purity of the nutritional brew

Murray emphasized that Torutein is not grown on methanol, paraffin, or on any petrochemical that has ever shown harmful substances in the final product. "Torutein," he said, "is *not* a petroprotein." He contrasted Torutein with most other foods as a purer product, due to the chemical purity of the nutrient brew, free from contamination by pesticides, herbicides, or radioactive residues. Amoco's plate-counts show from 25 to 150 times less bacterial activity in Torutein than in competitors' products.

"There are no cancer-producing chemicals in Torutein," Murray said. "It contains no benzopyrene. We have checked for all heavy metals, and any which might be present are beyond the limits of detection of the instruments—which is .02 milligrams per 100 grams. It is not a petroprotein, and there are no hydrocarbons used in the process."

Amoco Foods last year won two Putnam Awards, for the product and for the process of making Torutein. The awards, given biennially by the Putnam publishing firm, are granted by a panel of 25 food industry executives. Torutein is the first to win simultaneous awards both for product and processing.

Nevertheless, the *Mother Jones* article had its effect. Murray reported that Amoco Foods lost about half the volume of its business in the health food industry as a result of the article. But they did not lose the Loma Linda account, although there is a "Mother Jones file" at Loma Linda.

All the "dried yeast" now listed among the ingredients of Loma Linda foods is Torutein, from Amoco, according to Dr. Oliver Miller, Vice Presidnet of Research and Development at Loma Linda in Southern California. He described Torutein as "the finest quality torula on the market."

Loma Linda, producing vegetarian foods to serve as meat substitutes, is engaged in a constant search for ingredients which will yield a "meaty" flavor. Their taste-evaluation tests give the best marks to Torutein, especially because it lacks the bitter taste sometimes found in similar products. "We haven't been able to detect a chemical difference in this and other torula yeasts," Miller said, "but I assume there must be some chemical difference because there are some flavor differences." He attributes the difference to the substrate— the growth medium.

# NO LANDSLIDE

Dr. Miller indicated that a "landslide" in correspondence had been anticipated at Loma Linda as a result of the *Mother Jones* article, but "there has been little correspondence, and certainly no effect on our business."

Golden California Company was mentioned in the article along with Loma Linda. Golden California received four letters prompted by the article, but any potential affect on sales of their Torutein-based breakfast food Crunchy Yeast is in the realm of guesswork. The manufacture of Crunchy Yeast was canceled due to production problems before the article was published.

Stan Meckler, Golden California's Vice-President of Marketing, expressed disappointment at the production difficulties, which allowed the manufacture of Crunchy Yeast only in small amounts. "The initial marketing on it was exceptional," he said, "and it was an outstanding product."

Meckler expressed satisfaction that Torutein is a pure, healthy food, and said he hopes the production problem will be solved, so Crunchy Yeast can be marketed in the future.

The selling of Torutein provides a good example of the obscurities of labeling and advertising. Within FDA regulations, Torutein can be listed among the ingredients as "torula yeast," "dried yeast," or as "natural flavoring." Amoco Foods advertises Torutein as a "natural food," despite the computers, controlled chemistry and artificial environment created for the entire production process.

"It is a natural food, really," Don Murray said. "What we've done is move the natural process indoors, into a controlled environment that beats the problems found in nature." He contrasted yeast, a natural organism, to laboratory-synthesized foods, such as artificial flavorings, and food-analogs, such as those sold as "bacon bits."

Dr. Miller, Loma Linda's R&D head, expressed a common difficulty when he said, "I'd be hard-put to define 'natural.'" But Loma Linda's products are presented as vegetarian and wholesome—not as "natural."

"Torutein is derived from a natural source," Miller said "but it certainly has been processed, as is true of all torula yeasts on the market. I'd be very hesitant to call it natural, but I would say that it's a perfectly wholesome, nutritious food."

Stan Meckler at Golden California said, "What's natural? We don't consider ourselves to be a natural foods company. We do, however, offer products which are as pure and wholesome as possible."

# NATURE PLUS TECHNOLOGY

Perhaps a precise definition of "natural" is of far less importance than complete, precise knowledge of what is in the foods we eat, and of the processing our food is subjected to. It is safe to say that *Candida utilis* is as natural an organism as any, and that the elaborate technology used to produce Torutein and other torula yeasts is as artificial as any. And, while yeast grown on methanol or paraffin may be harmful to man and beast alike, there is no available evidence that Torutein contains any harmful contaminants.

No evidence of harmful contaminants

But a mystery still remains, hidden by the terms of labeling, frustrating the buyer who wants to know the source and history of the food he or she lives by: What other companies, selling in health food stores, are using Torutein in their products? Dan Murray at Amoco Foods would not say. "It should be their decision to make that disclosure," he said.

That leaves only one thing for concerned buyers to do when the ambiguous "dried yeast," "flavor enhancer," or "natural flavoring" appears on labels of products. Ask.

# Consumer's Guide

When vitamins occur naturally in foods, they are accompanied by other nutrients, synergistic factors such as coenzymes and trace minerals. Vitamins are manufactured by chemically isolating them from their natural source or by synthetic production. Not all the synergistic factors survive the isolation process, and synthetically produced vitamins are generally accompanied by other nutrients. Potency levels must be accurately labeled, but the only way to be sure if a vitamin is an isolate or a synthetic is to ask the manufacturer.

- It is cheaper to produce a synthetic vitamin than to isolate one from its natural source. Inexpensive drug store and supermarket vitamins may contain artificial colors, preservatives, sugar, shellac and polyvinyl plastic fillers.

- All high-potency B vitamin formulas contain synthetic B vitamins.

- Chewable vitamins are coated with fatty acids and usually contain sweeteners (sucrose or fructose) and flavorings.

- Ascorbic acid is a highly-processed vitamin C derived from glucose or corn dextrose. Small amounts of rosehips or acerola are added to synthetic ascorbic acid, and provide bioflavinoids which help make the vitamin C bioavailable.

- Vitamin E, tocopherol, is the only vitamin whose full name provides a clue to its origin and composition. D-tocopherol is a vitamin E that occurs in nature; dl-tocopherol is a synthetic. Tocopheryl indicates that the alpha compounds in the vitamin (thought to be the most active compounds) have been isolated from other compounds such as beta, gamma and delta; tocopherol indicates that the alpha compounds have not been isolated. If the vitamin has been combined with other compounds to increase its stability, the word tocopherol will be followed by *acetate* (for liquid vitamins) or *succinate* (for tablet or dry capsule vitamins).

- Sustained-release vitamins may contain cellulose, sugars, and starches. Ask the manufacturer for full disclosure.

264

- Vitamin tablets may be coated with zein, a corn protein, to prevent discoloration and moisture absorption.

- While most gelatin capsules contain preservatives and are derived from an animal source, some companies have capsules which are without preservatives and are from vegetable sources.

- The labels of liquid vitamins must state the percentage of alcohol, if any, in the formulation.

# LECITHIN

Lecithin is used in many products as a convenient emulsifier. Because of its current popularity, the lecithin normally put into a product as an emulsifier may be promoted as a wonder ingredient. A close look at the ingredient list will show if lecithin is a major ingredient or is merely added in minimal amounts as an emulsifier.

- Bleached liquid lecithin has fatty acids added to make it more pourable.

- Lecithin has a high phosphorus content and may cause an imbalance in the human system of calcium and magnesium.

- Fillers, binders and other ingredients in lecithin tablets must be listed on the label.

# YEAST

Yeast is a major source of naturally-occurring B vitamins and trace minerals. All forms of commercial yeast have been processed by a high level of technology, with chemical compounds used as nutrients for the yeast cells.

# Section X: Natural Foods as a Business

The consumer who walks into a natural foods store is not involved only in a flow of products which include various ingredients and are the result of many different kinds of processing. Natural foods retailing, wholesaling, manufacturing and growing are businesses. They operate on profit margins, regardless of their individual styles, and survive only if customers are induced to buy the products they offer. Advertising, packaging, displays and other forms of marketing are an essential part of the business, which is intended to have a direct effect on the would-be purchaser.

Shoppers seldom get a chance to eavesdrop on people in the food business as they talk about the marketing of their goods. Although this section of the *Natural Foods Guide* tells little about the ingredients and processing of food, it has special value to the consumer in spotlighting merchandising tactics and strategies on a local and national level. This section also shows the scope of the industry as a whole, and includes observations on some possibilities for the future.

Businesses in the natural foods trade obviously want people to buy their products. Either deliberately or by chance, they create an image, whether slickly designed by a sophisticated advertising agency or hand-made by a retailer who sells only bulk foods from barrels in a down-home funk atmosphere. In this section of the *Guide*, the reader will find the sorts of considerations weighed by business people whose aim is to move their products off their shelves onto the kitchen tables of consumers.

Marketing on a grand scale is the chief subject discussed by Wyck Hay, who was in charge of advertising for Celestial Seasonings, one of the most successful new companies in the natural foods trade. In contrast to nationwide merchandising, produce department manager David Findlay in another chapter tells how to sell fruits and vegetables in a small store, down to the details of how to stir the customer's appetite to have a papaya for lunch.

It is common knowledge that the total food business in the United States is gigantic, but little has been known until recently about the relative importance of natural foods within that vast industry. The shopper in the local natural foods store usually has no clear idea of the place such shops have in the shadow of the supermarkets—except for a vague impression that natural foods enterprises are small but growing. To help illuminate this dim picture, the over-all size and financial status of the industry is presented below in the *Annual Report on the Industry*, from the July 1978 issue of *Whole Foods* magazine.

267

In another chapter, the *Natural Foods Guide* comes full circle, back to the broad problems and prospects of organic farmers. In *New Age Agribusiness*, the topic is looked at as part of shifting economic, technological and ecological factors which may have a significant impact on the patterns of food production and consumption in America.

# 57

# *First Annual Report on the Industry*

In preparing **Whole Foods** First Annual Report on the Natural Foods Industry, we have drawn upon the responses of 928 health and natural food store owners and managers from all 50 states. Our Report, then, is based on the largest sample of health and natural food retailers ever undertaken or published to date.

Our 1978 survey of the industry brought many surprises. Both the total number of retail outlets and the changing pattern of their ownership and management were different from what we had expected. There are 6,400 (give or take 150) health and natural food retail stores in the 50 states. If we add to that some 1,500 to 2,000 food co-ops and buying clubs which also purchase natural foods in volume, we can get some idea of the actual scope of our industry. For the purpose of this report, we did not include the natural foods restaurants, supermarkets, gourmet and specialty food stores, schools, hospitals and other institutions, or vending machine sales of health and natural foods products.

Health and natural food retail store sales totaled $1,152,365,000 in the past 12 months. The average sales volume of the responding stores was $180,000. Of greater interest were the differences in the average sales volumes among the four broad regions of the country— West, Midwest, South and East. Average retail sales in the West ($171,000) and the Midwest ($168,000) are below the national average, while the South ($189,000) and the East ($200,000) are above it. It is also interesting to note that the national average retail sales for health food stores of $189,200 is higher than the average for natural food stores at $172,500.

As might be expected, the Western states dominate the industry. There are 2,630 health and natural food retail stores in the West, or 41.1 percent of the total. These stores account for 39 percent of the national total retail sales volume, or $449,730,000. California leads the nation in total number of stores with $1,250. At the other end of the spectrum, Rhode Island and Delaware have the fewest number of stores.

Generally, a store's purchasing decisions are made by the owner/manager. The most notable difference between health food retailers and natural foods retailers is the role of women as decision-makers. Among health food store owner/manager, 50.2 percent are men, while 32.6 percent are women and only 17.2 percent are man-and-wife teams. In

EAST
1,420 Stores
$284,000,000
Retail Sales

WEST
2,630 Stores
$449,730,000
Retail Sales

MIDWEST
1,260 Stores
$211,680,000 Retail Sales

SOUTH
1,095 Stores
$206,955,000 Retail Sales

U.S.A.
6,400 Stores
$1,152,000,000 Retail Sales

contrast, men's participation at the top decreases to 49.2 percent of the total for the younger natural foods retailers. Women run a surprising 40.2 percent of the natural foods stores, while co-owned stores account for only 10.6 percent of the total. Many co-owners indicated that they were not married partners. Both sets of figures tend to show little support for the mythical dominance of the industry by the "mom and pop" store.

Mom and Pop stores a myth

# NEW STORES

New retail stores are opening at a rate of 400 per year. Using current industry figures on opening inventory positions, the typical new store has a $16,500 opening stock in trade. This means that new store openings alone account for $6,600,000 or more in total industry sales. Store closing are more difficult to track, but it would seem that the going out-of-business rate is between 180 and 200 stores per year. These factors, plus the difficulty in compensating for nearly 10 percent annual inflation in retail food prices, make it hard to get a completely accurate figure for the real growth of the industry from year to year.

When it comes to reporting the intimate financial details of their operations, natural food store managers are more responsive than health food store managers. Only 18.4 percent of the natural food stores and 24.8 percent of the health food stores responding to our questions would not share financial data on their operations. The most open were the natural food folk from the Western states, with only 8.8 percent not responding. East Coast and Southern health food stores were the least communicative, with 29 percent not responding. Even so, we did obtain operating results for 708 stores, or 76.3 percent of all stores responding.

Natural food stores give more financial details

To simplify and highlight our findings, we first present our results for the country as a whole. Then, on the following pages, we report on each of the four major regions. Finally, we analyze the operating expense figures for the "typical" retail stores in the industry.

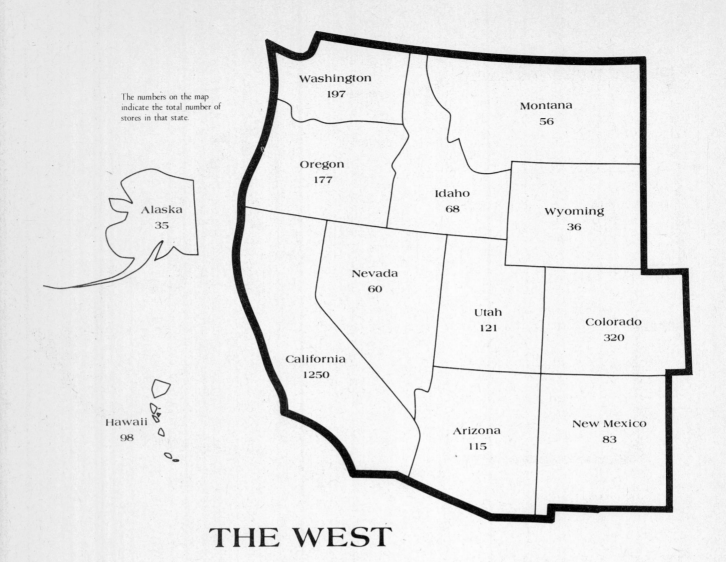

The numbers on the map indicate the total number of stores in that state.

Washington 197

Montana 56

Oregon 177

Idaho 68

Wyoming 36

Alaska 35

Nevada 60

Utah 121

Colorado 320

California 1250

Hawaii 98

Arizona 115

New Mexico 83

# THE WEST

### $449,730,000 Total Retail Sales
### 2,630 Health & Natural Food Stores
### $171,000 Average Annual Sales

**More new stores in the West**

The Western states, including Alaska and Hawaii, dominate the industry. There are 2,630 health and natural food stores (41% of all stores) in the 13 Western states. They accounted for $449,730,000 in retail sales ($39\%$ of the total) during the past 12 months. At $171,000, the average annual sales of stores in the West is 5 percent lower than the national average of $180,000.

California, with 1,250 stores, and Colorado, with 320 stores, account for 60 percent of the retail outlets in the 13 states. The lower average sales volume in the West may be the result of intense competition among the many stores in these two states. Another contributing factor to the lower dollar volume per store could be that there is a higher percentage of newer stores in these states. Older, established stores tend to have higher average sales volumes.

Natural food stores in the West have average annual sales of $165,000 compared to $174,000 average annual sales for health food retailers. Health food stores outnumber natural food stores 53.3 percent to 35.5 percent of the Western retailers responding, while 11.2 percent either declared that they fit both categories or did not respond. A total of 321 retailers in the West responded to our questions, or 12.2 percent of all retailers in this region.

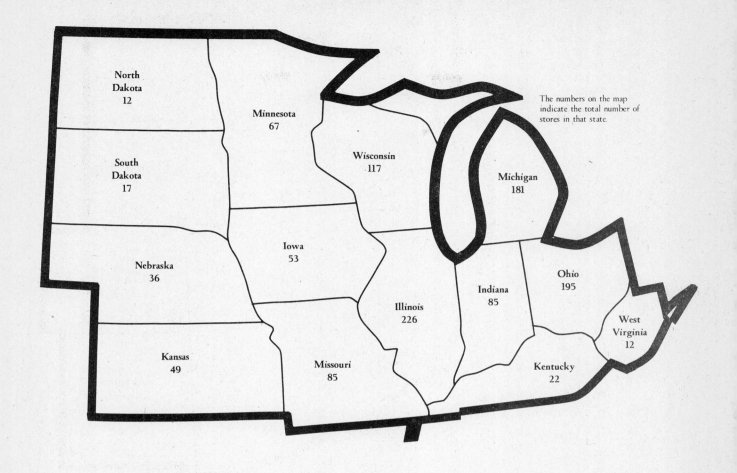

The numbers on the map indicate the total number of stores in that state.

North Dakota 12

Minnesota 67

South Dakota 17

Wisconsin 117

Michigan 181

Iowa 53

Nebraska 36

Ohio 195

Indiana 85

Illinois 226

West Virginia 12

Kansas 49

Missouri 85

Kentucky 22

# THE MIDWEST

### $211,680,000 Total Retail Sales
### 1,260 Health & Natural Food Stores
### $168,000 Average Annual Sales

The 14 Midwestern states support 1,260 health and natural food stores totaling $211,680,000 in retail sales (18.4% of the total) during the last year. As a group, stores in the Midwest have the lowest average annual sales. At $168,000, these stores fall 6.7 percent below the national average of $180,000 in annual retail sales for all stores reporting.

The over-all regional average is brought down by the relatively poor performance of natural food stores in this region. While health food retailers averaged $177,800 in annual sales, natural food stores averaged only $156,000—the lowest average for such stores in any region. These figures would tend to support the thesis that there is a lower "food consciousness" in the Midwest than in other parts of the country.

Illinois, Ohio and Michigan leads the region in number of stores, accounting for 52 percent of all stores in the Midwest. North Dakota, South Dakota and West Virginia are at the bottom of the list for the region, accounting for only 3.5 percent of the total.

A total of 196 Midwestern stores responded to our questions, or 15.5 percent of all retailers in the region.

**Lowest average annual sales in the Midwest**

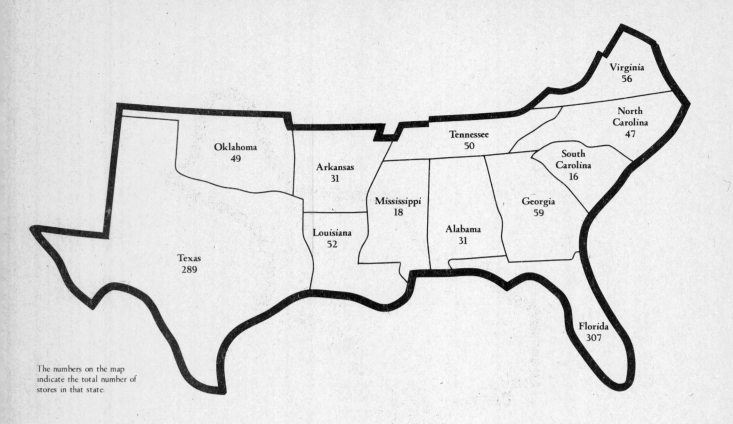

The numbers on the map indicate the total number of stores in that state.

Virginia
56

North Carolina
47

Tennessee
50

Oklahoma
49

Arkansas
31

South Carolina
16

Mississippi
18

Georgia
59

Louisiana
52

Alabama
31

Texas
289

Florida
307

# THE SOUTH

**$206,955,000 Total Retail Sales**
**1,095 Health & Natural Food Stores**
**$189,000 Average Annual Sales**

**The fewest number of stores in the South**

As a region, the South has both the fewest number of stores (1,095) and the lowest total retail sales volume ($206,955,000, or 18% of the total). However, the average annual sales of health and natural foods retailers in the South, at $189,000, is 5 percent above the national average. Health food stores in the South do quite well, reporting average annual sales of $203,400, as do natural food retailers with annual sales of $173,500.

Florida and Texas lead the South in number or retail outlets, accounting for 59.3 percent of the total between the two. Mississippi and South Carolina trail the region with only 3.4 percent of the total between them.

The story of the South seems to be told in the success of health food retailers in Florida, with its large retirement communities, and Texas, with its large and relatively prosperous population. It should also be noted that the average natural food store does about as well as the average natural food store in the West and considerably better than similar stores in the Midwest and East.

A total of 187 Southern retailers responded to our questions, or 17.1 percent of the total.

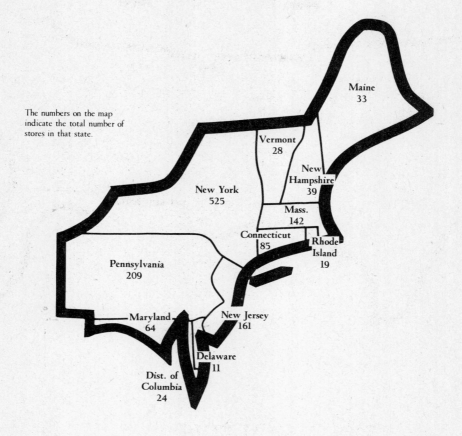

The numbers on the map indicate the total number of stores in that state.

Maine
33

Vermont
28

New
Hampshire
39

New York
525

Mass.
142

Connecticut
85

Rhode
Island
19

Pennsylvania
209

Maryland
64

New Jersey
161

Delaware
11

Dist. of
Columbia
24

# THE EAST

**$284,000,000 Total Retail Sales**
**1,420 Health & Natural Food Stores**
**$200,000 Average Annual Sales**

With 22.2 percent of the industry's retail outlets, health and natural food stores in the East account for $284,000,000, or 24.6 percent of the total retail sales during the past 12 months. This higher percentage of retail sales volume is due to average annual sales of $200,000 per store in this region which is 11.1 percent above the national average. Higher per capita incomes and a higher percentage of older, established stores in the East tend to account for the noticeably higher average annual sales.

New York leads the Eastern region with 525 stores, followed by Pennsylvania, New Jersey and Massachusetts in that order. These four states account for a whopping 73 percent of the regional total of 1,420 retail stores. Rhode Island and Delaware have the fewest number of stores, accounting for only 2.1 percent of the total between them.

A total of 224 Eastern retailers, the second largest group in our sample, responded to our questions. This amounts to 15.8 percent of the total health and natural food retailers in the East.

**Older, established stores
in the East**

## Average Retail Sales Volume

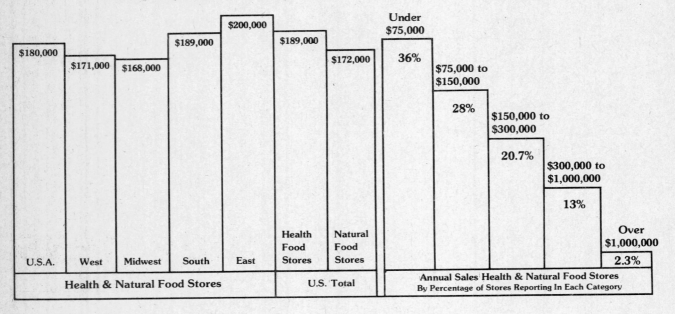

Health & Natural Food Stores: U.S.A. $180,000; West $171,000; Midwest $168,000; South $189,000; East $200,000

U.S. Total: Health Food Stores $189,000; Natural Food Stores $172,000

Annual Sales Health & Natural Food Stores By Percentage of Stores Reporting In Each Category:
Under $75,000 — 36%; $75,000 to $150,000 — 28%; $150,000 to $300,000 — 20.7%; $300,000 to $1,000,000 — 13%; Over $1,000,000 — 2.3%

---

## First Annual Report On OPERATING EXPENSES

*Operating Expenses For The "Typical" Store*

**Average Annual Sales $180,000**
**Average Inventory at Retail Value $22,225**
**Annual Turnover Rate 8.1 Times**
**Average Margin on Selling Price 36.5%**
**Average Annual Profit $18,785**

| | |
|---|---:|
| Cost of Good Sold | $ 114,300 |
| Gross Profit | $ 65,700 |
| Wages & Salaries | $ 23,400 |
| Rent | $ 7,200 |
| Utilities | $ 3,240 |
| Advertising | $ 3,150 |
| Supplies | $ 2,430 |
| Depreciation | $ 2,250 |
| Insurance | $ 1,530 |
| Legal & Accounting | $ 900 |
| Maintenance & Repair | $ 810 |
| Auto or Truck | $ 720 |
| License Fees & Permits | $ 450 |
| Miscellaneous | $ 835 |
| **Total Expenses** | **$ 46,915** |
| **Net Profit** | **$ 18,785** |

# 58

# *New Age Agribusiness*

## by Jim Schreiber

New age *agribusiness?*

For good reasons, many people who farm and distribute organically grown foods object to having their work called "agribusiness." That word, after all, summons up images of immense, impersonal corporations which operate factory-style farms that stretch one crop as far as the eye can see, growing plants addicted to chemical fertilizers, herbicides and pesticides. That is surely not what *we* are doing.

And the words "new age" bring up a range of images that defy rigid definition, applying to a mixed family of attitudes which may have no single element in common, including a revived interest in acupuncture, whole grains, ecology, pyramids, herbology, meditation . . . The "new age" seems to have something to do with a view that many things are connected together in ways which have often been overlooked—holistically, some would say—and that the strict analytic-synthetic methods of science give an incomplete and distorted picture of the world. The new age is biodegradable.

Our use of the phrase "new age agribusiness" is deliberate. It is intended to suggest a paradox: The interaction of new age attitudes and conventional agribusiness know-how can, and does, create alternatives which include the best features of both. If the time comes when each family, neighborhood or community grows and shares its own foods, then the paradox—and our industry—will vanish. Until that time, food production is business, and in our industry is sometimes nationwide business.

This business of supplying food, whether organically or chemically grown, rests on the same limited supply of consumer dollars. Businesses, whether operated by saints, scoundrels, or more usual people, engage in the same sorts of economic transactions. Unless it attains a certain level of efficiency, and delivers the goods to the table, an agricultural business cannot survive.

There is a popular notion that, for consumers, organic grains and produce must be more expensive than their commercial, chemical cousins. That notion may soon be due for a change. The very "efficiency" of industrialized, energy-consuming agribusiness is

The new age is
biodegradable

showing clear signs of tottering on its one leg, at the very time when new age alternatives are gathering momentum. The growth of organic styles in agriculture does not rest solely on good conscience. Any environmental, moral, or nutritional advantage which may go along with organic methods would mean little if the foods were simply too costly to farm and too expensive for the consumer to buy. But the *economic* balance now seems to be tilting in favor of new age, organic styles in agribusiness.

A tilting economic balance

Studies published recently in the *American Journal of Agricultural Economics* and the *Journal of Soil and Water Conservation* indicate that organic and conventional farms generally produce the same yields per acre, and that organic farming operations cost about the same as conventional ones. A significant difference was that the conventional farms used more energy—often more than two times as much—than the organic farms.

# SMILE AT THE GAS PUMP

Headlines which repeatedly promise increasing oil shortages in the near future also point to an increased advantage for organic growing techniques. "The production of chemical nitrogen fertilizers competes with other demands for fossil fuel," a 1975 USDA booklet points out. "Calculations of the energy required to spread organic materials, such as farmyard manure, on cropland indicates that efficient spreading systems require less energy in terms of tractor power and machinery manufacture than would an equivalent amount of chemical nitrogen fertilizers. Where efficient systems of loading, transportation, and spreading can be developed, the use of animal manures and sewage sludges may provide a valuable method of conserving fossil fuels." This means that the rising costs of gas and oil provide an increasing economic incentive to switch to organic methods. The price you pay at the gas pump may serve as an index of the rate at which farmers will move away from petrochemical agriculture.

Fuel shortage is an incentive for organic farming

Immediate financial advantage has not so far been the major reason for farmers' turning to organic methods. A survey reported in the November/December 1977 issue of *Compost Science* shows the reasons given by 150 people for switching to organic farming: 32 percent mentioned livestock health; 30 percent had soil problems; 25 percent referred to the cost of chemicals; 23 percent said chemicals were not effective; and 22 percent expressed concern for human health.

# TOPSOIL DISASTER

Secretary of Agriculture Bob Bergland said that, under conventional farming methods in the USA, "we are on a collision course with disaster." He pointed out that 15 tons of topsoil are washing out of the mouth of the Mississippi River every *second*. Erosion of various kinds removes up to 50 tons per acre of our topsoil every year. Since colonial times, one-third of the American topsoil has eroded away. This process is speeded up by the methods of conventional agribusiness, and when the crunch comes, with its obvious immediate effects on the pocketbook, farmers will need alternatives.

A collision course with disaster

It's easy to imagine all of it coming to a head at once. Nitrites from excessive use of fertilizers pollute underground water supplies—erosion and urban sprawl dangerously reduce useable farmlands—agricultural petrochemicals make crops easy prey to hungry pests and diseases—a scarcity of oil supplies makes conventional agribusiness an economic disaster. In such a too-possible world, new age agribusinesses would stand out as a remarkable example of sanity.

Organic farming does not pollute the environment. Organic composting and mulching methods create a living soil which holds water and does not blow away in the breeze. Organic growing methods, including crop rotation, result in plants which are not easily ravaged by insects and diseases. Organic farming does not depend heavily on the economics of petrochemicals. In the long run, both as a local business venture and as a response to the problem of hunger on a planetary scale, organic methods appear to be the only way out of the horror-story being written now by industrialized chemical farming.

Even the factor of size supports the new age perspective. The USDA itself has determined that the highest yields per acre and the most efficient use of farmland, in the USA and in the rest of the world, is found on farms of less than 25 acres. The famed efficiency of large-scale, factory-style agribusiness in the USA is a myth.

If small-scale farming is indeed efficient, then what at first seems to be a romantic fantasy may actually be an economic reality: Get a horse. Late in 1978 the *Wall Street Journal* reported a renewed interest in horses as draft animals. The article told of Richard Turner, a Tennessee farmer who got rid of his tractors five years earlier and has been farming 177 acres with nothing but horses ever since. Turner reportedly remarked that he can plant seeds in muddy or hilly ground that would halt a tractor. Other advantages cited in the article include these: A tractor may cost about $25,000; a good horse, from $2000 to $5000. A horse will produce up to 15 tons of fertilizer per year, runs on farm-grown fuel, and a mare can produce about 10 colts, which can be used on the farm or sold. Disadvantages? "Horses just aren't feasible for the large-scale operations that produce the bulk of this country's food."

Get a horse

# FORGING A FOOD CHAIN

The new age agribusiness has countless advantages over conventional agribusiness, but is only a tiny link in the vast American food chain. Supermarkets bulge with commercial produce, but it is often hard to find a single organic carrot. When well managed, organic farming is already just as economical as commercial farming, but the consumer usually pays a premium for organically grown food. A countryside quilted with small-scale farms using horse-drawn plows seems to be a sensible alternative, but we still see mechanized fields flung from horizon to horizon. What is going on here?

The imbalanced success and power of Big Business in agriculture is an obvious answer. Large corporations, including the agrichemical suppliers, do have a vested interest in maintaining "conventional" industrialized farming, and they are very good at selling their wares to farmers and to legislators. But that is not the whole story.

Although the large-scale farm may not be as efficient as the smaller one, the large-scale distribution system linked with mega-farming is more efficient, so far. It is more economical to haul a fully-loaded semi-trailer from coast to coast than to carry one box of broccoli into town in a pickup. That, as farmers will be glad to point out, is where much of the cost comes in—between the fields and the retailer's bin. In many ways, distribution of organic production may be the weakest aspect of our industry.

Distribution—a key to efficiency

The firms which focus on distributing organic produce are only a few years old. On both ends of their routes, they are often dealing with other businesses which also have only a few years of experience. The growers, distributors and retailers are often people who are still in the process of learning how to operate most effectively, do not have extensive backgrounds in business, and are exploring nonstandard ways of doing their work. The companies themselves are often relatively small, labor-intensive, and staffed by people whose world-views influence their business practices. While all these factors may lead to a kind of harmony arising from a sense of common purpose, they have not yet resulted in widespread economic efficiency. The parts of this alternative food chain do not link up.

A case in point: On one hand are organic growers who are begging to find outlets for their production. On the other hand are the organic growers described by Daniel Zwerdling in *The Progressive* (December 1978): "They sell most of their crops to conventional agribusiness corporations, who mingle their organic produce with chemically grown crops and sell them incognito at conventional supermarkets . . . So while agribusiness experts warn you that organic farming would put food prices out of reach, you're buying organic foods at your local supermarket already—and you don't even know it." Zwerdling mentions organic table grapes sold to Safeway, Food Fair, and Kroger.

The network to catch these organic products and carry them to outlets within our industry is being woven slowly. Two successful examples, Sunburst Farms on the West Coast and the New England Organic Produce Center, are looked at elsewhere in this book.

# 59

# Produce is a Living Business

## by Janice Fillip

Finding an orange that tastes like an orange is about as easy as finding the right guru or a good ten cent cigar. The mass produced produce available at supermarkets may look tasty, but rarely has any flavor. Natural food stores too often offer little improvement. A limp carrot doesn't attract the customer, even if the carrot was organically grown.

But every now and then you run into an exception to this bleak picture. Such an exception is the produce section at Living Foods in Mill Valley, California. The reason is an exceptional produce manager, David Findlay. He shared his ideas with **Whole Foods,** for the use of readers interested in the selling of fruits and vegetables.

**JANICE: I notice that you are always available to discuss produce with your customers, and explain how a vegetable can be used, and recommend things which are especially fresh and tasty. I've seen very few produce people who have such a direct relationship with their customers. Is this merely an extension of your personality, or is it a conscious business technique?**

**DAVID:** When I was working at a truck stand on the Avenues in San Francisco, all I had money to buy was small, undersized, but very tasty pears in damaged boxes. I realized I was going to have to do something or I would go out of business. I knew they were excellent fruit, so I started giving samples of pears to every single person who came there. I was basically hustling the pears. I started selling about 15 boxes a day just on the basis of taste and presentation.

I realized that I had to completely re-do my whole presentation. I began to make connection with people, very sincerely, customer by customer. I began practically to design people's whole menus for them. I would have no qualms about investigating what they needed, and presenting it to them is such a way that they could use it.

Since then I've become less intrusive, especially in the store. You don't want to create a realm of theater in the store to the point where people are distracted or offended. But it's

Hustling pears

essential to put yourself in the position of the consumer. I don't do anything whatsoever without considering how the consumer is going to respond.

**JANICE: As well as stocking a complete line of familiar produce, you are continually introducing unusual fruits and vegetables. How do you go about introducing new items?**

**DAVID:** What is unique about my particular business is taking elements of ancient cultures, combining them with what I know about natural foods, and presenting them in such a way that a vision is captured. There's an exotic element that's also practical and nutritious. I always have an eye for that kind of thing.

An exotic vision

For instance, yesterday one of my partners mentioned that we should put the seaweed in the produce deparatment. So I investigated seaweed. Then I created a salad with it: I squeezed some lemon on the dulse, put some brown rice vinegar on it, cut some ripe papaya onto that, added some snowpeas and some fresh peas out of the pod. It was very good. It totally transformed everyone's notion. It was something that would not have occurred to them apart from my presenting it to them.

I always have something a little obscure. I've felt some response to macrobiotic vegetables. so I'm going to have lotus root and daikon. In the past, two of the stores I've worked in have been Filipino and Latin American, so I bring in Philippine and Latin American vegetables which people can try.

If you're going to do that, your presentation must be perfect. You're merchandising an entirely new product. The customer needs historical description, encouragement as far as taste, and a description of use. Otherwise, only a very marginal number of people will buy.

# CREATIVE DISPLAYS

**JANICE: Display is an important part of your approach. Are there any special techniques you use in creating your displays?**

**DAVID:** My produce reefers (refrigerators) have two tiers on them, an upper and a lower. For anybody who is investing in a new business, I'd absolutely recommend that style of refrigeration. When you have those two tiers, you can create a whole spectrum of qualities you can't get in the conventional one-level refrigerator.

A spectrum of qualities

Usually I have all my light, leafy, salad, cucumber, tomato things in one entire section. In the other section I have the heavier cooking vegetables and roots.

Color in display makes an incredible difference. If I need some color in the grapes, I'll put in a cauliflower to contrast. Apart from that, I incorporate elements that are botanically related. It's interesting to know how the vegetables are derived botanically. When you put them together in patterns of display, the historical development in botany is immediately apparent.

**JANICE: What inspires your displays? Are they thematic?**

**DAVID:** Last Saturday I got a shipment of organic vegetables from Southern California. Included in it were some daikon and some organic turnips. Conventionally speaking, neither one of those elements would sell. I'd heard little tidbits from people interested in macrobiotic foods that the Japanese considered daikon a tremendous blood purifier. This inspired a vision to create a display of daikon, red cabbage and green cabbage that was penetrating. All day people remarked on it. All it was was lowly cabbages and radishes, and it completely penetrated everybody's psyche.

Penetrating displays

**JANICE: You haven't yet mentioned fruit displays. Your fruit is put in the store window. Is there a reason for that?**

**DAVID:** That's what attracts people. In the window, you have to put something that's immediately available for consumption, make it accessible.

# PRICING

**JANICE: How do you determine what to charge for your produce? Is it predetermined, or does it fluctuate with each shipment?**

**DAVID:** I do not do an incredible volume of sales. My prices range from ten percent above to ten percent below supermarket prices. When I get a case in, I look immediately at what the wholesale price was that day. Then I estimate its value. I'll quickly look over the quality and predict how much of it will sell and how much of it will waste. If I get a 32-pound box of tomatoes in from Mexico that are pink, I know I'm going to have to ripen them in the basement. Chances are I'll lose three to seven pounds. So I make my estimation based on 25 pounds of tomatoes. From that basis, for the volume I'm doing, I charge double what I paid for them.

**JANICE: Eggplant always seems to jump back and forth between a unit price and a per-pound price. How is that determined?**

**DAVID:** That's tricky. If it's summertime, and I'm in a neighborhood where I know people can go through some eggplant, they're $4 a box for 24—if I go three for $1, I can get $8 back on them. But if it's wintertime, and eggplant's in short supply, and people don't seem to be very interested in it, and I don't have time to make a presentation of it which will insure that it sells, then I'll go for a per-pound price. It seems modest, but will in fact cost the customer probably 75¢ for the eggplant.

**JANICE: As a customer, I've noticed that. So, basically, you charge what you think you can get from the market, considering time of year and availability?**

**DAVID:** Right. I've worked in stores in the San Francisco Mission District where I never sold tomatoes for more than three for $1, no matter how much they cost. Even if I was losing money on them. That's the nature of that area: there's just not enough money around. That business totally depended on volume.

**JANICE: What percentage of Living Foods' business volume is in produce?**

**DAVID:** Our store sells between $2,000 and $2,500 worth of merchandise a day. In the winter, my average produce sales are $500 a day. That is not high based on the kind of return most stores—particularly natural food stores—make. But I have almost zero waste. And I do double my money on almost every item. At its weakest point, in its first winter, the store was making $4,000 a month on produce. At maturity, the produce department will probably earn between $10,000 and $15,000 a month.

# PROFITABILITY

**JANICE: Do most natural food stores make a profit from selling produce?**

**DAVID:** I've noticed almost without fail that natural food stores seem to regard produce as more trouble than it's worth. The few stores in the Bay Area—which I'm sure are some of the oldest in the entire country—that are modestly successful with produce are doing nothing compared to what they could be doing.

The main reason is that they don't have professional people working in the produce department. The owners and managers don't seem to have any idea of the possibilities, both monetary and in terms of the general intense attraction, that a good produce department has. When people open a natural food store, they almost invariably lose a lot of money on produce because they don't know what they're doing and because produce depends on a day-to-day response. I had five years of experience, plus a very hard winter in another location prior to opening this store, and we still lost $1,000 on our store opening.

**Estimating produce prices**

**Unit and per-pound prices**

**More trouble than it's worth**

I learned a lot of ways to be conservative, but still show a good face.

**JANICE: Aside from showing a good image, or "good face," what else do you need to succeed in produce?**

**DAVID:** A willingness to really stick your neck out in terms of variety, in terms of availability, and an absolute willingness to give the produce away or throw it out the moment you know that it doesn't have life in it any more. Everything has to be kept alive. Nobody wants to buy anything that's even the slightest bit dead.

# PROFESSIONALISM

**JANICE: You mentioned the lack of a professional produce person. Is it really necessary to have an employee who deals only with produce?**

**DAVID:** I can't stress how important the employee aspect of it is. To slide along at a marginal level or with no profit or in the red is ridiculous. It's completely possible to make produce a lively, intense, money-making part of the store. And that is dependent upon finding an employee who can be completely, individually responsible for turning a profit in that department. It shouldn't have to fall back to the manager to supervise some new and inexperienced person who's going to do nothing but cost the store money.

In supermarkets, an old-timer will break in a new person in the traditional way. He'll teach the new employee how to do brunt labor and prep to the point where the new person is mature enough to be responsible for things like ordering, display, pricing—the whole spectrum of possibilities that a produce manager has.

But in natural food stores the tendency is to just throw it in the reefer and several people will take care of it. That approach will never make a profit. It won't even break even: it'll cost you money.

If I were opening a new store, or had a store that was doing badly on produce, or wanted to really do it up right, I would hire a mature middle-aged person who had specific experience in commercial produce work. Because it would take at least one year of very intense work in this field for an inexperienced person to be able to responsibly turn a profit.

**JANICE: Would a full-time produce employee pay for himself after a year?**

**DAVID:** It depends on the person. If the person is creative, attentive to the needs of the store, and in the right vocation, he would easily pay for himself. But not without either a very strong intuitive sense of merchandising and how organic things work, or else a very specific training in it by somebody who did have that sensitivity.

# FINDING HELP

**JANICE: Where does a store owner find someone like that?**

**DAVID:** That's a good question, because I've looked for employees before. To find someone who is really interested in making it a vocation is very difficult. There are a number of possibilities open. One is to hire a middle-aged professional and be willing not to skimp on his salary. Or to find a retired produce man who is willing to come in a few days a week and very specifically train your existing staff. I did that once and learned an incredible amount.

Some supermarkets have a franchise arrangement where the produce section is rented to an independent produce person at a certain rate. I'm not sure what the economics of it are. The person pays for the spot and uses it to sell produce. This is another possibility for a natural food store, but the person who would be leasing the space should be thoroughly investigated. It would work with someone whose incentive was to make a living, who wasn't just doing it as a sideline.

**JANICE: About half the produce you carry is labeled "organic." How do you find sources for organic produce?**

**DAVID:** In the Bay Area there are at least three natural food distributing companies which have a very high level on integrity: Fowler Brothers Distributing Co., Sunshine Distributing, and Sun Country. There are probably a few others that I don't know about. I've done business with Sunshine Distributing and the Fowler Brothers. In both cases, there's absolutely no doubt in my mind about what kind of merchandise they were sending me

**JANICE: It's easy to claim things are organic. Do these distributors have any verification that the produce is in fact organic?**

**DAVID:** They have very specific standards with legal affidavits as to the origin of the produce, and signed statements from the growers which are legally endorsed by a notary.

# OTHER SOURCES

**JANICE: What do stores do if they don't have access to produce distributors? Or in the winter when produce is limited?**

**DAVID:** As to what a store should do in an area that didn't have a natural food distributing company and a sophisticated development of organic growers, I do have some suggestions. In my store, I have a display which begins at the lower level with parsley, watercress, cilantro or fresh coriander, and climbs into mung sprouts, lentils—every bean I can sprout—and eventually finishes with two huge trays of alfalfa sprouts. That display in itself earns me about $150 a week.

Herbs are fragile, but you can obtain parsley almost anywhere in America in the winter. All these other sprouts I grow in plastic tofu buckets right beneath my produce reefers. They're literally no increased difficulty to me. I can water them while I work. They're fresh and they make incredible profits. I sell them for $1.25 a pound, and they probably cost me 30-40¢ a pound to make. And I sell 10-20 pounds of each variety a day.

In Minnesota, in the middle of winter, an idea could be extended into all kinds of possibilities. Tomatoes available in the United States in the winter are almost all from Mexico. There are very few good hot-house tomatoes around, if any. Mexican tomatoes are usually shipped completely green to the produce terminals and then put in a hot room and gassed with ethylene to ripen.

Well, if you have storage space and warmth, you can buy the tomatoes when they first arrive and ripen them to an incredibly rich flavor. It's the same with avocados and bananas. But it's dependent on your willingness to supervise the whole event, or else you'll lose everything.

It's important to have a strong face as the seasons change. So many people who come into the store are bound by ritual habits of buying—we all know what our own tendencies are in this area. Customers may mention that there's not much produce around this time of year, when in fact the produce reefer is full. They just aren't seeing what they're used to buying.

So I'll say, "Have you ever had chard?" They may say, "I don't think I like it." My responsibility at that moment is obvious: I create it for them. I say, "Here's how I do it: cut it up, steam it, make a garlic butter sauce, and serve it with another brightly-colored vegetable—maybe some carrots—and just put a little bit of vinegar on it." Now it's a fifty-fifty shot. A lot of people will experiment.

In the middle of winter, broccoli often comes in with enormously thick stalks because the crops have been rained out except for the very mature vegetables. In a case like that, I unband the broccoli and sell them separately. Sometimes I walk down the aisles and notice everybody snapping the heads off and leaving the stem. What I do is educate people as to how tasty the stem is in a salad if you peel the thick, hard membrane off and slice the inner core.

Here's the kind of thing you have to do: Suddenly in the middle of January there are no more bunch radishes. The only radishes available are commercial radishes in plastic packages which are not going to sell and are definitely not going to make a profit. I had the inspired idea of setting baskets of loose radishes—taken out of the plastic bags—in the middle of my lettuce display. They sold like lightning. People like to be able to choose the number they can buy.

# ADS BY HAND

**JANICE: I had stopped eating pears because I could never find any with taste. I figured pears were something they didn't make anymore. You had a large display of pears, and on the sign you penned in, "The juice runs down your chin." It sounded good, so I tried the pears. They were delicious.**

**DAVID:** You have to capture the essence of the origin of the produce and its true potential. It's advertising, basically. That's as sophisticated as I get, but it's very effective. When I'm opening a case of pears, I'm seeing the pear back on the tree. I know where it came from, I know what its relationship to the universe is. I don't want to get too philosophical, but, literally, I know the growing area, what the weather conditions are likely to have been, and what it's like to taste like. It's just a matter of attention.

The cosmic connection

That's the fun of the produce business, that's what makes it exciting: to get excited when your own order arrives and communicate that excitement of the season to the buyer. They don't want to come in and see some half-dead stuff with organic signs on it. They want lusty displays.

**JANICE: I'd like to talk about produce waste. The obvious place to start is with the refrigeration. What type of reefers do you recommend?**

**DAVID:** When we built our store, one of the major expenses was compression and refrigeration. We bought used equipment, and still our produce department cost at least $20,000. Now, I wouldn't want to work with any less than that, but I don't know the economics of everyone's case.

What I recommend is the very best refrigeration equipment, installed by professionals. Natural food stores are always buying used equipment—maybe not even produce reefers, but old meat refrigerators—and having them installed by non-professionals. That always ends up in complication. Refrigeration is not something that you can compromise with.

If you have your refrigeration installed in the fall by non-professionals, perhaps it will go fine through the winter. But as soon as the summer comes along, the coefficient of cooling is reduced by 50 percent, and you're heading for breakdowns and complications. It will end up costing a fortune.

If you don't have specifically designed produce reefers, the produce will be kept too hot or too cold, or will be dried out by the type of air circulation that the machine has. I used to buy beans in the winter and put them in old meat refrigerators with poor temperature control. I couldn't even leave them out one night without obvious deterioration. With high-quality refrigeration, those same beans would look absolutely perfect for four, even five days. That makes an incredible difference in both sales and economy.

Proper refrigeration prevents waste

Refrigeration is expensive no matter how you look at it. In one store we ran the produce department without refrigeration—we didn't even have a walk-in. We bought every day and we were not afraid to throw out what was not in prime condition. This

NATURAL FOODS
AS A BUSINESS 283

worked very well, because the economy of it depended only on what we had to throw out. Eventually we had enough money to buy good-quality refrigeration.

# PREVENTING WASTE

**JANICE: How do you prevent waste?**

**DAVID:** Part of it is not putting yourself in a position where you end up with stuff that doesn't sell. You have to have a good face, but at the same time there are many things you can do to present that face without losing whole cases.

In touch with natural laws

You have to know the cycles of deterioration of all the food you're dealing with, and where to place it relative to temperature and conditions in the store. Organic things follow natural laws, and you have to get absolutely in touch with those laws.

Part of it depends on either having a good broker or else doing your buying yourself. Most natural food brokers deliver once or twice a week, so very careful planning is necessary. There should be no arbitrary, random guesses about how much you're going to need. You have to take into account conflict with other people using the walk-in, too. You have to know how much your walk-in can hold, how much you can manage, and schedule it so that the dairy, the dry goods, and the produce don't all arrive at the same moment.

For instance . . . when I get papayas in, the professional way to do it is to break open the case as they deliver it, and quickly see what the condition of every papaya is. Now, if I don't have other papayas out, and the papayas are green, I might put them where they'll ripen further. If they are extremely green, then they have to stay in the box, or enough heat will never accumulate to ripen them. The same applies with bananas—most tropical fruit. If you take extremely green fruit out of the box, it will stay starchy.

Turning loss to profit

If the papayas arrive completely ripe, they immediately go under refrigeration. If there were damaged papayas in the box for which I couldn't get credit, then I've devised a means of even turning a profit on those: I immediately slice the papaya long the line of breakage or bruise, eliminate that area, and wrap it in cellophane. I don't mark it down. I cut a thin wafer of strawberry, place it on top of the papaya underneath the cellophane, and sell it for more. Somebody on their lunch hour comes in, doesn't have any idea what they want to eat. They see the papaya, it's just what they want, and it has a beautiful strawberry on top to boot.

I don't sell things which are old, unless I specifically give them away or sell them at ridiculously low prices for juicing or soups or whatever. Old produce should not be sold as fresh produce—which seems to happen a lot in health food stores.

# SECONDS BECOME FIRSTS

**JANICE: Do you sell seconds in your store?**

**DAVID:** In my store there's very little interest in seconds. I turn seconds into first all the time. The other day I got a case of artichokes in, and the quality had changed dramatically. My broker had been buying from one grower who was sending beautiful chokes. They were selling as fast as I put them on the shelf. I had visions of ordering twice as many, to do it again. So I said, "I only want them if they're the same good chokes." He sent up the artichokes: They weren't the same chokes.

Sell the old ones first

Here I am with three cases of artichokes that I'm going to have a difficult time getting rid of. I took all the worst ones out of the box—not the worst tasting, the worst looking—trimmed them up and presented them at a ridiculously low price.

I developed a theory on the truck stands: You don't want to have to sell your old ones last. While the funny-looking ones are fresh, I bag them up immediately, present them to a customer who's right in front of me at the moment, and say, "I'll give you these at cost."

What's he going to say? Of course he'll buy them, because they're fresh. But you try to do that three days from then!

You've got to do it with some personality, with some presentation. It's like the papayas: You can make a silk purse out of a sow's ear in the produce department.

**JANICE: Do you have any more tricks up your sleeve?**

**DAVID:** When I open a case of citrus, I go through the case and take all the best fruit out. I have a mechanical citrus juicer in my citrus display. Any fruit that is undersized, overripe, punctured or has something wrong with it gets pumped into the juicer. That is turned right into profit. Some of them I cut in half and enclose in cellophane and put in the middle of the display.

More tricks

The papayas recently were very high priced, very small and green, but good fruit inside. No one was buying them. I cut some open so people could see inside. Their confidence was restored, and they bought the papayas.

Broccoli I sell loose, celery I cut in half, eggplant I cut in half. Everybody thinks eggplant is going to turn brown when you cut it in half, but if you squeeze a little lemon on it and wrap it in cellophane, it will stay white for a whole day, at least.

# LESS IS MORE

To avoid waste on apples once they get into the far end of their season—about eight months from when they're picked—I won't put the whole case out. I put half a case out, fake it in terms of volume, and put the rest back in the walk-in. I know people don't want to come home with a mushy apple.

When you're building your display cases for fruit, the angle should be shallow or, at the window, flat. Most natural food stores are not going to sell the kind of volume that warrants deep bins. It's much better to have a shallow display with the fruit in layers, rather than the fruit filling up a depression.

The same for your vegetable reefers. They usually have settings to make them shallow or deep. Make them shallow. Unless you have the volume to warrant it, keep your display shallow but full. You can make half a case look most lusty and delicious than a full case. Your broker can help you here. If your volume is slight, and you know you're not going to be able to sell a whole case, buy half a case. The broker should be sensitive to what you need.

A lusty display

**JANICE: Do you buy from growers, or from brokers?**

**DAVID:** I go entirely through brokers. To make a good living, to have a healthy business, you need to be at work every day. It's always been that way with produce. No matter how much I streamline my operation, I can't imagine a time when I'm not working at least five days a week, ten hours a day minimum, to keep everything under control. So I don't spend time going out to growers.

It's going to be a long time before there's natural food widely available. We have some strong beginnings on the West Coast. There are a nominal group of growers who produce lettuce weekly, almost without fail, almost throughout the whole winter. There are three or four really strong growers who are capable of distributing to the entire Bay Area all but four months of the year. But it'll take a long time, in my estimation, before organic food will truly become a reality.

My experience in farming is fairly marginal: I've spent two years farming. The investment required and the learning period required is so long and so large that it seems like only either middle-aged farmers who have switched to organic methods or else large spiritual communities are capable of becoming mature, reliable producers. That's why brokers are so important. That's why the whole natural food business has to mature. The romantic notion of some guy growing something in his backyard is simply that. I'm constantly besieged by customers who want organic this, organic that. But they have no conception of what would be involved for it to be in the store. We need strong growing systems, we need good brokers.

The Sunburst Farm has become sophisticated to the point where they employ the use of a semi-trailer twice a week from Santa Barbara to San Francisco. They drive that up loaded with their own produce and brokerage of other things they gathered together, and take a load of things they can't get—like apples and dried fruit—back down to Santa Barbara.

That's the kind of powerful movement that's going to be required before there will be truly organic food and not so many lies in natural food stores.

**Beyond a romantic image**

# 60

# *Celestial Reasonings*

## by Steven Haines

Over the last decade, Celestial Seasonings has emerged as one of the most successful new faces in the natural foods industry. A key factor in Celestial's rapid growth has been a series of colorful ads with commercial, as well as aesthetic, appeal. This ad program originated from the tea company's in-house ad agency, Celestial Reflections. Which brings us to Wyck Hay, Celestial's vice president of advertising and the creative force behind its multi-media ad program.

This marriage of ad and product was so happy that it seemed destined to last forever. Then, in the fall of 1977, rumors began circulating that the tea company had taken its account away from Celestial Reflections and given it to a major, national advertising agency. Ripples of concern, fear and panic began to spread among the alternative magazines that had come to depend upon Celestial's four-color ads. Rumors became fact and speculation began. Who was Dancer-Fitzgerald-Sample anyway? Why would Celestial choose that agency in San Francisco, so far away from its home base in Boulder, Colorado? What would the change mean for Celestial's image and direction in the market place?

On a more personal level, there were questions and concerns over Wyck's future. To many in the industry, Wyck Hay is a friend. To many more, he is something between a myth and a legend. In any case, Wyck Hay was the one source best equipped to answer the many questions raised by the change at Celestial Seasonings. So **Whole Foods** publisher Steve Haines went to Boulder and talked to Wyck Hay.

**Marriage of advertising and product**

# WHY THE CHANGE?

**STEVEN: Wyck, what was the thinking behind the decision to take the Celestial Seasonings ad account away from Celestial Reflections? What is the status of Celestial Reflections? Why was the decision made to go with a major national ad agency?**

**WYCK:** We had Reflections going here for three years. We did, as far as most people were concerned, a lot more than aesthetically adequate work for the tea company. We attempted to embody the artwork and the philosophy that was on the packages in our advertising. And it worked out pretty well. You know, in the course of the last couple of years doing our own ads relatively well, we won a couple of awards here and there. But I think the advertising is basically a reflection of the product. A lot of it works the other way, the product is a reflection of the advertising. That's because most products are not as aesthetically packaged, as informative, or as naturally oriented or whatever.

But when I started taking a look last year at the advertising dollar we were going to be spending this year, and I saw that all being jobbed out of a one-room office by two guys, it looked to be a little bit more than I was really willing to handle.

Number two, I figured that I had learned pretty nearly as much about advertising as I was going to learn in the little town of Boulder. It was starting to become a situation where people were coming to us and—not really milking us, but asking us. We were passing out a lot of free information, which was great. I loved doing it, but it was also taking a lot of time out of the way. Deadlines are something that I have never met in my life. They're not the friendliest people I know. My partner, Balfour Patterson, and I just looked at each other one day, and I said, "Bal, let's get out of this thing."

We had never really completed one contract that we had started. Halfway through the contractual period, we would either not be able to produce enough product or the hybiscus flowers we got were not good enough, or any one of a number of problems. So Mo and I would have to back off on whatever that contract was.

Even though I had established a strong rapport with whatever person I was buying my space from, I could never really keep that continuously strong rapport. I always had to call them up maybe 50, 60, 70, 80, maybe 90 percent of the way through the contract and say, "Well, listen, I'm really sorry, but we have to go on allocation because there's a coffee boycott going on and everybody's buying herb tea," or "UPI released a story and now everybody's buying our product," or "We just started advertising a lot in San Francisco, so I don't need to buy *New West* anymore," or whatever the story happened to be.

It was nerve-wracking to try to set up personal relationships with those people and then have to sever them because of a business relationship. In other words, folks that I knew at whatever publication we happened to be dealing with were always still friendly, but we could not really end up completing that business circuit 100 per cent. That was a reason.

# RUNNING IN CIRCLES

Another reason was it got to be really aggravating trying to get everything done out of this one-room office. Bal was working on getting the separations done or getting the black and white artwork shot to a particular line screen, getting it there, talking to the art department, getting the bills back. It was my responsibility to come up with the concept, and either go down and produce the radio spot or contact the artist to produce the art, get it back here, write the copy, get the copy set, get it all done to the aesthetic level that I thought would marry itself to the rest of the tea company line so that it really completed the circle.

That went on with everything, including my first tv spots, where I had no idea what was going on. It worked out really well, and I learned just humongus amounts, as anybody would in their inception of going into television production. It was phenomenal for me to sit down and write the piece — to just take it from soup to nuts except for pushing the button on the camera, and realize when it was finally done, yeah, indeed this is a pretty good ad which does not replace our market of loyal people with another market. I wanted to be very sure that we didn't jump into housewifery and leave all our really close market by the wayside and replace them with the Country Squire set. That's not what I wanted to do.

In the ads we put out, everything kind of fit what our loyalists would assume would be our advertising campaign. That's what I wanted to do. It makes the product—not elitist—but almost "chic," I guess, so that people want to migrate over toward our mindstream. That was good for us because it created almost a strange fascination for our product. It made it almost "in" to drink our product. But the problem with that is that, as soon as something in, it's out, and food, as far as I'm concerned, is not a fad.

Natural foods will never be a fad. Personal health, bodily cleanliness and day-to-day health awareness are not fads. We're trying to make our product as creditable in the way that it's presented through media as it is in its presentation in somebody's kitchen.

Creating a fascination for the product

# CHOOSING AN AGENCY

**STEVEN: How did you select Dancer-Fitzgerald-Sample? Were there many agencies that you invited to bid, or did you just throw it open?**

**WYCK:** We had hired a new marketing director at the time. He was very perfunctory, very full-on, straight-forward, very astute, good businessman, who wanted things "just so." I couldn't really envision myself being the agency responsible to a marketing director that needed 14 different examples of copy. That was just too much for me to do. First of all because I'm not that creative a person, I'm not a copywriter. I write short stories and I write songs and I'm in the middle of writing a movie — but to put it in straight New Yorkese, I couldn't stand the aggravation. I didn't need that problem. So one day I said, "Agency." He said, "Great."

I've been studying advertisements for years, because advertising to me is a real in-depth look at sociology. One thing that I intensely dislike about advertising is the consumer manipulation that goes on. Bracketing people into demographics is a very scarey thought.

Advertising and consumer manipulation

When I say we've got a certain loyalistic group of people that buy our products, that's great because those people have evolved with us and their headsets are maneuvering around and coming to a point where the sand settles on the bottom after all the scrambling of the late '60s. Those are the people that I think are buying our product. And there's also a lot of older people who are buying our product. But to try to change the headset of somebody who. . .I don't even want to put them into an age bracket, but the people who do those kind of things that I would label so-called middle-class, and even saying that kind of a catchall is not a positive. . .trying to change those people's minds is very difficult. Really difficult. Unless you do it with hype. Most people do it with lies.

The problem I think we have here at the tea company is that we don't believe in lying. We don't believe in misrepresenting the truth. First of all, we don't want to misrepresent it because the FDA gets on our case. Second, we don't want to misrepresent it because, what's the point? The truth is there, and if somebody wants to unearth it, they're going to unearth it. We may as well tell them the truth and take it at that. Most people won't believe you when you tell them the truth, that's the problem.

We don't believe in lying

Bal and I looked at the problems of the agency business. I started looking at the idea of who are we going to get? I've got all my *Ad Ages* lying around, so I'm constantly reading about what's happening and what's creatively being done in advertising, who's doing it and why they're doing it. I go to a lot of seminars. I listen to these people that I read about and hear what they have to say about the changing climate of the advertising world.

# SETTING THE CRITERIA

So we started looking. I pulled out my *Ad Ages*, and looked at the top five hundred and sixty agencies in the world. I had read books by Jerry Della Femina and by David Ogilvy, so I wanted to find out what they were all about. So we put them on the list. The marketing director and I drafted a seven-page letter establishing certain criteria, introducing our products, sending out samples, *et cetera*. And we sent that letter out to the agencies we were interested in, both in New York and San Francisco. I think there were a dozen in all.

A lot of them dropped us because our billing was not large enough. Scali-McCabe had another client who was putting out an iced tea product. In the final analysis, it came down to Foote-Cone-Belding or Dancer-Fitzgerald-Sample. We went out to San Francisco for two days of eight hours one day with these guys and ten hours the next day with those guys. It was no question. Dancer was really interested and involved in the integrity of the tea company. The morality. The decision between caffeine and non-caffeine. They really wanted to trigger us.

**Who buys the product— and why**

Although we did look at a few agencies out of New York, we wanted to work out of San Francisco because I think the country is looking at San Francisco, and we all know that. But by the same token, we didn't want to get a boutiquey little agency. What we really wanted to do was find out in actuality, demographically, who is buying our product and why. So our initial move with these people was not: O.K., create us something that's four-color Dr. Pepper. We weren't looking for that. We were looking for the agency that was going to come in and be aware of our problems.

Getting down to the final day, the Dancer people said, "We're aware of your problem. You don't know who you're selling to. You don't really know how to go about doing it. You're having vacillation problems in product production, i.e., do you want to go into a line of coffee extenders, coffee enhancers, or do you want to establish your own category of herb tea? Do you want herb tea to be known as the migration between Ovaltine and tea, or is it somewhere between tea and coffee?" And they decided, "No, you want to establish your own generic. You are your own Electrolux. You are your own Kleenex. Celestial Seasonings equals herb tea. Herb tea does not equal coffee, does not equal coffee expander, coffee extender, or even coffee substitute. It equals itself." Dancer saw that, and they really got into our headset.

They showed us the man hours, the creative time that they would have to put into it, the market research, the art direction, the copy, the reviewing of this, the driving back and forth, you name it. They said, "We're going to be losing money on you." I said, "Well, yeah, this year you're going to be losing money on us." They said, "We completely realize that. But be aware of the fact that you are basically below our minimum billing." Although they didn't really *say* that, they make you feel that, without saying it, which is also part of the agency game. They always make you feel it without saying it, right?

# THE AD BUDGET

**STEVEN: Wyck, you've avoided being specific about the ad budget. Is that because of preference, you'd just as soon not say what the budget is?**

**WYCK:** What our ad budget is? I don't think it's really good policy for companies to talk about dollars. At Celestial, we're talking about consumer service being what we're trying to do first. We're trying to put out a product that's not overpriced, that's the best quality we can get our hands on. Maybe somebody else can get their hands on something better, but I don't know where it exists.

**Ad budget guidelines**

**STEVEN: What I was trying to get at is that many of the companies in the industry didn't exist ten years ago. Now they look around and all of a sudden they're big companies. They're doing four, six, eight, ten million dollars worth of business and**

they don't have any guidelines, except what the other guy does, to come up with ad figures like that. I know that in the last seven months, doing research to put Whole Foods **together**, probably the most frequent question asked of me was: "What should our ad budget be?" How do you develop a feeling for that?

**WYCK:** To directly answer that question, initially we started out two or three years ago working on about 3½ to 4 percent. But our sales were growing in such exponential forms that we didn't even really have an ad plan. We'd do co-op ads in Madison and in Ann Arbor or wherever. Now we do exactly 4.7 percent of our overall projected net sales. So we're spending, just on advertising, a little under one-half million. That's only in ad placements. That doesn't count things like in-store stuff that we're doing, mail-outs to distributors, mail-outs to natural foods stores.

That's one thing that I'm working on right now. We were having one heck of a time trying to reach the person in the middle. When I talk about the person in the middle, I'm talking about the person who owns the natural food store. The one who's between the distributor and the consumer. We can get to our 55 or 60 distributors on the phone in the course of a week. We're talking to those folks, O.K. And I'm talking to the consumer because I'm advertising in *East West* and *New Age* and *Mother Earth* and *Prevention* and *Organic Gardening* and *Let's Live*. Practically every health food magazine that we can target, we've been targeting. As a matter of fact, this year we've dropped all major consumer advertising. We're not advertising in *New Times*, *New West*, or any of those. It's going right into the natural food area. But that leaves this person in the middle. And the person in the middle is probably the most important person.

**Reaching the middle-man**

# SELLING THE PACKAGE

For example, here's our sample pack. Now the sample pack can have all kinds of different things in it. It's going to have pictures of herbs on the inside — you know I have to do a little product sell here — it's going to have these really nice cards with vanishing flowers and herbs, and six different products in here. But if I'm only announcing it to the trade, the distributors know about it, the consumers know about it, but the person in the store does not realize what an opener that could be for somebody walking into the store. If I had a health food store, I'd take this thing and cut the price down on it about 20 percent, put it on a special in my store and watch what happened to my herb tea sales. Because it could go bananas. But retailers are not going to know about it, unless I tell them about it.

You're a health food store owner in Corte Madera, O.K? All of a sudden there's an article in the *Pacific Sun* talking about these wonderful herb teas. And you have this new sample pack. It's even got a picture of it in the food section, story written by Olga Housewife. Next thing you know, there's nine or ten people coming into your store that following morning. Well, that store owner does not know that somebody's coming out to do any P.R. in the area. He hasn't been contacted by the company that's doing the P.R. He should be. And he should be, at the same time, aware that there's going to be an article in this paper.

**Coordination of advertising and store promotion**

Maybe he wants to run a special on teas, or maybe he wants to have a copy of that article put up on his cash register, or maybe he doesn't want to have anything to do with the whole scene whatsoever. He's doing fine selling plenty of vitamins and he couldn't give a flying sea otter about herb teas. Maybe he's pushing Seelect and doesn't care about us.

I would still like to find out whether he does or whether he doesn't. Just for my own edification, to find out how high is up in the health food business. Because the message that we're trying to put out with the tea goes in a lot of different directions. We are trying to talk about new methods of farming. We like to tell people about the new warehouse we're building which will run on solar energy. There's a lot of different little things outside of the health aspect of the whole thing that we are putting into our boxes. And, further on down the road, you'll be seeing more and more of them from Celestial.

# INTO GROCERY STORES

There are some markets where we are into grocery stores. The reason we're into grocery stores is because we can't find out how high is up in the health food stores. We don't really know what kind of saturation we've got out there in lieu of having somebody on the road and visiting 5,700 stores. We can't afford to do that.

When I'm introducing in a grocery area, like we are right now in Boston, I've got to not only back up our broker, but I've got to make sure that I'm taking care of Erewhon. Because I don't want what happened to so many granola companies—I don't want to have our products walk into a grocery store shelf and completely undercut the natural foods people in that area. Then we are being the biggest hypocrites of them all, as far as I'm concerned.

**A pioneering effort**

Right now, Celestial is basically pioneering by going into grocery stores on a good-size level. And not into the little health food section either. I'm talking about going into the tea shelf. What a great consumer market place!

Once you put your foot in that door, one thing that you are doing, obviously, is getting a lot more consumer exposure. Number two, your price is looking a little more realistic. Number three, your problems of being out of stock in a grocery store are a lot less than they are being out of stock in a health food store. Number four, it is such an assistance to our cash flow—to get paid in net ten rather than net forty.

Planning means being able to have that cash flow to make those decisions ahead of time. It's six or seven months from the time those rose hips leave the dock in New York until they get to Chattanooga Natural Foods, until the money gets back to the distributor, until the distributor gets the money to us. It's a long, long process. The grocery stores—that's kind of where it's at on a cash-flow basis.

We don't intend to have the grocery stores be the catch-all of our whole business. The natural food business is growing rapidly. And we like to think of ourselves as being one of those products in the natural foods industry that is trying to help move things along. One thing that we have been trying to prove lately is that, when we put our product into a grocery store, the natural foods sales of our product escalate at the same time. They don't go down.

**Consumer confusion**

By the same token, you're dealing with different classes of trade. You're dealing with the health foods business, you're dealing with gourmet specialty shops, you're dealing with grocery stores. In one shopping center, for example, you could be in Alpha Beta at one price, you could be at a gourmet cheese shop around the corner at another price, and be at the health food store across the corridor in the mall for even a different price. Talk about consumer confusion!

# RADIO SPOTS

**STEVEN: The little bit I've gotten from the account people at Dancer indicates there is going to be a sizeable emphasis on broadcast media, especially select radio.**

**WYCK:** Yes, it's going to be a fairly major part of it.

**STEVEN: Is this a change from what you've been doing?**

**WYCK:** Not really. For the last three years in Denver, we have averaged, over the course of the winter, at least 18 to 24 spots a week on three or four stations. Last year, we put about $25,000 or $30,000 into television in Denver as a test. We also bought ad time on five radio stations in San Francisco, two in Boston.

**Radio— good media**

We just bought—it started about two days ago—time on seven radio stations in San Francisco and six here in Denver. Radio is a good media for us. If you go into Safeway and you don't give the Safeway buyer or broker some advertising to play with, give him some in-store stuff to have, you might as well not be on the shelf. First, the consumer doesn't know what natural foods are. They are completely confused when they look at this line of multicolored boxes. They don't have any kind of reference point—and I don't mean seeing it in a natural food store. And that's what radio does. They walk down an aisle and say, "Oh yeah, I heard about that stuff." It's a product, and we want to get the message of that product out to the consumer marketplace. Media is very, very important.

We are also sponsoring a natural food recipe show that will be syndicated across the country, which we can turn into a television program. It really explains what is going on in the world of natural foods instead of just: "Put water in here, add your pinto beans, put it in the blender, and you're out." It's an educational program.

Health and natural food education program

We're not throwing a lot of money into the media. We are putting a minimal amount of advertising dollars into the areas where we're going into the grocery stores. The reason that we're going into those areas is because, demographically, they break out as places that tea sells well and our tea has sold well: San Francisco, Boston, Chicago and Denver.

Yesterday afternoon, I had some people in here. We were talking about the maladies of Saturday morning television, and how that's going to manifest itself 25 years on down the road. So I am working with Dancer on allocating a certain amount of money to put into Saturday morning television. This may sound a little bit farfetched, but I think that we could—well, not change the course of humanity, but certainly alter a few headsets in the adolescent awareness that evolves by pinpointing something very positive into Saturday morning. What I'm working on now is a health and natural foods educational program which might be animated. We're not really sure. Make it very exciting, something where we do the show. Eventually, it goes into a classroom in a junior high or in a fifth or sixth grade. Then we introduce it further on down the road in Saturday morning. But time is so competitive there and everything is set to a rock beat. It's very scarey to think what those people are growing up with.

# NEW MARKETS

**STEVEN: How about other local markets, like Austin, Ann Arbor, Madison. Are they too small?**

**WYCK:** No. To pinpoint them does not really make any sense for us right now. For one thing, we could go around the country and sell well in Eugene, Austin, Tucson, Ann Arbor, Santa Barbara, Santa Cruz, Madison, Boston, Philadelphia, Columbus. We could just go around to the big college towns across the country. But when you want to go into a market place where you can really get a track record on selling your teas, it's just a spit in the ocean, as far as a buyer's concerned, that you've done well in six college towns. He wants to know have you ever tried to go into the Des Moines area, or have you ever done well in a number-two market like San Francisco.

A spit in the ocean

Another reason we went with Dancer in San Francisco is because they could give us assistance should we need it in opening the door at Lucky's and keep rapport strong with the natural foods people. So now, the next logical step is to establish a beachhead on the East Coast. Erewhon is so cooperative in working with us, it's phenomenal. If, as we go into new markets across the country, we have half the cooperation that we've gotten from Erewhon—I mean Erewhon has allowed us to establish a precedent which has been equitable for them and very equitable for us.

**STEVEN: Do you think that Celestial has had to compromise its philosophy in order to grow in the marketplace?**

**WYCK:** I like to look at our company as being good marketeers. We keep our philosophy with us as we market the product. I don't think we've lost anything of our philosophy over the course of the last couple of years. I don't think our integrity has really suffered. For that, I'm very thankful, and I want that to establish a precedent for anything we do in the future.

There are so many companies that are a lot like ours. In talking to them, we all decided that we've got to be very professional in everything that we do — so much so that we're not making mistakes, either verbally or in the marketplace, that we're going to be sorry for. We don't want to go rushing headlong into how to market our product at the grocery store level unless we can establish track records on how to deal with distributors and whatever classes of trade we happen to be dealing with in those particular areas.

**Establishing a foothold**

Establishing a foothold is very, very important for the natural food industry right now. Because, as we know, it was a dying issue essentially from 1940 to 1965. That doesn't mean to say there were not a lot of people who were buying good food. I mean that the whole national awareness had not peaked to the level that it's peaked to now. It's funny, because when I went on a sales trip four years ago, people were saying, "Yeah, I'll probably buy the product now, but I know it will be off the shelf in another couple of months because the health food fad is going to end." This fad is not ending because there is no end to a healthy body.

**STEVEN: One question I've got to ask you. You know rumors are rife. They run around all over the place. The ones that I particularly love are the set that go something like: Celestial Seasonings has secretly been acquired by Coca Cola or it's being financed by Lipton. . .**

**The Celestial family**

**WYCK:** Bullshit. That's all bullshit. You know what else I heard? I was in a gourmet store in Cambridge trying to get the guy to help sponsor our natural foods recipe show. A girl came up to me and said she'd read an article in the *Daily News* or something that we were owned by Sun Myung Moon.

The truth is that Celestial is all family owned—let's put it that way—not the Hay family or the Siegel family; it's all owned by the Celestial family.

# *About the Authors*

**David Armstrong** is a freelance writer whose column American Journal, syndicated by Future Associates, appears in 30 newspapers across the country. For two years, David was editor of the *Berkeley Barb*, in Berkeley, California. Prior to that, he was the managing editor for the *Syracuse New Times*. David has written for the *Columbia Journalism Review*, *East West Journal*, *MORE*, *New Times*, *Politicks*, *Whole Foods* and a variety of alternative publications. Currently David is writing *A Social History of the Alternative Media*, to be published by J. P. Tarcher, Inc.

**Robert C. Carey** is co-founder and Chairman of the Board of Bima Industries, a sprouting seed and equipment company in Seattle, Washington. During his fourteen years as a management consultant, Robert has written numerous articles on all forms of management. Involved in the natural foods industry for the past six years, Robert studies nutrition with Dr. Jeffrey Bland.

**Jacques de Langre,** master baker, operates a whole grain bakery in Chico, California, where he originated the technique of miso-leavened bread. A recent immigrant from France, Jacques has been involved with the macrobiotic movement for years. Jacques is the moving force behind Happiness Press, located in Magalia, California, which publishes books and pamphlets on natural grains and baking from a macrobiotic point of view.

**Larry Eggen** is founder, president and general manager of New Life Foods in Tracy, Minnesota. A distributor of a wide range of organic grains, New Life Foods' organic certification standards are considered the finest in the natural foods industry. For two years, Larry was president of the Soil Association of Minnesota, an organic farmers organization, where he started the Association newsletter. He is also a member of the Soycrafters Association of North America. Larry has written articles for *Acres, USA*; *Organic Gardening and Farming*; and *Whole Foods*. He has also contributed to *Tofu and Soymilk Production*, a book by William Shurtleff, published by New Age Foods Study Center in Lafayette, California.

**Scott Fickes** is an organic chemist interested in chemical research on substances which increase biological potential, and in natural product research. Scott is president and founder of Herbalanimal, an Oakland, California company which manufactures ecologically responsible household products. As technical director of Ecosafe Laboratories, Scott offers his services for product ecology and safety evaluation, truth-in-labeling investigation, and product development. Scott has written articles for *Daily Planet Almanac*, *Well-Being* and *Whole Foods*.

**Janice Fillip** is associate editor of *Whole Foods* magazine. Prior to becoming a journalist, Janice was a paralegal researcher in the law offices of economist/reformer Louis Kelso, and an educator in elementary and secondary schools in California and Spain. A freelance writer, Janice has also written for *Holistic Health Review*. She is currently working on a book about women who own businesses.

**David Findlay** describes himself as "totally fascinated with the earth's capacity to produce food." Having created what he calls a "produce personality" in eight natural food stores in the San Francisco Bay Area, David currently manages the produce department at Living Foods in Mill Valley, California. David is also forming a wholesale produce brokerage company which will offer an apprenticeship program to train produce personnel. The monthly columns which David writes for *Whole Foods* have recently been compiled in *The Produce Department*, a pamphlet published by Whole Foods Press.

**Gary M. Garber** is public relations director for Community Action of Laramie County in Cheyenne, Wyoming, where he was in charge of developing Cheyenne's solar greenhouse. Gary serves on the National Board of Directors for the Solar Lobby, and is Chairman of the Wyoming Solar Alliance. He has written articles for *Solar Greenhouse Digest*, *Whole Foods*, and a number of local newspapers. A chapter written by Gary will appear in *Eco-Communities: Resettling America*, a book edited by Gary Coates, soon to be published by Rickhouse Press.

**Steven Haines** is the publisher of *Whole Foods* and *Professional Sports Journal*, both located in Berkeley, California. Beginning his career as an investigative reporter for the *Chicago Daily News*, (where he was nominated for a Pulitzer Prize in 1963), Steven has written for a variety of business and consumer publications including *Automation in Housing* (where he received the ABP's Jesse H. Neal Award for outstanding journalism in 1967), the *Berkeley Barb*, the *Berkeley Tribe*, the *Ann Arbor Sun*, *Earthwatch*, *East/West Journal*, and many others.

**Leonard Jacobs** is publisher of *East West Journal*, for which he writes a Questions and Answers column on natural health practices. Leonard is studying and teaching macrobiotics through the East West Foundation and the Kushi Institute in Boston, Massachusetts.

**David Johnston** is a staff reporter for the *San Francisco Bay Guardian*. A freelance writer with an emphasis on consumer reporting, nutrition, labeling and fairness in advertising, David's articles have appeared in the *Berkeley Barb*, *Coast Magazine* and the *Milwaukee Journal*, among others.

**Fern Kozer** is the cost accountant for Green Mountain Herbs in Boulder, Colorado. During her four years in the natural food industry, Fern has acquired an extensive knowledge of herbs and herb products. Fern has also written a monograph on psycholinguistics for the Academy of Science in Colorado and Wyoming.

**Jeff Kronick** is president and cofounder of Auro Trading Co. in Santa Cruz, California, which imports and distributes ginseng and other products to the natural foods industry. Jeff began his involvement in the natural foods industry six years ago, when he helped start a food cooperative in Lake Tahoe, California. Jeff studies homeopathic medicine and is a songwriter.

**Richard Leviton** is the founder of the New England Soy Dairy (formerly Laughing Grasshopper Tofu Shop) in Greenfield, Massachusetts. A pioneer in the soyfoods industry, Richard is a founding member of Soycrafters Association of North America, and of SANA's publication *Soycraft*.

**Kurt Paine** is vice president and co-founder of Auro Trading Co. in Santa Cruz, California, which imports and distributes ginseng and "esoteric and neglected personal care products" to the natural foods industry. Kurt began his involvement in the industry five years ago, as a truckdriver for Pure & Simple Foods. Pursuing his interest in ginseng, Kurt has visited ginseng farms in China and Korea.

**Rick Purvis** has been an organic farmer for three years and is currently preparing to augment his degree in environmental studies with a graduate degree in agriculture. Rick has been director of a community garden project in Sacramento, California and served on the Board of Directors of the Sacramento Natural Food Cooperative.

**Warren Raysor** is president and co-founder of Abracadabra, a botanical seed and natural cosmetics company in Guerneville, California. Warren describes himself as a student of psychology, nature, and the mineral kingdom. An expert on clay, Warren has written articles for *East West Journal*, *Whole Foods* and a number of local newspapers.

**Machmud D. Rowe,** co-founder of Bima Industries in Seattle, Washington, pioneered investigation into methods of seed sprouting and has extensively researched the food values of a variety of sprouting seed mixtures.

**Jim Schreiber** is editor of *Whole Foods* magazine. Formerly, Jim was editor of the *Berkeley Barb* and the *Berkeley Tribe*, was a reporter for the *Livermore Independent*, a stringer for the San Francisco Bureau of *Time* magazine, and a copy boy for the *Oakland Tribune*. His freelance writing has appeared in the *East Village Other*, the *Los Angeles Free Press*, *Paperbag* magazine and *Fiction West*. Jim also spent two years teaching journalism and other writing courses at Simpson College in Iowa.

**Ellin Stein** is a freelance writer whose articles on nutrition and related topics have appeared in a variety of San Francisco Bay Area publications, and in *Whole Foods*.

**Howard Summerfield** is a freelance journalist experienced in covering the Washington, DC scene, focusing on the government's role in agriculture and other food-related issues.

**Dennis M. Warren** is an attorney in Sacramento, California, and legal counsel to The Platonic Academy in Santa Cruz, California. Dennis was formerly with the Consumer Protection Unit of the District Attorney's Office in Sacramento County. He has written articles on "preventative legal medicine" for *Health Foods Business* and *Whole Foods*.

# Sources and Resources

## ORGANIZATIONS

**American Soybean Association,** P.O. Box 158, Hudson, IA 50643.

**Bio-Dynamic Farming and Gardening Association,** 17240 Los Alimos St., Granada Hills, CA.

**California Certified Organic Farmers,** P.O. Box 812, Soquel, CA 95073.

**Center for Science in the Public Interest,** 1755 S Street, NW, Washington, DC 20099.

**Consumers for Nutrition Action,** 3404 St. Paul, Ste. 1-B, Baltimore, MD 21218.

**Feingold Association of the United States,** 56 Winston Drive, Smithtown, NY 11787.

**George Ohsawa Macrobiotic Foundation (GOMF) Inc.,** 1544 Oak St., Oroville, CA 95965.

**Graham Center,** Rte. 3, Box 95-F, Wadesboro, NC 28170. (Information on seed sources.)

**The Herb Trade Association,** 4302 Airport Blvd., Austin, TX 78722

**Jojoba World Trade Association,** 332 Kalmia, San Diego, CA 92101.

**National Academy of Sciences, Food and Nutrition Board,** 2101 Constitution Avenue, NW, Washington, DC 20418.

**National Nutritional Food Association,** 7727 South Painter Ave., Whittier, CA 90602.

**New Age Foods Study Center,** P.O. Box 234, Lafayette, CA 94549.

**Northern Regional Research Laboratory, USDA (NRRL/USDA),** 1815 North University St., Peoria, IL 61604.

**Northwest Alternative Food Network,** 1505 - 10th Ave., Seattle, WA 98122.

**The Platonic Academy,** P.O. Box 409, Santa Cruz, CA 95061.

**The Safe Food Institute,** 301 Surrey St., San Francisco, CA 94131.

**Society for the Preservation of Old Mills,** P.O. Box 435, Wiscasset, ME 04578.

**S.O.S. Foundation,** 510 Concord Dr., Menlo Park, CA 94025. (Information on sprouting and seeds.)

**Soycrafters Association of North America,** 305 Wells St., Greenfield, MA 01301.

**U.S. Office of Consumer Affairs,** 621 Reporter's Bldg., Washington DC 20201.

# PERIODICALS

*Bestways,* 466 Foothill Blvd., La Canada, CA 91011.

*Cascade, Journal of the Northwest,* P.O. Box 1492, Eugene, OR 97401.

*CoEvolution Quarterly,* POINT, P.O. Box 428, Sausalito, CA 94965.

*East West Journal,* 233 Harvard St., Brookline, MA 02146.

*Farmstead Magazine,* P.O. Box 111, Freedom, ME 04941.

*Food Monitor,* P.O. Box 1975, Garden City, NY 11530.

*The Herbalist,* P.O. Box 62, Provo, UT 84601.

*Let's Live,* 444 North Larchmont Blvd., Los Angeles, CA 90004.

*Millstream: A Natural Food Baking Journal,* P.O. Box 8584, Parkville, MD 21234.

*Mother Jones,* 607 Market St., San Francisco, CA 94105.

*New Age,* 32 Station St., Brookline Village, MA 02146.

*Organic Gardening and Farming,* Organic Park, Emmaus, PA.

*Prevention,* Rodale Press, Emmaus, PA.

*Seriatim, Journal of Ecotopia,* 122 Carmel, El Cerrito, CA 94530.

*Soybean Digest Bluebook,* American Soybean Association, P.O. Box 158, Hudson, IA 50643.

*Soycraft,* Soycrafters Association of North America, 305 Wells St., Greenfield, MA 01301.

*Vegetarian Life and Times,* Ste. 1838, 101 Park Ave., New York, NY 10017.

*Well Being,* P.O. Box 1829, Santa Cruz, CA 95061.

*Whole Foods, The Natural Foods Business Journal,* 2219 Marin Ave., Berkeley, CA 94707.

*Yoga Journal,* 2054 University Ave., Berkeley, CA 94704.

# BOOKS

*Bailey's Industrial Oil and Fat Products*, Daniel Swern (ed.), Interscience Publishers, Inc., New York, NY.

*A Barefoot Doctor's Manual*, Cloudburst Press, Seattle, WA.

*Birthright Denied: The Risks and Benefits of Breast-feeding*, Environmental Defense Fund, 1525 18th Street, N.W., Washington, DC 20036.

*The Book of Garlic*, Lloyd J. Harris, Panjandrum Press/Holt, Rinehardt and Winston, New York, NY.

*The Book of Kudzu: A Culinary and Healing Guide*, William Shurtleff and Akiko Aoyagi, Autumn Press, Brookline, MA.

*The Book of Miso*, William Shurtleff and Akiko Aoyagi, Autumn Press, Brookline, MA.

*The Book of Tofu: Food for Mankind*, William Shurtleff and Akiko Aoyagi, Ballantine Books, New York, NY.

*Brand Name Guide to Sugar*, Ira L. Shannon, DMD, MDS, Nelson-Hall, Inc., Chicago, IL

*The Changing American Diet*, Letitia Brewster and Michael F. Jacobson, Center for Science in the Public Interest, Washington, DC.

*The Chico-San Cookbook*, Cornellia Aihara, GOMF, Inc., Oroville, CA 95965.

*The Complete Book of Ginseng*, Richard Heffern, Celestial Arts, Millbrae, CA.

*Consumer's Dictionary of Cosmetic Ingredients*, Ruth Winter, Crown Publishers, N Y, NY.

*Diet & Nutrition: A Holistic Approach*, Rudolph Ballentine, MD, The Himalayan International Institute, Honesdale, PA.

*Dry It—You'll Like It!*, Gen MacManiman, MacManiman, Inc., Fall City, WA.

*The Farm Vegetarian Cookbook*, The Book Publishing Co., The Farm, Summertown, TN

*Food Oils and Their Uses*, Theodore J. Weiss, AVI Publishing Co., Westport, CT.

*Food For People, Not For Profit*, Catherine Lerza and Michael Jacobson (ed.), Ballantine Books, New York, NY.

*Graham Center Seed Directory*, Graham Center, Wadesboro, NC.

*Guide To Bees And Honey*, Ted Hooper, Rodale Press, Emmaus, PA.

*Herb Walk*, LeArta Moulton, The Gluten Co. Inc., Box 482, Provo, UT.

*The Herbal Dinner, A Renaissance of Cooking*, Rob Menzies, Celestial Arts, Millbrae, CA.

*High Level Wellness, An Alternative to Doctors, Drugs and Disease*, Donald B. Ardell, Rodale Press, Emmaus, PA.

*The Holistic Health Handbook*, Berkeley Holistic Health Center, And/Or Press, Berkeley, CA.

*Kick The Junk Food Habit With Snackers*, Maureen and Jim Wallace, Madrona Publishers, Inc., Seattle, WA.

*Kitchen Cosmetics: Using Herbs, Fruits and Edibles In Natural Cosmetics,* Jeanne Rose, Panjandrum/Aris Books, San Francisco, CA.

*Laurel's Kitchen: A Handbook for Vegetarian Cookery and Nutrition,* Laurel Robertson, Carol Flinders and Bronwen Godfrey, Nilgiri Press, Berkeley, CA. Available in paperback from Bantam Books, New York, NY.

*Major Medicinal Plants, Botany, Culture And Use,* Julia. F. Morton, Charles C. Thomas Publishers, Springfield, IL.

*The Merck Index -* available at major libraries. Provides the chemical names of chemicals and drugs, tells how they are made, how they work, their uses and toxicity.

*Miso Fermentation,* K. Shibasaki and C. W. Hesseltine, NRRL/USDA, Peoria, IL (pamphlet).

*Miso: Preparation of Soybeans for Fermentation,* K. Shibasaki and C. W. Hesseltine, NRRL/USDA. (pamphlet).

*A Modern Herbal,* Mrs. M. Grieve F.R.H.S., Jonathan Cape, London, England.

*Northwest Directory of Natural Food Stores and Co-ops,* CAREL, Box 1492, Eugene, OR

*One Straw Revolution,* Masanobu Fukuoka, Rodale Press, Inc., Emmaus, PA.

*School of Natural Healing,* Dr. John R. Christopher, Bi-World Publishers, Inc., Provo, UT.

Select Committee on Nutrition and Human Needs, U. S. Senate, *Dietary Goals for the United States.* Second Edition, December 1977, Government Printing Office Stock Number 052-070-04376-8. Supplemental Views, November 1977, Government Printing Office Stock Number 052-070-03987. Available from the Superintendent of Documents, Government Printing Office, Washington, DC 20402.

*Soybean Diet,* Herman and Cornellia Aihara, GOMF, Inc., Oroville, CA.

*Soybeans As A Food Source,* W. J. Wolf and J. C. Cowan (eds.) CRC Press, Cleveland, OH.

*Soybeans: Chemistry and Technology: Volume 1—Proteins,* (Revised Second Printing), Allan K. Smith and Sidney J. Circle (eds.), AVI Publishing Co., Inc., Westport, CT.

*Soybeans and Soybean Products,* Klare S. Markley (ed.), Interscience Publishers, Inc., New York, NY.

*The Sunburst Farm Family's Cookbook,* Woodbridge Press, Santa Barbara, CA.

*Technology of production of edible flours and protein products from soybeans,* (Agricultural Services Bulletin 11), S. S. De. Agricultural Services Division, Food and Agricultural Organization of the United Nations, Rome.

*Traditional Fermented Foods,* C. W. Hesseltine and Dr. Hwa L. Wang, NRRL/USDA, Peoria, IL (pamphlet).

*Wellness,* Cris Popenoe, Yes! Inc., 1035 - 31st NW, Washington, DC.

# Index

# KEEP UP TO DATE
# ON NATURAL FOODS

All the information published in this *Natural Foods Guide* came from the pages of *Whole Foods* magazine. Issued every month, *Whole Foods* continues to look into the products, problems, and business practices of the natural foods industry. Products scheduled for study during 1980 include fructose, carob, bottled water, capsuled herbs, minerals, bread, and nut butters. Business reports include an examination of price structures and a new inquiry into organic farming. If you found this book to be of value, *Whole Foods* magazine can keep you up to date. Subscriptions cost $24 per year. If you would like to subscribe, please send your name and address, and a check or money order for $24 to:

Subscription Department
Whole Foods
2219 Marin Avenue
Berkeley, CA 94707